Regulating Style

Regulating Style

Intellectual Property Law and the
Business of Fashion in Guatemala

Kedron Thomas

UNIVERSITY OF CALIFORNIA PRESS

Earlier versions of portions of chapter 1 were published as "Corporations and Community in Highland Guatemala," *PoLAR: Political and Legal Anthropology Review* 37, no. 2 (2014): 231–245; and "Economic Regulation and the Value of Concealment in Highland Guatemala," *Critique of Anthropology* 35, no. 1 (2015): 13–29. They are reprinted with permission.

An earlier version of chapter 2 was published as "Intellectual Property Law and the Ethics of Imitation in Guatemala," *Anthropological Quarterly* 85, no. 3 (2012): 785–815. It is reprinted with permission.

An earlier version of portions of chapter 3 was published as "Brand 'Piracy' and Postwar Statecraft in Guatemala," *Cultural Anthropology* 28, no. 1 (2013): 144–160. It is reprinted with permission.

University of California Press, one of the most distinguished university presses in the United States, enriches lives around the world by advancing scholarship in the humanities, social sciences, and natural sciences. Its activities are supported by the UC Press Foundation and by philanthropic contributions from individuals and institutions. For more information, visit www.ucpress.edu.

University of California Press
Oakland, California

Library of Congress Cataloging-in-Publication Data is available at https://lccn.loc.gov/2016033503

ISBN 978-0-520-29096-9 (cloth : alk. paper) |
ISBN 978-0-520-29097-6 (pbk. : alk. paper) |
ISBN 978-0-520-96486-0 (ebook)

Manufactured in the United States of America

25 24 23 22 21 20 19 18 17 16
10 9 8 7 6 5 4 3 2 1

Contents

Illustrations

Acknowledgments

This book is the result of the incredible generosity of the people of Tecpán, Guatemala. I refrain from thanking particular individuals here in the interest of protecting anonymity, but I am deeply indebted to the dozens of people who shared their lives with me and made me feel at home in Tecpán and to the many who continue to enrich my life with their friendship. People in various other cities and towns throughout Guatemala contributed their stories to this research as well. I am grateful to Claudia, Marvin, Ana, and Silvia, who worked with me as research assistants and, in many ways, made the fieldwork possible. I also thank Te Ix'ey, Lajuj B'atz, and the other teachers and mentors at the Oxlajuj Aj Kaqchikel Maya Institute for their instruction and for introducing me to so many aspects of highland life.

A number of agencies and institutions provided generous funding support for this project: the Fulbright-Hays fellowship program, the Charlotte W. Newcombe fellowship program at the Woodrow Wilson Foundation, the Foreign Language and Area Studies program, the Weatherhead Center for International Affairs and the David Rockefeller Center for Latin American Studies at Harvard University, the Harvard University Graduate School of Arts and Sciences, the Harvard University Department of Anthropology, and the Department of Anthropology at Washington University in St. Louis.

I am indebted to the anthropology faculty at Harvard for guiding my scholarly and professional development during my time in graduate school. For the lively intellectual debate that I experienced within my cohort and across the graduate student community, I want to thank, in particular, Naor Ben-Yehoyada, Alireza Doostdar, Alex Fattal, Garner Gollatz, Kate Mason, Troy Montserrat-Gonzales, Wrick Mitra, Juno Parreñas, Sabrina Peric, Miriam Shakow, Noelle Stout, and Parker Van-Valkenburgh. I appreciate the support provided by the department's staff members as well, who were so generous with their kindness, time, and expertise.

Various scholars of Guatemala and the wider Maya region dialogued with me on issues related to this work and offered insights and guidance as this project unfolded. They include Regina Bateson, Michelle Bellino, Jennifer Burrell, David Carey, Quetzil Castañeda, Monica DeHart, Avery Dickins de Girón, Deborah Greebon, Anne Kraemer Díaz, Deborah Levenson, Walt Little, Judie Maxwell, Diane Nelson, Tal Nitsan, Tom Offit, Sergio Romero, Carol Smith, and Tim Smith. I especially want to thank Pakal B'alam, Carmelina Espantzay, Rebecca Galemba, Carol Hendrickson, and Kevin O'Neill for their friendship, comments, and criticisms of this project, and Ted Fischer, who has provided mentorship since my undergraduate years at Vanderbilt University, and without whose friendship, advice, support, and feedback I never would have been able to carry out this research or writing.

The semester that I spent at the Universidad del Valle de Guatemala as a visiting professor was indispensible to this project, and I particularly thank Andrés Álvarez Castañeda for his support and my remarkable students for their stimulating engagement. Thank you also to the staff members of the Universidad del Valle, Universidad de San Carlos, Universidad Mariano Gálvez, Universidad Rafael Landívar, Centro de Investigaciones Regionales de Mesoamérica and Facultad Latinoamericana de Ciencias Sociales for making the library resources of their institutions available to me.

This book has benefited enormously from the questions and comments that I have received after various presentations of the work over the years. I presented early drafts of chapters at Leiden University's Department of Cultural Anthropology, the Center for Latin American Research and Documentation at the University of Amsterdam, the University of Chicago's Department of Anthropology, Washington University in St. Louis's Department of Anthropology, the St. Louis University School of Law, the annual meetings of the American Anthropological Association and Latin American Studies Association, the Congreso de Estudios Mayas at Universidad Rafael Landívar; conferences sponsored by the Guatemala Scholars Network, Wuqu' Kawoq, Free University Berlin, Royal Museum for Central Africa, Free University Brussels, and Catholic University of Leuven; and graduate student conferences at the University of Pennsylvania and Yale University. I am deeply indebted to people who read and commented on early versions of chapters and to those who provided crucial insights regarding the themes and ideas developed in this book. They include José Carlos Aguiar, Bettina Bruns, Michael Chibnik, Alex Dent, Alex Dubé, Monica Eppinger, Andrew Graan, Karen Tranberg Hansen, Stuart Kirsch, Brent Luvaas, Gordon Mathews, Ellen Moodie, Constantine Nakassis, Cristiana Panella, Janet Roitman, Josephine Smart, and Rebecca Wanzo.

At Washington University in St. Louis, the support provided by the staff members and my faculty colleagues in the Department of Anthropology is truly remarkable, and I am especially grateful in this regard to John Bowen, whose intellectual and professional guidance has been invaluable. Thank you to the faculty and graduate student participants in the Latin America Reading Group, Ethnographic Theory Workshop, and Social Studies of Institutions group, including my colleagues at the University of Amsterdam and École des Hautes Études en Sciences Sociales, for commenting on various portions of this work. Anita Chary, Andrew Flachs, Natalia Guzman Solano, Rebecca Hodges, and Jessica Ruthven generously read early versions of the full manuscript and gave excellent feedback. Maria Mata and Caroline Buhse supported the project as research assistants during the writing and editing stages. In St. Louis, I am also fortunate to have a fantastic writing group that has included Talia Dan-Cohen, Jean Hunleth, Jong Bum Kwon, Stephanie McClure, Bruce O'Neill, E. A. Quinn, Lihong Shi, and Priscilla Song. Their advice and criticism was absolutely indispensable to this book's evolution.

I am eternally grateful to my dissertation committee members for their years of mentorship and unwavering support. Kimberly Theidon set an example of ethical and courageous research, scholarship, and engagement in Latin America that continues to inspire me, and I cannot thank her enough for directing my studies. Thank you to Michael Herzfeld for keeping me grounded in the big, bold questions of anthropology, shaping me into a professional anthropologist, and facilitating my continued growth as a scholar. The critical questions that Ted Bestor asked of this project along the way have made it a much more robust and sound work.

It has been a pleasure to work with the University of California Press. Thanks to Reed Malcolm for his enthusiasm for this project and to

Stacy Eisenstark for ushering the manuscript through much of the publishing process. I appreciate the Press's careful selection of such thoughtful and engaged reviewers, whose critical insights and generous suggestions helped me sharpen my arguments and improve the overall quality of the work. Thank you to Cindy Fulton for overseeing the production process, Genevieve Thurston for her careful copy edits, Bill Nelson for his cartographic skills, and Sharon Sweeney for preparing the index.

Thank you to my mom and Patti for daily encouragement and for being there when I needed them. Finally, this book is dedicated to Pete, Manny, and Henry. Thank you to Pete for his inestimable contributions to this project and for introducing me to anthropology and to Guatemala, tirelessly supporting me and sustaining our family through the years of study, research, and writing, and giving careful attention and brilliant thought to this book in all of its iterations, and to Manny and Henry, who unwittingly inspire me to be a braver scholar and a better person.

Introduction

Tecpán, the highland Guatemala town where I carried out the ethnographic research for this book, stirs with activity each evening. The central plaza, a paved square edged by a colonial-era Catholic church and town hall, bustles after sunset with taco and tamale vendors offering cheap dinner fare. Adolescent boys kick soccer balls back and forth across the pavement. Old women sell *atol,* a hot beverage made of rice or corn, from heavy baskets and wooden carts. Dozens of young men lounge against the basin of the empty fountain or stroll the plaza. They all wear *sudaderos,* sweatshirts with oversized hoods, which they wear pulled up over gel-drenched hair. Each of these sweatshirts features a brand name—Abercrombie & Fitch, Hollister, Ecko—splashed across the front. A pair of torn and faded blue jeans with wide legs and shiny black leather shoes—freshly polished by one of the younger and poorer boys who lug around wooden shoe-shine kits and shout "lustre, lustre!"—complete the look.

The sweatshirts these young men wear are part of what many fashion industry executives, policy makers, law enforcement officials, and representatives to international institutions—including the World Trade Organization (WTO)—call the global piracy trade. "Piracy" is the official term used to describe the unauthorized, illegal reproduction of registered trademarks owned by multinational corporations. Pirates are fascinating figures in the Western social imaginary. The word calls to mind the seafaring renegades who troubled mercantile trade routes during Europe's "golden age" of colonial expansion (Konstam 2008). "Historically," notes Talissa Jane Ford (2008: 13), "pirates were deemed *hostis humani generis,* the 'common enemy of mankind,' and therefore outside the law." This book is concerned with the everyday experiences of people who are dubbed "pirates" under new international legal regimes that claim to promote and protect intellectual property.[1] The application of this label to people who appropriate fashion brands without permission implies a context of rebellion, thievery, bad intentions, and deviant behavior. Proponents of strict intellectual property (IP) law enforcement draw on such imagery to moralize against brand pirates and justify the criminalization of these pirates' livelihoods. I offer a portrait of piracy that pushes back against these moralizing narratives. Specifically, I situate the unauthorized use of brand names and logos as part of the routine work of making and marketing fashionable clothing in highland Guatemala, as in many world regions, and argue that brand piracy is integral to the contemporary production of style. "Style" is a keyword in my analysis, and I use the concept to discuss the fact that brand names and logos used to adorn clothing are an important part of material culture and thus a resource through which people constitute aesthetic repertoires, participate in projects of group identification and differentiation, and express politics. I analyze IP law and its accompanying discourse of piracy as a means through which states, corporations, and international institutions regulate style, and I seek to understand just what is at stake for them in doing so.

The past two decades have seen unprecedented international efforts to standardize IP laws (including those that govern trademarks); strengthen the protections they offer to authors, artists, designers, inventors, product developers, and brand owners; and ensure their enforcement. Because of the prominent role that trademarked brand names play in the organization of the fashion industry and the marketing of fashion, IP law is now central to how the industry regulates its global business operations and cracks down on the unauthorized reproduction of looks and labels. In Guatemala, the IP push has resulted in more extensive trademark protections and more coordinated efforts to prevent and punish brand piracy. There are highly publicized, periodic raids on street markets in the capital city, where knockoff fashion is sold; media campaigns that hype the detrimental effects of the presumed problem of piracy on the national economy and public moral integrity; and ongoing industry-led attempts to consolidate and strengthen IP protections through international trade agreements and national legislation.

FIGURE 1. Market vendor in the Guatemalan highlands wearing a traditional *huipil* (woven blouse) and selling t-shirts featuring pirated brands, 2008.

The criminalization of brand piracy adds new dimensions to the anthropology of dress and the interdisciplinary field of fashion studies. The historical and ethnographic investigation of clothing has been important for understanding the globalization of particular fashion styles and for apprehending dress as a marker of social distinction. Clothing is a cultural practice through which gender, class, sexuality, national and religious identities, race, and ethnicity take shape and find diverse expression.[2] Anthropologists have demonstrated, for example, how blue jeans have come both to feel "comfortable" and to signify comfort, class status, gendered belonging, and leisure time for wearers (Miller and Woodward 2012). At the same time, dress is wrapped up with power and politics, such that the production and consumption of blue jeans implicates large-scale political economic processes and increasingly involves consumers, activists, and fashion industry insiders in serious ethical debates about labor rights and the environmental impacts of cotton agriculture, textile dyeing, and clothing waste, for example (Brooks 2015). Anthropologists, historians, and cultural studies scholars have also demonstrated how clothing has figured centrally in hegemonic political projects of control and subordination. Jean

Comaroff (1996: 24) has written, for example, of the importance of clothing to nineteenth century British colonialism, when Protestant missionaries and colonial administrators viewed the adoption of Western dress as "a sign and an instrument" of the transformation of African peoples into Christians and colonized subjects.[3] A century later, British youth rebelled in the streets of London against the constraints of class and clothing by adopting punk and mod styles that pushed dress and its codified meanings to the point of ribald absurdity (Hebdige 1979).

As a mode of expression, a means of social control, and a tool of resistance, clothing is an essential material with which people craft culture and society. My research demonstrates that, in highland Guatemala, changes in fashion reveal a great deal about changes that are taking shape in class composition, gendered spheres of politics and work, practices of indigeneity, and ethnic and racial affiliation and differentiation in a region where the overwhelming majority of people identify and are identified as Maya. The knockoff fashion trade has emerged as part of a postcolonial field in which issues of mimesis and alterity (Taussig 1993) already structure national and regional debates about what it means to be indigenous and how indigenous people figure into projects of modernization and development. The liberal politics of the late nineteenth and early to mid-twentieth centuries emphasized the cultural, ethnic, and racial assimilation of indigenous people in Guatemala and posited native or traditional dress styles as signs of backwardness (Grandin 2000). In recent decades, international movements have proclaimed and institutionalized the rights of indigenous peoples to their dress, cultures, land, and languages. Charles Hale (2005) has characterized the political effects of indigenous rights movements in Guatemala in terms of "neoliberal multiculturalism," whereby the nation-state guarantees a minimal set of rights for indigenous groups and celebrates cultural diversity exhibited in dress and language without addressing the historical injustices, persistent violence, deep socioeconomic inequalities, or structural processes of marginalization that affect the country's indigenous population. Neoliberal multiculturalism is a powerful discourse through which conditions of precarity and insecurity are naturalized in terms of cultural difference and poverty is read as a "traditional way of life" and justified as such to international audiences and within the development industry.

The emergence of the knockoff fashion trade in the highlands troubles the state's efforts to relegate Maya people to the disparaged domains of "culture" and "tradition," since fashion branding is a decidedly modern sphere of marketing and commerce (English 2013). At the same time, international IP laws that seek to control and criminalize "the copy" feed into neocolonial narratives that accuse Maya people of being "inauthentic"—of employing mimicry, trickery, and double-talk to conceal their "real" intentions of using what the national elite consider to be questionable claims to indigeneity and difference to obtain special rights; undermine the power, privilege, and authority of nonindigenous Guatemalans; and disrupt processes of economic development and national progress (Nelson 1999, 2009). Investigating the dynamics of the knockoff fashion trade in highland Guatemala and international efforts to regulate and restrict "the copy" is thus a way of drawing critical attention to contemporary "controlling processes" (Nader 1999) that have pernicious effects in a postcolonial context where race, gender, and dress have long been subject to control and regulation and where issues of assimilation, modernization, and development and questions about copying, imitation, and authenticity have long been contested and at stake.

"THERE IS NO ORIGINAL"

Indigenous Maya people in highland Guatemala are not just consumers of fashion knockoffs. They make branded apparel and sell it in regional markets and city streets to wholesalers, retailers, and traders, who sometimes transport the products across Central American borders. Situated on the Pan-American Highway about an hour's drive from Guatemala City, Tecpán is an important and regionally well-known center of nontraditional clothing production for the Central American market.

The majority of Tecpán's approximately twenty thousand residents are Kaqchikel Maya,[4] and the town has been a key node of indigenous cultural and political activism in the wake of Guatemala's internal armed conflict, which officially ended in 1996 and included a genocidal military campaign against Maya people (Fischer and Brown 1996; Fischer and Hendrickson 2002; Fischer 2001; Warren 1998). Today, there are hundreds of indigenous-owned garment workshops in and around the town. Distinct from the weaving tradition in which so many Maya women and some indigenous men in the highlands participate to make the colorful garb that the term "Maya" generally brings to mind, the nontraditional apparel trade has a much shorter history and a more industrialized present. Apparel workshops in Tecpán are usually located in spare rooms built onto residences and equipped with a few industrial

Guatemala, showing the locations of Tecpán and several other towns that are important manufacturing and marketing centers in the highland apparel trade.

knitting and sewing machines. The male head of the household is considered the workshop's owner and principal decision-maker, even if women and other men are involved in production in various capacities. Producers with the largest businesses employ dozens of workers at sewing machines and own high-capacity knitting machines that can turn out a hundred sweaters per day. Most of the fashionable clothing they manufacture features brand names such as Converse, Lacoste, and Tommy Hilfiger or, in the case of children's clothing, cartoon characters trademarked by Walt Disney and Nickelodeon.

FIGURE 2. Young men working at sewing machines in a garment workshop in Tecpán, 2009.

In 2006, I embarked on an ethnographic investigation to understand the work of the Maya men who make and sell these clothes. I spent twenty-one months living in Tecpán—including carrying out a full year of fieldwork in 2009—observing the design, production, and marketing process as it unfolded across garment workshops and retail sites, and getting to know workshop owners, their employees, wholesalers, and others involved in the apparel trade. For two months, I worked on an unpaid, flexible basis in two garment workshops, sitting for eight to ten hours a day at an industrial sewing machine or sometimes mending knitwear and cutting out patterns. I recorded interviews in Spanish and Kaqchikel with more than a hundred people working in the trade and also directed surveys of more than two hundred clothing vendors in municipal markets and retail stores throughout Guatemala.

I focused my investigation on the ways that Euro-American IP laws that have now become globalized standards have been institutionalized at a national level in Guatemala and how enforcement efforts are unfolding in the highlands. I also documented the alternative and vernacular conceptions of property, ownership, and authorship that animate Guatemala's apparel trade. People who make knockoffs and sell clothing in highland Guatemala and people who purchase that clothing do not necessarily share the definitions of "original," "copy," "real," and "fake" that are written into IP law. A substantial amount of historical and ethnographic work on IP piracy and counterfeiting has now demonstrated some of the cultural contours of the global market in knockoffs and fakes and the fact that people in different world regions bring disparate understandings of the relationship between originals and copies to this multibillion-dollar trade. For example, Elizabeth Vann (2006) showed that Vietnamese consumers evaluate whether a branded good is "real" or "fake" based not on an authentic or verifiable relationship to a corporation or manufacturer but rather on whether or not the product works as intended—that is to say, whether a purse is sturdy or a beauty product is effective for achieving a certain look. Yi-Chieh Lin's (2009, 2011) work in China and Taiwan—the geographical heart of the global piracy and counterfeiting trade—demonstrates that people who participate in the "bandit" economy understand themselves as integral to economic development in the region and part of innovative efforts to define cultural politics in ways that do not line up with international IP law.[5] Piracy is a location from which diverse populations actively work out "various ways of being modern" that are rooted in "concrete local ways of 'being human'" (Eckstein and Schwarz 2014: 18; Newell 2012). The idea that brand pirates are simply doing something illegal and immoral discounts the reality that they are doing something innately human by making meaning, producing material culture, and forging an existence in the world in ways that make sense within local worlds where the connotations and politics of culture, identity, ownership, authenticity, and property are not reducible to or the same as those built into globalized IP frameworks.

This critical argument, which comes from ethnography and history, is important because the notion of an "original" branded garment does tremendous ideological work for the promotion of intellectual property as a seemingly common-sense legal framework and political economy. The presumed existence of an "original," whether in fashion branding, art, music, or industrial design, seems to justify the legal protections that are afforded to some but denied to others who are not considered to merit them because they merely reproduce things in ways that are said to violate the rights of creative individuals and organizations. In this way, the divide between originals and copies in IP law implies a sociological divide between people who create and people who copy.[6]

In the chapters that follow, I explore the meanings of terms such as "original" and "copy" as used among Maya workshop owners to describe various aspects of making, selling, and purchasing fashionable clothing in Guatemala. Apparel producers routinely emphasized the creativity inherent in their design and manufacturing processes, even if the resulting clothes feature brand names for which the producer does not own the rights. During my interviews and conversations with producers, they conveyed to me the importance of developing fashionable looks that participate in existing trends but also offer something distinctive and exciting for buyers. Some critiqued the very idea of "original" fashion designs. For example, a workshop owner and designer in his midtwenties—a young man who is an upstart in the local industry— stressed to me that knowing what to copy and how to copy is part of what makes a good businessman. "Imitamos las cosas buenas" (We copy the good stuff), he explained. We sat across from one another at his kitchen table as the steady hum of sewing machines reverberated through the room. Half a dozen young indigenous men were assembling hooded sweatshirts embroidered with Hollister logos on the other side of the concrete-block wall that separated the producer's home from the workshop. He pointed out the multicolor striped cotton shirt I was wearing that day and explained that design is a process of finding something you like and then figuring out what makes it appealing. Is it the color combination? The pattern? The cut or shape? The logo printed across the front? To be able to discern what is interesting and what might thus be profitable about a particular item of clothing is the first step in crafting a new design that will satisfy clients and contribute to a sense of the self as innovative, industrious, and entrepreneurial. What he and other producers told me, in essence, was that a brand name might be one part of what carries over from an existing garment to a new design, but the aim is to put together a complete look, which features many different elements, rather than just reproduce a logo (cf. Thomas 2013). International IP law, however, focuses narrowly on the logo and construes piracy in terms of the pilfering of these signs and the corporate value attached to them. When IP law criminalizes such copying, this young man explained to me, it indicates to him that the law does not understand how fashion and style actually come into being. "No hay primero" (There is no original), he insisted.

Ethnography can be useful for understanding why and how people in different world regions might perceive and enact property relations and business ethics in fundamentally divergent ways. In this young man's case, copying and appropriation are essential to engaging in a creative process and to making a complete look. These acts are also part of a multisided project having to do with attachments to economic goals and aspirations, as well as cultural frames of moral personhood and hard work. I show in later chapters how copying and imitation are business practices that are wrapped up with commitments to ethnic solidarity, family, community, and development. The point is that careful and sensitive assessments of something derided on an international scale as "piracy" reveal locally legitimate and indeed ethical ways of "being modern" and "being human."

Anthropologists and other scholars who are wary of the criminalizing discourses that have accompanied IP law's globalization tend to hold up cultural difference in defense of populations now dubbed "pirates." Legal scholars, economists, and others who advocate stronger IP laws and stricter enforcement tend to see culture—a term that, for them, indexes tradition, backwardness, rootedness, and a lack of cosmopolitan ethics—as part of the problem that must be overcome in order to successfully achieve the international rule of law and an ordered global economy.[7] There is something larger at stake here, though, than the question of cultural specificity. Anthropological theory has long held that borrowing, appropriation, imitation, and mimesis are fundamental to the elaboration of meaningful material worlds—that culture, in fact, depends on these processes.[8] Historians of fashion and cultural studies scholars have demonstrated that copying is intrinsic to the normal functioning of the modern fashion system (Mason 2008; Stewart 2008; English 2013), and a handful of historians, philosophers, legal scholars, and economists have recently made the case, sometimes in direct response to the expansion of IP law and the intensification of enforcement efforts, that imitation is an undervalued aspect of how creativity and innovation happen.[9] If we take seriously, then, this young Maya man's assertion that "there is no original" in fashion—that anything considered to be an "original" in fashion has already and of necessity been influenced by something that preceded it, and that the trademarked logo is just one design element among others in the contemporary fashion system—and consider the growing body of scholarship that seeks to rescue copying and imitation as necessary and valuable human activities, questions emerge as to why tremendous political and law enforcement resources are being mobilized around the promotion of certain kinds of copying and the prohibition of others. The chapters that follow thus explore the cultural and political dimensions of when, how, and with what justifications distinctions between "good" copying and "bad" copying are drawn at multiple scales, from the regional knockoff economy in highland Guatemala to the globalized discourses of piracy on which international legal regimes are being constructed.

FASHION BRANDS AND THE PRODUCTION OF STYLE

The IP laws that render the activities of Maya apparel manufacturers criminal claim to protect corporate property in the form of trademarks—the brand names, logos, taglines, and other signs and sensory experiences that have come to comprise the "imagery of commerce" (Coombe 1998: 6). Trademarks are the legal technologies on which modern branding and marketing rest. The monopoly protections that registered trademarks have been afforded in the United States and Western Europe since the late nineteenth century have incentivized businesses to invest in these marks as property. Marketing departments and advertising agencies now organize corporate identities, advertising campaigns, brand messaging, and retail interactions around the trademark form.

The big business of branding has been the subject of several sociological and anthropological investigations of late (Lury 2004; Mazzarella 2003; Dávila 2001; R.J. Foster 2007). Another set of studies has examined the diverse meanings that are attached to popular brand names and logos in local contexts and the ways that brands figure into all kinds of cultural and political projects. Robert J. Foster (2008), for example, has explored the reach of the Coca-Cola commodity chain into Papua New Guinea and detailed the brand strategies worked out in corporate offices to integrate the soft drink into everyday consumption routines in that country and imbue the company's trademarked logo with locally salient meanings and values. Rosemary Coombe (1998) draws attention to the role brand names and logos play in contemporary social movements, as activists in the United States and Canada turn recognizable corporate symbols into potent rallying points for political struggles.[10]

The anthropological investigation of branding has often foregrounded the sign-function of trademarks—that is, the way trademarks relay meanings and messages between corporations and consumers. The idea that trademarks are first and foremost vehicles for communicating corporate identity, value, and meaning to potential purchasers of a good or service, to shareholders, and to other kinds of publics is also central to the arguments made by industries, business and legal scholars, and economists in favor of increasingly stringent trademark protections. Brand piracy, the story goes, threatens to disrupt, muddle, and confuse that communication circuit. My research in highland Guatemala suggests that trademarks have other roles in cultural life that are just as central as their signifying capacities. Building on and contributing to a conversation about brands in anthropology that includes the important insights gleaned from semiotics, I propose an approach that also appreciates trademarked fashion brand names and logos as material culture. Trademarked brands are design elements, part of the material repertoire through which people engage in aesthetic projects of identity formation and social organization. In contemporary fashion in particular, the prominent display of brand names and logos on the front of sweatshirts, the back pockets of jeans, and the sides of sneakers is a crucial component in the design and production of fashionable looks that have broad commercial appeal. Trademark law, from this material culture perspective, regulates people's abilities to participate in style.

I use the term "style" to refer to the social production of a particular look and feel that is also a product of multiple and diverse acts of copying, interpretation, collaboration, and contestation. In its colloquial usage in English, style refers to a "way of doing" (Hodder 1982). Archaeologists, cultural studies scholars, and a range of social theorists have found the concept of style useful for exploring how certain confluences take shape in how people do things—especially how they dress, act, or otherwise express themselves—in specific times and places.[11] My own analysis of style in highland Guatemala is influenced heavily by Dick Hebdige (1979), who drew on the concept to explore how class, race, and gender were constituted through material culture in postwar Britain. Hebdige analyzed, among other subcultures, the punk movement of the 1970s. "Rather than presenting class as an abstract set of external determinations," he explained, the goal is to show "it working out in practice as a material force, dressed up, as it were, in experience and exhibited in style" (78). The semiotic and material aspects of style were not separate for Hebdige, who saw in the ripped jeans and safety pins of punk teens a practice of signification that disrupted the social codes of white, middle-class identity and materiality. The sociology of class could not be understood without careful inquiry into the materials themselves and the identities, struggles, disputations, and expressions that materialized in dress and distinctive ways of doing things.

The same is true of knockoff fashion in highland Guatemala, where the young men who grease their hair and wear oversized hoodies with bold brand names are using "stuff" (Miller 2010) to craft new senses of indigenous masculinity and complex relationships to tradition and modernity.[12] IP law encourages a reductive evaluation of the dress

FIGURE 3. Knockoff t-shirts for sale in the municipal market in Tecpán, 2008.

practices of Maya youth, positing that these teenagers are merely copying or mimicking signs of status that properly belong to brand owners
in North America and Western Europe, but such a framing misses the
ways that branded fashions are part of regional processes through
which class, gender, race, and ethnicity are being expressed and contested in the highlands. This is not only a story of the globalization of
brands and the far reaches and echoes of corporate marketing
campaigns—although mass-mediated images of fashion and celebrity
do influence style in highland Guatemala, just as they do in any other
part of the world. Nor is it about localization—how commodities and
signs produced elsewhere become meaningful in a particular setting or
marginal place. Rather, this is a story about how highland Guatemala
rightly belongs to the global arena of fashion and style. It is a place with
its own fashion industry that has been built up and embedded over the
course of decades in relation to shifting regimes of regulation and technologies of rule that govern trade and economics in Guatemala and
around the globe. Tecpán is a town where fashion is crafted through the
same processes of copying and creativity that drive design in Paris,
London, and New York and where youthful consumers get excited

about the appearance of new designs on the tables and racks of outdoor markets and corner shops and then show them off in the central plaza. They stand around and stand out as part of an elaborate cultural scene and stylized space, participating in aesthetics that are combinatory and contextual. This book tells the story of a local industry that contributes meaningfully to the elaboration of what is and could be fashionable in the world. Highland Guatemala is a place where creativity and productivity are thriving, even in the midst of entrenched poverty, violence, and corruption; discrimination on the basis of indigeneity, gender, and dress; and persistent efforts on the part of states, corporations, and international institutions to regulate, relegate, marginalize, and criminalize the work that Maya people do.

Style is about practice, performance, and identification. It is about appropriating and using material culture in ways that make statements and articulate positions within and across social and political landscapes. At its core, style involves a dialectical relationship between instantiation and interpretation (Hodder 1990). When a Maya manufacturer designs a garment, for example, he both instantiates a particular design and interprets the aesthetic genres that are already available. His interpretation references what has come before, participates in an aesthetic and material milieu that is wrapped up with broader cultural meanings and processes, and reveals future possibilities for how people might dress and identify in highland Guatemala and beyond. Style is thus manifest in the flow of social life and is an iterative process through which identities and subjectivities take shape in relation to evolving materialities and cultural contexts. In order to be recognizable as style— to have social and aesthetic significance—any expression must refer to a more general patterning and engage a dynamic temporality and historical formation that unfolds across multiple materializations. This theory of style applies equally well to the highland apparel trade and the fashion industry at large. Each "new" design is admittedly, on the part of so many US and European fashion designers and brand owners, an interpretation of extant cultural forms and not an isolated event or a pure creation that comes from nowhere (see Hilton et al. 2004; Raustiala and Sprigman 2006; Hemphill and Suk 2009). It is indeed only through acts of interpretation, repetition, association, and differentiation that a design becomes available and recognizable to consumers and critics as "fashion," as Roland Barthes (1990) so poignantly argued.

By "regulating style," I mean two things. First, I use the phrase to describe the work that IP law does to control, delegitimize, and constrain the momentum and dynamism of fashion and style—to regulate ways of making, dressing, expressing, and contesting that are evident in diverse settings. Building on scholarship in critical legal studies, cultural studies, postcolonial studies, and political and legal anthropology, I argue that IP law participates in the neocolonial segregation of world regions and racialized populations according to categories of authenticity and mimicry, real and fake, and creative minds and copycats. The authority granted to multinational corporations and nation-states to set the parameters of what counts as creativity and originality and what does not has the effect of perpetually relegating marginalized and subordinated groups to the wrong side of development and modernity in a way that may never be overcome, creating a scenario in which Maya people are potentially able to imitate the styles of dress, business, and entrepreneurship that are promoted in First World development schemes and nationalist projects but will never obtain equal footing with the officially and legally authorized progenitors of globalized standards and models. In relation to the "real" fashion industry presumed to be located in North American and Western European metropoles that also house the international finance, trade, and legal institutions that structure a global economy, Maya people involved in making and wearing branded fashions are, at best, "almost the same, but not quite" (Bhabha 1984: 126), and, at worst, criminal actors seeking to undermine law, progress, and modernity.

The second sense in which I use the phrase "regulating style" in this book has to do with the fact that the trade in knockoff fashion in highland Guatemala is regulated on a regional level according to well-developed business ethics, modes of organization, and styles of work in spite of official portraits of the trade as an "illegal" and "informal," or unregulated, economy. Maya workshop owners style their employment practices, business relationships, and design and marketing strategies in accordance with regional norms related to kinship and felt contours of community and belonging; past and present experiences of state violence, violent crime, and corruption; and globalized discourses of entrepreneurship and development that are variously taken up, enacted, and contested by state agencies, NGOs, and workshop owners themselves. The chapters that follow thus contribute in important ways to conversations in economic anthropology about the diversity of ways that capitalist activities and industrial labor are organized around the world (often in the absence of or in spite of "formal" regulation) and the importance of culture, morality, norms, and values to economic practice and systems of production at multiple scales. It is at the intersections of the aesthetics of everyday life, the politics and meanings of dress, the racialized and gendered structures of control in a postcolony, and the creative, productive, and controlling processes through which material worlds and economic systems take shape that the study of style becomes most anthropological and, thus, most compelling for me.

HIGHLAND STYLE

Fashion brand names and logos derive meaning and value from the fact that they are incorporated into processes of stylistic and stylized production, consumption, and interpretation that implicate the clothing designs to which a brand name or logo is affixed, but also from the material, aesthetic, and semiotic contexts in which the design materializes and the broader milieu of cultural politics that influences expressive forms. In other words, brands take on meaning in relation to the styles of which they form a part, and the emphasis on individual ownership, accountability, and originality promoted in the fashion industry and enshrined in IP law obscures the collective, historical, and political aspects of how style is constituted as a social fact. Working in a way that owes much to Hebdige's study of style and culture, I argue that appreciating brands in terms of style means situating the use of brand names and logos within the relevant context of cultural production, apprehending the historical currents that shape material culture and aesthetic sensibilities in a given place and time, and engaging ethnographically with the politics of identification and differentiation that contour style and social life in diverse worlds.

Branded fashions are just one part of a vibrant scene. They fit into a generalized look and feel—a world of style—in highland Guatemala that is colorful and loud. The secondhand school buses imported from the United States and operated by private transportation companies are famously painted in bright hues of blue, red, and green with streamers, reflective stickers, stuffed animals, blinking lights strung inside and out, and high-powered speakers blasting *norteña* music. The same goes for *tuc-tucs*, the motorcycle taxis imported from India that fly about the streets of towns like Tecpán sporting brightly colored decals, bold paint jobs, and custom electric horns that blast a popular song or a humorous sound effect. This aesthetic effervescence also includes and links together the Christmas Eve fireworks that are shot off from every home in town; the enormous speaker systems rented out for birthdays, baptisms, and weddings that force entire blocks to share in

FIGURE 4. Secondhand school bus, brightly painted in red, blue, and yellow, carrying passengers in the Guatemalan highlands, 2009.

the celebrations; and the reflective decals proclaiming "¡Dios Es Amor!" (God Is Love!) on the front of highway buses. The use of brand names on oversized hoodies is part of this broader context of style and substance, a way of doing and dressing and expressing that is more flourishing and festooned than concepts of imitation, mimesis, or copying would suggest. An Abercrombie & Fitch logo on the front of a sweatshirt is a reiteration of an effusive aesthetics that makes life in the region visually arresting and baroque. And each example given here is a mode of expression and an affective moment in which people are saying something about themselves and their relationships to a wider world but also doing something ordinary—fitting into and being part of a scene that has creative momentum and intensity.

Highland style stands out against the backdrop of deep economic poverty and precarity that also characterizes the postcolonial space within which the buses and *tuc-tucs* motor about and the birthday parties take place. More than half of the country's 13 million inhabitants live in poverty. Guatemalans attend school for an average of four years, and the country has the second-highest illiteracy rate in the western hemisphere, after Haiti. Nearly half of children under the age of five suffer from chronic malnutrition (World Bank 2015; United Nations Development Programme 2015). In a country with one of the highest rates of inequality in Latin America, these numbers look much worse for indigenous Maya men and women. Indigenous people make up 50 to 60 percent of the national population. They are more than twice as likely to be poor than nonindigenous Guatemalans (Cabrera et al. 2015).

Compounding the situation of poverty and inequality are rising violent crime rates and rampant impunity. The internal armed conflict sparked by a US-led coup d'état in 1954 ended in 1996 with peace accords negotiated by the United Nations. Still, everyday life for many Guatemalans is fraught with violence. The country has the sixth-highest murder rate in the world, due mostly to drug trafficking between South America and the United States and indicative of a regional spike in transnational gang activity over the past fifteen years that has been driven in part by the US-led War on Drugs.[13] There are political assassinations, drug traffickers wage brutal turf wars, and gang members command extortion rings that target businesses (O'Neill and Thomas 2011), including apparel workshops in Tecpán. Everyone I spoke with over the course of my field research had been witness to or a victim of crime, from the armed robberies that are daily occurrences on highway buses to holdups outside banks and ATM machines in the capital city.[14] These incidents are an ordinary part of life in Guatemala.

Government officials and the World Bank characterize Guatemala as a "developing" nation and lament its weak institutions, meager tax revenues, and general lack of the rule of law. These assessments are, in a sense, an attempt to describe the difficulty, danger, and limited life chances with which most Guatemalans contend, but they generally obscure the ways that histories of colonialism and First World interventionism and the contemporary coupling of the rule of law with unfair and austere economic schemes and modes of militarization organized around failed drug policies conspire to produce the very conditions of poverty and insecurity that contour daily life in the region. They also fail to acknowledge the way that style serves as a potent and valuable resource for people who occupy the margins of a global economy, those for whom the promises of "development" continually fall short. In the midst of very difficult circumstances, highland residents craft a way of doing and of relating to one another and to the world that is fundamentally creative and expressive. Highland style is imbricated with everyday precarity, and its effervescence in no way excuses or resists the ongoing subordination of indigenous Guatemalans within an unequal and unjust political economy. Rather, highland style emerges out of these histories of violence and takes shape in relation to the workings of power at multiple scales. As I explain here and elaborate on throughout this book, style cannot be separated from regional, national, and international structures of difference that have shaped class, gender, race, and ethnicity in the highlands.

Highland residents are quick to distinguish ornate sweatshirts, jackets, and shoes from types of clothing that, while they may be just as colorful, are considered "traditional," as *tecpanecos* put it. Traditional clothing, or *traje*, usually worn by Maya women, is part of the same vibrant and elaborate scene described above, with festive and nuanced designs that include intricate flowers, bold geometric patterns, bright stripes of red and purple, or rich tones of maroon and gold, depending on the origin, status, and tastes of the wearer. But the young people, mostly young men, who sport Hollister tees and hoodies are choosing to wear something decidedly *other* than indigenous dress. This is salient because race, ethnicity, and gender are key axes of differentiation in highland Guatemala, and they are marked perhaps most powerfully through what people wear. The *mujer maya* (D. Nelson 1999) enveloped in her handwoven *huipil* (blouse) and *corte* (skirt) not only symbolizes indigeneity for Maya cultural activists (see Otzoy 1996) but also serves as a basis for Guatemalan nationalism. Maya women in *traje* adorn the pages of guidebooks and illustrate tourism websites and advertising. The Maya—many of whom were killed during Guatemala's internal armed conflict because they exhibited visible signs of ethnic difference, which were read as communism to justify a genocidal military campaign—and their textiles are now the primary means by which Guatemala attracts foreign investment and tourism dollars and elaborates a fantastical image of itself as having a ready-to-consume cultural heritage. The state and private enterprise capitalize on culture to create a national brand around indigeneity, part of a worldwide trend that John and Jean Comaroff (2009) call "Ethnicity, Inc."

For example, the online advertisement from Guatemala's National Tourism Institute shown in figure 5 displays the crisp blue waters of Lake Atitlan, a favorite tourist destination, and reads, "With your vote, we'll be one of the Seven Natural Wonders of the World!" The ad references an online contest sponsored by the United Nations. However, it is not entirely clear whether the "natural wonder" the text references is the volcanic lake or the indigenous woman pictured in the foreground of

FIGURE 5. Online promotion from Guatemala's National Tourism Institute, encouraging people to vote for Lake Atitlan in an international contest, 2011.

the advertisement wearing her *huipil* and *corte*. She stands with her back to the audience, gazing out across the lake, and carries an infant on her back, tucked snugly inside the shawl cinched around her shoulders. Naturalized as a static custom, her clothing serves as a reference point for tradition and a counterpoint for what it means for Guatemala, and Guatemalans, to become modern and developed, that is, not part of a natural landscape. She is, quite literally, the progenitor of Guatemala's national culture and, at the same time, a symbol of the country's native past, with her back turned to the modern viewer and the digital age he or she inhabits. The visual codes and rhetorical strategies exemplified in this marketing message are central to the project of neoliberal multiculturalism in Guatemala that at once celebrates cultural and national difference and conceals the deep historical and ongoing marginalization of and discrimination against indigenous people in Guatemala. The advertisement also illustrates how indigenous clothing is treated as a kind of property, the cultural property of the state, which can be packaged and sold to foreign audiences.

Maya *traje* is "a symbolically rich, polyvalent and visually stimulating domain of representation," writes Edward F. Fischer (2001: 117). Carol Hendrickson (1995: 193), an anthropologist who has long studied traditional clothing in Guatemala, notes that, for many Maya men and women, "there is an ideological and emotional identification with *traje* such that dress is inextricably associated with the person's very being." There is a felt "equivalence between dress and cultural heart," she writes (193). *Traje* is an important marker of geography, ethnicity, and aspects of experience and identification that are part and parcel of what it means to be Maya in Guatemala. Nearly every highland town has its own distinctive *traje,* and, in the past, the color, design, and manner of wearing traditional dress signaled the municipality from which the wearer originated (51). Today, it is increasingly common for Maya women to wear designs from various towns, a trend promoted by leaders of the pan-Maya movement, a loose affiliation of cultural rights activists, during the peace process that ended the internal armed conflict to encourage a sense of commonality and solidarity among indigenous Guatemalans regardless of regional, linguistic, or historical differences (Fischer and Brown 1996).

Indigeneity in Guatemala is contrasted in everyday discourse and practice with a constellation of ways of dressing, looking, behaving, and belonging—a style—signaled by the term *ladino.* In the early nineteenth century, a "complicated colonial racial scheme" involving numerous categories and distinctions was collapsed by the political class and economic elite into this dualistic racial and ethnic division between *ladinos* and *indios* ("Indians," a pejorative term in Guatemala; Grandin 2000: 83–85). Today, *ladino* describes any Guatemalan who does not identify as indigenous. Not wearing *traje,* not speaking a Mayan language, not having a recognizably indigenous surname or exhibiting stereotypically indigenous phenotypes, residing in urban spaces, demonstrating relatively high socioeconomic status through consumption, being relatively well-educated—Guatemalans take into account any and all of these characteristics when making a determination about a person's location within an ethnic and racial scheme. Both categories, *indígena* (a term used by my informants to describe themselves and others perceived to share Maya heritage) and *ladino,* are somewhat flexible, and modes and tactics of identification may change depending on social and geographical context, as I will detail in later chapters.

Given the strong personal, cultural, and political significance of *traje* in Guatemala, it may seem curious that many Maya youth and adults choose to wear *vestido,* the "common clothes" that Carol Hendrickson (1995: 66) described twenty years ago as involving a "foreign element in clothing merchandise and fashion (inspiration)." This style or preference might seem to be an outright rejection of tradition or a mundane mode of mimesis. It matters to Maya consumers that nontraditional, industrially manufactured clothes are often cheaper than handwoven *traje.* There is also the fact that most indigenous Guatemalan men have been wearing European-inspired pants and shirts for a long time, due primarily to sumptuary laws and the politics of passing and belonging that characterized the colonial and early postcolonial periods. Perhaps young Guatemalans want to be viewed by their peers as in-style or on-trend, and in Guatemala, as in many other places, this means adopting clothing that is popular within the global fashion system. The privatization and consolidation of media, the rise of transnational capitalism and mass marketing, and the proliferation of communications technologies conspire to pare down the kinds of messages and images to which people are exposed, leaving youth around the world with a rather homogenous vocabulary for expressing taste (see Nakassis 2016). This pattern of "taste transfer" from center to periphery certainly fuels the globalization of consumption patterns (Appadurai 1993: 419). Youth in Guatemala are regularly exposed to the brand names and looks that are promoted as fashionable in advertisements, on television, online, and in department stores. They listen to Latin and US pop music during the day and watch Argentinean, Mexican, and US cable channels at night. They head to Internet cafes after school or work to download music, watch movie trailers, play video games, and surf entertainment sites. The fashions donned by soccer players, singers, film stars, and television actors—none of whom are identifiable as "indigenous" in the sense that term has acquired in Guatemala, but who all fit into the racial schema that defines elements of whiteness and class status associated with being *ladino*—become topics of conversation, saturate the public culture, and influence what people make and wear.

While the globalization and homogenization of fashion is part of this story, what interests me is how fashion branding fits into the experiential world of style and styling in which Maya men and women actively produce material culture and elaborate an aesthetic richness and meaningful existence. Maya people interact with globalized media and material culture as participants in a vibrant local fashion industry, one that has its own legitimate and legitimating ontology and that is certainly connected to the production, marketing, and consumption of fashion in other places and at other scales. James Ferguson (1999) conceptualized the dress habits, ways of speaking, and norms adopted by urban Zambians in terms of "cosmopolitan style" and argued that an orientation toward the Other and the outside largely defined how young people in the capital city represented themselves to fellow Zambians, especially their similarly situated peers and rural kin. Migration and mobility are also important to Tecpán's fashion scene and the local industry. Maya men and women who travel to work in places such as New Jersey, Florida, and California return to the highlands having adopted elements of Latino, Chicano, and other styles and, in turn, influence trends in their hometowns. Cosmopolitanism and cognate senses of modernity, urbanity, and middle-class-ness are constitutive of stylistic sensibilities in the highlands, which do take shape in relation to what is perceived as traditional or *not* fashionable. But style in highland Guatemala is not simply a function of what is happening somewhere else or reducible to a theory of cosmopolitanism. Rather, the styles that young Maya men participate in and that they often also labor to make as workshop employees have developed in relation to the general look and feel of highland life, trends unfolding in the media and across peer groups, and aesthetic movements happening within the local industry and amid national and regional political conversations about the markers and meanings of indigeneity. Even when indigenous apparel producers told me that the popularity of clothing styles depends on how the original is "moving" or selling (*como se mueve lo original*), they did not use the term "original" to reference an authorized brand name or "authentic" garment that had come from the United States or Europe. Instead, the distinctions they drew between "original" fashions and what they called "imitations" indexed all kinds of attributes, especially price, the quality of materials and construction, and the specific retail location where the garment was sold. As I discuss in later chapters, these attributes are meaningful to Maya apparel producers and highland consumers because of how they map onto, reflect, and produce regional class inequalities and ethnic and racial divisions. These structures of difference that have emerged out of multiscalar histories and political and economic processes matter for how fashion is made in Guatemala, and they influence cultural contestations over what people wear and what it means.

THE REGULATION OF STYLE

There is a great deal at stake for institutions, including states and corporations, in the regulation of style. Managing the patterning and meaning of dress, for example, is also a way to shape culture, politics, and economies in specific directions. Dress codes and sumptuary laws popularized in late medieval Europe and integrated into colonial projects in Latin America and other parts of the world were instrumental to the making of gender, class, market systems, and colonial worlds and, at the same time, provided a mechanism through which style could be interpreted as a static marker of difference and a measure of deservedness (Hunt 1996; John L. Comaroff and Jean Comaroff 1997; Garber 1992). The chapters that follow advance the claim that IP law is another important domain for analyzing and assessing the regulation of style (Beebe 2010, 2013; Ponte 2009). Just who holds the rights to produce and reproduce material culture, to promote particular ways of dressing and doing, and to consume and interpret style has wide-ranging consequences for how social relations, politics, and markets take shape.

In recent decades, anthropologists looking at the globalization of IP law have debated, on the one hand, the potential benefits of expanding the regime to protect forms of property that matter to indigenous people and other marginalized populations and, on the other hand, the incommensurability of IP frameworks with the diverse ontologies, property systems, and ways of life evident among various social groups. Rosemary Coombe (1998) has argued that IP mechanisms could be a powerful tool for indigenous peoples struggling against exploitative market forces (see also Benthall 1999; Brush 1993; Brush and Stabinsky 1996). Demands for copyright or patent protections for native art forms, tribal names and other ethnic identifiers, and agricultural knowledge and seed varieties, for example, have become important "axes of mobilization" in the larger sphere of indigenous organizing (Hayden 2003: 38). At the same time, Stuart Kirsch (2004) and others (M. F. Brown 1998, 2005; Aoki 1998; Hirsch and Strathern 2004) question whether granting indigenous groups rights and protections based on the international IP framework primarily expands the reach of Western institutional and market logics with little demonstrated regard for indigenous concepts of property or ownership and in ways that may actually further disadvantage indigenous peoples in relation to multinational capital and bureaucratic states. Creative projects that stretch back through time and across entire communities—folklore, performances, and oral histories, for example, what legal scholar Susan Scafidi (2005) calls "cultural products"—do not easily fit into hegemonic IP models.[15] Partly in response to such criticism, the WTO and the World Intellectual Property Organization (WIPO)—the United Nations agency charged with promoting international IP law and administering various multilateral agreements—have turned greater attention in recent years to developing alternative IP frameworks built around native concepts and practices, including special protections for "cultural expressions" and "traditional knowledge." Anthropologists remain skeptical, however, since the effectiveness of such frameworks still depends on the translation of local cultural norms into a set of legal rights that can be harmonized with international law, leaving important questions of incommensurability by the wayside (Kirsch 2004; Povinelli 2001).[16]

The fact that most discussions taking place within international institutions such as the WTO and WIPO about the property rights of indigenous peoples focus on traditional knowledge, folklore, and the management of biodiversity reflects stereotypical assumptions about who indigenous people are and what they do (i.e., they are agriculturalists or ritual specialists) and their relationship to the world and to technology (i.e., they are sources of raw materials that may be converted into modern technologies, but they are not themselves part of the modern world system). That indigenous populations actively participate in transnational movements of goods and ideas, are integrated into national and global economies (often sitting at the bottom of the socioeconomic order), and increasingly live in cities (Morgan and Gulson 2010) is overlooked in such discussions. Current property debates do not take into account either that indigenous peoples are more and more confronted with IP, not as benefactors of special copyright and patent protections but as producers and consumers of criminalized classes of goods, as in the case of the knockoff fashion trade that I describe.

Attention to style, as I conceptualize the term, offers an important corrective to this mode of stereotyping and expands anthropological debates about property and indigeneity in important directions. International IP law has the effect of limiting who has access to certain material cultural forms and the styles of which they are a part. When poor people are criminalized for wearing fake Nike shoes or Levi's jeans, for example, trademark law functions to reproduce a "system of consumption-based social distinction and the social structures and norms based on it" (Beebe 2010: 814) even as the broader development and modernization framework aims to cultivate consumer desire and orient people toward market participation as a means of fulfillment and a mode of exercising citizenship rights. Indigenous populations can be caught in the middle of these social and institutional dynamics, since they are simultaneously compelled by nation-states and the development industry to "update" their ways of life and conform to recognizable, "modern" styles but then denigrated as imposters when they attempt to do so. Elizabeth Povinelli (2002: 13) recounts the double bind faced by indigenous Australians in this regard: Australian state authorities recoil from "encounters with difference they consider abhorrent, inhuman, and bestial," but they also balk at encounters "with differences they consider too hauntingly similar to themselves to warrant social entitlements—for example, land claims by indigenous people who dress, act, and sound like the suburban neighbors they are."

International IP law regulates access and consumption, but it also influences who can do what in life, who can be recognized as a legitimate creator and progenitor of recognizable ways of doing, and who can fill landscapes with aesthetic and material projects and forms of expression and experience. IP law draws a line between "good" and "bad" copying that is also about separating the so-called rightful participants in creative industries and high-status consumer classes from populations that are racialized and marginalized as Others, associated with tradition or backwardness, and viewed as not properly modern in their ways of making and using certain material cultural forms. The limits that IP law places on production and consumption are important aspects of how the culture industry and contemporary consumer capitalism generate what Bourdieu (1984) calls "distinction," or the differential access to cultural capital that permits some populations, defined by their already privileged economic—but also racialized, ethnicized, and gendered—social positions, to convert style into economic profits and increase their social advantage. IP law polices the boundaries of who can make and own style, market it, display it, and, in turn, use it to further influence systems of status and privilege. My investigation of IP law and the regulation of style thus has broad implications for understanding global economic development and the uneven distribution of property and power in the world. It directs our attention to the ironic fact that people who innovate, conduct business, and undertake creative and entrepreneurial activity are often opposed, devalued, and denigrated at the same time as they are said to be "resource-poor" and in need of "development."

Hence, an important dimension of the regulation of style explored in this book has to do with the production of particular economic rationalities and market relations that are also an explicit component of what the international expansion of IP law is supposed to accomplish. Business scholars and economists contend that IP law enforcement and education efforts are necessary to spur innovation, drive technology change and economic growth, and cultivate proper business and consumer ethics in societies that are seen as having problematic "cultures" of copying or collectivism (Maskus 2000, 2012; Fink and Maskus 2005; Helpman 1992; Lai 1998; Chen and Puttitanun 2005; Gould and Gruben 1996;

Husted 2000; Marron and Steele 2000). Understanding how enforcement efforts are taking shape and what effects they are having on markets and business practices in a place like highland Guatemala could offer a lot to these scholarly conversations, which also drive policy implementation and structure normative frameworks.

I conceptualize business practice and business ethics in highland Guatemala—the ways of making, marketing, managing, and moralizing that are part of the knockoff fashion trade—in terms of a regional "regulating style" that is challenged and undermined by IP enforcement efforts. International economic and legal frameworks have a "regulating style"— a way of seeking to control and shape business activities—but so do indigenous apparel manufacturers who must negotiate, contend with, and conform to the knowledge systems and business practices that are idealized in the development industry and in master narratives about modernization. For my analysis of these styles, I draw on recent anthropological writings on economic regulation, especially a set of ethnographies that have focused on what social scientists since the 1970s have termed the "informal economy." This label has been used to describe economic activities—ranging from domestic work and craft production to peddling, smuggling, and piracy—that fall outside the purview of state agencies and escape bureaucratic attempts at regulation and revenue extraction. Anthropologists have been interested in how work is organized and how proceeds and profits get distributed within informal economies, as well as the tendency among states and corporate interests to disparage informal sectors—which are most often comprised of poor and marginalized populations that are structurally excluded from formal education and enterprise—sometimes equating them with organized crime rings and often framing their activities as illegal.[17]

Along these lines, Janet Roitman (2005: 18) demonstrated that informal economic sectors, including the smuggling circuits she researched in Central Africa, often turn out to be sites of the "pluralization of regulatory authority" rather than spaces devoid of governance or unregulated by authoritative and normative frameworks. In other words, nonstate modes of regulation come to predominate in these arenas. This is indeed the case with the apparel trade in highland Guatemala, which is largely hidden from state agencies but nonetheless involves a wide array of actors, including national and local police (who extort rents from apparel producers and raid market stalls selling knockoff fashions); gang members (who also extort rents and threaten the physical safety of producers); wholesalers, retailers, and other market intermediaries (who help determine prices, regulate market access, and distribute business risk); and workshop owners themselves. All of these groups exercise control over the accumulation of wealth, the distribution of resources within and beyond the trade, and the moral implications of what it means to copy designs and produce styles. Apparel producers are caught up with various other people and institutions in social and market networks as well as with cultural dynamics related to kinship, reciprocity, and concepts of moral personhood and professionalism, and their work involves processes of business accounting and accountability that often contradict or depart from state forms of discipline and control or the norms and business styles that are globalized in regimes of IP regulation.

National and international law, in fact, carry little weight with apparel producers in the highlands. From the perspective of many highland residents, whose most immediate experiences of the state have been in the form of a cruel and bloody war in which they were the targets of a genocidal military campaign, the normative frameworks built into state law seem culturally relative and intimately wrapped up with elite power and privilege. The efforts of international institutions to promote a liberal political framework and the rule of law since the armed conflict ended seem contradicted by contemporary realities of government corruption, violent crime, and deepening economic inequality. In this context, apparel producers have met recent attempts by state agencies to impel formalization, collect taxes, and prohibit trademark law infringement largely with suspicion or disdain. And the mandate of formalization efforts and IP law enforcement not only ignores the socially embedded, if "informal," modes of regulation and business ethics that already make the apparel trade an important and productive economic sector in the highlands but also deems that business style criminal and illicit.

The anthropological study of informal economies suggests another key direction for understanding the intersection of IP law and business style in the highlands. Recent ethnographies have explored various implications of the fact that economic activities that fall outside the purview of state bureaucratic apparatuses have, over the past few decades, been revalued by international financial institutions and nongovernmental organizations as sites of tremendous growth potential in the so-called developing world. In highland Guatemala, there are now tens of thousands of development NGOs, microfinance agencies, and public-private partnerships oriented toward the promotion of rural enterprise and small-scale business (Rohloff et al. 2011). In recent years, entrepreneurship has become a powerful discourse through which the income-generating activities of poor people in many places are evaluated by an international development industry made up of international institutions, state governments, NGOs, and private investors and through which disciplinary interventions in the lives of the poor are articulated and justified (Elyachar 2005; Freeman 2007; John L. Comaroff and Jean Comaroff 2009; Isik 2010; DeHart 2010). Neoliberal economic reforms, including structural adjustment policies implemented in Guatemala in the early 1990s, have aimed at liberating "individual entrepreneurial freedoms" by liberalizing market relations and restricting government "interference" in the form of public works, social services, and tariffs and other trade restrictions (Harvey 2005: 2). The "figure of the entrepreneur," as Carla Freeman notes (2007: 252), is "considered neoliberalism's quintessential actor" (see also Bourdieu 1998) and the solution to all kinds of social and economic ills (Cassis and Minoglou 2005; A. Smith 2005). Microloans to poor individuals, for example, have been favored by the World Bank as a way of solving problems ranging from poverty in sub-Saharan Africa to potable water shortages in Latin America.[18] Development economists consider IP protections central to the promotion of conditions that allow "entrepreneurship" to thrive (Casson and Godley 2005).

Entrepreneurship—understood as a set of meanings and values globalized via discourses of neoliberal development, integrated into the practices of diverse institutional actors, and deeply entangled with IP law's rationalities—has ethnographically visible regulatory and disciplinary effects on the lives of Maya workshop owners. The producers of knockoff fashions could be viewed as just the sort of microenterprise owners and creative individuals who can fuel developing economies. But their business styles are more often evaluated by multinational capital and state agencies as being outside of the acceptable range of rationalities, orientations, and activities that are deemed legitimate and effective in economic growth models and development goals. As anthropologists have repeatedly shown, the meaning of "development" entails the international and institutional advocacy of a moral project that aims to craft particular subjectivities—styles of self, practices of comportment, and models of behavior—that lend themselves to a capitalist business ethos and work ethic and yield easily to entrenched and hegemonic forms of governance, surveillance, order, authority, and extraction (J. Ferguson 1990; Escobar 1995; Gardner and Lewis 1996; Mitchell 2002; Li 2007; James 2010). The international development industry wants to produce people who follow the law and work hard as individuals to maximize profits, clearing the way for the invisible hand to work its magic. The pursuit of this goal—the production of sufficiently "modern," enterprising, and otherwise appropriate subjects within colonial and postcolonial contexts of rule and regulation—involves ordering the technological and material worlds that people inhabit (Mitchell 1991, 2002; Keane 2007; Chakrabarty 2000; Sundaram 2010). In the chapters that follow, I examine various aspects of the material world of business in Tecpán—from the distribution of machinery and other forms of capital to the use of receipts and other calculating tools (Callon 1998)—and the modes of regulation that surround them in the highlands. IP law and the wider discourse of development dismiss the regulating style of Maya businessmen and disparage the normative frameworks that structure the production of fashion in the knockoff trade. Maya apparel producers are criminalized for breaking the law by producing illicit and illegal "copies," but, in my view, the real threat—deeper and perhaps more covert—that the IP regime guards against is the potential for racialized and subordinated populations, such as Maya men, to disrupt the processes of spatial and temporal boundary making that relegate brown and black bodies to the past, to backwardness, and to being something less than and other than modern and to instantiate new social and material worlds that show up the arbitrariness of the forms of privilege and authority that divide the globe into creators and copycats.

THE STRUCTURE OF THE BOOK

In the course of this book, I lay out my findings regarding the contexts of production and regulation that describe the business of knockoff fashion in highland Guatemala. These findings implicate grand histories of legal and economic globalization, the evolution of trademark law and corporate strategy, and transnational trends in fashion and branding. I also trace the histories and recent experiences of people struggling to come to terms with a violent past and to earn a living amid rampant insecurities and ongoing upheaval. I have organized these discussions into five chapters and a brief conclusion. Chapter 1 tells a story of how the apparel-manufacturing trade in and around Tecpán came to be, paying special attention to its historical relationship to shifting national and international regulatory contexts. I draw out a dialectical relationship that is key to the unfolding of business style in the highlands—namely, a tension between the sharing of knowledge, resources, and information in the trade and the value of concealment for Maya manufacturers who actively and strategically hide their work from state agents. I describe transformations in the trade since the 1960s that are related to the internal armed conflict and the more recent advent of free trade regimes that privilege multinational capital and especially *maquiladoras* (large-scale garment-export factories) over local industry. This history, recounted via the life stories of Maya workshop owners, builds on anthropological work on regulation and challenges evolutionary models of economic "development" that assume economies move naturally and progressively from less formal to more formal relationships to the state and that such an evolution brings about material benefits for the regulated, "developing" populations.

Having described the historical contexts of the local industry, chapter 2 broadens out to a story about the political and legal processes through which the globalization of IP law has taken place, and then I get down to describing the everyday work routines of Maya apparel workshop owners and employees. Copying, borrowing, and appropriation are part and parcel of the elaboration of style in the highlands. These practices are also the subject of ongoing ethical debate in Tecpán. I argue that workshop owners evaluate "copying" in light of norms and values that differ significantly from those promoted in IP law. These normative models—which revolve around ideas about envy, individualism, and fair and unfair competition—and the market strategies evident among Maya businessmen parochialize official portraits of business ethics and innovation built into the IP regime and challenge assumptions about progress, improvement, and ordering on which the wider development industry is based.

Chapter 3 delves into the world of brands and branding. Scholarly analyses and bureaucratic approaches to IP law tend to treat brands primarily as communications media that relay information from corporations to consumers. Trademark protections are justified largely as measures that protect and promote the efficient transfer of information along this route and in terms of the legal doctrine of "brand dilution." In the chapter, I question that framing by analyzing brands as design elements that derive their value and meaning from the contexts of material culture and social practice in which branded goods circulate, drawing evidence from the design and marketing strategies of Maya apparel workshop owners. I critically engage with the sociology and anthropology of dress and examine the branding strategies of several multinational fashion firms, especially Abercrombie & Fitch. I make the case that the globalization of trademark law is, among other things, an attempt to concretize and naturalize neocolonial divides along the lines of geography, race, ethnicity, and gender, which positions some populations as rightful creators and stylish consumers and others as mere copycats or deviants. In the last sections of the chapter, I describe the efforts of some Maya workshop owners who have embraced technical-legal discourses of intellectual property to market their goods using unique brands that reference their indigenous identity, and then I explore the political implications and consequences of such marketing moves and the lessons it has for the anthropology of IP law.

I foreground and explicate my analytical approach to material culture in chapter 4, where my focus is on the material technologies and techniques of business accounting. The chapter explores a government campaign that urges Guatemalans to "Ask for your receipt!" after every economic transaction. The campaign disparages business owners and service workers who fail to conform to models of professionalism and modernity associated with economic formalization and encourages consumers to demand that businesses adopt a more professional style premised on the use of paper. The chapter includes a discussion of how the international development industry—including microfinance and microloan programs—similarly privileges the use of certain modes of calculation, accounting techniques, and methods of documentation in the promotion of neoliberal, entrepreneurial forms of development. While Maya workshop owners worry that receipts accede to authority and concede their businesses to the state, they have their own charged debates about the accounting styles of neighbors and competitors and the place of documentation in their trade. People working in the regional apparel trade assess how their fellow clothing producers record transactions, set prices, manage debt, and figure profit in relation to and in the form of a gendered discourse on what it means to be a good businessman and a good citizen.

Chapter 5 is devoted to security—a topic that I have explored elsewhere in depth (see O'Neill and Thomas 2011). I draw on framings from medical, legal, and economic anthropology to understand how Maya workshops owners and other highland residents alternatively take up or contest the language of human rights and rule of law in a context of everyday violence and widespread social suffering. Amid rising violent crime rates, the emergence of extortion rings, and endemic government corruption, workshop owners have recently adopted private security measures that are sometimes termed by scholars, journalists, and activists as "indigenous law." This characterization implies a relationship to the past and to tradition and can obscure the complex relationship between enterprising forms of security evident in Maya communities and neoliberal ideologies of entrepreneurial freedom, transnational "security talk" (Goldstein 2007) and discourses of national security, and deep histories of state violence and discrimination against indigenous people. My analysis of community-level security measures and the discourses of blame that circulate among Maya workshop owners also reveals the importance of space and scale in how people make sense of insecurity and lay claim to forms of work, membership, and belonging that they understand as decidedly not criminal or immoral, such as the work of brand piracy.

The book closes with some reflections on the concept of style. Piracy is disparaged everywhere as the mere reproduction of something that has already been done, but the ethnography of knockoff fashion in Guatemala demonstrates that copying is part of the dialectical movement of style, out of which something "new" is created. I discuss the temporality of style and its relationship to race, indigeneity, tradition, and modernity in Guatemala, taking my cue from Edward Said's (2006) writings on what he termed "late style." My hope is that readers come to see that Maya participation in the fashion system is a dynamic engagement with globalized material culture and a thriving local industry, realities that upturn the notion that indigenous people are defined by the past. That the criminalized, moralized, and politicized category of "pirate" gets attached to their activities (and the production and consumption activities of so many other groups around the world) reflects historically rooted structures of power and a gap between international development frameworks that promote indigenous and "ethnic entrepreneurship" (DeHart 2010) as the way forward and legal regimes that criminalize copying and actual forms of enterprise, innovation, and business. Apprehending this contradiction and understanding its foundations are central to ongoing debates over law, fashion, and the place of ordinary people and diverse populations in the global economy.

CHAPTER 1

Economic Regulation and the Value of Concealment

Guillermo Ordóñez owned one of the garment workshops in which I spent time cutting and sewing garments in Tecpán Guatemala in 2009. A forty-year-old Kaqchikel Maya man, Guillermo specialized in making youth sweaters and sweatshirts featuring the logos of globally popular fashion brands, such as Abercrombie & Fitch and Hollister. Typical of the regional trade, his business occupied a cinder-block room built onto the back of his home. Teenage boys rode their bikes from the outskirts of town or from nearby hamlets each day to operate the half-dozen Juki sewing machines imported from Japan and the two Universal knitting machines from Germany, shouting to one another in Kaqchikel, the primary indigenous language spoken in this part of Guatemala, over the mechanical noise.[1] Although it could barely be heard, the radio played bachata and reggaeton music.

Guillermo's relationship to the apparel trade was forged in the early 1970s, when his father purchased a knitting machine from a salesperson in Guatemala City. For the next ten years, his father made baby hats and blankets at their home in Xenimajuyu', a small hamlet outside of Tecpán. He would leave the village late at night to arrive early in Guatemala City on market days. Guillermo's mother, Doña Eugenia, explained in Kaqchikel, "My husband walked the path from Xenimajuyu' to Tecpán. He carried the hats and blankets in a bag. Then he rode to Guatemala City to sell to *mayoristas*"—here, she used the Spanish word for "wholesalers"— "and some of the hats would go to El Salvador." Her eyes lit up when she talked about how the little hats she helped her husband make ended up in another country. "There was no market for baby clothes around here back then because everyone made their own. But in El Salvador, they didn't make these things, so we could always sell what we made." At that time, the capital served as an international trading post for the Central American market. In many such stories that people told me about the early years of the apparel trade, Guatemala City is remembered as a vibrant center of economic life and a gateway to distant places.

Things changed quickly for Guillermo and his family when, in 1982, at the height of the country's internal armed conflict, his father was killed not far from their rural home. His body was discovered in the woods outside Xenimajuyu'. Guillermo's father was one of many in the region to meet his fate at the hands of soldiers, state-sponsored death squads, and armed civil patrols acting on government orders (Comisión para el Esclarecimiento Histórico 1999). The military strategically targeted indigenous professionals and business owners, though the particular circumstances surrounding Guillermo's father's death remain unknown.

This chapter recounts Guillermo's story—the history of his family's involvement in the apparel trade and the business style on which his modest success is based—and that of several other apparel manufacturers as a means of giving historical and ethnographic shape to an industry that is today largely and strategically hidden from outsiders. Maya manufacturers who once carefully conformed to state regulations now conceal their work from tax agents, police, and other state authorities, and sometimes also from one another. The regional trade has been transformed by state-sponsored violence and the more recent advent of free trade regimes that privilege multinational capital over local industry and encourage state government to target informal enterprises as sites of criminality and delinquency. The transformation of the trade from a state-regulated sector to one operating out of sight of state agencies runs counter to the master narratives that are so central to international projects of modernization and development, which tell of economies moving naturally and progressively from less formal to more formal relationships to the state. These narratives also include the idea that such an evolution brings about material benefits for the regulated, "developing" populations. At the same time as the historical processes and transformations evident in the apparel trade disrupt such neat accounts, the characterization of the trade as "informal" obscures ongoing and important relationships to the state and to legal regimes and ignores the regulatory practices of multiple sets of actors who exercise control over apparel manufacturing, markets, and meanings of work on regional and national levels. This chapter draws on social scientific analyses of the informal economy in Latin America and anthropological studies of economic regulation to parse out the "regulating style" that structures highland business practice and business ethics, a style that contrasts with the models of development and regulation enshrined in international trade and legal agreements. This chapter thus contributes to economic anthropology by analyzing the historical embedding of an industry and particular modes of regulation and ways of doing business amid dynamic social and market processes and in view of a local moral world where norms and values other than those privileged in international development and IP law shape the kinds of work that people do and the business ethics that they espouse.

While Maya manufacturers place tremendous value on secrecy and the concealment of their business practices from outsiders, they also actively share business knowledge, information, and resources across networks of kin and neighbors in Tecpán and the surrounding region, and they teach what they know to younger Maya men, whom they encourage to start their own workshops. What I term the "pedagogical imperative"[2] is as much an ethical dictum as it is a means to several ends, including the spurring of what indigenous manufacturers describe as economic development in Tecpán and the maintenance of long-term social relations. In this chapter and the next, I describe the moral contours of sharing and pedagogy and demonstrate how this commitment has its own regulatory effects on the trade. I argue that the tension between, on the one hand, secrecy and concealment and, on the other, sharing and pedagogy conditions the dialectical movement through which business and regulating styles are elaborated in the highlands. This tension will be important in later chapters for understanding how copying matters for and is evaluated by Maya workshop owners.

ORIGINS

Guillermo's family history is typical in many ways. Beginning in the late 1950s, Maya men and women in several highland towns—such as Totonicapán, San Francisco El Alto, Quetzaltenango, and San Pedro Sacatepéquez, to name the most prominent—took up nontraditional apparel production. Such activities were structured either as cottage industries or as small-scale, independent manufacturing firms (C. A. Smith 1984, 1989; Hendrickson 1995; Ehlers 2000; Fischer 2001; Ortez

2004; Goldín 2009). It was around 1960 that a handful of indigenous men in the rural hamlets around Tecpán bought semi-industrial knitting and sewing machines from dealers in Guatemala City. Many of these manufacturers focused their production on baby clothes or men's and women's sweaters in the early years, and the town continues to be well known for those items, even though workshops produce a wide variety of garments today. Tecpán's centrality, in relation to the capital city (88 kilometers to the southeast along the Pan-American Highway) and Western highland markets (Quetzaltenango, currently Guatemala's second largest city, sits 116 kilometers away), facilitated the integration of these businesses into Central American commercial networks. The burgeoning industry, which has been an "economic revolution for Tecpán," as one gray-haired manufacturer put it to me in 2007, offered new opportunities for Tecpán's indigenous population, whose traditional household economy, based in subsistence agriculture, was under threat by state-corporate alliances and a growing population.

As Carol A. Smith (1984) documents, more and more indigenous Guatemalans were being pushed out of traditional agriculture in the mid-twentieth century through land privatization schemes orchestrated by the state in tandem with large-scale agricultural enterprises that were investing in export production for US and European markets. Wage labor options were historically limited to seasonal work arrangements on the highland coffee *fincas* and coastal sugar and cotton plantations (Fischer 2001). Unlike plantation labor, garment manufacturing allowed *tecpanecos* control over the means of production, an important cultural and moral value among Maya peoples (Watanabe 1992). Manufacturers need no formal education, which is important, since only half of the Maya children in the department of Chimaltenango (where Tecpán is located) who enroll in school complete their education through the sixth grade (Ministerio de Educación de Guatemala 2008). Also, the trade requires minimal capital investment. In 2009, a used manual knitting machine cost around one thousand quetzales (US$125), and thread, yarn, and cloth distributors routinely sell on credit.

After Guillermo's father's death, Guillermo's mother, Eugenia, moved the family into Tecpán's semi-urban core, onto a small lot that a brother-in-law had purchased several years before. Their relocation from rural village to town center reflects wider trends in the apparel trade, and in Guatemala's history more generally. The initial wave of growth in the apparel trade took place in a handful of rural hamlets outside of Tecpán, though most manufacturers eventually moved their operations into the

FIGURE 6. Photograph from the early days of the highland apparel trade, featuring a workshop owner, his employees, and a young boy posing with semi-industrial knitting machines in a rural hamlet outside of Tecpán, 1960s. (Photograph courtesy of CJ)

town center. Sometimes, these relocations were economically motivated; workshop owners wanted to be closer to bus routes and potential customers, have more space for employees, and hook up to electricity to run the newer, more industrial machinery that had become available by the early 1970s. However, a massive earthquake hit central Guatemala in February 1976, forcing many of the small-time clothing producers who were still living in the hamlets surrounding Tecpán out of their crumbled adobe homes. Concrete-block structures organized around central courtyards and painted in vibrant shades of green, blue, and yellow—in keeping with the aesthetic effervescence of highland style— became the new architectural model for Tecpán thereafter.

Other producers, including Guillermo's father, remained in the hamlets until the late 1970s, when genocidal violence against the Maya people began as part of the internal armed conflict. Between 1979 and 1983, the Guatemalan Army stepped up its so-called counterinsurgency campaign. Official reports issued by the Catholic Church and the United Nations estimate that two hundred thousand Maya people were killed during the conflict, most of them during this four-year period of intensified violence. Indigenous business owners and political activists (individuals were often

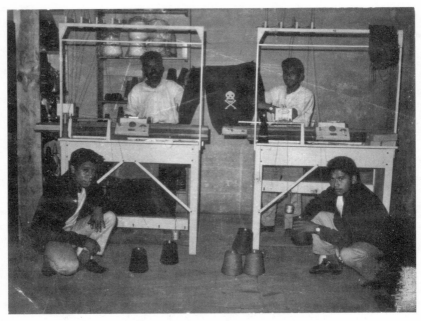

FIGURE 7. Another photograph from those early days, featuring workshop employees displaying a sweater with a skull-and-crossbones design, reminiscent of a pirate flag, in a rural hamlet outside of Tecpán, 1960s. (Photograph courtesy of CJ)

both) were frequent victims of kidnappings and killings (Comisión para el Esclarecimiento Histórico 1999). Rural indigenous populations were more likely to be suspected of guerrilla activity, and many families who had had some success in garment manufacturing in the hamlets moved to Tecpán's urban core at this time, attempting to escape the threat of the military's combination of scorched-earth tactics and targeted assassinations. The town has continued to grow at a rapid pace; the population doubled between 1996—when the peace accords that ended the war were signed—and 2010. These movements follow a broader trend of urbanization in Guatemala, as rural people migrate to towns and cities with the aid of kin connections, seeking new possibilities for education and wage-based work (O'Neill and Thomas 2011).

Guillermo's mother eventually built a small house, where she continued to make children's clothing, which she sold in Guatemala City to support her family, making her one of only a few women in Tecpán, past or present, to manage her own clothing business. Men are positioned generally as owners, managers, and salespeople within the regional trade. Young men operate the machines. Women are relegated to doing hand-embroidery work, sewing on adornments, finishing seams, or packaging garments, tasks that are considered either more delicate or easier than the jobs the men do. Eugenia's five children worked alongside her in their home, each of them learning first how to sew buttons and mend sweater-knit fabric. Eventually, the three boys took over the role of operating the growing number of knitting and sewing machines in their workshop. When the children were old enough to attend primary school, their morning classes and afternoon homework took priority over garment production, as Eugenia considered education to be the primary means for the next generation to better its economic standing. She had learned to speak Spanish only after her husband's passing, when market dealings in Guatemala City demanded it. She learned to read and write in Spanish under the patient tutelage of a wholesaler in the capital, who, as she explained, "felt sympathy for her." Guillermo attended some university courses in the capital before marrying a Kaqchikel woman, at which time he received gifts of capital from his mother and uncle, which he invested in a set of well-worn industrial sewing machines. His sisters pursued teaching careers, but his brothers also remained in the garment industry. In 2009, one brother operated a set of industrial embroidery machines used to adorn other people's clothing stock with popular brand names, sports insignia, and cartoon characters; the other marketed school uniforms around the highlands. Guillermo's family history traces the rural-urban migration path followed by so many apparel producers in the early decades of the industry, and it highlights the importance of kin in the growth and expansion of the trade. The entanglements of state-sponsored brutalization and economic aspirations that drove these trends continue to shape how apparel manufacturing is organized and regulated at local and regional levels. An enduring ethos of sharing, networking, striving, and overcoming defines the industry in many ways and lies at the core of what it means to be a Maya businessman in Tecpán and throughout the highlands.

THE PEDAGOGICAL IMPERATIVE

The apparel trade in the highlands has expanded in large measure through kinship and apprenticeship connections. A commitment to training others and sharing knowledge, skills, and even material resources between individuals and across generations powerfully shapes the business style of indigenous manufacturers. As with Guillermo's family, people who are already established in the business help younger men get started, teaching them the necessary skills and providing gifts of capital and loans.[3] Kinship patterns in Tecpán are patrilineal, favoring the father's line (Fischer and Hendrickson 2002: 46). A new bride commonly goes to live with her husband and his family. It is customary for the new couple to remain with the husband's family until a proper home has been prepared for them on the family's land; due to this system, the plots get smaller with each successive generation. More commonly in Tecpán's semi-urban center, new rooms are built onto the house to allow space for the expansion of the family. In Guillermo's case, by the time he got married, his mother's house had already been added to and divided up twice in order to accommodate his older brothers' wives and children. Somewhat reluctantly, therefore, he and his mother agreed that he would build a house on land owned by his new wife's family (her parents had no sons to inherit the plot). This arrangement has been particularly difficult for his mother, who longs for him and his children to be under the same roof with her and as attentive as the other family members with whom she shares living space. Nevertheless, Eugenia is proud that the difficult years she spent making and selling clothing in a market dominated by men provided Guillermo and his two brothers with sufficient resources to earn a living.

Passing on not just capital but also the skills needed to earn a living is common across apparel manufacturing families, where sons work alongside their fathers (or mothers, in Guillermo's case) in their youth and are often given machinery and cash when they marry. Such an arrangement is part of a constant, informal flow of gifts and loans among parents and children in Tecpán and is not limited to the apparel trade, also extending into agriculture and other modes of livelihood (Fischer 2001: 174). From an early age, male children are expected to "pay back" the "life-giving generosity" of their parents through household labor, and in adulthood, the children are expected to demonstrate "filial piety in the form of gifts," including money, to their parents (144). This reciprocity may reach beyond blood relatives. If a new bride's family views her husband's work prospects as paltry, her parents or other kin may intervene to provide training and capital to get the couple started. For example, Guillermo recently gifted a rusty knitting machine, some lessons on how to use it, and a market contact to his wife's sister's husband, whose widowed mother had little to offer the young man and his wife.

Mutual aid relationships also extend to employees. Workshops generally employ young men of meager means and little education from the town center or, more often, surrounding hamlets. Employers often teach

FIGURE 8. Teenage workshop employee seated at a serger machine, which is used to finish the edges and seams of knit fabric, Tecpán, 2009. Note that he is wearing a knockoff Abercrombie & Fitch sweater.

what they know about operating and repairing machinery, crafting designs, and marketing to these teenage workers, many of whom eventually leave the workshops to start out on their own, sometimes taking along an old machine and a capital loan. This is again true of Guillermo's case. From my first day of work in his *taller* (workshop), it was clear that Guillermo had a distinctive bond with one employee in particular, Angel.

When the other employees took their bicycles home in the evening, Angel stayed on to dine with Guillermo's family and slept on a palette in the workshop during the week. Nineteen years old, tall and lanky, with sharp features and fashionably gelled hair, Angel had started working for Guillermo three years prior and had since been taken in by the workshop owner and his family as something of a son and brother. The distance between the workshop and Xeabaj, the rural hamlet where Angel's parents and younger siblings resided, only partly explained his stay overs in Tecpán. Guillermo saw something in this young man: a drive, some kind of energy, and a willingness to learn. In the case of some workers, he explained to me in Spanish[4] during a trip to Guatemala City to sell clothing, "you have to tell them everything they're supposed to be doing, but Angel finds work to do. If he finishes one thing, then he looks to see what else needs to be done."

Angel's dependability and work ethic were not the only reasons for the affinity between the two men. Simply put, Guillermo and Angel got along. They enjoyed joking with each other during the workday and playing soccer on the weekends. And one more thing: "With Angel, I speak mostly Kaqchikel," Guillermo told me, "but not with the others. They know how to speak it, or at least they understand it, but some of them are embarrassed to speak Kaqchikel. For me, it's an honor to have learned it, because it's a language that we all should learn." Guillermo appreciated and respected the fact that Angel spoke his indigenous language without shame, when others had seemingly internalized discriminatory attitudes that associate speaking Kaqchikel with being backward or uncouth. As I learned from my participation, observation, and interviews, the fact that the apparel trade is organized as an indigenous Maya industry populated by Maya (not *ladino*) business owners and employees mattered for Guillermo and for many other producers. Guillermo interpreted Angel's style of self-presentation through language as concomitant with his own pride in being Kaqchikel Maya, the kind of pride that has been promoted by indigenous activists for several decades. In this way, the industry is informed by and connected to the social movement that took shape in the 1970s and achieved international attention and a measure of success in the 1980s and '90s as indigenous Maya community leaders and activists—a significant number of them from Tecpán and nearby towns and hamlets—protested the state-led violence and advocated for a set of cultural and political rights based in international law. The shaping of a powerful sense of ethnic solidarity in the midst of that movement and through the ongoing efforts of Maya activists, scholars, and indigenous political parties is part of what the sharing and networking so important to the growth of the industry are all about.

Three years into their working relationship, Angel had learned every part of the garment-production process from his employer. When Angel first arrived, Guillermo told me,

> He could knit, but he had no experience in cutting, no experience in packaging, and his first few weeks were difficult. But my mom said to me, "Don't rush him because you need something and it's not getting done; have some patience." And now he has become specialized in this type of work. When he's not in the workshop, I worry. If there's cutting that needs to be done, it might not happen if he's not there. And when I work alongside him, in knit-

ting or sewing or cutting, it used to be that I showed him how to do it, and now he shows me! And this is a lot easier, because he is really specialized, and that's why I miss him if he doesn't come in one day.

Angel's "specialization," the term Guillermo used to describe his employee's skill in the various steps involved in making sweaters and sweatshirts, not only guaranteed that Guillermo had someone who could manage production when he was on the road making sales in marketing centers in the Western highlands or the capital city but, in Guillermo's estimation, also mattered for Angel's future. Angel had accumulated sufficient knowledge of the garment trade to set up his own workshop if and when the time came. The teenager had a "serious" girlfriend, someone he had been seeing for nearly a year at the time I was working with him, and there was some expectation on the part of Guillermo's family that Angel would soon want to get married, perhaps rent a house in town, and get his own machines to start a workshop business. As noted above, this kin-based, lifecycle-linked trajectory is a pattern of expansion that *tecpanecos* have witnessed since the earliest days of the trade. "A lot of the time, an employee's workshop is bigger than his old boss's," remarked a manufacturer whose children's clothing business had been the launching pad for at least three relatively successful enterprises.

When the state-directed violence of Guatemala's armed conflict subsided in the mid-1980s, the garment trade took off. Employers, their sons and other kinsmen, and their well-trained former employees opened hundreds of small-scale workshops in the later years of that decade and throughout the 1990s. Edward F. Fischer (2001: 218) estimated that, in 2001, there were "between seventy-five and one hundred small sweater factories that employ[ed] between one and twenty workers." Based on my own counts and input from local producers, I estimate that there are now one hundred workshops in Tecpán's semi-urban core and perhaps two hundred more in the *colonias* on the outskirts of town and the hamlets that are part of the municipality. A yarn and thread distributor in Tecpán reported to me that he had around four hundred clients in 2009, although this number included workshops throughout the department of Chimaltenango (there are a few dozen just in the department capital) and some in the nearby departments of El Quiché and Sololá, whose owners travel to Tecpán to buy their inputs. Still, he estimated that about 80 percent of his clients are from Tecpán, putting the number of workshops in the town above three hundred. Tecpán has become as important to the domestic apparel trade as more traditional centers of tailoring such as San Francisco El Alto and Guatemala City (C. A. Smith 1984; Goldín 2009). Nearly every family in Tecpán has some connection to the apparel trade, and entire families are sometimes employed in the workshops. The growth of apparel manufacturing has also led to the establishment in town of a slew of machinery importers, screen-printing shops, and textile and thread suppliers that deal in natural and synthetic fibers imported mainly from India, Peru, and Mexico.

The model of employee "specialization" that has underwritten the growth of the regional trade in highland Guatemala differs dramatically from the Fordist model of mass production that has defined the globalization of apparel manufacturing since the 1970s. Once-vibrant manufacturing sectors in North America and Western Europe have been outsourced over the last half-century to free trade zones in the so-called developing world, where low wages and lax labor and environmental regulations permit scales of profit accumulation and modes of profiteering and exploitation that union organizing, consumer advocacy, and robust state oversight tend to challenge and constrain in "developed" countries.[5] Exempt from local and state taxes and tariffs on trade by special economic agreements, these large-scale garment factories that have been set up along the US-Mexico border and in postcolonial settings throughout Latin America, South and Southeast Asia, and, more recently, sub-Saharan Africa produce an incredible volume of clothing for export to consumer markets around the world, and especially in the Global North. While the opening of China's economy to liberalization in recent decades and the expiration in 2005 of an international trade instrument (the Multi-Fiber Agreement) that imposed restrictions on apparel imports to North America and Europe from China mean that the southern coastal region of China is now home to the largest apparel-export industry in the world, Central America has been an important site of sweatshop labor and export production since the 1980s.

In Guatemala, *maquiladoras* (as garment export factories are known in Latin America) line the Pan-American Highway and are a major part of the contemporary export-driven economy. But to indigenous Maya businessmen involved in small-scale manufacturing in Tecpán, there are striking moral as well as material differences between *maquiladoras* and their own workshops. Attending to the distinctions related to worker training, compensation, and community embeddedness that these producers are inclined to make between their trade and the *maquila* industry also reveals that the kinship and apprenticeship models described above are not just a matter of course for indigenous manufacturers but also carry the weight of an ethical imperative. Looking at where and how the two trades overlap in everyday practice is also helpful for explaining and situating the use of globally popular brand names by Maya producers within a broad picture of fashion and the fashion industry.

Maquila expansion in Guatemala, fueled mainly by US and South Korean capital, was rapid once the violence of the internal armed conflict subsided in mid-1980s (Petersen 1992). The number of export factories nearly doubled between 1992 and 1996. By the mid-1990s, 130,000 Guatemalans were employed in almost five hundred textile and garment factories, and 99 percent of the products they manufactured were exported to the United States (Traub-Werner and Cravey 2002). By 2005, Mexican and Central American *maquiladoras* supplied nearly 20 percent of all apparel sold in US stores (Abernathy et al. 2005). Yet this "flexible" industry has always been volatile. In the late 1990s, nearly one hundred *maquiladoras* closed and moved elsewhere in search of lower wage rates and more favorable regulatory climates (Goldín 2001), even as other factories were opening. Closures have accelerated in recent years, leaving only around 30,000 Guatemalans employed in the garment-export industry (Muñoz 2012). Factory closings are often sudden, and stories abound of employees showing up to work and finding the factory locked up, leaving them with no way to collect their final paychecks.

Maquiladoras make clothing for North Americans and Europeans. In theory, they do not compete with the Maya-owned *talleres* that supply Central American markets with less-expensive clothing. The small-scale workshops are connected to *maquiladoras,* however, via complex material networks. Rolls of cloth with minor imperfections, the rejects of the *maquila* industry's tight quality control systems, sell cheaply in highland markets and retail stores in Guatemala City and constitute an important source of inputs for some Maya manufacturers. And since *maquiladoras* contract directly with foreign brand owners or their licensed subsidiaries or are subcontracted by production-sourcing firms or other authorized intermediaries, they often have stockpiles of tags and labels printed with the official, trademarked logos of popular, multinational clothing companies. These are sometimes smuggled out of *maquiladoras* by employees and end up in Maya-owned workshops, where they are incorporated into garments that are sold to Guatemalan consumers. Economists and law and business scholars refer to these movements of materials between authorized manufacturing and distribution sectors, such as the *maquila* industry, and informal economic sectors, such as the highland apparel trade, as the "grey market." Grey markets in materials are common throughout the globalized apparel industry (Hiebert 1994). The term captures the sense that, from corporate and legal perspectives, although the materials are "real" and "authentic," the local markets where they end up are unauthorized and illegal (Mackintosh and Graham 1986; Phau et al. 2001; Huang et al. 2008). While Maya manufacturers sometimes benefit from the low-cost rolls of material and the branded tags and labels that flow out of *maquiladoras,* other aspects of the grey market trade challenge the competitiveness of the domestic industry. *Maquiladoras* often dump imperfect, finished garments and overruns into local markets, even though production contracts and state law generally prohibit this practice and demand that overruns and imperfect garment be disposed of in other ways. *Maquiladoras* thus undercut the highland trade by illegally flooding the marketplace with name-brand clothing made with high-quality materials that often sells at lower prices than the knockoffs and other fashions made by Maya workshop owners.

But these material connections and networks, although salient to the production and marketing decisions that Maya producers make, are not necessarily the most important relationships between the *maquila* industry and the highland garment trade that small-scale manufacturers cited in interviews and casual conversations. After an hour spent observing and chatting with the young men intensively engaged at the dozen sewing machines that made up his workshop, I walked with Roberto Tecun through the dusty courtyard of his home toward the kitchen door. Roberto and one of his brothers have done considerably well in the apparel trade due in large measure to a well-timed capital investment made possible by the sale of ancestral farmland (an option not commonly available to often-landless workshop owners). Their surname, which is associated with modestly priced children's clothing and fashionable, screen-printed t-shirts, is now well known around town and across highland markets.

Pulling a chair up to the table, where his wife had arranged an assortment of pastries for Roberto and me, I inquired if any of his employees had worked in the *maquila* sector before coming to work for him. "Well, no. The problem with the *maquilas,*" he replied between sips of watery instant coffee, "is that they don't pay what they should. They exploit people, and when they decide to leave town, they go without paying their debts [to employees]." He continued, "The other problem is that they don't teach you very much." At this point, he began to draw a sharp contrast between *maquiladoras* and Tecpán's *talleres,* concentrating on a pedagogical imperative evident among workshop owners—

namely, that they impart knowledge and skills to the young men they employ that go beyond task-oriented training:

> In the *talleres*, you have to learn how to finish a whole piece—a shirt, for example. You learn to attach the collar, the sleeve, the cuffs, bodice, buttons— everything that makes up a shirt. So, this person [trained in a workshop] could find work anywhere. But in the *maquilas*, the *muchachos* [boys] don't know how to work. He might be able to run one kind of machine, but *real* work is making a whole garment.

Roberto then recounted how he had just finished training a seventeen-year-old young man from one of the hamlets outside of town, who rode his bike to the workshop and then home after each ten-hour workday. As he told the story, Roberto fell into a steady rhythm of contrastive terms, emphasizing differences between the two types of garment manufacturing but also spatializing those differences in a way that drew attention to the fact that he himself belonged to a production community identified as indigenous and proximate:

> Here, a person learns how to work. And my way of thinking is this: if a young man works with me and learns how to work, that's good. He doesn't have to work with me all his life, maybe two years. He does the work, and he leaves. Because then I've helped in his education; he has the tools he needs, the knowledge, and no one can take that away from him. But in a *maquila*, he could stay five years working, and [learn] nothing. Here, it's a question of putting together a bit of money and setting up his own workshop, and then he starts working on his own. He can take care of a family that way. There, in the *maquila*, if he made money, took care of his family, maybe even bought a few things . . . but when the *maquila* cuts him loose, what does he know how to do?

Moving back and forth between "here" and "there," Roberto outlined important boundaries of social membership. Far from simply referencing the spatial coordinates of our position at the kitchen table, he marshaled a spatial metaphor that situated him comfortably within a particular kind of moral and geographical community, a thriving industry built on forms of sharing and networks of association, with a definite socio-moral meaning and ethical seriousness that is lacking on the assembly lines in the big factories.

Roberto was simultaneously reporting on the practical differences between the *maquila* industry and his own and participating in a genre of talk about community-centered "development" (Thomas 2012) that I discuss in more detail in the next chapter. He was also outlining shared parameters of gendered, moral personhood. As Richard Eldridge (1989) has explained, the fact and experience of moral personhood revolves around one's ability to make sense of one's actions in light of held principles and to render oneself capable of self-responsibility and of "incarnating" values (78; see also Frimer and Walker 2008). Anthropologists have used the concept of moral personhood to describe the particular ways in which responsibility and ethical decision-making figure into what it means to be a person and part of a given community (Jaffe 2009). I find that Maya clothing manufacturers discursively posit multinational corporations as foils against which their moral personhood appears unblemished, allowing them to craft a story about a sense of community and a trajectory of collective upward mobility through reference to shared values and imparted practices and to establish a sense of a proximate and responsible self in contrast to multinational corporations. For Roberto, learning a trade, teaching others, taking care of family, consuming, and knowing "how to work" all defined what it meant for him to be an effective head-of-household, an ethical employer, and, simply put, a good man.

As our conversation continued, my curiosity about how Roberto imagined the *maquila* industry and why he thought its approach to employee training was so different grew. When I asked him about it, I could tell from his quick response that he had given the topic some thought. Young men and women trained in *maquiladoras* sometimes came by his home seeking employment in his workshop, but he had been reluctant to offer them work because of their specialization in only one particular task. He explained to me,

> This [type of training] works to the benefit of the owner of the *maquila,* and this is what you have to think about: that it's better for the owner if the worker doesn't know everything, because in a little while, that worker is going to open his own workshop, going to need his *own* employees, and he's going to call on those that are in the *maquila.* This is why the Koreans and the Chinese don't teach everything, and this is why I don't fault the *maquilas,* even though I'm not in agreement with them.

While Roberto did consider *maquiladoras* to be a "problem," it was not because they might take workers from the highland apparel trade (a concern that other producers in Tecpán communicated to me). Furthermore, he did not criticize the *maquila* system on the same grounds as international social movements, which draw attention to the routine violation of workers' rights to fair compensation, reasonable hours, and job stability within the sweatshop industry. Rather, Roberto found fault with *maquiladoras* for not contributing to the process of development that interested him (and other Maya manufacturers), one that is premised on training and supporting young men in ways that move them from workers to owners and employers in keeping with the growing needs and responsibilities presumed to come with getting older and getting married.

However, Roberto did not fault *maquila* owners in the same way that he might fault a fellow Maya producer if that person instituted a similar system of limited training and support. It seems to me that, for Roberto, export factories exist as part of a different social sphere, or even a distinct moral world (Kleinman 1999).[6] He believed that the Koreans and the Chinese (he insisted on this national and perhaps also geopolitical, ethnic, or cultural difference, emphasizing several times as we talked that he was certain most of the *maquila* owners were Korean) were concerned with protecting their market position and ensuring a surplus labor pool. While these are business basics in neoclassical economics, they do not mesh with the kind of moral personhood and the spatialized sense of corporate community (Wolf 1957) and mode of development that preoccupied Roberto and his neighbors. The pedagogical imperative manifest in the practices of Maya manufacturers and highlighted in their talk about the industry's success and value formed part of their shared expectations for how neighbors would conduct business and thus shaped how business got done. It is one part of the plural regulatory context in which apparel production happens in highland Guatemala.

DISCLOSURE

The apparel trade in Guatemala is nothing more and nothing less than a set of stylized interactions among workshops owners, employees, wholesalers, retailers, consumers, extortionists, government agents; the kinship structures and debt relations that build up among and around individuals from these groups; the technologies that make their way to the highlands; and the technical routines and material qualities of production and marketing. As decades of research in economic anthropology and sociology have demonstrated, social and material relations are just as important to market systems as dynamics of supply and demand, if not more so.[7] Moral imperatives related to kinship, community, and a particular kind of development have helped structure Tecpán's apparel trade in ways that might escape neoclassical economic analysis. Moreover, regulatory mechanisms related to senses of morality and personhood have been meaningful at a time when the market for low-cost garments has been largely and effectively unregulated by state authorities.

State tax agents sometimes visit large towns in the highlands to look for unregistered businesses, levy fines, and demand back taxes, but these officials seem to be fighting a losing battle. Partly because of the investigative practices of these agents and partly in spite of them, most garment workshops did not display business signs on their doors at the time of my fieldwork. Marketing activity was limited to face-to-face interactions in municipal markets and the wholesale districts of the capital city. My entry into the field was facilitated by introductions to several families involved in the apparel trade by fellow anthropologists who had conducted research in the region for some time. Once I established rapport with these families, they generously introduced me to kin and neighbors who operated workshops. After several months of fieldwork, I attempted to expand my network with the aid of two research assistants from Tecpán. We spent countless hours walking through the streets of town. Treading slowly, we went block by block, listening for the hum of knitting and sewing machines, obscured by music blaring from radios, through the concrete walls. When we located what seemed to be a workshop, I would knock at the door.

The Guatemalan government—especially the department-level offices that administer and enforce tax policy in the highlands—does not have the resources to carry out this kind of careful, time-consuming investigation. If the owner happened to know my research assistants or their families, my knock was met with a friendly invitation to see the workshop. More often, however, my inquiries were rebuffed with a suspicious look and a mumbled question about my possible affiliation with either the SAT (Superintendencia de Administración Tributaria, the state tax administration) or Nike (a frequently copied brand name). My *gringa* appearance led to questions about whether or not I worked for a North American apparel or footwear company. Such questions were generally followed by repeated denials that any business was operating inside the home (cf. Crăciun 2013).

Historically, workshops were not so difficult to find. In an earlier era, many indigenous producers reportedly regarded registering their businesses and paying taxes as a routine part of the trade. First-generation workshop owners who began to make clothes in the 1960s and early '70s recounted in conversations with me that they had registered their businesses with the state as a matter of course as their workshops grew from family operations to employers of up to forty young workers. The trade has thus undergone what some social scientists call a process of "informalization" (Portes et al. 1989; Meagher 1995). When asked about their personal biographies and the history of the apparel trade, workshop owners and others I talked with in Tecpán indicated that what began as a market sector more or less subject to state authority now operates overwhelmingly out of sight of state officials. But to say that the apparel trade has become less formal over time risks obscuring the relatively definite "form" that the sector has taken around the defining tension between sharing and concealment.[8] Calling the trade "informal" also ignores the significance state institutions have had in shaping the everyday practices of apparel producers (as discussed below), however hidden these businesses might be from state agents.[9]

The classic social science explanations of informalization link the phenomenon to macroeconomic processes. For example, Manuel Castells and Alejandro Portes (1989) have proposed that the expansion of the informal economy in many world regions in recent decades—following a long period of state regulatory control over industrial sectors—is a symptom of advanced capitalism (see also Fernandez-Kelly and Garcia 1989; Benería 1989; Meagher 1995; F. Wilson 1993). Informalization, they contend, is largely an effect of the reorganization of global capital that has taken place as the capitalist elite has strategically attempted to undercut labor power in formal sectors. When unionization rates increase, for example, industries shift to informal work arrangements, with people laboring out of their homes and from other unregulated sites, and, in this way, avoid state labor laws and union contracts that cut into corporate profits.

However, that explanation does not describe the particular history of Guatemala's apparel trade. The formalized relationships that apparel producers had to state agencies in an earlier era were never an inevitable feature of Central American industrialization. Nor were those relationships the result of a strong or efficient state bureaucracy that supported formal employment as part of a national development strategy, even though informalization in the country has coincided since the late 1980s with a neoliberal program of devolving regulatory authority to local and regional government officials who are often without the necessary funding to carry out their mandates. Rather, as I detail below, the fact that apparel producers formally participated in the market had to do with the aggressiveness of authoritarianism and the technologies of surveillance employed by a dictatorial, militarized state during an internal armed conflict.

The concept of informality is itself problematic, and the sense of dissatisfaction with the term that I share with other anthropologists and social scientists reflects both the broadness and fuzziness of the term. Lisa Peattie (1987) argues that the concept says more about the difficulties economists and governments have faced in trying to quantify and capture the value created through smaller-scale, less privileged, sometimes more "casual" and less successfully surveilled forms of work than it says about the organization of economic practice in a given setting. Indeed, Keith Hart's (1973) original use of the term was, at least in part, a response to the inadequacy of concepts in economics to account for the "complex" income and expenditure patterns that he observed in his fieldwork among poor residents of Accra, Ghana. He understood the informal sector to comprise all forms of self-employment in urban Ghana, from petty capitalism to petty theft, which he interpreted as ways people made do in a city beset with rampant poverty and inequality. Initially a critique, then, of economists' focus on the problem of "unemployment" at the expense of richer conversations about marginalization, urbanization, and the uneven distribution of resources in the Third World, the concept was soon picked up by development economists and international institutions, especially the International Labor Organization (1972), to describe a sector that was understood to be outside of the "real" or "regular" economy and considered to be a barrier to economic growth and modernization.

A short time later, as Julia Elyachar (2005) highlights in her historical and ethnographic study of squatter settlements and small businesses in Cairo, the "informal economy" took center stage in national and international economic growth and development strategies, fueled by Hernando de Soto's (1989) popular argument that the entrepreneurial potential of the poor would be unleashed if government regulations were swept out of the way and land titles and business licenses were distributed freely to squatters and the self-employed. In the 1980s and '90s, Elyachar (2005: 74) wrote, "[international organizations] supervising the state's retreat from the economy realized that the practices through which the poor in Egypt had always managed to survive were a good thing, and could become the basis of a 'safety net' for those who might fall through the holes made by [structural adjustment programs]."[10] International institutions thus had a vested interest in promoting and developing the "informal sector," a project states could be recruited to help with via a simple change in vocabulary. Whereas the language of "informality" called attention to the state's failures to fully regulate its national economy, the language of "microenterprise" that came to replace it in development discourse played on state sympathies for business promotion. Rather than focusing on the extra-legality of the poor, the term "stresses individuals and their entrepreneurial qualities" (82). In Guatemala, support for microenterprise and entrepreneurship has

come through a series of initiatives, programs, and foundations established by the World Bank, the United States Agency for International
Development, and the Inter-American Development Bank.[11] A host of
private, nongovernmental microloan agencies also operate throughout
the country, offering credit and business training programs alongside
monitoring, evaluation, and reporting procedures (see chapter 4).

Even though microenterprise and small business ownership are promoted in Guatemala as keys to economic development, "informality"
continues to be targeted by government officials and international institutions as a source of inefficiency, illegality, and noncompliance. Reform
programs directed by the national government and supported by the
same development institutions and agencies referenced above focus on
regularizing and formalizing relationships between the state and the private sector, increasing tax revenue from small businesses, and shutting
down illegal piracy and counterfeit markets. The story of the highland
apparel trade is not a simple tale of "informalization," but the neoliberal turn to the promotion of microenterprise does not fully describe the
situation that Maya apparel manufacturers face either. Rather, the history of the industry winds through an authoritarian past and a present
in which the business style of Maya "entrepreneurs" continues to be
targeted and evaluated by states and international institutions as "not
quite" right (Bhabha 1984: 126), and sometimes even as utterly antithetical to national progress and global economic development.

In spite of the difficulties and costs that applying for a business license
and paying taxes entailed (compounded by limited access to formal
education and a low degree of literacy among many manufacturers), it
was important, older producers told me in interviews, that each manufacturer operating an apparel workshop in the 1960s and '70s had
papers with him during the weekly trips made up and down the Pan-
American Highway to visit clients in various market towns. Police frequently intercepted indigenous businessmen with their bundles of garments packed into sedans or microbuses or loaded on the top of
passenger buses to ask for a set of documents that included a business
license and receipts detailing the purchase of supplies and sale of goods,
which, according to the producers with whom I spoke, were meant to
prove that the goods were not stolen. Police officers were said to have
harassed folks who did not have their papers "in order."

In at least one case, that of Carlos Reyes, a producer who fled his
small rural hamlet outside of Tecpán for Guatemala City in the late
1970s after being denounced to the army as a *guerrilla* supporter, these

papers were an answer to the deadly demands of the counterinsurgency apparatus. After learning that the then president Efraín Ríos Montt had offered amnesty to *guerrilleros* and their supporters,[12] he sought to redeem himself in the eyes of the army so that it would be possible for him to rejoin his family members who were living in Tecpán. He recalled,

> When Ríos Montt came to power and issued the amnesty, then families could come back to their homes, and I went straight to the military commissioner. I told him, "I'm working here in Guatemala City. I'm not doing anything wrong." "No," [he replied], "the people say that you are a *guerrillero*. How can you prove that you're not?" . . . Well, when I had first arrived in Guatemala City, *gracias a Dios*, I had gone to register with the fiscal authorities to get my papers. So I went to the commissioner again, and I showed him my papers.

"Why had you even obtained papers in the first place?" I interjected. "To be legal," he responded, "to show that I was not a *guerrillero*. To say, 'Look, I am a workingman. I spend my time working.'" The papers, plus a hundred-quetzal note to grease the commissioner's palm, were sufficient, in this instance, to get Carlos's name erased from the list.

Apart from the security and mobility that papers could provide apparel producers, registering with the state was also part of an entrepreneurial culture framed around practices of disclosure, where business success depended on building a reputation through publicity. Sometime in the early 1960s, Elías Cua began making sweaters on a used knitting machine and selling them in Guatemala City. At the time, he was living in a wood-framed adobe house in a rural hamlet outside of Tecpán, with a wife and three young sons. He walked two kilometers to the center of town each Thursday morning, carrying a bundle of finished sweaters on his back, to catch the bus to the capital city and sell his wares. By the early 1970s, Elías's business was growing faster than his rural home could accommodate. A location in the center of town would better facilitate transportation to and from Guatemala City and provide him the opportunity to market his goods locally as well. So he built a concrete-block house in Tecpán with a two-room workshop attached to it and rented out a retail location next door. His family settled into their new home, and Elías named the factory and retail shop after his newborn daughter, Carmen. He hung a sign and applied for a business license with the help of a local accountant. Elías quickly became known around town for the quality and stylish colors of the sweaters, hats, and baby clothes he made and sold.

Maya manufacturers who set up their operations in Tecpán around this time tended to give their businesses names (which also served as brands for their clothing lines), to pay regular taxes to state and local governments, and to secure business licenses. Some of these businesses remain today, and their brand names are well known and generally respected across the highlands among wholesalers, retailers, and, in particular, older consumers.

I asked many active garment producers why older manufacturers had incorporated their businesses and traded under unique brand names while the current generation generally avoids these modes of disclosure and publicity. Younger manufacturers offered varied, sometimes nostalgic responses, explaining that the older generation complied with the law and paid taxes because they felt a sense of duty to "cumplir con sus compromisos" (meet their obligations). Older producers replied to similar questions by mentioning the importance of papers relative to interactions with police and military. They also indicated that the size and prominence of their businesses, together with the fact that there were only a few dozen workshops in operation at the time, made it impossible to hide their activities. Fewer than forty clothing workshops were operating in Tecpán's semi-urban core in the early 1980s (Cadenas 1981). Furthermore, they insisted, the publicity that came with advertising one's location and products via prominent signage was more important than avoiding taxes. Transactions often took place on market days, when people from the surrounding hamlets and larger towns along the Pan-American Highway came to Tecpán, a regionally significant market for many decades, to trade and shop. Signs hung over doorways and tags displaying family names sewn into sweater collars helped to guide clients to the right merchandise.

There were other strategic reasons for producers to register their businesses in those early decades. For example, having a formal relationship to the state was a prerequisite for doing business with retail shops and also with many wholesalers in Guatemala City and larger highland towns. These buyers demanded numbered receipts for all transactions—the kind of receipts or invoices (*facturas*) that list the manufacturer's name, contact information, and tax identification number. This continues to be an important impetus for larger producers in Tecpán to maintain registration. As one manufacturer whose family name is displayed above the doorway to his home and workshop explained, "The system demands it. I can't buy or sell to important clients, to lucrative clients, if I don't use *facturas*. If the municipal government wants a thousand shirts, let's say, if I can deliver that with a *factura,* then I can get the contract." Working with government agencies, formal retailers, Guatemala City wholesalers, and nongovernmental organizations on a contract basis makes it easier for larger workshops to maintain regular cash flow and plan capital investments because these clients generally pay on delivery or within thirty to sixty days. Workshop owners who do business with regional wholesalers and market vendors that operate outside the purview of state authorities must consign goods to their buyers on credit. These wholesalers and market vendors may not pay their consignment debts on time, and sometimes they do not pay at all. There is little recourse for manufacturers when this happens, and some workshops go under when debtors fail to pay (Thomas 2009).

Therefore, according to this research, disclosure of one's business to the state emerges as a historically strategic marketing and financial decision, a defensive tactic to avoid harassment (or worse), and an important mode of publicity. In the face of so much evasion of state authority in the contemporary marketplace, older producers often explain and perhaps justify disclosure as an inevitable part of doing business—a teleology that, to their minds, simply has not played out yet for younger manufacturers. As one rather well-to-do clothing producer who had started out in the 1960s explained, "Today, most of the businesses are not registered, and it's because they are very small and don't produce very much. So, after all is said and done, they don't have much [money] left to pay taxes. What happens then is that they get larger and larger, and eventually they register and, when their time comes, begin to pay." The implication here is that each business begins small but eventually prospers to an extent that paying taxes becomes possible or inevitable; when the workshop owner has the means to pay taxes, he moves ahead with registration and properly reports his business activities to state authorities. In the historical context of the 1960s and '70s, and in the particular cases of the producers who got off to a strong financial start in those decades, this was indeed the story. But the idea that manufacturers today have the same opportunities for rapid growth and the same reasons to (eventually) comply with state law does not accurately reflect contemporary market conditions and state-citizen relations.

CONCEALMENT

As J. T. Way (2012: 7) writes, the informal economy in contemporary Guatemala "would be more appropriately called *the economy* itself." In 2009, out of the hundreds of workshops that were active in and around Tecpán, no more than a few dozen operated with business licenses and factory names or utilized accounting practices in line with state requirements (on these accounting practices, see chapter 4). The ones that did have formal regulatory relationships with the state were generally the second or third generation instantiations of that first wave of workshops that opened in the 1960s—businesses that needed to continue as formal enterprises because the state already had them on its rolls. These were typically the largest and best-known operations in town as well, such that history, size, and reputation combined to structure how a given workshop interfaced with the market and the Guatemalan government.

In recent years, concealment has emerged as a value and a normative framework that shapes the apparel marketplace in highland Guatemala and forms part of the regulatory context in which production happens. In the next chapter, I discuss the ways that norms about egalitarianism and ethnic solidarity encourage people to keep their business success a secret. These norms have been described in Maya communities for a long time, but they have come to matter differently as the "regional class system" (C.A. Smith 1984: 194) has undergone rapid change due to the sheer number of indigenous men involved in capitalist enterprise in towns such as Tecpán. In this section, I attend to structural conditions such as population growth and increased competition within the apparel marketplace that encourage concealment from state agents and other regulatory authorities. Castells and Portes (1989) contend that informalization takes place in relation to structural dynamics and a changing capitalist landscape, but their focus on the tension between labor and capital and rational choice logics of profit maximization does little in the way of explaining the specific conditions that have led apparel producers to avoid and evade state bureaucratic surveillance. The relationships to the state and ways of doing business that are evident in the highland apparel trade have been shaped more powerfully by racialized patterns of discrimination that limit educational and employment options for indigenous people than by a generalized structural contradiction between increasing labor power and the profit motivations of capital. Even the conditions of increasing competition that I describe here demand a culturally sensitive and historically particular analysis of business practice in order to be understood. As anthropologists have shown, competition is not a uniform experience or condition across cultural settings, but rather a set of social relations defined by senses of community and belonging and interpreted in light of values, norms, and expectations that take shape over time and in relation to diverse modes of rationality and cultural logics.[13] What is more, the relationship of indigenous business owners to state agents and to the idea of "the state" cannot be understood without taking into account the decades of military violence that these men and their families have endured.

Secrecy and informality are questions of degree rather than kind. Even among apparel workshops registered with the state, it is common for some aspects of the production and marketing processes to be out of sync with state law and out of sight of state agents. During my field-work, I observed that labor practices were not generally in compliance with state guidelines having to do with work hours, vacation days, or employer contributions to social security. Most workshops also relied to some extent on household labor—even if they employed a dozen or more wageworkers from outside the household—and so could be classified as "informal" in that sense as well (see Hart 1973). As I detail in chapter 4, workshop owners were selective about when they issued receipts and when they did not and about which earnings they reported to the tax administration and which they kept off the books.

There are practical reasons for owners to hide their workshops and not to comply with state mandates. In Tecpán, population growth has led to increased business in the areas of construction and commerce and to an expanding municipal market, but it has also meant that there are a large number of people concentrated in a few economic sectors—one of these being apparel production. The growth of the trade since the late 1980s—which has been premised on limited employment and education options for young indigenous men, low market-entry barriers, and the model of kinship and apprenticeship outlined above—means that apparel manufacturers today can take advantage of expansive production and marketing networks. At the same time, the rate at which new workshops are opening has contributed to difficult feelings of competition among neighbors, and the crowded marketplace makes it hard for most people to grow their businesses beyond an average size of two to ten employees. Most businesses never achieve production scales sufficient to attract state surveillance, so concealment comes easily. As a small-time producer whose workshop occupies a corner of his home expounded, "The SAT doesn't bother small workshops. It doesn't even know about them." There are also distinctive strategies for ensuring that one's workshop does not draw attention. In order to conceal business activities from the state, workshop owners encourage their employees to park their bicycles inside the home-workshop's courtyard rather than out in the street, for example. And the loud music blaring from old radios inside nearly every workshop serves to both distract the workers from their tedious tasks and camouflage the noise of the sewing and knitting machines, which helps keep unsuspecting government employees away.

Competition at an international level—the consequence of free trade initiatives that have prioritized foreign investment in *maquila* production over domestic industrialization and allowed the influx of low-cost imports—also motivates against the disclosures that accompany formal market participation. When I asked active producers why they did or did not use a company name to publicize their workshop, they did not talk about branding in terms of marketing strategy, even though the older, formalized workshops built up their reputations for quality and stylishness based on their use of family names as brands. A second-generation manufacturer told me that it used to make sense to have a company name as a way to promote your business. "After a long time, everyone knew the name and paid more for your products," he conceded. "But most people don't put their name on the products now because [registering a business or brand name is] expensive, and no one knows the name anyway. The *consumidor final* [end user] does not care if something says, 'Made in Tecpán.'" This producer sensed that the proliferation and popularity of global brand names in the Guatemalan marketplace had made it difficult for local brands to yield any market advantage for the producer, in spite of the fact that "Made in Guatemala" and authentic indigenous identifiers might be important aspects of branding traditional woven goods for tourist markets and international consumer publics (Nash 1993; Little 2004). In this way, the globalization of the apparel industry has had the effect of inhibiting impulses to conduct business in "formal" ways and has motivated producers in places like Tecpán to perceive more value in globally recognized brands than in local labels. These are crucial factors, as I continue to describe in later chapters, for understanding why and how piracy happens.

The impetus to work with one's own brand name, and thus to have that name registered with the state as a business entity, has given way over the past twenty years to the use of globally popular brands. The grey market trade with *maquiladoras* has facilitated the use of tags and labels by domestic producers at the same time that these foreign-owned sweatshops dump imperfect (but branded) garments on the national marketplace, increasing the visibility of popular brands in highland markets and city streets. The flow of secondhand clothing into Guatemala also significantly impacts the regional apparel trade, bringing authentic, branded goods to market at prices that are affordable for a wide swath of the indigenous population.

The worldwide trade in second-hand clothing has grown exponentially over the last four decades. Between 1980 and 2001, global revenue from the sale of secondhand clothes increased from US$207 million to nearly US$1.5 billion. The United States is the world's largest exporter of used clothing, and it is the largest exporter of these products to Guatemala. Between 1990 and 1997, worldwide exports from the United States more than doubled, from US$174 million to US$309 million (Hansen 2004). In 1997, Guatemala ranked tenth in the world in the amount spent in the used clothing trade (US$1.5 million) and fifth in the world in metric tons of clothes imported (Ehlers 2000). Countries such as India, Indonesia, and the Philippines have banned the importation of used garments because of what are viewed as adverse effects the trade has on domestic textile and apparel industries (Hansen 2004). In interviews, garment producers in Tecpán often lamented the low price and availability of used clothes in the highlands. Tracy Ehlers (2000), writing about domestic apparel production in another highland town, documented that the influx of *paca,* as second-hand clothing is called because of the thousand-pound bales (*pacas,* in Spanish) in which it arrives to Guatemala City importers, has put many garment workshop owners out of business. It has also contributed to a decline in the number of indigenous women wearing traditional *huipiles* and *cortes.* Whereas a handwoven *huipil* costs anywhere from several hundred to several thousand quetzales (up to a few hundred US dollars), and a sweater made in either San Pedro Sacatepéquez (where Ehlers carried out her research) or Tecpán runs from 40 to 150 quetzales (approximately US$5 to US$20), it is easy to find a secondhand blouse or sweater for 5 or 10 quetzales (US$0.75 or US$1.50). In addition to the used-clothing retail stores, with names such as Megapaca, in Guatemala City and other urban areas, vendors and shopkeepers throughout the highlands buy bundles of *paca* from capital city distributors to break open on market days. Brand-name jackets, sweatshirts, sweaters, jeans, and shirts that are in good condition are sorted by size or style and displayed on racks in shops and on sidewalks. Lower-quality *paca,* including socks, ragged t-shirts, and worn-out pants or shirts are piled on tarps in the middle of the street and often sold for a single quetzal apiece. Not only must Maya producers compete with *paca* pricing, but they must also compete in terms of the perceived stylishness of brand-name garments, albeit used ones.

The importation of new clothing also shapes the brand landscape in Guatemala and makes informality and illegality a sensible business strategy. Imported clothing threatens the viability of small-scale domestic manufacturing. Mexico and China are Guatemala's two largest trading partners after the United States and the Central American Common Market countries. Mexico supplies approximately 11 percent of Guatemala's imports, and China supplies more than 7 percent. While clothing has been entering Guatemala from Mexico for a long time, Maya workshop owners reported to me that the quantity and quality of clothing being imported from other countries began to impinge on their own businesses in the late 1980s. Free trade agreements signed with Mexico in 2000 and Taiwan in 1997 and 2005 ensure that textiles and apparel continue to be significant imports to Guatemala from these regions. Between 2000 and 2014, imports to Guatemala from China increased by more than 1500 percent, with upwards of US$1.8 billion worth of products arriving in 2014 alone, including US$430 million in textiles, apparel, and footwear (Observatory of Economic Complexity 2016). Markets, city streets, and retail shops throughout the highlands are full of Mexican sweaters and East Asian casual clothing, some of it from brands that are not marketed globally (such as Victoria from Mexico, Vanessa from Korea, and Gardenr from Taiwan), and some of it with unauthorized reproductions of brands such as Levi's, Diesel, and Nike. Chinese and Korean immigrants are also active in the wholesale garment markets in Guatemala City, where they deal primarily in imported goods. Arab immigrants from various countries operate wholesale clothing businesses in the capital as well and often trade in East Asian imports brought to Guatemala from the free trade zone in Colón, Panama. *Tecpanecos* told me that imported garments are of variable quality and price, but many agreed that Chinese and Taiwanese imports, for example, are constructed of better-quality material than what is available in Guatemala yet sell for lower prices than domestic goods. Mexican sweaters, which have been very popular among Maya women, who match them by color and style with their *huipiles* and *cortes,* are generally more expensive than locally made sweaters and are commonly said by both producers and consumers to be more stylish, especially the plush acrylic designs that are valued both for their softness and warmth and for the brilliance of the yarn colors. Tecpán's manufacturers work with some Mexican yarns, but they complained that they do not have access to the same range of inputs as their Mexican counterparts. Even so, they often tried to replicate the look and feel of the Mexican designs. Replicating these imported garments, a process I describe further in chapter 3, often involves copying a logo or brand name.

More frequent encounters with brands have been coupled with the greater availability of branding technologies. Used screen-printing and embroidery machines became affordable in Guatemala in the 1990s, a result of North American and European textile and apparel manufacturing sectors closing their doors at the same time as free trade agreements opened Guatemala's borders to European and US technology imports. In this context of *maquiladora* overruns, imported knockoffs, and US hand-me-downs, it has become difficult to sell a garment in Guatemala without a brand name that has recognizable currency in a globalizing marketplace. Family names and other local business monikers simply do not have the same cachet. And businesses that copy popular brand names have no interest in having a relationship with a state that has recently criminalized this practice. The ubiquity of branded garments in the Guatemalan marketplace, then, motivates activities now labeled "piracy" and contributes to a context in which concealment has become a mode of regulation and part of a regionalized regime of economic value, aesthetic styles, and practices of business building and marketing.

"THE STATE" AND OTHER TROUBLES

The majority of highland clothing producers I spent time with talked about state law and tax codes as unnecessary burdens that were to be avoided. More localized styles of reasoning about justice, rights, and business ethics held sway, but state laws and regulations were not matters of great concern. The government seemed distant to most manufacturers, but when it got close, it appeared threatening. Police patrols on the Pan-American Highway continue to stop workshop owners and inspect their goods, and many producers reported that the police attempted to extort bribes from them regardless of whether they had their papers in order, which is consistent with research on postwar policing (Glebbeek 2009). In discussions about law and crime, producers repeatedly commented to me that their primary concern was not with their own possible legal transgressions but rather with the state's failure to address the country's rising violent crime rates and rampant impunity for violent crime. In other words, they politicized the meaning and reach of the state and the visibility of what seemed to them to be a dire situation of dysfunction and disorder.

A producer who operated a registered workshop helped me understand how contemporary crime and violence motivated some workshop owners to conceal their activities. Many business owners around the highlands have received extortion threats related to their businesses in recent years. This particular workshop owner relayed to me that gang members look for signs of prosperity or business activities and then call up the proprietor to levy threats against his family members (whom the caller claims to have been following for some time). These threats and perpetual payments of *impuestos* (taxes) to extortionists have come to constitute a form of nonstate regulation and redistribution within the apparel trade and across the country. The Guatemalan judiciary, plagued by police corruption, citizen mistrust, and overcrowded prisons, has been unable to respond effectively to the problem. In Guatemala City and in large towns such as Tecpán, extortion has become part of everyday life for bus drivers and business owners and an increasingly common cost of doing business, and many apparel producers prefer to hide their work and their profits behind plain facades and razor-wire fences than to expose their families to potential harm.[14]

Several apparel producers I spoke to about extortion compared these threats to contemporary police bribes and the road blocks set up along the Pan-American Highway during the armed conflict, where soldiers demanded money or valuables in exchange for passage. Jean and John L. Comaroff (2006: 5) have interpreted the proliferation of illegal activities carried out by state and nonstate actors in South Africa as a symptom of the "troubled dialectic . . . of law and dis/order" in the postcolony, meaning that liberal politics and the rule of law too often prop up and justify exploitative economic systems that perpetuate the marginalization of formerly colonized populations. People who are excluded from systems of accumulation within neoliberal capitalism, as the Comaroffs explain, do not always or even usually rebel or resist legal and market logics; rather, they often create "parallel modes of production and profiteering, sometimes even of governance and taxation, thereby establishing a simulacra of social order" (9). In Guatemala, bribes paid to gang members function as a sort of cash-transfer program, a system of regular payment to an urban underclass that moves perpetually in and out of prison with no hope of gainful employment in formal, legal sectors and has a relationship to the state that has been characterized over time by equal parts of authoritarianism and abandonment (O'Neill 2011). Gang membership and extortion rackets cannot be understood without taking into account the structural and societal conditions that perpetuate a situation of deep economic insecurity and precarity throughout the country (Benson et al. 2008; O'Neill and Thomas 2011).

Some Maya workshop owners pay *impuestos* more faithfully to gang members than to state agencies, a fact that some have resigned themselves to and others justify in terms of the corruption of government officials and institutions. "A million quetzales in the pockets of some official are gone in under a year, spent on failed projects and luxuries," said one manufacturer. "A hundred quetzales in the pockets of an entrepreneur," he continued, "it multiplies. The official who steals is really the guilty one." Rachel Sieder (2003: 141) has made the point that "most Guatemalans rightly [tend] to see the law as something that operates to the benefit of powerful individuals and groups." Her observation helps contextualize the fact that the current situation of physical and social insecurity in Guatemala does not compel people to seek out the state and the legal protections it might offer. One might assume, for instance, that business owners facing extortion threats and robberies along the highways they travel to sell their goods would file police reports, bring lawsuits, and otherwise intensify their relationships to the state in order to secure some measure of safety. This sort of strategy is not too far afield from the one adopted by a previous generation of workshop owners, which sought to comply with bureaucratic and authoritarian demands for documentation in order to preserve their lives and livelihoods. To the current generation, however, even those who are registered with state agencies, a recent history of direct state violence and contemporary conditions of impunity and widespread corruption make the idea that the nation-state wields legitimate authority and administers the law according to a set of rationalized premises seem rather peculiar and even menacing.

Understanding the history of apparel production—why and how the regulation of this trade has been reconfigured over the past fifty years—reveals a great deal about law, ethics, citizenship, and the state in Guatemala. The fact that highland apparel entrepreneurs have come to avoid state regulation (rather than simply remaining part of a formal market structured by the business practices of a previous generation) says something about how economic reforms designed to promote international competition, together with the limited kinds of economic opportunity available to so many residents and the violence of the country's internal armed conflict—a war in which people "both acted on and acted with . . . weapons of concealment, secrecy, and masquerade" (D. Nelson 2009: xxii)—have generated both citizen mistrust of the state and practical indifference to the state's regulatory functions. In the midst of these conditions, informality and illegality have become effective business strategies.

On its website, the state tax administration represents tax evasion as a problem of education, efficiency, and communication (Superintendencia de Administración Tributaria 2013). The Facebook page devoted to the administration's Cultura Tributaria (Tax-Paying Culture) initiative reads:

Since 2005, the Superintendencia de Administración Tributaria has developed an integrated program for the development of a tax-paying culture, a program intended to inform, educate, and raise awareness among Guatemalans about taxes, but, especially, about the values that underwrite conscientious compliance with one's tax-related obligations. (Superintendencia de Administración Tributaria 2014a)

The characterization of this program and of the tax administration's mission more generally in terms of the targeting and transformation of a culture of noncompliance misses the point of entrepreneurial concealment. As Georg Simmel (1906: 450) wrote in his sociology of secrecy: "Confidence, as the hypothesis of future conduct, which is sure enough to become the basis of practical action, is, as hypothesis, a mediate condition between knowing and not knowing another person." In the case of Tecpán's apparel producers, it is precisely their knowledge of the state that has undermined their confidence in state institutions. Simmel continues: "[A] knowing process often goes on with reference to another so automatically, its result often presents itself so suddenly and unavoidably, that the best intention can do nothing to prevent it" (456). Educational campaigns about paying taxes and other public relations efforts aimed at concealing that which "presents itself so suddenly and unavoidably" about state governance in Guatemala (i.e., a history of violence and terror and compounded conditions of inequality and insecurity) fail to address the structural conditions and dilemmas that lead apparel producers into informality in the first place.[15]

It is in the face of so much historical and practical knowledge about the state (in the context of systems and structures that continue to marginalize Guatemala's indigenous population) and in relation to forms of community and morality that matter more dearly than national forms of citizenship that highland apparel producers have strategically concealed their businesses and earnings from formal authorities. As intensifying competition at local and global levels layers onto conditions of physical, financial, and sometimes existential insecurity, hiding one's business from both state agents and private factions has come to not only make sense but also take on an air of decency and discretion, with gauche displays of economic success judged, at times, as evidence of improper if not occult dealings, a theme I explore in the next chapter. The dynamics of concealment evident in the apparel trade thus trace both a history of violence and the practical reshaping of regulatory power and business style in the postwar period.

CHAPTER 2

The Ethics of Piracy

As one workday ended, Guillermo Ordóñez loaded his Mazda microbus with black garbage bags full of finished garments carefully folded, stacked, and bundled by the dozen. He would leave at four the next morning for San Francisco El Alto, a town in the western highlands with a lively wholesale garment market. Dozens of other producers from Tecpán make the same trip each week. Guillermo and I sat in his kitchen for a cup of coffee, and he complained about rising levels of competition among these producers over designs and pricing, competition that he said was unfair and disrespectful to one's neighbors. "The apparel business has made people in Tecpán very individualistic. People are envious and only watch out for themselves," he said. "So you have to watch out for yourself." He contrasted the garment trade in Tecpán with other modes of livelihood in neighboring towns—San Juan Comalapa's artisanal traditions in weaving and painting, and Patzicía's broader agricultural base—claiming that residents in those towns had been able to maintain a sturdier sense of cooperation and solidarity. In giving this analysis, he was clearly nostalgic about what he felt had been lost in Tecpán, where envy and individualism seemed to him to be thriving.

In this chapter, I examine what garment manufacturers such as Guillermo meant when they said that people have become envious and individualistic. In chapter 1, I outlined the pedagogical imperative—an ethic of sharing resources and information across kin and employees that structures, in large measure, the day-to-day workplace interactions at knockoff fashion workshops. How is it that accusations of envy and individualism arise among business owners who are so committed to pedagogical and reciprocal relationships with employees, relatives, and neighbors? To answer this question, I introduce a set of globalized legal processes and locally salient normative frameworks that complement the value regimes related to pedagogy and concealment discussed in chapter 1. I continue to flesh out what June Nash (1981) called the "ethnographic aspects of the world capitalist system" as it manifests in Guatemala and the business style of the highland apparel trade. I find that processes of legal globalization shape a changing "context of accountability" (Douglas 1992) in Tecpán's clothing industry, with its differently positioned participants and its ambivalent relationships to the past and to the nation. Accusations of envy among garment manufacturers and within the wider community function as nonstate regulatory mechanisms that organize marketplace interactions. Business owners themselves serve as regulatory agents when they gossip about their neighbors' market dealings and evaluate competitive behavior in terms of normative ideals of pedagogy, reciprocity, and community that are inflected by longstanding commitments to class-based solidarity among Maya people, commitments that were forged in the face of deep structural inequality and ethnic and racial discrimination against indigenous Guatemalans. These findings emerged from extended conversations with manufacturers about what is right and wrong in business, about the concept of economic development, and about the practices and effects of entities that Maya workshop owners characterize as "the state" and "the law." I find that the normative models and business practices evident among garment producers parochialize official portraits of business ethics and innovation promoted in neoliberal policy agendas and international law and challenge assumptions about progress, improvement, and ordering on which the global development industry is based.

In the highland apparel trade, accusations of envy often emerge alongside moral evaluations of pervasive practices of copying and imitation. Examining the ethics of copying within this trade provides analytical purchase on a set of anthropological questions related to the recent problematization of brand "piracy" in international trade and legal frameworks. Below, I detail the process through which the World Trade Organization's Trade-Related Aspects of Intellectual Property Rights (TRIPS) Agreement, signed in 1995, has been implemented in Guatemala. The agreement, which tied international trade policy to intellectual property law, signaled a new era in the globalization of IP protections. Practices of sharing, appropriation, and copying—some of which qualify as piracy under national and international law—have a lengthy history in Guatemala. Maya garment manufacturers have long borrowed from and copied one another in addition to incorporating global trends into their designs. Certain acts of copying have also been viewed by manufacturers as manifestations of envy and therefore disparaged, even in the absence of strict IP enforcement. Tracing the contours of when and how copying is regulated within the local industry is helpful for apprehending the business style of highland apparel manufacturers and the relationship of the trade to the regulatory impulses of the IP law regime.

As TRIPS was rolled out in the late 1990s, international institutions, states, and corporations suddenly identified "piracy" as occuring all over the map, but especially in the Global South. New legislation and intensified policing have had little success, however, in curbing copying. "We have seen little evidence—and indeed few claims—that enforcement efforts to date have had any impact whatsoever on the overall supply of pirated goods," a recent study of digital media piracy explains (Karaganis 2011: iii). The piracy of music and films comprises upward of 85 percent of the market in many developing countries. The unauthorized reproduction of fashion brands represented a $350 billion market worldwide as of 2004 (Hilton et al. 2004), and that market has continued to grow. Authorized goods often sell at price points that many people simply cannot afford (Karaganis 2011). As described in this book's introduction, anthropologists have demonstrated that diverse cultural understandings of authenticity, originality, and ownership also guide consumption habits and complicate the implementation of IP frameworks. Ethnography is useful for understanding the failures of implementation efforts and the limitations inherent in globalized property regimes, as well as apprehending the regulating style through which a relatively successful fashion industry has taken shape in a marginalized economic setting.

INTELLECTUAL PROPERTY VALUES

As a signatory of TRIPS and the Dominican Republic–Central America Free Trade Agreement (DR-CAFTA), which were implemented in Guatemala in 2000 and 2006, respectively, the Guatemalan government moved to remake a legal context in which "there was little effective protection for intellectual property" (Godoy 2013: 59) into an enforcement regime fully harmonized with international law and enforcement standards. As part of this process, the national legislature expanded trademark protections covering brand names and logos, the kinds of words and images that highland apparel manufacturers often copy. The TRIPS Agreement, negotiated in the Uruguay Round of the General Agreement on Tariffs and Trade (GATT) in 1994, built on earlier treaties, namely the Paris Convention for the Protection of Industrial Property, originally signed in 1883, and the Berne Convention for the Protection of Literary and Artistic Works, first accepted in 1886, which established international unions to facilitate mutual recognition of patent and copyright protections, respectively, for rights holders from all signatory countries. The TRIPS Agreement largely integrated these early treaties with obligations established in the Rome Convention (1965) covering copyrights related to audio performances and recordings and in the Washington Treaty (1989) on patents for integrated circuits while supplementing these conventions with additional protection standards and enforcement requirements. What clearly distinguishes earlier conventions and the TRIPS Agreement, however, is the fusing together of trade issues with IP protections (Correa 2001: 79–80). Each of the nearly 130 nations that were party to the Uruguay Round was required to implement the TRIPS Agreement along varying timelines, depending on development status (as a "developing country," Guatemala had until January 1, 2000). The Uruguay Round also resulted in the establishment of the WTO as the international institution responsible for overseeing ongoing multilateral trade negotiations and resolving member disputes. TRIPS violations are thus subject to review under a WTO system that allows for significant trade sanctions against countries not abiding by or enforcing IP protections.

Under pressure from corporate lobbies, the United States had pushed hard for the inclusion of IP protections in the Uruguay Round. Indeed, the TRIPS Agreement's basic approach to linking trade and property rights had first been tested in US trade policy in the 1980s, when intellectual property lawyers, the film industry (concerned at the time with media piracy primarily in the Caribbean Basin), and pharmaceutical companies (interested in manufacturing drugs abroad cheaply without the threat of their formulas being "stolen") had organized lobbying efforts. Their representatives had convinced members of Congress and US delegates to the World Bank and the International Monetary Fund that intellectual property was a key indicator of a country's economic viability and that a country's enforcement record should be taken into account in making trade policy and lending decisions (Braithwaite and Drahos 2000: 66). By 1994, the United States had negotiated a number of bilateral agreements linking trade and IP protections and had success-fully coerced states including India, Thailand, and South Korea—states that had previously promoted alternative property rights approaches based on ideas such as "common heritage" (Sell 1995: 318)—to adopt or enforce Western IP laws by threatening trade sanctions. By the time of the Uruguay Round, international opposition to the US model of private property rights enforced via trade mechanisms had largely been squelched through such bilateral negotiations (Braithwaite and Drahos 2000: 63). A set of protections that are "suitable for industrialized countries, or, more precisely, for certain industrial sectors in which firms based in such countries dominate" had been universalized (Correa 2000: 5).

The TRIPS Agreement significantly expanded international trade-mark protections. Trademarks—defined as any sensorially perceptible signs that distinguish the good or service of one entity from that of another entity—can be words (such as a company name or the name of a particular product or service), graphics or images, tag lines, or packag-ing designs, and they may also include color combinations and fonts pertaining to a company's name, logo, or graphic scheme. Even smells and sounds may be considered for trademark protection. Whereas the Paris Convention had required that a trademark be in use in a given country in order to merit protection there, the TRIPS Agreement also protects marks that are not in use in a WTO member state but are none-theless publically recognizable because of marketing and promotion. These are referred to as "well-known marks." For example, even if the Gap retail chain does not operate in Guatemala, the Gap brand name and logo merit protection in Guatemala because Guatemalans have been made aware of the company and its brand through the company's mul-tinational marketing campaigns and promotional tie-ins to popular media vehicles. This is, in effect, a legal recognition of the fact that cor-porations and marketing firms have reconfigured and repurposed the brand form over the last several decades as a mode of publicity rather than a mark of origin. Another key extension of trademark protections under the TRIPS Agreement has to do with the association between marks and particular goods or services. An entity can now be prosecuted for trademark violation (and the state held accountable for infringe-ments) if it uses a mark that resembles that of another company, even if the companies market completely different categories of products. The Paris Convention gave limited protection to marks based on the goods or services in connection with which the mark had been registered. Now, a beverage marketed in Guatemala under the brand name Nike might be found to violate the IP rights of Nike Inc., even though Nike is not (at the time of this writing) in the business of selling beverages.

In the aftermath of TRIPS, the United States continued to push for even tougher IP regulations and enforcement procedures through a series of bilateral and multilateral free trade agreements, including DR-CAFTA. Besides reducing tariffs and eliminating quotas for US exports to the Central American region, DR-CAFTA tightened patent restrictions for pharmaceutical drugs, a move that was in direct violation of the Doha Declaration on TRIPS and Public Health that had been approved by WTO member states in 2001 and a subsequent WTO decision in 2003 to allow the importation of generic drugs to countries with limited domestic manufacturing capacity (Fink 2005). DR-CAFTA also extended copyright protections an additional twenty years (TRIPS had set the limit at the author's life plus fifty years) and required tougher IP enforcement protocols, such as the policing not only of imported goods but also of exports and transiting goods. Furthermore, whereas TRIPS limited the imposition of fines to the monetary damage suffered by rights holders, DR-CAFTA required the imposition of fines in the case of copyright or trademark piracy, irrespective of actual damages. Finally, the TRIPS Agreement did not include any specific obligations with regard to the allocation of state funding for IP enforcement. DR-CAFTA, on the other hand, spelled out that "resource constraints cannot be invoked as an excuse for not complying with the agreements' specific enforcement obligations" (Fink and Reichenmiller 2005: 296). In a country like Guatemala, where law enforcement budgets are severely limited and already strained by efforts to combat violent crime and drug trafficking, this provision means that the state has had to reorganize priorities in order to be in compliance with the agreement and qualify for favorable trade relations with the United States. Despite popular demonstrations against DR-CAFTA across Central America in 2005 and 2006, concerns among US congressmen regarding the treaty's net impact on both the US economy and Central American states, and pushback by Guatemala's then president Oscar Berger regarding the agreement's limitations on generic drug importation, production, and sales, the administration of US president George W. Bush was successful in pushing the agreement through in the United States and in each of the five Central American states and the Dominican Republic.

The inclusion of IP law in multilateral trade negotiations reflects the interests of powerful corporate lobbies working for the fashion, film, music, pharmaceutical, and software industries, which claim that the worldwide explosion in piracy and counterfeiting since the 1980s drastically impacts their profitability. Although copying can sometimes help more than hurt trademark owners (see chapter 3), IP law is now a core feature of the international economic development agenda. Economists, legal scholars, and business scholars claim that IP law encourages innovation by making new ideas profitable and that innovation drives economic growth (Grossman and Helpman 1993), contending that firms are unlikely to invest time and resources in building a brand or developing technology if these are not protected. This view presumes a competitive market environment in which decisions related to innovation and growth are based on the potential for profit. "Competition is anticipated, even imagined," within the IP framework, notes Marilyn Strathern (2002: 254). Meanwhile, neoliberal economists and allied international institutions strategically compel competition through the design, promotion, and enforcement of market-based systems that reward states and businesses for minimizing immediate costs and maximizing economic returns on private capital. The implementation of legal frameworks such as the TRIPS Agreement encourages and, indeed, enforces particular political-economic relationships and modes of behavior.[1]

Given the empirical failures of enforcement efforts, business and legal scholars commonly blame "culture" for piracy's continued proliferation. For example, marketing scholars Robert Green and Tasman Smith (2002: 92–93) write: "Many of the countries where counterfeiting flourishes are highly collectivist in nature, as opposed to the more individualist West. . . . Collectivist societies place less value on the role of any individual person or company's contribution and place a premium on the benefits to society . . . . Recent empirical studies have found a significant relationship between a country's level of individualism and the extent to which intellectual property rights are protected." As exemplified in this quote, culture is used to stereotype various world regions as a means of advancing market objectives and legitimizing uneven development (J. Ferguson 2006; Cooper and Stoler 1997). IP scholarship frequently draws on reductionist portraits of "national cultures" (Husted 2000) that are supposedly "fixed, simple, and unambiguous" (Herzfeld 1992: 73). The result is a map of the world where national boundaries represent stark and stable differences that are utterly discontinuous with one another (see Gupta and Ferguson 1997). Scholars and practitioners rank these culture groups hierarchically according to their degree of affiliation with the West and modernity, a neocolonial approach that calls to mind Dipesh Chakrabarty's (2000: 27) critique of the "given, reified categories, opposites paired in a structure of domination and subordination" that underwrites Orientalism. Scholars such as Green and Smith begin their analyses from the biased position that all humans are, or ought to be, self-interested individuals whose decisions follow the logic of market capitalism. The ethnographic case detailed below troubles this assumption. In fact, Maya apparel producers whose actions are labeled "piracy" under the globalized IP regime complain that the "individualism" evidenced in the business practices of their neighbors and competitors impels unethical modes of copying, and they simultaneously advocate a business ethics premised on modes of sharing and cooperation that Green and Smith might understand as "collectivist."

The notion that private property rights are not a universal principle could provide a starting point for critical discussions among legal and business scholars, policy makers, and regulators about the globalization of IP frameworks (Hann 1998). In fact, "culture" and "traditional knowledge" have become keywords in development discourse, and the WTO and WIPO have instituted negotiations regarding alternative, sui generis property rights systems that purport to take communal forms of ownership and local relationships to knowledge and natural resources into account. Some anthropologists and legal scholars applaud the resulting registries and protections afforded to, for example, alternative medical systems and healing traditions in India and indigenous agricultural knowledge and crop diversity in countries including Mexico, India, and Brazil as important for addressing global inequalities in the distribution of rights, assets, and status (Benthall 1999; Brush 1993; Brush and Stabinsky 1996; Downes 2000; see also World Intellectual Property Organization 1999).

When it comes to populations that participate in piracy and counterfeiting, however, cultural difference more often serves as evidence of moral shortcomings, as if imitative, "collectivist," and other approaches to property were indicative of a faulty ethics. Alexander Nill and Clifford Shultz (1996: 39) explain the benefits of educational campaigns against piracy and counterfeiting as follows: "People are made aware of the ethical issues involved; awareness is a prerequisite for ethical reasoning." It is presumed that people who participate in piracy—who are characterized as deviant, aberrant, and criminal in the business literature (Albers-Miller 1999)—can be reoriented toward a new culture and ethics if the law is clearly explained to them. This is a different sort of pedagogical imperative, one where difference is deemed acceptable only if it can be managed as part of the expansion of an overarching set of

Western understandings of property and rights (Mohanty 1988). Anyone who reads the law, it is assumed, will come to an identical conclusion about the problem of piracy; ethical behavior seems possible only in the context of formal legal governance, and respect for the law ought to be independent of socioeconomic status and other conditions of life or citizenship. As US vice president Joe Biden stated in 2010 when announcing the release of the US Joint Strategic Plan on Intellectual Property Enforcement: "Piracy is theft. Clean and simple. It's smash and grab. It ain't no different than smashing a window at Tiffany's" (Sandoval 2010).

In many places, however, the law is anything but clean and simple. Rachel Sieder (2003: 141), writing of "the historical legacy of citizen mistrust of the law" in Guatemala, describes the postwar state judiciary as "bereft of legitimacy in the eyes of the majority of the population." Given the lack of accountability related to wartime atrocities—the peace process, concluded in 1996, granted blanket amnesty to the perpetrators of the deaths of two hundred thousand Guatemalans, most of whom were indigenous (Comisión para el Esclarecimiento Histórico 1999)—the promotion of antipiracy laws and the penal logics ensconced therein reflects a rather foreign concept: that crime is crime. Considering the rampant criminal impunity in the country—in 2009, less than 2 percent of homicides in Guatemala resulted in a conviction (M. Wilson 2009)—the idea that modern state sovereignty is defined by the punishment of crime seems misguided. A culturally peculiar criminology, premised on the notion that punitive law prevents crime and improves civic life and governmental and economic efficiencies (Pasquino 1991), shapes the ideological context in which arguments in favor of the expansion of IP protections are often couched in terms of the spread of democracy, progress, and prosperity to nations that are seen as politically, ethically, and culturally backward (Lippert 1999; Bettig 1996).[2]

The Guatemalan state has responded to international pressures concerning IP enforcement through various efforts, including the appointment of a special prosecutor for IP rights and the implementation of sporadic, well-reported raids during which police confiscate illegal compact discs, DVDs, and clothing sold in Guatemala City streets (Mauricio Martínez 2004; Larios 2011). Certain national actors have taken up the discourse of IP protections, even if the cultural presuppositions of the IP regime do not hold up to empirical scrutiny. The police charged with enforcing IP law, for instance, are not paragons of law and order in Guatemala. The many street vendors I interviewed in 2009 told me that, following raids, the underpaid police fenced the seized products for their own gain.[3] The government recently removed most of these vendors (and the clients who depend on their cheap goods) from the sidewalks of Zone 1, the capital city's historic center, as part of a larger public-private partnership to convert the area into an upscale entertainment district (Véliz and O'Neill 2011). The street vendors have been relocated to an interior space in a multistory building, making product piracy a less conspicuous feature of the capital city's urban landscape. The United States Trade Representative's (2010) report on international IP rights infringement urged the Guatemalan government to "extend its efforts to pursue raids and prosecutions, not just against small-scale sellers, but also against manufacturers of pirated and counterfeit goods." In one of these coordinated production raids in April 2011, eight people were arrested in two capital-area homes, where millions of compact discs and dozens of computers and CD and DVD burners were confiscated (*Prensa Libre* 2011a). Representatives of US trade associations such as the Business Software Alliance, the American Chamber of Commerce in Mexico and in Guatemala, and the International Intellectual Property Alliance regularly comment in the media on economic losses associated with the piracy trade (see, e.g., *Prensa Libre* 2008; Marroquín 2010; *Prensa Libre* 2011b; Leonardo 2011; Coronado 2013; Patzán 2014; G. I. Ramírez 2015) and have also participated in public roundtables in Guatemala City to discuss the "nature, causes, and consequences of piracy, and viable alternatives" (*Prensa Libre* 2011c, my translation). Reporters for the country's major dailies characterize people who manufacture and sell unauthorized reproductions of copyright- and trademark-protected materials as lawbreakers—"mercenaries of illegality," as one national newspaper called them, "who cost the Guatemalan state millions in lost taxes" (Menocal 2005).

In 2011, a representative of El Zeppelín, a large domestic clothing manufacturer based in Quetzaltenango, estimated that between 40 and 60 percent of apparel sold in Guatemala is pirated, and he was quoted in a national newspaper saying: "[Piracy] is bad, slows down economic growth, doesn't pay taxes, and robs market niches from the national textile industry and impedes its development. It sells at lower prices but without the backing of a company and no quality, and the client can't complain" (*Prensa Libre* 2011c, my translation). He added, "Lo barato sale caro" (Cheap stuff is expensive), a colloquial phrase meaning that one ends up paying more in the long run when buying inexpensive, low-quality goods that do not last. This company representative nicely sums up the attitude toward piracy that some formal business owners in Guatemala have adopted in the wake of so much attention to IP protections over the past decade.

The criminalization of piracy converges in everyday conversation and media reports with ideologies of race, ethnicity, culture, and class in ways that make already marginalized populations available for new kinds of blame. Because street vendors hawking pirated goods in the capital city are socially and spatially proximate to street crime (e.g., pickpocketing, mugging, and assault), piracy is lumped into a generalized portrait of deviance and violence as an intractable part of urban life. The fact that street vendors generally belong to an urban underclass and are often indigenous (Offit 2011) also fits with stereotyped portraits of delinquency that blame poor, rural people, whom many nonindigenous *ladinos* say become "corrupted"—that is, drawn into a life of crime— when they move to the capital city (Camus 2011).[4] This stereotype and ubiquitous "talk of crime" (Caldeira 2001) in Guatemala have emerged partially out of brutal realities. But an alarming rise in violent crime rates since the armed conflict ended more accurately reflects the influx of transnational drug gangs into the capital city and widespread conditions of poverty and insecurity that make life precarious for most Guatemalans (O'Neill 2011). Sensational media accounts conflate piracy with organized crime, violence, and even international terrorism, a line of argument promoted by the US government and international industry associations (*Prensa Libre* 2011b; see also Aguiar 2010; Dent 2012a; Treverton et al. 2009). Such characterizations of piracy belie the fact that crime is not a homogenous category and discourage sophisticated analysis of the factors that underpin the physical insecurity that many Guatemalans currently face (Benson et al. 2008). Pirates do not always or even usually belong to drug gangs, and piracy is a widely accepted practice, indeed a staple, of Guatemala's marketplace. As much as 80 percent of software used by Guatemalan companies is pirated, even though there have been dozens of court cases that have resulted in private businesses being fined (Marroquín 2010). Pirated goods are sold openly on urban streets and in highland market towns. In large towns throughout Guatemala, retail shops with names such as El Estreno (Premier) and La Nueva Moda (The New Style) feature clothing with pirated brand names and logos. Maya manufacturers involved in piracy do not see themselves as "bad people" engaging in criminal behavior, although most are aware of the discourse against piracy that echoes through national newspapers. They do not view their activity as something that undermines the health of the economy either. A simple criminology of piracy overlooks the ways that multiscalar normative regimes intersect to produce the "profound moral—even righteous" (Bourgois 1996: 41) ethical codes that so often underlie criminalized behavior.

THE RUMOR MILL

The following story, recounted by anthropologist Edward F. Fischer (2001: 38), is but one of the more colorful rumors linking wealth and witchcraft that circulate in Tecpán: "A successful but greedy local businessman possessed a strongbox full of gold that, no matter how much was spent, always remained full; anyone other than its owner who looked inside, however, would see only a tangled mass of black snakes, a clear sign of its nefarious origins." Assumed to be motivated by envy (*envidia*), wealthy people are often suspected of accumulating their wealth through occult, unethical, or illicit means. The word *envidia* combines meanings of covetousness, jealousy, and greed. *Envidia* is understood as a dangerous affective disposition, a malicious personality, and it is associated with *mal de ojo*, the evil eye. In Tecpán, people say that falling under the stare of an envious person will result in your being bewitched, which will bring you illness or other misfortune; this is a common belief across many peasant and petty capitalist societies (G. M. Foster 1972; Dow 1981). Talk of envy has a long history in the highland region (Tax 1957) and is a dominant discourse used to express and evaluate the moral hazards that have accompanied rapid industrial change and transformations in Tecpán's social organization in recent decades. The discourse of envy also offers Maya manufacturers an important frame for evaluating practices of copying and imitation in the highland apparel trade. As discussed below, garment producers attribute certain forms of copying and competition to envy, understanding those practices as the result of a greedy and jealous disposition. Comprehending the social meanings of envy is indispensable for tracing the intersections and divergences between international IP law and the normative frameworks that regulate practices of sharing, appropriation, and imitation within the regional trade.

Closely associated with material accumulation and processes of class stratification, envy is often regarded in the anthropological literature as a negative mechanism for the maintenance of egalitarian social and economic relations. George M. Foster's (1965) seminal work on envy explains its ubiquity and power in terms of a worldview shared among Latin American peasants founded on the "Image of Limited Good."

Peasants regard resources such as wealth and prestige as finite and scarce, and this creates a "zero-sum game" in which people who accumulate more than is customary are seen as taking away from other people (Taussig 1980: 15). Emphasis on class and ethnic solidarity among a subordinated population has been theorized by a long line of anthropologists working in the Maya region (e.g., Vogt 1961, 1969; Annis 1987) as evidence of what Richard Wilk (1983: 103) called a "fierce egalitarian ethos," which enjoins the distribution of material resources across indigenous communities through well-organized political and religious institutions. The fraternal *cofradía* system, for example, has historically required families to contribute regularly to communal coffers for the upkeep of the images of patron saints, facilitated joint land holdings, served as a source of local political leadership, and provided a system of loans as well as mutual aid for families and individuals in need (G.M. Foster 1953; Wolf 1957; Warren 1978; Brintnall 1979). My fieldwork revealed a changing politics of fairness and equality in Maya communities that is rooted in a cultural tradition but not determined by it. Egalitarianism emerged from my study not as a static trait but as a contested norm, a fraught reality, and a normalizing discourse.

The accumulation and concentration of wealth yields accusations of envy in Tecpán, where relatively well-to-do manufacturers are accused of having obtained their wealth by nefarious means and having violated a property regime that allows for certain forms of sharing, copying, and imitation. As discussed in chapter 1, cooperation among kin and neighbors has been an economic resource for *tecpanecos* since the early 1960s, when employers began sharing resources with kinsmen and training employees in apprentice-like relationships to prepare them to start their own garment manufacturing businesses.

I sat down with Manuel Chicoy, one of the earliest apparel producers in Tecpán, to talk about former employees of his, not to mention two of his sons, who left his workshop over the years to start their own businesses. Manuel specialized in women's sweaters. He was about seventy years old when I spoke with him in 2009 and was dividing his time between overseeing the garment workshop, where his youngest son managed the day-to-day operations, and supervising the two-story hotel that he had built near the center of town with his profits from the apparel trade. As we talked in the hotel office, I asked Manuel about the growth of the trade. He replied in a style of Spanish that is common in indigenous towns such as Tecpán, where, for most people of Manuel's generation, Spanish is a second language. Sentences are often short, and due to the influence of both Christianity and traditional Maya spirituality, ordinary conversations often involve parables and moral lessons. Clean-shaven and neatly dressed in tailored pants and a collared shirt, Manuel sat across from me at the table in his otherwise bare office and related this story to me with great intensity and conviction: "It's like this. You encounter a man in the street, and he says, 'I don't have work. My family is hungry, and I don't know what to do.' So you say to him, 'Come with me. I'll give you work.' Years later, he says that he wants to start his own workshop. You say, 'Very good, here's your capital. Buy what you need.' That is what we have to do—help each other, help our neighbors."

Knowing from previous conversations with workshop owners and town residents that such moral tales generally conveyed an ideal rather than reported a factual state of affairs but also aware that the number of workshops in town had indeed grown through kin and apprenticeship relations, I pressed him on the question of whether he felt that more workshops in town meant greater competition and whether that might challenge the sustainability of his own business. Manuel did not give my inquiries much thought before he continued: "I think it is development [*un desarrollo*] for everyone. The more production we have, the more business, the products just get better and better. I don't see it as competition. It's a way for all of us to better ourselves. That's the kind of development we should pursue."

This genre of talk about neighborly kindness and mutual obligation that underlies the pedagogical imperative in Tecpán's apparel trade echoes religious themes that circulate globally and manifest in particular ways among practitioners of Catholicism in Guatemala and the country's booming neo-Pentecostal movement (O'Neill 2009). Protestant pastors have advocated "participation in the new community of 'brothers and sisters' who work towards the common goal of self-betterment" and promoted a "new ideology [that] emphasizes individualism, competition, personal improvement, and social and economic progress" as positive values (Goldín and Metz 1991: 334). Both Protestants and Catholics involved in commercial enterprise have increasingly embraced these values (Goldín 1992), though not without protest. Many garment manufacturers I spoke with bemoaned the general ethical shift away from solidarity and toward individualism. A medium-sized producer complained in an interview: "We in Tecpán are very individualistic. We dedicate ourselves to our work, to our own affairs, our own commitments . . . everything that has to do with our family and our business, and that's it." He blamed individualism for many problems, from fights among neighbors and family members to *delincuencia,* a general term for disrespectful or criminal behavior perpetrated by town youth. The integration of commercial enterprise with social institutions such as religion, family, and economy is never simple. However, anthropologists note that the discourse of competition and self-betterment promoted within Protestantism and now widespread among highland Maya people is often grounded in appeals to "fundamental Maya values associated with community solidarity, support, and guidance" (Goldín and Metz 1991: 334). This kind of hybridity was readily apparent among the apparel manufacturers I got to know, whose livelihoods involve competitive market behavior but who are nonetheless expected to integrate themselves into networks of reciprocity and, in a model reminiscent of the older *cofradía* system, support the success of neighbors and kin through financial as well as spiritual and moral assistance. As the uncertainties of capitalist enterprise have put a strain on communal ties and induced further competition, producers have sometimes grown nostalgic about lost values of solidarity and egalitarianism, sentiments that are, in turn, interpreted in some anthropological accounts as evidence of a sullied past. Ideas about how the past differs from the present and how individualism contrasts with authentic indigeneity have thus shaped how Maya apparel producers style themselves in relation to one another and in relation to the marketplace.

Manuel cautioned against the destructive nature of competition even as he extolled commercial enterprise as a source of self-improvement and community development. I climbed the tiled stairway with him from the lobby of his hotel to the second-story rooftop. Looking out over the neighboring houses, Manuel pointed out the home-workshops of other manufacturers he had trained or assisted over the years. He returned to his earlier point about the importance of helping others and then added: "Not everyone understands it as development. Instead, they take it as envy, as competition. But if someone asks you for something, you give it to them. People come into town and ask me where a different workshop is because they want to buy something there, and I tell them. If I were to say that I don't know where it is just because I don't want them to buy from a different workshop, that's pure envy." At least in part, Manuel was positioning and politicking. Helping one's neighbors and sharing one's resources were common refrains among *tecpanecos,* who are constantly negotiating their standing given that garment manufacturing has led to some socioeconomic stratification (Thomas 2009). Manuel literally sat above most of his neighbors in his two-story home and workshop and the adjacent hotel. He and others who got their start before *la violencia* (as the bloodiest years of Guatemala's internal armed conflict are known) capitalized on the new markets opened up by apparel manufacturing and amassed small fortunes, in relative terms—enough to build a large house, buy a car, send a child to college in the capital city, or open a second business. Manuel thus drew on a shared moral economy and business ethic in our conversation to both explicate a felt normative regime and stave off potential accusations against him.

As described in chapter 1, constraints on employment and educational opportunities for indigenous people meant that scores of men in Tecpán opened up workshops after the genocidal violence of the armed conflict subsided in the late 1980s and throughout the 1990s. The kinship and apprenticeship model of social reproduction has enabled growth despite the seeming contradictions between its emphasis on both reciprocity and solidarity and the neoliberal model of entrepreneurship promoted on a global level. Yet, the rate at which new workshops have opened and the market pressures impelled by structural adjustment and free trade have all contributed to intense feelings of competition among neighbors. The crowded marketplace makes it difficult for anyone to earn a "minimum income" (Scott 1976), the level of economic security that petty capitalists seek to maintain amid market pressures and given sentiments of community solidarity. Neighbors look at the wealth that older manufacturers like Manuel display in multistory houses and late-model cars and wonder how anyone could achieve that level of success without dealing in the occult or engaging in unscrupulous behavior. Indigeneity as a mode of identification and belonging is also at stake here. When it comes to how Maya men and women see upward mobility, there is often suspicion about assimilating into nonindigenous culture. As anthropologist Linda Green (2003: 56) notes, economically successful Mayas have sometimes been accused of "acting as agents" of racism and oppression, a sentiment that anthropologist Liliana Goldín (1992: 112) attributes to the fact that *ladinos* are "thought to be wealthy (or wealthier than Indians) from the exploitation of poor Indians." As for Manuel, he appealed to neighborly ethics in a context where the specter of conspiracy and neocolonialism was hovering over some houses and workshops more than others.

Ethnic and racial classificatory schemes in Guatemala are somewhat flexible; for example, indigenous people often attempt to "pass" as *ladino* outside their home communities to avoid discrimination (Warren

FIGURE 9. Garment workshop with industrial knitting machines in the La Giralda neighborhood of Tecpán, 2009. Note that the rudimentary concrete floors and wooden construction of this workshop contrast significantly with the tiled floors and painted concrete-block walls of the workshop pictured in figure 10, illustrating a degree of socioeconomic stratification within the highland apparel trade. I discuss the social dynamics surrounding La Giralda's relationship to Tecpán's more central barrios in chapter 5.

1998: 10–11). Carol Hendrickson (1995: 33) wrote of "relative ethnicity" in Tecpán, by which she meant that people were often said to "act like" a Maya or a *ladino* "in certain contexts and for particular reasons." During my fieldwork, the more successful manufacturers in Tecpán were, somewhat jokingly, referred to by other manufacturers and town residents as *medio-ladino* (half-*ladino*), implying an aspiration to associate with and adopt the public markers of distinction that set apart this economically and politically more powerful group. The label sometimes also connoted a sense of ethnic betrayal. The adoption of a nonindigenous style—which was variously defined as engaging in more extravagant consumption habits, wearing less formal or more expensive clothing, displaying an air of conceit in relation to indigenous peers, even using an indoor shower rather than the traditional *tuj,* or sweat bath— was often interpreted as a loss or rejection of traditional values. In short, saying that someone was acting *ladino* generally meant that the person

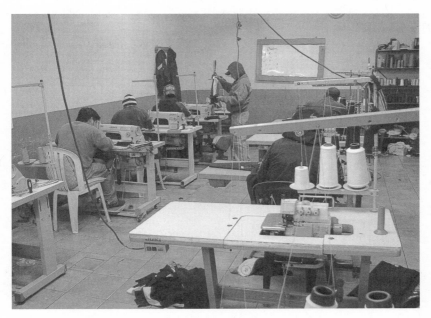

FIGURE 10. Sewing machine operators in a garment workshop in Tecpán, 2009.

was behaving selfishly, was taking advantage of people, or thought himself to be above or better than his indigenous peers (Hendrickson 1995: 18). This haughtiness can be comical when the person is unmistakably indigenous to local people because of family ties, a Kaqchikel surname, or physical features socially inscribed as indigenous traits. One producer commented that another man was becoming "like the *ladinos*" because the man was consumed by greed, had built a fancy house with an ostentatious brick façade, and had grown out his curly hair, an unusual style among middle-aged indigenous men. Another producer referred to a neighboring manufacturer as *medio-ladino*, explaining that the man had two cars, including a late-model SUV, and was wearing "*original* clothing," by which he meant more expensive garments purchased in urban retail shops. If ethnic boundaries are somewhat flexible in Guatemala, it is also the case that there are well-defined modes of policing indigenous style and maintaining boundaries and also latent assumptions and anxieties about who belongs where and how race and ethnicity are related to morality, propriety, and social class.

Talk of envy has genres. I noted that individuals often explained the tragic and unfair collapse of collective ventures, especially economic ones, by pointing to the envious behavior of others. For example, a group of Maya garment manufacturers formed a cooperative in the late 1980s to more efficiently source raw materials. After some initial success, the cooperative began to struggle and was eventually dissolved. I talked with dozens of manufacturers about why the cooperative failed. They told me that a national thread and textile firm had opened a retail outlet in Tecpán, basically eliminating the need for the cooperative. Many people then added that the real problem was *envidia*. They alleged that the cooperative's directors were envious and paradoxically did not like seeing the members benefit from the group's services, so they ran it into the ground. They claimed that some of the directors even stole money from the cooperative's accounts. There are dozens of stories like this in my field notes, stories where an economic outcome that social scientists might explain in terms of apolitical market dynamics was explained by apparel producers as having more to do with the moral stakes of the marketplace. The point is that, for Maya workshop owners, market dynamics are moral. One young apparel producer complained to me that another manufacturer had beaten him out of several lucrative production contracts to make school uniforms. In contrast to the vagaries and crediting demands of the wholesale and municipal market trades, these contracts guarantee the sale of a specified quantity of items and promise full payment within thirty to sixty days of delivery. The producer who had lost several contracts described his competitor:

> This man has a workshop in one of the *colonias* on the edge of town. Not just a workshop, it's a *media-maquila*. He wins contracts because he deals in prices that are much lower than what we can offer. The truth is, I think he's a *narcotraficante*. He walks around with a pistol, and that's why I say, maybe he's a drug trafficker, and he has this *maquila* in order to throw people off his trail, because he sells everything at prices that are way too low to make a profit.

In a contemporary twist, it was not the devil with whom this entrepreneur had allegedly made his pact (Nash 1979; Taussig 1980) but rather the murderous drug gangs who threaten Guatemala's capital city and border provinces. The fact that the manufacturer in question was known to have significant advantages of scale did not prevent speculation that his pricing was simply too low for a legitimate, profit-earning enterprise. Fantastical tales about his shady dealings were made more believable to local residents by the fact that he lived "on the edge of town," had no known family connections in Tecpán, and seemingly appeared out of nowhere a few years previous.

One of the wealthiest, best-known workshop owners in town was also a frequent target of rumor, with talk circulating that he cheated neighbors for personal gain and was ultimately motivated by *envidia*. He was one of the first producers to invest in high-capacity knitting machines, and thus one of the first to significantly increase his scale of production. Many workshop owners in town said that he was the main reason for declining prices, intensifying competition, and all kinds of economic hardship. The most egregious acts he was rumored to have committed related to the armed conflict, however. It was said that he led guerrilla fighters and received money from the government as part of the peace settlement. Yet instead of disbursing the funds among his troops, he reportedly pocketed the total amount, using it to establish himself in the apparel business. This rumor reflected, among other things, a sense of uneasiness about the peace process and concerns about who benefited and how the promises made regarding assistance for indigenous communities affected by violence had or had not been kept. This man's success was marred by suspicions of theft and betrayal.

The impersonal workings of the market economy, the mastery that some entrepreneurs develop over the skills and dispositions necessary to accumulate capital, and the structural forces that make it difficult for many to do so become ordinary or eventful in the idiom of envy. This sociology of symptoms and suspects is itself symptomatic of the influence of various cultural frames and historical burdens. The military's strategic targeting of indigenous professionals and business owners during the armed conflict fueled rumors that people turned one another over to the state out of envy (Fischer and Hendrickson 2002; Sanford 2003). More than petty gossip, rumor has emerged in the postconflict era as a key medium used by national and local officials to generate uncertainty about who precisely is to blame for the shortcomings of Guatemala's peace process while localizing blame onto amorphous troublemakers who are said to be responsible for disrupting community life (Benson 2004). Rumors about envy and accusations of individualism fold in a great deal of suspicion related to "that odd fusion of . . . hope and hopelessness, of utility and futility, of promise and its perversions" that characterizes millennial capitalism in general (Jean Comaroff and John L. Comaroff 1999: 283) and postwar national development policy in Guatemala in particular. Entrepreneurship, promoted by international institutions, national officials, and nongovernmental organizations as the key to ending poverty and achieving First World modernity, does not always or even usually lead to economic security, and it also entails moral and legal hazards. Envy provides an interpretative frame for *tecpanecos* as they attempt to make sense of the promises of entrepreneurial success, on the one hand, and the difficult realities of postwar social life and economic struggle, on the other. The discourse of envy is part and parcel of the apparel marketplace. It regulates the activities of the trade's participants and makes the marketplace what it is, such that simple dichotomies between morality and economy and between norms and practice seem untenable.

THE ETHICS OF THE COPY

There has been an explosion in the amount of foreign goods coming into Guatemala since the armed conflict ended. Mexican-manufactured clothing, Chinese and Taiwanese imports (much of it featuring pirated brands), and secondhand clothing from the United States spills out from Guatemala City's brightly painted concrete-block shops onto the sidewalks in the wholesale garment district along La Bolívar, one of the city's major avenues. The influx of these products puts downward pressure on prices; imports may be of higher quality, but they are often cheaper than Guatemalan-made goods. The globalization of the Guatemalan clothing market has also given highland manufacturers access to new designs and brand names. Copying is the most basic and ubiquitous mechanism through which these manufacturers develop their product lines; they sometimes even copy copies, since they frequently base their designs on pirated apparel from China.

Alberto Ixim, a thirty-two-year-old Maya man, owned one of the workshops in which I worked in 2009. After I had spent a long day in the concrete-block room, wedged into my seat in a row of five young men, all of us guiding sweater-knit fabric and fleece material through industrial sewing machines, it was a welcome change to accompany Alberto to his home for late afternoon coffee and a chat about his business. He complained to me on one such occasion that wholesalers had lost interest in the children's clothing designs he was producing. He had been embroidering Winnie the Pooh and Spiderman figures onto little shirts and pants, but many manufacturers were using the same popular cartoon characters on their garments. So he wanted to set himself apart from the competition. Alberto reached across the kitchen table to grab a small fleece shirt and said, "This is what I want to do." I asked if the garment was a *muestra*, a sample he was working on to show potential buyers. He replied that it was a Mexican import that he had purchased a few days before on La Bolívar. Alberto explained: "When I go to the capital city, I look at what the Mexicans are doing. I prefer to copy the Mexicans or the Chinese. A lot of people just copy what their neighbors are doing. But you make enemies that way."

Alberto sold to wholesalers on La Bolívar every Friday morning. One Friday, we arrived very early, before some of the shops had opened. He told me that he had hoped to get there before anyone else from Tecpán: "When everyone is walking around at the same time, people see your newest designs. They see how many bundles you're delivering, how much you're selling. They might be envious. Some will come along right behind you and ask the wholesaler how much you charged him. And they'll say, 'I can make that for less.' That's how the *copiones* work." The term *copión,* which means a copycat in the classroom, was commonly used to disparage garment manufacturers who copied other producers in ways that were considered unethical. For example, if a producer did not make some kind of change when copying someone else's design, if he did not introduce some creative element, he was called a *copión.* This teasing out of the dialectic through which style gets produced both recognizes that copying is inevitable and necessary and also specifies the modes of copying that can result in socially legitimate styles of fashion and of business practice.

There are similarities here to the norms related to copying and imitation that anthropologists have documented among handicraft vendors and traditional weavers in highland Guatemala. Walter Little (2004: 120), for example, has written that "[handicraft] vendors try to give tourists the impression that they are not in competition with each other." Yet, Little continued, "unsuccessful vendors are jealous of successful vendors and say derogatory things among themselves about those who consistently have high sales, and they try to copy successful designs. . . . Showing jealousy, trying to steal customers and otherwise attempting to demean competing vendors in front of tourists is considered to be not only poor taste but wrong" (120). Outward displays of ethnic solidarity thus emerge as an economic strategy, since foreign tourists often go looking for "Indians"—people who belong to a presumably homogenous and harmonious group defined "in relation to both tourists and to Ladinos" (119). Feelings of "jealousy," which I refer to in this chapter by the term "envy," challenge vendors' abilities to live up to globally circulating stereotypes about the "perceived steadfastness" of traditional communities (Dudley 1996: 47), since these feelings inspire what is perceived to be unethical behavior, such as the direct copying of competitors' designs. Likewise, Carol Hendrickson's (1995) work on Mayan weaving showed that knowing what designs to imitate was a matter of pride for weavers, as was adding some creative inflection to these designs that demonstrated their particular skills.

Garment manufacturers also take pride in improvising on designs they see in malls, online, and at the markets and shops where they sell. For example, Alberto might take a fleece romper design that he sees on the Baby Gap website and substitute sweater-knit fabric for the material of the bodice—partly because he can make knit fabric with his machinery, so it is cheaper for him, and partly because this improvisation will be a selling point for him in the market. A young manufacturer from another apparel-producing town noted proudly in an interview that his family deals in *imitaciones*. "We copy it, but we make it better," he said, explaining that they start with popular youth styles they see on websites and in upscale commercial centers and tailor them to the local market, producing garments that suit their clientele in terms of price but also in terms of color palette and overall design. It is common for highland producers to mimic certain elements of their neighbors' designs as well, but they are expected to make changes that set their garments apart in a meaningful way. A producer might copy the cut and brand of a cotton t-shirt that his neighbor is manufacturing, for instance, but change the color scheme and also screen-print the logo rather than sewing it on. This would be seen as a legitimate form of borrowing and appropriation. Although directly copying a neighbor's design is admittedly easier, it takes advantage of an already open system in which producers acknowledge the economic and moral legitimacy of copying and imitation.

Those labeled *copiones* do not just copy exactly what someone else is selling. They also sell the product for less than what the other manufacturer is charging. Alberto was trying to evade *copiones* during our early-morning visit to La Bolívar. "It is a normal reaction for people to get angry with one another," one producer explained, "especially when you are offering the same product at a lower price to the same buyer. That is when people get really upset." Another producer told me that he had begun travelling to more distant markets to avoid meeting up with other manufacturers who might steal his designs. Already part of what Carolyn Nordstrom (2004) might term a "shadow economy" because of the largely informal and often illegal nature of the trade, this producer referred to his strategy as "selling undercover" (*vender escondido*). He told me that, if he didn't do so, "they [other producers] will copy what I am selling and then come back and offer it to my buyers at a lower price.

It always depends on what kind of machinery you have and your talents, but everyone tries to copy everyone else." Alberto and many other garment manufacturers interpreted price-based competition—a predictable and rather ordinary business strategy in neoclassical economics—as both unfair, since everyone suffers when prices go down, and morally problematic, evidence of the kind of greed, jealousy, and maliciousness that Maya people in Tecpán describe as *envidia*.

Part of why the copying of global fashion brands is socially acceptable throughout much of Guatemala is because of the hard realities of poverty and inequality. The expensive products sold by multinational fashion firms are beyond the reach of most Guatemalan consumers. Gross national income per capita in Guatemala is approximately US$3,340, a figure that overestimates the buying power of indigenous people in the highland region. In 2006, the last year for which data are available, the richest 40 percent of Guatemalans earned nearly 80 percent of the national population's total income and purchased nearly 80 percent of the total value of goods and services consumed. And as poverty rates in Guatemala are climbing, according to national and international poverty standards, indigenous people and rural populations are increasingly likely to live below the poverty line (World Bank 2015). All of this adds up to a highland population that has relatively little, if any, expendable income and depends on secondhand markets, cheap imports, and locally made knockoffs for nontraditional clothing.

Another factor accounting for the persistence of what international IP law labels as "piracy" production is the idea common among Maya garment manufacturers, wholesalers, and consumers with whom I spoke that foreign manufacturers do not know what local people want to buy. Highland workshop owners say that it is therefore up to them to tailor designs to local tastes. Copying the look of an imported garment or a style made popular by a foreign company, which may involve copying a trademarked logo, is seen as part of the business, an intelligent design strategy, and also a good way to avoid the moral dangers of directly copying one's neighbors. People who resorted to copying the products being offered by neighboring producers were, from the perspective of many Maya workshop owners, considered to be unskilled, indiscriminate, and not savvy. Moreover, foreign corporations and manufacturers seem distant. Driving through Tecpán at the close of another workday, Alberto and I passed by a clothing shop with several Abercrombie sweatshirts displayed on clothes hangers in the entryway. Alberto, who was wearing a knockoff Lacoste polo shirt, turned to me

FIGURE 11. Knockoff Abercrombie & Fitch sweatshirt
for sale in a retail store in Tecpán, 2009.

and commented: "You see a lot of clothing that says Abercrombie on it.
Abercrombie is not here." Then he began to laugh. A critique of Guatemala's position in the world system—as a country that is not home to
the Abercrombie & Fitch corporation or any other firms that market
globally popular brands and that never could be because of macroeconomic policies and transnational processes that have made Guatemala
peripheral to fashion and modernity—this comment simultaneously
made a joke out of the fact that the Abercrombie name and logo are
indeed everywhere in Tecpán and in Guatemala more generally. For
several years during my fieldwork, Abercrombie & Fitch hoodies were
some of the most popular garments made in highland workshops and
worn by Maya women and men, especially young men, in the highland
region.

"Do you mean that Abercrombie is not from Guatemala?" I asked to
make sure I got the joke, and he laughed even harder. "It is definitely
not from Guatemala, and definitely not from Tecpán," he replied.

This exchange with Alberto was typical of my conversations with Maya apparel producers about the brand names they affixed to the clothing they made and wore. These small-time manufacturers often drew attention to the sociopolitical and geographical distances that separate Maya people who make and consume fashion from the places represented as the true sources of fashion in global marketing campaigns and official discourse, including in development narratives and antipiracy propaganda.

It is not, as some legal scholars assume, that Maya entrepreneurs are unaware of how they are connected to international markets. Rather, producers such as Alberto are all too aware of how historical legacies of the political and economic subordination of indigenous Guatemalans and contemporary trade arrangements, from the elimination of tariffs on imported goods to the subsidization of multinational manufacturers instead of domestic producers, challenge the sustainability of their regional trade. Producers respond to these conditions in ways that are contextually and ordinarily ethical given their obligations to kin and community. A normative order that privileges and protects the proximate is evidence that values other than those assumed to be natural or superior within the international development agenda exist, even in places that have a longstanding relationship to development discourse.

During my fieldwork, once I had established a relationship with a manufacturer and overcome initial suspicions about my possible affiliation with governments or rights-bearing corporations, it was uncommon for that manufacturer to hide from me the fact that he knowingly copied popular brands and fashion designs. In spite of a lot of talk about copying, the term "piracy" surfaced only intermittently in my conversations with manufacturers. In an interview, one small-scale producer suggested that the *copiones* are just like the *piratas* (pirates) he had read about in the newspaper—people who sell CDs and DVDs containing unauthorized content in the capital city streets. "The people who make the original discs complain because they can't sell them for the price they want," he explained. This producer, who traded in pirated brand names himself, interpreted the criminalized problem of piracy in line with the localized ethics of copying. His view was that piracy harms some producers because it undercuts their ability to earn a living when others copy digital material and engage in unethical and immoral price cutting. This is different from the claims about authorship, ownership, and originality that condition IP law. He did not evaluate the mere act of copying as problematic, nor did he express concern regarding the property rights that content producers might have for their creations. Within a moral economy committed to sharing and a community of practice dedicated to the production of style, he and others accepted some forms of copying as appropriate, legitimate, and ethical while simultaneously denouncing business practices that they perceived as motivated by *envidia,* such as the kinds of cutthroat competition that detracted from the ability of community members to earn a living and that thus seemed morally and financially threatening to the overall stability of a local industry.

Another producer, Mateo Cali, found some humor in the moralizing campaigns against piracy that he heard about in conversations with other apparel manufacturers. Mateo's one-room workshop was neat and tidy, not cluttered with remnants, fabric scraps, and old machine parts like so many of the neighboring *talleres.* He prided himself on running an orderly business and liked to work on a contract basis with wholesalers in Guatemala City rather than with the market vendors who demand that producers supply them with goods on credit. Yet Mateo told me that he copies just like everyone else. As we discussed the garment design he was working on during one of our conversations—a t-shirt with the Adidas logo screen-printed across the front—Mateo commented to me that companies like Adidas have offices in the capital city where producers are supposed to pay for *el derecho* (the rights) to use their logos. He had read in a national newspaper about crackdowns on market vendors selling "pirated" goods and seemed keen on assuring me that he knew and understood the law. When I asked if anyone from Tecpán ever pays for these rights, his face lit up with a broad smile. He exclaimed, "The market is pure piracy, pure Captain Morgan" (puro pirata, puro pirata Morgan)!

Mateo's joke says a lot about the relationship between small-scale producers like himself and the multinational corporations that hold the rights to the brand names and logos that adorn high-priced, exclusive consumer goods. Captain Morgan rum, a brand that plays neatly on the pirate history of the Caribbean system, is heavily marketed in Latin America on television, online, and in print media. Perhaps, in citing Captain Morgan, the Welsh privateer turned storied pirate hero who wreaked havoc on Spanish fleets and colonial settlements, Mateo was calling up centuries of struggle against Spanish imperialism and First World interventionism in Central America. Perhaps he meant to draw a parallel between the appropriation of intellectual property by Guatemalan Mayas and the ransacking and potlatching of colonial wealth by Morgan and his men. Or perhaps he was just making a clever joke by referencing salient and ubiquitous signs. What is certain is that Mateo echoed a public discourse about "piracy" that one reads about in the pages of the country's major dailies and sees in the televised coverage of industry-funded, antipiracy, public relations campaigns. Mateo played on this label ("pirate") that has been given to him and his neighbors, the implication being that he might be outside the law and just as disruptive of sovereignty as a Caribbean pirate, when his tidy workshop more accurately reflected the entrepreneurial spirit celebrated in neoliberal development discourse at national and international levels. A modern businessman as much as a "modern pirate" (see Thomas 2009), Mateo was also citing his capacity to (in)cite an international brand, to invoke the symbols and structures of the global economy, and calling attention to his participation in it. Ravi Sundaram (2010) uses the phrase "pirate modernity" to describe how increasing mobility, extensive urbanization, expanding media access, and the widespread availability of digital technologies make copying and reproduction central features of the cultures and economies of postcolonial settings even as Western states and corporations attempt to extend their sovereignty through the regulation and marketization of intellectual property. Five centuries of evolving pirate modernity came together in Mateo's wry evocation, which was also a reflection on how IP law makes people into "pirates" (cf. Gallant 1999).

IP FOR PIRATES?

In spite of media coverage, police crackdowns in markets and city streets, educational campaigns, and some tension around the question of "piracy" among highland manufacturers (which I discuss further in chapter 3), it should be clear that Maya workshop owners in Tecpán have not adopted the normative stance toward copying that is institutionalized in IP law. Yet the discourse of the *copión* has a somewhat uncanny relationship to the problematization of piracy in international law. The *copión* is conceptually distinct from the legally defined "pirate." The discourse of piracy rests on the ideological privileging of isolated, individualized acts of creativity carried out by IP owners and a notion of originality that contradicts the practical realities of sharing and the dialectical production of style that defines fashion and enterprise. The discourse of the *copión* delineates the ethics of copying in relation to a powerful sense of community and a normative commitment to sharing and fair competition that has taken shape alongside the growth

FIGURE 12. Computerized embroidery machines operated by young men in a garment workshop in Tecpán, 2009.

of capitalist enterprise in the highland region. Maya business owners who complain about copycats seek to protect not so much their individual investments in unique designs, although that is part of it, but the contours and experience of a mode of community-centered development that (ideally) permits a large number of people to earn a decent living. This sometimes leads manufacturers to adopt defensive strategies such as selling in more distant markets or selling at odd hours of the day to protect their designs and their livelihoods from would-be copycats. It can also lead to more direct claims of ownership. For example, Pedro Serech, a Maya man who owns an embroidery shop in Tecpán, explained to me that some of the characters, figures, and logos he stitches onto clients' garments are "owned" by those clients. Pedro bought a used eight-head embroidery machine from a dealer in Guatemala City in 2004 with loans from the bank, his father, and a sister who works as a secretary in Guatemala City. Almost all of the embroidery designs he uses come from compact discs loaded with digital images of cartoon characters, popular fashion logos, and sports team logos (especially those of soccer clubs). Pedro customized these images on his desktop computer and then reproduced them on fabric by loading them onto the computerized embroidery machine.

As we looked through the images stored on Pedro's computer, he showed me how he had organized the files into folders and explained, "There are folders for each one of our clients. For example, if someone wants embroidery for a [school] uniform and we made it for them before, I have it right here. And in this folder," he said, pointing to the screen, "I have everything that is of general use for baby clothing. Here," he pointed to another folder, "I keep everything that doesn't have an owner." He double-clicked the mouse and opened the folder to show me this last group of images, which included everything from Disney characters to Reebok logos. "These are the ones that I can sell to anyone," he told me. "They aren't exclusive designs." He then opened a folder labeled with the name Alberto Ixim and stated, "Here are some that belong to Alberto." Knowing that I had spent time sewing in Alberto's workshop, Pedro felt comfortable using the manufacturer to illustrate his point, and he showed me several digital images that I recognized from Alberto's garments. There were teddy bear and flower designs that Pedro said he and Alberto had worked on together, starting with just a pencil-and-paper sketch or a generic clip art file. There were also trademarked cartoon characters. "So this folder is just for him [sólo es de él]," he declared.

I inquired as to whether this meant he would not reproduce the images on garments he embroidered for other customers, trying to understand how this kind of protection worked given the seeming ease with which people in the regional trade copied one another. "No," he confirmed. "I don't want to sell these to other people. I have all these others that I can give to whomever wants them. I maintain—I try to maintain that difference because you can't trust other people, because the competition is always like this: at any time, they can copy you. So we at least try to help out our clients."

In the embroidery business, Pedro was able to differentiate himself from his competitors by providing a measure of property protection. He tried to "help out" his clients by protecting them from the copiones. In a subsequent conversation, Alberto explained to me that he usually asked Pedro to hold a particular design in reserve, just for him, for a period of two or three months. After that length of time, either the design was no longer in demand or, if it had been successful, people had noticed and begun copying it, regardless of Pedro's safeguarding (it is easy to have another embroiderer reproduce an image), and it was time to move on to another design. This is the dialectic of style at work in the highland apparel trade. Pedro's respect for individual ownership of designs led him to offer at least some measure of protection, albeit short-lived, for his clients and established him as a trusted supplier who would provide an element of privacy. And he, like Alberto, attributed the need for this kind of protection to the moral dispositions of certain apparel manufacturers, the kind of disposition associated with *envidia* as a generalized and pervasive feature of the community and the market: "You can't trust other people, because the competition is always like this."

Kathleen Gordon (2011: 37), in discussing the convergence of market vendors' strategies in highland Bolivia and globalized "neoliberal ideologies" promoting entrepreneurship, competition, self-interest, and self-reliance as innate human impulses, argues that the parallel apparent in such cases "emerges from the context . . . and from the kind of work that they do—from the labor process." Gordon writes, "Vendors, because they rely on their own resources and face competition in the marketplace, must be entrepreneurial and competitive" (37). Her point, which applies equally well to the similarities between Maya apparel producers' attitudes regarding ownership and some of the principles that underlie IP law, is that indigenous people in developing countries often adopt strategies that seem to confirm a set of assumptions about human nature that have been used to justify and promote free trade and structural adjustment programs since the 1980s (i.e., that humans are rational, self-interested, maximizing economic actors). And yet, if we situate indigenous people's behavior within a historical and ethnographic context, we find layers of nuance and interplay among social structures, cultural meanings, and market realities that influence a regulating style and the strategies people adopt to make ends meet.

What an overly simplistic correlation between the discourse of the *copión* and the discourse of piracy would miss is that acts of copying, imitation, and appropriation do not bring two objects into an aesthetic relationship—in which one is the original and one is a copy—as IP law posits. Copying, part of the dialectical movement of instantiation and interpretation through which style gets produced, is a moral relationship between aesthetic forms *and* their producers.[5] In highland Guatemala, the normative contours of this relationship are defined in relation to the proximity of producers to one another and their mutual participation in a vital local industry. There is no perceived social relationship, no shared ethical space, between highland apparel producers and the makers of international fashion designs. Maya manufacturers regulate copying within the regional trade, however, because the producers share a sense of belonging to a particular place, an ethnic community, and a community of practice. In a somewhat ironic turn (apropos of the assumptions built into the IP framework), manufacturers interpret copying one's neighbor and selling the same design for a lower price as violating an ethic of sharing (rather than as a transgression of individual property rights, as IP proponents might expect). From the perspective of many *tecpanecos,* as Pedro's comments and his efforts to protect his clients' designs illustrate, acts of betrayal perpetrated by *copiones* are moral failures that go hand in hand with participation in some forms of capitalist enterprise. Market-based competition inspires envious stares and unethical behavior, and it becomes fiercer precisely because of such behavior. Competition is thus perceived as an inevitable and vicious cycle in which people must protect themselves—not only their market position, but also their moral integrity—from the dangerous forms of individualism and envy that are part and parcel of the social field that market participation so often elaborates and entails.

IP protections are one set of legal mechanisms by which Guatemala is supposed to demonstrate that it is on the "progressive path" toward development and becoming a fully modern nation-state (Vann 2006: 289) and by which its citizens are to be reoriented toward formal, rational market participation. Maya businessmen are not strategically engaging in illegal behavior because of a proclivity toward crime, however. The values that inform their design, production, and marketing decisions cannot be described accurately in terms of a dualism between collectivist societies and Western individualism, as if concern for one's neighbors and an ethic of sharing were antiquated features of a precapitalist or otherwise primitive national culture. Guatemalan apparel producers are not defying the law out of some kind of simple self-interest either. In point of fact, they are actively constructing an industry and a marketplace for fashionable garments in highland Guatemala at a felt distance from the rights-bearing corporations that seem so troubled by their "lawbreaking."

To put it another way, the social lives and livelihoods of Maya apparel producers depend on the successful management of the production of style in relation to shared senses of community and belonging. This is not unique to indigenous Guatemalans. Anthropologists, historians, and other scholars looking at various production contexts and marketplaces similarly demonstrate that the regulation of borrowing, appropriation, and inspiration—euphemisms that sidestep the preponderance and inevitability of *copying* in the fashion industry and other creative fields—is grounded in norms and values that differ from or exceed the normative frames and interpretations provided by IP law.[6] Maya apparel producers face criminalization not because they are exceptional in their reliance on copying but because they are structurally positioned as informal and illicit actors, even in the context of economic programs that promote, as the key to national progress, just the kind of entrepreneurship in which they engage.[7] In Guatemala, one encounters not so much a "culture of piracy" (Condry 2004) as a shifting context of accountability centered on envy and individualism, what Mary Douglas (1992) might refer to as an unfolding "forensics" of blame in the context of deeply entangled political and economic processes and ordinary ethics (Lambek 2010) that regulate the distribution of legitimacy, risk, and responsibility.

CHAPTER 3

Brand Pollution

In this chapter, I analyze significant gaps between how brands are synthesized, deployed, and understood in highland Guatemala and how brands figure into international projects of legal harmonization. Most critical engagements with brands are analytically oriented toward contexts in which branding logics presumed by trademark law seem to hold up: where, for example, trademarked brand names and logos are understood to connect corporations, commodities, and consumers through webs of affect and meaning. For example, in her sociology of branding, Celia Lury (2004) draws on the history of corporate marketing and advertising to argue that brands mediate the capitalist marketplace by organizing information about product qualities for consumers and coordinating the use of that information across successive purchasing decisions. Adam Arvidsson's (2006) analysis of corporate brand strategy reaches a similar conclusion: that brands embody the logic of a mode of capitalism premised on the value of information. My concern is with how brands figure into the lives of people who reside on the outskirts of brand ideology, beyond the smoke screens that emanate from advertising agencies (Mazzarella 2003) and corporate marketing departments (R.J. Foster 2007), in places where the rationalities promoted in IP law and the flow of information from companies to buyers cannot be taken for granted and where the existence of something called a "brand" that exceeds the material inscriptions of trademarked logos demands proof.

A thorough history of the concept of the "brand" and the rise of a set of corporate practices now conceptualized as "branding" is beyond the scope of this book and can be found in other works in history, sociology, and anthropology.[1] It is important for my purposes to note that the particular role of brands in the organization of mass consumer society and the emergence of branding as part of the functioning of the modern corporation have been central considerations in legal scholarship on intellectual property and have influenced relevant case law in US and European courts, thus shaping the IP regime that has been globalized in recent decades. As early as 1927, law professor Frank Schechter questioned whether longstanding justifications for trademark law that treated trademarks as indications of a product's origin were still relevant. "Owing to the ramifications of modern trade," Schechter (1927: 814) reasoned, "the source of origin of the goods bearing a well known trademark is seldom known to the consumer." Schechter did not dismiss the importance of trademark law based on this observation; rather, he argued that the trademark had acquired a new and vital function. Well-known marks had come to replace or stand in for the consumer's relationship to the product's origin instead of communicating information about that origin. Put another way, trademarks had assumed the ideological function of bridging the physical and experiential distance between the conditions of production (where and how goods are made) and the contexts of consumption (the phenomenologically accessible social locations where consumers purchase goods and put them to use). In this way, trademark law had become an important legal tool for producing broad-scale consumer markets, allowing corporations to ratchet up the manufacturing, marketing, and circulation of consumer goods to national and even global scales while still connecting with consumers in intimate and meaningful ways by imbuing trademarked signs and images with particular marketing messages.

Expanding on Schechter's foundational arguments, contemporary legal scholars contend that what trademark law actually serves to protect (and has served to protect for some time) is the corporate investment in *branding* rather than the actual signature or mark of a producer (Magid et al. 2006; Swann and Davis 1994; Lemley 1999).[2] The trademark has become one part of a "brand," which also includes meanings, values, sensations, associations, and perhaps even a personality. Because of the trademark's role in modern branding, Barton Beebe (2004: 625) argues, it has lost its traditional referents—a trademark does not need to identify any particular producer, source, or even commodity to receive protection, because the trademark is itself a commodity produced through the branding process. It derives its exchange value from the immaterial meanings, sensations, and affects promoted through marketing and advertising, and it remains important to corporate branding strategy because it serves to anchor the brand in a materialized form to which a corporation can claim exclusive legal rights (Nakassis 2013: 152). The Nike logo, for instance, is a vehicle for conveying a bundle of ideas, affects, and relationships to consumers through marketing campaigns, and it is that complete bundle that trademark law protects when it limits the use of the logo to the Nike corporation. In sum, the trademark is useful and valuable because it communicates brand image, has a protected legal status, and easily attaches to (and detaches from) all kinds of marketable commodities (Troutt 2004: 1143; see also Lury 2004; Arvidsson 2006; Mazzarella 2003; Beebe 2008; Davis 2008).

At the same time as scholarship on brands and branding that follows this line of reasoning has revealed essential dynamics in global capitalism, including the importance of image and affect for the production of consumer markets and corporate profits, my fieldwork in highland Guatemala's apparel trade compels the view that trademarks have other functions and roles in addition to serving as the legal and material anchoring of brand image. For example, in their day-to-day activities, Maya garment producers interact with trademarked brand names and logos as material culture. Specifically, they treat logos as design elements whose significance is constituted in large measure by the material qualities of the garments that display them, the styles into which the logos get incorporated, and the broad sociological contours of the contexts in which branded fashions circulate. While transnational marketing messages and corporately managed brand image are part of the story, the value of trademarked brand names and logos to the regional fashion industry operated by Maya apparel producers also derives from more locally salient structures of racial, ethnic, and gendered difference and associated patterns of exclusion that make certain designs, certain ways of dressing, and certain other modes of style more highly esteemed and more economically profitable within the highland marketplace. Thus, in this chapter, I approach trademarks not as signifiers whose meanings are fixed by corporate marketing departments and whose mere appearance conjures corporate brand values—an understanding of brands that animates much scholarship on the topic and also underwrites international trademark law enforcement efforts—but rather as part of the material repertoire through which designers and manufacturers actively produce style and make fashion.

ORIGINAL GAPS

I often traveled with Alberto Ixim to municipal markets where he sold his products. On one occasion, we delivered several bundles of children's sweaters and pants sets to his regular customers in the open-air market in Chimaltenango, the department capital, about a half-hour bus ride from his workshop in Tecpán. We then set out for Chimaltenango's retail stores—boutiques that line a main street and, like the market stalls where Alberto sells, showcase clothing that incorporates popular brand names in ways that are deemed illegal under national and international IP law. A spatialized hierarchy means that the youth styles these boutiques acquire from highland workshops or Guatemala City wholesale distributors of Chinese imports are of higher quality and sell at higher prices than what one finds in the municipal market, which caters to lower socioeconomic classes.

Our next stop was a mall built in 2006, with plenty of parking, a fried chicken restaurant, a Taco Bell, and a Bulock's, a national retailer with sixty stores that sells clothing priced just above that sold in municipal markets. Alberto told me with pride that he sometimes bought clothing there for his three young children. The sweatshirts and t-shirts featured logos that read "Arthur & Campie," "Holistar," and "Hollinger," obvious imitations of the popular US brands Abercrombie & Fitch and Hollister. Bulock's also sells clothing under the Basic Editions label, a discount line available at Sears and Kmart stores in the United States. These garments are made in the *maquiladoras*. As noted in chapter 1, overruns and imperfect garments assembled in these large-scale export factories often find their way into retail stores and street markets in Guatemala.

At the other end of the mall, we stopped in front of a store that I immediately recognized. The sign hanging above the doorway featured the dark blue square and slim Arial lettering of the ubiquitous US clothing chain Gap. However, a second look revealed that the sign actually read "GAP[PS]," as if this iteration of the store were a postscript to the US version. Alberto was hesitant to enter the store, stressing that the clothing was very expensive. He was perhaps concerned about not being welcomed there, since long-standing structures of discrimination discourage Maya men and women from entering spaces seen to belong more appropriately to well-to-do, nonindigenous Guatemalans (D. M. Nelson 1999:

249–250). Indeed, spatial imaginaries, class structures, and institutional-ized practices of discrimination in Guatemala have historically linked urban space, formal institutions, nonindigenous *ladinos,* and "moder-nity" on the one hand and rural space, informal enterprise, indigenous people, and "tradition" on the other (Thomas 2009: 8; Fischer and Brown 1996: 10–11). The merchandise at this store was expensive: jeans were priced at 299 quetzales (US$35), compared to 49 quetzales (US$7) at Bulock's. The styles were similar to those sold at US Gap stores, the quality was high, and each garment displayed the Gap logo. But Gap Inc., the corporation headquartered in San Francisco, California, does not have retail outlets in Guatemala. As we left, I could not resist point-ing this out to Alberto. "It's not real," I said. "That store is an imitation of the real Gap stores in the US." Alberto was unfazed. "Those clothes are originals," he remarked. "Didn't you see how expensive they were?"

What "original" and "originality" mean in this context is interesting and nuanced. Maya garment manufacturers readily acknowledge that the products they make are *imitaciones* (imitations), not *originales* (origi-nals). At the same time, local understandings of what makes a garment "original" disclose a disjuncture between international legal frameworks and the brand ideologies that they prop up on one hand and how Maya people in Guatemala experience the apparel marketplace on the other hand. The term *imitaciones* indicates that the garment is a copy, a more or less faithful reproduction of an original, and implies inferiority in terms of quality and desirability. But the term *originales* does not neces-sarily imply to Maya clothing producers or consumers a formal, legal relationship to a fashion firm or an authentic and authorized link to a point of origin. Furthermore, highland residents do not use the term *orig-inales* to reference a meaningful connection to a brand image or the eco-nomic value imbued to a trademarked name or logo through corporate branding campaigns. For certain, corporate investments on the part of Gap Inc. in proliferating and promoting the Gap brand around the world are part of why the logo has a degree of recognizability in places such as highland Guatemala and why it is widely associated with fashion and stylishness. But marketing campaigns and corporate investments do not neatly determine the originality of a garment and the meaning and value of a logo. Rather, for highland residents, originality is an index of the gar-ment's exclusivity, meaning the garment's position in the marketplace as a function of the context in which it is sold—its price, quality, and spatial location in relation to other goods—and thus who can and cannot con-sume it. Merchandise sold in urban retail shops and commercial centers, whether it would be deemed "original" by IP standards or not, is considered more original, more prestigious, and more fashionable by Maya garment producers and consumers than what most indigenous people buy in highland markets because the politics of social, cultural, and economic difference in Guatemala make those spaces more difficult to traverse and the products offered in them too expensive for most to afford. Alberto did not interpret the store we visited and its products in terms of the Gap brand. Rather, the store's location as a predominantly nonindigenous and exclusive space and the quality of the garments and their price and overall stylishness gave the Gap logo its meaning and value and, in this case, made the knockoff store into an "original." Contexts of consumption, then, are also sites of cultural production and the generation of social and economic value. In markets and malls, the significance of the materialized brand is open to interpretation.

Proponents of strong trademark protections take for granted that successful branding, grounded in the protections provided through trademark law legislation, enforcement, and prosecution, is vital to corporate profitability. Critics of contemporary capitalism generally make the same assumption. The worldwide prominence of brands such as Gap and the enormous resources that corporations pour into branding efforts have been blamed by some critics, including most famously Naomi Klein (2000), for obscuring ongoing and unjust transformations in capitalist relations of production. In her bestselling book, *No Logo*, Klein diagnosed the globalization of trade and the disarticulation of production chains (what had, in the early twentieth century, signaled to Schechter a new role for the trademark and which had reached a frenzied pace by the late twentieth century) as a problem of brand power. The emergence of the brand form as a source of social meaning and market value, she argued, had freed up corporations to focus on reputation building and image management rather than the human dimensions of commodity production and mass consumption, such that brand image and reputation (e.g., the good feelings associated with the trademarked Nike swoosh or Gap's blue box and white lettering) functioned to obscure the exploitation of natural resources and manufacturing labor in the Third World. It is a familiar and powerful argument about ideology, culture, and capital.

But interestingly, Klein's argument supports the notion that corporations have something real and economically valuable at stake in trademark protections. Most legal scholarship generally characterizes this "something" in terms of "brand dilution," a term introduced to the legal literature by Schechter (1925). Dilution has come to denote the decreasing capacity of a trademark owner to charge a premium based on the brand's image or reputation due to the trademark's circulation beyond authorized boundaries (Kort et al. 2006; Reid 2004; Magid et al. 2006). Knockoffs, counterfeits, pirated goods, and other copies that circulate outside the confines of corporate control are dangerous, so the argument goes, because they indirectly threaten corporate profitability. If one is arguing on the side of corporate capitalism, brand dilution provides a justification for antipiracy campaigns and law enforcement efforts. If one is critical of brand-centric capitalism, the circulation of knockoffs and pirated goods appears as a form of resistance and usurpation that has the potential to undercut corporate profits and power and challenge exploitative structures.

The dilution metaphor implies a kind of scientific and apolitical assessment of the weakened purity and potency of a brand whose trademarked signs are circulating beyond authorized boundaries, an assessment that can justify trademark enforcement and might determine specific legal cases. The idea is that the brand loses material and symbolic value as it gets spread out too thinly. My ethnographic research suggests an alternative formulation of brand value and its relationship to the trademark. Brands are not inherently pure or dense. They are not initially and innately potent compounds of meaning, affect, and value, synthesized in the boardroom, stabilized, and then distilled into society. They do not start out with a fixed formula that gets watered down during circulation. In contrast, they become valuable precisely through the circulation and contextualization of trademarks and via a process that requires a great deal of interpretive and affective labor on the part of consumers, who attach particular connotations to the trademark depending on the context in which the mark appears. The ability and propensity of trademarks to soak up their surroundings through this process is the source of the cultural and economic power of the brand form and the reason why marketers continuously put trademarked logos and names in places and into relationships that will contribute to the positive valuation of the brand by target consumer segments. Marketers do not stop advertising or associating brands with meanings once the trademark is circulating, and this is because the meanings and values are never definitively stabilized. Celebrity endorsements that build associations between a brand and a particular personality and premiums paid to outdoor advertising companies for prominent billboard space in hip neighborhoods are sources for the perpetual creation of brand meaning and value, sources that marketers cannot do without, but so are the unauthorized appearances of fashion brand names and logos on personal style blogs, in pop music lyrics, and on bodies moving through city streets (Aoki 1994).

Appreciating the ways that brand image and value are actively constituted as trademarks circulate, meet with resistance, link up with other and ongoing projects of meaning making and value creation, and become "originals" or "imitations" within local contexts throws into relief and challenges the ideology of corporate trademark owners and marketing departments and IP proponents, who claim that brands are or should be ontologically and semantically stable forms that can be owned.[3] As Rosemary Coombe (1998: 8) writes, "the mass-reproduced, media-circulated cultural form [the brand] accrues social meaning in a multiplicity of sites." Yet, according to trademark law, "the meaning is produced exclusively at a mythic point of origin." Trademark law, industry propaganda, and marketing ideology purport that brands are the creative property of specific owners and that the orderly functioning of the marketplace depends on those owners having exclusive control over the meanings and values with which they imbue their trademarked properties (see also Lury 2004).[4] In contrast, the anthropology of branding makes clear that brands have meaning and value only insofar as they circulate as materialized signs in contexts that are chock-full of sociological significance.

THE LOOK OF PIRACY

I return to the concept of originality later in the chapter to put the meanings of the concept evident among Maya people in Guatemala in conversation with how multinational fashion firms attempt to manage market value and regulate style. In this section, however, I examine additional dimensions of how highland apparel producers interact with and interpret trademarks, including why and how they incorporate them into the styles they make and sell, to reveal further gaps in IP law's rationalities.

Each time we prepared to leave Martín Cua's garment workshop to sell his goods in highland markets, the ritual was the same. Martín, who was in his late thirties, sells mostly to wholesalers in the Western highland market of San Francisco El Alto. Before loading the garments into his beat-up Toyota sedan, he carefully inspected the stacks of folded sweatshirts—individually packaged in clear plastic bags, bundled by the dozen, and tied with a strip of fabric. This way of preparing garments for market is essential to what manufacturers call *presentación,* the way the garments will look to clients and, ultimately, to consumers. *Presentación* also entails sewing labels into the collars of shirts and the waistbands of pants. These labels commonly feature trademarked brand names, although there is often little attention paid to which brand name is used; the important thing is that there is one. Producers source labels from print or embroidery shops or use labels and tags that are smuggled out of *maquiladoras.* As discussed in previous chapters, IP law frames piracy as willful deception and bad faith (Green and Smith 2002). The criminalization of copying is said to punish people who steal and dilute the property ("brand value") of multinational corporations and thereby separate out good entrepreneurs from bad actors. But the use of labels in this context is part of a cultural practice and business ethic where the formal and professional presentation of goods is also about the self-presentation of the producer as a moral person who cares about his work. The use of pirated labels is also an entrepreneurial strategy for realizing some measure of business success in a marketplace dominated by a cadre of popular brand names due to fashion marketing, globalized media, and free trade. In highland Guatemala, as elsewhere, it is difficult to sell a garment without a label, and more specifically, without a label that affords some competitive advantage due to it featuring a form that is recognizable as a globally popular brand.

In addition to labels and tags, many clothes made in Tecpán include a pirated logo or brand name stitched to the outside of the garment, as is the case with hoodies that feature an Abercrombie & Fitch logo across the front. Importantly, manufacturers do not see trademarked logos primarily as signs of corporate ownership but instead view them as design elements, similar to a stripe or color combinations (cf. Luvaas 2013; Nakassis 2012). Brand names are not add-ons, as they are treated in international trademark law, but are considered to be integral to the constitution of a particular look. Maya garment producers use the Kaqchikel word *ruwäch*—a polysemous term that, in this case, means "the look" of the garment—to talk about design. The same term is used in Mayan weaving. For instance, the word *ruwäch* refers to design elements such as the zigzags and stripes on a traditional *huipil* from Tecpán. The term also refers to how these elements are distributed across the garment and combine to make the overall design. Carol Hendrickson's (1995) work demonstrates that, among traditional weavers, the imitation of designs and techniques indicates respect for past

FIGURE 13. Knockoff Abercrombie & Fitch, Hollister, and American Eagle sweatshirts for sale in a highland market, 2008.

generations and acknowledges a weaver's participation in a community-based form of production. What carries over from traditional weaving to garment manufacturing is the sense of design practice as combination and appropriation, as well as the conceptual interdependence of the part (a design element) and the whole (the overall garment design). Both are captured in a single term, *ruwäch,* which indexes linguistically what cannot be separated practically.

One of Martín's staple products in 2009 was a hooded sweatshirt cut from fleece material, featuring a zipper, pockets, and the word "Hollister" spelled out across the chest in felt letters. When I asked Martín why he used the Hollister logo on these garments, he replied, "Lleva menos letras que Abercrombie" (It has fewer letters than Abercrombie). When producers decide which logo to include, there are many things they take into consideration, such as current trends, the difficulty involved in replicating a given logo, and the cost of materials. If a brand name has fewer letters (e.g., Hollister versus Abercrombie), it means lower costs for the manufacturer. My analysis, however, points to the most important factor being the need to conform to a recognizable

FIGURE 14. Finished knockoff Lacoste polo shirt in a garment workshop in Tecpán, 2008.

look, an instantiation that has been made generic and has thus become readily available for innovation and interpretation. This is the process of producing style. Martín's garments had to feature either Abercrombie or Hollister because the Abercrombie & Fitch corporation (which actually markets both brands) took the basic hooded sweatshirt, made it baroque and graphic with characteristic lettering across the front, and popularized that look among young people worldwide in the 1990s and 2000s. If Martín made polo shirts, he would use either a Ralph Lauren pony or a Lacoste alligator, because those companies made the soft-collared shirt embossed with an animal figure popular globally. IP law protects trademarks, but fashion companies actually sell a combinatory "look and feel," as these examples illustrate (Bharathi 1996: 1668). In contemporary youth fashion, logos such as the stylized lettering on hoodies and the animal figures on polo shirts have become prominent aspects of styles that are heavily marketed and have attained recognizable currency in markets around the globe.

There is contestation in IP law over the relationship between trademarked logos and fashion design (Hemphill and Suk 2009). Western legislative bodies and courts do not generally shelter fashion works in the same way that they protect industrial designs and artistic creations. European courts have been reluctant to grant copyrights for fashion designs, and in US law, clothing has been designated historically as a "useful article," meaning that courts did not recognize fashion design as an "artistic" practice qualifying for copyright protections (Raustiala and Sprigman 2006; Briggs 2002).[5] Hence, some fashion firms combat design piracy by making their trademarked logos more prominent features of their products, a strategy Louis Vuitton pioneered in the late nineteenth century by stamping his leather goods with a trademarked, stylized "LV." To copy the design, one had to copy the legally protected trademark, which is a prosecutable offense. In many contemporary Ralph Lauren designs, the small pony that has traditionally been embroidered on the polo shirt's left breast has become a large horse emblazoned across the entire left side. This transformation, the enlargement of the size of the trademarked logo, is no accident, and it is not purely aesthetic either. With the logo displayed prominently on the garment, pirates cannot copy the style—the "look and feel" of the piece—without also pilfering the logo, and this extends the company's authorship and ownership to more holistically include the design (Scafidi 2006; Blackmon 2007). Yet interestingly, while it strengthens the force of law, this trend does not abet trademark piracy, and it perhaps paradoxically encourages the practice, because producers in marginalized settings such as Tecpán aim to replicate this complete aesthetic, the globally marketed look and feel. When these manufacturers stitch "Hollister" across a sweatshirt, they are not simply attempting to capture or steal the value (i.e., the marketed meanings) of a trademarked logo. When consumers purchase that sweatshirt, they do not buy it just because it says Hollister, making a straightforward calculation related to the value and meaning of a marketed brand image. What are being bought and sold in highland markets are holistically conceived looks, designs, and styles, what the Maya call *ruwäch,* which is to say, fashion.

Fashion firms do not always and everywhere attempt to stymie the copying of their designs. Kal Raustiala and Christopher Sprigman (2012) demonstrate that fashion is generally and rather comfortably a "low-IP environment," where copying and imitation are part and parcel of the industry's normal operations and where the rapid and widespread availability of a design across market segments generally encourages the kind of forced obsolescence that, at least in part, drives fashion consumption and underwrites industry profitability (see also M. Wade 2011). Fashion styles emerge out of a dialectic of instantiation and interpretation, of copying and creativity, such that Ralph Lauren can be both a designer and a design hack, a victim and a perpetrator, depending on one's point of view, because even renowned designers borrow influences and elements from the fashion system (Nakassis 2013: 148).[6]

The difference between acceptable modes of copying and modes that the industry works to criminalize may rest on whether the copy threatens or blurs the divide between the original and the imitation, such as when fake Louis Vuitton bags are passed for the real thing on internet retail sites. What legal and marketing scholars label "counterfeiting" can threaten corporate profits if consumers are being tricked into spending their money on fakes. But the need to protect consumers from such trickery does not explain antipiracy campaigns and enforcement efforts. "Pirated" products do not attempt to pass themselves off as the real thing (Phau et al. 2001). The material qualities and circulatory context of pirated goods give away their imitative status, as is the case with Maya garment manufacturers who produce relatively low-quality, low-priced garments for "informal" markets where everyone knows that the products are *imitaciones*. Piracy thus presents a different case from counterfeiting. The reasons given by industry associations for piracy enforcement, the kinds of moralizing arguments presented in the previous chapter about how piracy production and sales rob states of tax revenues and provide funding for organized crime and terrorism, rely on hyperbolic figurations of pirates as bad people and security threats and discount the importance to economic development of industries such as the highland apparel trade.

Courts generally rely on the dilution doctrine to justify strong trademark protections. Yet a growing body of marketing research challenges on empirical grounds the assumption that brand piracy damages brand image and reduces corporate profitability. Recent studies find that the circulation of pirated goods yields "bandwagon effects" and "herding effects" as new consumer segments are exposed to the trademark. The increased visibility of the mark can boost demand, creating a "virtuous circle" in which sales of pirated goods drive up sales of authorized goods, and vice versa (DeCastro et al. 2008: 76; Raustiala and Sprigman 2006; Ritson 2007; Whitwell 2006). Piracy may also allow firms to charge a "snob premium" to elite consumers who want to buy the real stuff and thereby distinguish themselves from people who buy obvious fakes (Barnett 2005: 1384). It is simply not clear that piracy threatens a trademark owner's bottom line and is generally difficult to demonstrate (much less prove) such damage in trademark infringement cases. Courts in the United States, at least, tend to side with trademark owners anyway, mustering moral arguments against piracy that turn on "a desire to punish free-riding," where the unauthorized use of trademarks is figured as a problem of fairness and ethics (Franklyn 2004). But the facts of marketing research suggest to some scholars that pirates should be seen as innovators rather than market detractors, since they contribute to a "pro-competitive environment" and "possess skills and a creative capital" that may push trademark owners in new design and marketing directions (El Harbi and Grolleau 2008: 385; Barnett 2005).

At the same time as scholars are questioning whether piracy is really harmful to trademark owners, fashion companies are engaging in marketing practices that look to some observers and analysts like the very kinds of brand dilution that rights holders litigate against in trademark infringement cases. The trend in fashion over the past several decades has been for firms to expand product lines to reach out to new consumer segments, especially middle-class and bargain shoppers, and to license or franchise brand names to other corporations to boost awareness and increase market reach (English 2013). The extension of a brand name across a range of goods, manufactured with varying quality standards and sold at a range of price points to disparate sets of consumers, would seem to threaten the overall value of the corporate brand. Giorgio Armani, for example, has a high-fashion couture collection; a premium ready-to-wear line sold under the Giorgio Armani label; lower-priced lines marketed via the Armani Collezioni and Emporio Armani labels and geared toward upper-middle-class consumers; and a line called Armani Exchange that is sold in shopping malls to middle-class suburbanites (Raustiala and Sprigman 2006: 1694). All of these lines are part of the Armani brand portfolio. While some legal scholars argue that the use of different labels (Armani Collezioni versus Armani Exchange) sold at different retail outlets can mitigate brand dilution (Raustiala and Sprigman 2006: 1725), others caution that the variation in price, quality, and style that characterizes such a broad range of merchandise is confusing to consumers who might expect a certain quality standard and degree of exclusivity when they buy a product that carries the Armani name: "Now the counterfeiter is the fashion house itself and the potentially damaged party is the buyer of the good" (Hilton et al. 2004: 351; see also S.S. Nelson 2003).[7] The practices that fashion firms have taken up in recent decades, from making trademarked properties into prominent design features to extending product lines across multiple and divergent markets, seem to undermine the basic premises on which strong trademark protections have been justified. Meanwhile, my research supports the notion that the economic and moral arguments regarding the supposed problem of piracy are unfounded and reveals that the copying of trademarked brand names and logos is part of the creative and innovative process through which style gets produced in contemporary fashion design.

WHITE STYLE

Given that the logics that underwrite trademark law enforcement efforts do not hold up to scrutiny, my contention is that trademark law actually accomplishes something quite different from its stated aims. Antipiracy efforts have become a means by which fashion firms can police the racial boundaries that are part and parcel of the fashion system. The racial dynamics of IP law enforcement have drawn a great deal of attention from critical legal scholars, sociologists, and anthropologists in recent years. At a basic level, argues Carlos Correa (2000: 5), IP law positions countries in the Global North as innovators, owners, and authorized consumers while saddling governments in the Global South with the burden of "protecting" rights holders from the "pirates" and "counterfeiters" said to thrive in that region. The discourse of piracy is often couched in racist, civilizational terms, as when trademark law proponents argue that the collectivist East threatens the intellectual property of the individualist (and thus properly "modern") West (see chapter 2; Liang 2011). Fashion is also deeply entangled with racial politics and inequality. Clothing has played an important role in helping to define and demarcate racial and ethnic categories from the colonial period to today. Contemporary fashion branding and marketing builds on this history insofar as Euro-American fashion firms continue to participate in the consolidation of mass consumer markets around white style. By "white style," I mean the ways of looking, dressing, acting, and expressing that, over time, have come to signify whiteness. Whiteness is a racial identity that is generally taken for granted and that goes unrecognized because it is has the status of being normative and normalized. White style appears, in many contexts, to be "natural" or "normal," whereas other styles—those recognizable and distinguishable according to what linguists call "marked" racial and ethnic categories, including black, indigenous, native, and so on—seem divergent, different, and are often interpreted as deviant (Hill 2008; Hall 1999; Clifford 2000; Lipsitz

2006). Whiteness may be defined in contrast to other racialized styles that become salient in a particular place and time, such that being, looking, or acting white is understood as *not* looking or acting black or indigenous. This is the case in Guatemala, where *ladino* style involves a host of signs and practices that all share the common feature of *not* being signs and practices associated with indigeneity. But whiteness has positive content as well and is often wrapped up with markers of middle-class respectability, a certain level of educational attainment, and particular ways of expressing gender and sexuality and claiming national identity—in short, ways of dressing, speaking, and presenting oneself that conform to the norms and expectations produced and circulated within institutions, by the media, and through marketing messages as signs of status and privilege (Roediger 1991; Gilroy 1987). The fashion system has played a key role in defining and publicizing these markers, and fashion firms continue to strategically surround their trademarks with images of whiteness in order to appeal to the purchasing power of consumers in the Global North and also stoke the aspirational desires of emerging consumer classes in other regions. The corporate investment in whiteness as a major part of the "look and feel" of fashion has proven enormously profitable for the industry.

Piracy is perceived by fashion firms as harmful because it results in the circulation of trademarks outside of the prescribed boundaries of whiteness, putting marks in contact with people and places that are read as nonwhite because of how histories of social stratification and discrimination come together with skin color, class, gender, aesthetics, and material culture. Clothing touches the wrong bodies, and vice versa. The threat that piracy poses to fashion firms is not necessarily about *brand dilution,* which includes the watering down of meanings and values associated with whiteness. The threat is rather, with a nod to Mary Douglas (1966), about *brand pollution*—that is, the process through which trademarks absorb or take on meanings and values related to nonwhite styles. But the fashion industry and the wider legal and business community that supports antipiracy enforcement do not have to acknowledge race as a key diacritic of fashion branding or cite the policing of racial boundaries as a reason for their efforts. This is because trademark law provides an official, legal, and deracialized discourse about the protection of rights, the orderly functioning of the marketplace, and a seemingly self-evident distinction between originals and copies as meaningful justifications for the regulation of style. Although talk about the problem of piracy does not involve explicit references to race and its importance for the continued success of the fashion industry, antipiracy campaigns are couched in terms of, and come to seem like a common sense approach to, protecting the property and integrity of people who create from the immoral and illegal actions of populations who copy. Race is masked by crime as the main point of disputation and disturbance. In this way, the discourse of piracy provides ideological cover for a racialized system of distinction and corporate profiteering.

Clothing has been integral to the social construction of whiteness and the making and marking of certain populations as differently raced, as well as potentially polluting, since at least the colonial era. For example, Jean Comaroff's (1996) analysis of nineteenth century British evangelical missions to Southern Africa demonstrates the vital role that dress played in how missionaries and colonial administrators justified the colonial project and established both political authority and relations of economic dependency in the region. The "nakedness" that British colonials ascribed to the native population, an ascription that overlooked and denied the sophistication of existing aesthetic regimes and practices of adornment, served as evidence of the "backwardness" and "sinfulness" of Southern Africans. It was during the same period that industrialization and new forms of marketing were conditioning the rise of the modern fashion system in Great Britain, a system that encouraged people to see themselves as consumers whose purchasing decisions reflected their "good taste" and their social position within a society that the growth of textile and fashion manufacturing sectors were helping to stratify into professional and working classes. Missionaries and government officials traveling to the colonies took this changing relationship to dress with them, and the project of clothing African bodies "was driven by a clear sense that civilization was promoted by encouraging discerning consumption" (Comaroff 1996: 20). Native people's adoption of dark cottons and woolen garments manufactured in Manchester and Leeds was understood by the missionaries as vital to the cultivation of Protestant personhood and, at the same time, as proof of the spiritual rebirth and social transformation that British control over the region was enabling.

Dress lends itself easily to projects of racialized distinction perhaps in part because of the intimate relationship that it has to the body. Clothing touches the skin in ways that feel deeply personal, making "fit" and "comfort" important as ways of experiencing a garment and as a means of identifying with certain styles in terms of the fabrics, cuts, and constructions that are popular at a given moment (Miller and Woodward 2012). Dress shapes the perceived contours of the body as well, influencing how people experience physicality and intimacy and how they interpret their bodies as conforming to socially constructed frames of normalcy or as deviating from acceptable physical standards that are related to social distinction and frames such as race, ethnicity, gender, and class (Entwhistle 2000; Butler 1990). Because garments envelop and enfold the body, clothes are sometimes perceived to represent the stylized essence of the wearer. Comaroff's account speaks to this mimetic capacity of clothing to both represent the interior of an individual and take on social qualities associated with the individual or group who wears certain clothing in certain ways.

Take, for instance, the uneasiness and reprehension with which British missionaries responded to the "creative couture" (Comaroff 1996: 30) of Tswana men and women, for whom "European costume . . . opened up a host of imaginative possibilities" (27). Southern Africans mixed and matched. They blurred the boundaries of "civilized" and "uncivilized" that were supposed to remain tidy and assure a racialized division of morality and modernity in the colonial context. It became common, in fact, for Tswana people to combine the British fabrics and fits thrust upon them in the name of "civilization" with their own material repertoires, especially animal skins, and with aesthetic sensibilities that implicated color and cut in "fantastic shapes," as Comaroff (1996: 30) explains, citing Moffat (1842: 506). "Such 'eccentric' garb," notes Comaroff (1996: 30), "caused the Christians much anxiety." In keeping with Douglas's (1966) insights into the dangers associated with boundary crossing and category confusion, Comaroff finds that this miscegenation and syncretism came to be associated with dirt and contagion. Colonial health authorities conjectured that Africans who adopted some elements of British dress while maintaining other aspects of indigenous fashion "were most susceptible to serious disease," Comaroff (1996: 30) explains, citing Packard (1989: 690).

What is interesting to me about this historical case is the way that the fashion system taking shape in Great Britain influenced a colonial context of racialized subordination and directed the integration of Southern Africans into a globalized and exploitative commercial system in which they were expected to take their place as menial laborers in commoditized agriculture and extractive industry and as consumers of European style and senses of stylishness. British colonials promoted assimilation to a unified model of Europeanness, Christian piety, and whiteness through the adoption of certain ways of dressing. However, when Southern Africans took up practices of "discerning consumption," it did not make them "white" or "European" from the perspective of British colonials. Rather, it evidenced and ensured the effective control of their daily habits by and their submission to an evolving transnational political and economic order premised on the export of European taste and desires to new markets—in this case, a market comprised of an emerging African "peasant-proletarian" class and nascent "black petite bourgeoisie," as Comaroff (1996: 36, 29) puts it. Tswana people who assimilated only in part to this new social order were understood as threatening and polluting, and British missionaries worked hard to discourage and discipline any wayward "Tswana *bricoleur*" (30) who combined European styles with African aesthetics.

There are similarities here to the historical and present-day realities of the apparel trade in highland Guatemala. Maya people have also been racialized within colonial and postcolonial national social orders as uncivilized, backward, and nonwhite at the same time as government officials and global marketers have encouraged their relative "whitening"[8] through assimilationist policies and the promotion of cosmopolitan fashion styles and business styles linked to development and entrepreneurship. When the best efforts of highland Maya people to express taste and discernment and exhibit style in line with the modes of distinction promoted by the fashion system fall short—that is, when they mix and match, adapting popular designs to highland style and copying globally marketed trademarks as part of that process—they are labeled "pirates," talked about as threatening the health of the national economy, and blamed for illegally stealing the value and good name of European and North American corporations. The discourse of piracy ignores the fact that nearly everyone in Guatemala works and trades in the "informal" economy and leaves little room for discussion of how the structural disadvantages of poverty and the racialized marginalization of Maya people mean that high-priced, authorized goods are generally out of their reach and that their participation in formal, legal production systems and consumer markets is unlikely.

These cases from colonial-era Southern Africa and contemporary Latin America illustrate how white style has been promoted and sold to populations as part of efforts to establish relations of dependency and control and also how senses of pollution and threat surround the stylistic practices of groups racialized as nonwhite. Another dimension of the relationship between race and fashion is the way that certain dress styles associated with whiteness have been designated as off-limits to racialized Others, ensuring a clear set of visual demarcations between white and nonwhite populations even in contexts of forced assimilation. From the earliest days of the Atlantic slave trade, for example, Africans arriving in North America were "quickly clothed in European garb and made to conform to European concepts of decency" (White and White 1998: 8); this is similar to the way that British colonials compelled "civilization" through dress in Southern Africa. Only certain European-style cuts and fabrics, however, were deemed acceptable for enslaved, black bodies. The Slave Codes adopted in the American colonies restricted slave attire to "loose-fitting garments made of the coarsest available cloth" (White and White 1998: 9; see also Ponte 2009). Some slaves were able to access better textiles and finer garments via an underground economy in which slaves bought, sold, and bartered for stolen cloth and clothing, but the sight of black men and women dressed in apparel that approached the styles worn by whites was considered scandalous. As historians Shane White and Graham White (1998: 16) note, "such actions disturbed the nuanced social order that clothing was supposed to display, blurring the boundaries between black and white, slave and free." They assert that whites generally interpreted the appropriation by enslaved blacks of dress styles reserved exclusively for white people not so much as slaves "adopting white values" but rather as slaves actively "subverting white authority." It was understood as the privilege and right of white Americans to dictate dress as one aspect of their control over the lives and labor of black people.

Following the American Civil War and the end of slavery, sumptuary laws that had restricted the types of fabrics and styles of dress that were deemed appropriate for enslaved black men and women were reconstituted as informal, but no less enforceable, rules of dress under the Jim Crow system of social control. Discriminatory legislation combined with a system of vigilante justice to deny black people participation in democratic politics and other aspects of public life, institutionalize segregated systems of housing and education, and ensure high levels of black unemployment while criminalizing joblessness and poverty. As part of the Jim Crow social order, African Americans were also "required to dress, walk, comport themselves, and direct their gaze in a manner that registered uncomplaining subservience. Blacks understood, for example, that it could be dangerous to wear expensive clothes or, particularly in rural areas, to don Sunday attire during the week" (White and White 1998: 154). A black person who adopted sartorial markers of whiteness and upper-class status was vulnerable to the violent reprisals of white people who were deeply invested in a racial order rooted in white supremacist ideology. From the earliest days of the Atlantic slave trade to the end of the Jim Crow era, black men and women were thus disciplined to walk a fine line between, on the one hand, conforming to dress styles derived from the European tradition that were deemed appropriately modest and civilized and, on the other, carefully avoiding styles that might give the impression that they identified too closely with whiteness or were attempting to usurp the signs that separated whites from blacks within a deeply and racially stratified society.[9] Again, there are parallels between how this system monitored and subordinated black modes of dress and forms of expression and how antipiracy legislation and enforcement efforts attempt to modulate and regulate style today. While trademark law enforcement obviously does not depend on the forms of cruelty, violence, and overt racism that defined slavery and Jim Crow, it has the similar effect of enabling the promotion of white style (through branding and marketing) while also surveilling and limiting how various groups take up and put on markers of whiteness.

The promise that IP law could accomplish these goals became apparent to US fashion industry executives early on in the modern fashion system's elaboration. While the Jim Crow system of violent subordination was in force, the proprietors of fashion design firms and apparel manufacturing businesses were looking to IP law as a means of regulating African Americans' access to dress styles and maintaining the social boundaries marked by clothing. By 1914, legislative debates over who could and could not make and wear certain apparel designs were being framed in terms of "piracy." As Lucille Ponte (2009: 76) explains, citing Anne Theodore Briggs (2002: 204–205):

> The National Design Registration League, a fashion industry association, lobbied for the enactment of design protection laws, arguing that "[pirates] take that popular design of high-priced goods and reproduce it in cheap material and put it on the market, the result being that the ladies going into their laundries see the clothing of their colored cooks and wash girls trimmed with the same pattern of lace they use on their expensive garments. . . . [S]he will not wear the same style of lace and embroidery that is used by the servants in her household."

In making the argument for strict design protections, this league of fashion designers and manufacturers called attention to the ways that racialized and spatialized distinctions between black and white bodies were vital to their ability to entice white consumers and turn a profit. Dress was part of how women displayed class status and taste. It was also integral to the production and maintenance of a gendered and racialized division of labor. The "style of lace and embroidery" worn by white "ladies" was understood to mark them as properly feminine and as having a certain relationship to the kitchen, work, the household, men, other women, and the wider society. They were above the menial labor that was the domain of the "colored" women, who were seen not as women at all but rather as mere "girls." The industry executives' argument also relied on the notion that the industry's target consumer population—women with disposable incomes who were charged with making purchasing decisions for their households and who cared deeply about preserving and protecting their own whiteness from any crossover with "colored" styles—would be willing to pay a premium for exclusively white fashions.

The entanglements of race, labor, and consumption highlighted in this example are one part of the picture of how whiteness has mattered for the fashion system and how concerns over racial boundaries have animated debates over the application of IP law to fashion design. The National Design Registration League's requests for patent protections covering lace and embroidery and other design elements were unsuccessful. As noted above, patent and copyright laws in the United States and Europe generally do not protect fashion design from copying in the same ways that they do other industries. Trademark law, however, has proven useful for the fashion system in important ways related to the social construction of race, the restriction of access to designs, and the pursuit of profits, as I now discuss.

The consolidation of white consumer classes in North America and Western Europe that are concerned with racial difference and willing to invest in white style has been facilitated to some extent by trademark law. Rosemary Coombe (1998) argues that, beginning in the late nineteenth century, corporations strategically designed their marketing campaigns to encourage white Americans to see themselves as racially distinct from other groups and as belonging to a privileged class that could best express its national pride and hegemonic racial identity through consumption. Coombe describes how IP law was integral to this process, since trademark protections allowed US corporations to "own" stereotyped images of Native Americans (e.g., the feather-adorned Red Man used to market chewing tobacco) and racial epithets that disparaged African Americans (e.g., Nigger-Hair Smoking Tobacco) and employ those signs in advertisements in ways that reified racial categories, confirmed a sense of racial superiority, and made white Americans feel as though racial privilege and distinction was their rightful property, an entitlement, something that they were authorized to consume and enjoy.[10] Coombe's work thus illustrates how trademarks have been important for the construction and consolidation of whiteness alongside the promotion of consumer desires.

Fashion firms have sometimes relied on brand names and logos that stereotype racialized Others—Coombe (1998) references the Cherokee clothing brand and Red Indian jeans, for example—but they have more often worked to surround their trademarks with images of whiteness and leveraged the protections afforded by trademark law to limit the access nonwhite populations have to their designs. This is true of the very firms that own the rights to trademarks that have become popular design elements in highland Guatemala. Tommy Hilfiger, for example, whose clothes gained popularity among African Americans in the 1990s, and whose designs continue to appeal to diverse consumers in Latin America and other regions, is the subject of a persistent (although apparently false) rumor that he claimed he "wouldn't have become a designer" had he known that "black people" were going to wear his clothing.[11] A more substantive example of the contemporary relationship between race and fashion branding is provided by Abercrombie & Fitch.

Since its founding at the turn of the twentieth century, Abercrombie has built its marketing strategies around the celebration and marketing of whiteness, "a particularly privileged and leisure-class whiteness," according to cultural studies scholar Dwight McBride (2005: 66). For much of the century, the company promoted its clothing to well-to-do white men using images and values related to outdoor exploration, adventure, and tourism. After faltering financially and changing hands several times, the company found tremendous success in the mid-1990s, when newly appointed CEO Michael Jeffries launched a new phase in the clothing line's branding. As McBride (65) explains:

> [Jeffries] tapped superstar fashion photographer Bruce Weber (widely known for his Calvin Klein, Ralph Lauren, and Karl Lagerfeld ads) for the playful coed shots on the walls of Abercrombie stores. Weber would go on, of course, to become the photographer for the infamous A&F Quarterly [the company's clothing catalog] as well. The A&F Quarterly was launched in 1997 to, as one commentator put it, "glamorize the hedonistic collegiate lifestyle on which the company built its irreverent brand image."

Jeffries and Lager seem to have taken the lessons learned from Calvin Klein (whose renowned underwear ad campaign, launched in the 1980s, featured tanned, muscular, erotic, white men's bodies wearing only underpants printed with the designer's trademarked name) and Ralph

Lauren (who was selling fashion via scenes of white privilege, especially images of yachting, country homes, and of course, polo) and gone on to produce "a false radicalism" (McBride 2005: 65) that enjoined the "collegiate," sporting, leisure-filled, "lifestyle" with images of young men and women that were sexualized in ways that drew the ire of conservative groups, who viewed the company's catalog and advertising campaigns as scandalous and indecent (61). The images and meanings struck the right chord with teenagers and young adults, who recognized in Abercrombie the chance to flaunt social and sexual mores and push the boundaries of middle- and upper-class acceptability, but in ways that seemed, and were ultimately, white and innocent—a bit of youthful play still comfortably situated amid the trappings and privileges of whiteness, boys being boys.

What McBride finds so disdainful about Abercrombie's branding strategy—the title of his 2005 book is *Why I Hate Abercrombie & Fitch*—is not just the fact that Abercrombie has marketed whiteness (other fashion firms do the same) but that it has also sought in rather obvious ways to make its clothing the exclusive property of white people by limiting contact between the brand and nonwhite bodies and populations. By the mid-1990s, Abercrombie had institutionalized white style as a basis for employment, a requirement made more or less explicit in the company's *Look Book,* the manual given to all retail employees. Here is an excerpt from the 1996 edition:

> Exhibiting the A&F Look is a tremendously important part of the overall experience at the Abercrombie & Fitch stores. . . . The combination of our Brand Representatives' style and our Stores Visual Presentation has brought brand recognition across the country.
>
> Our people in the store are an inspiration to the customer. The customer sees the natural Abercrombie style and wants to be like the Brand Representative. . . .
>
> Our brand is natural, classic and current, with an emphasis on style. This is what a Brand Representative must be; this is what a Brand Representative must represent in order to fulfill the conditions of employment. (McBride 2005: 67)

The stylistic constraints on employees' appearances that the *Look Book* goes on to delineate matter for the company's branding strategy and profitability because brands get continually produced and reproduced through the material, aesthetic, and social contextualization of trademarks and clothing designs. Glossy photos in magazines and catalogs are one part of how Abercrombie has sought to position itself in the marketplace, but the construction of the retail space as white space and the workforce as white has been another crucial part of the iterative process of performance, imitation, and appropriation through which the Abercrombie brand and style have been produced over time and across consumer populations. The *Look Book* urges employees to keep in mind that the customer buys the firm's clothing because he or she "wants to be like the Brand Representative," a form of copying and imitation on which the company depends for its success. The importance of the "experience" of the store and the "style" of the employees to Abercrombie's branding and profitability, as emphasized in the *Look Book,* challenges arguments in social science scholarship and the legal and marketing literatures about the communicative function of trademarks and their role as conduits of information connecting corporations and consumers. The logo matters for consumers and signifies whiteness in particular ways because of the marketing images that surround it *and* its materialization in a context of overwhelmingly white style.

White style gets marketed and capitalized on by Abercrombie and other fashion firms through the exclusion of forms of embodiment and modes of expression and affect that are deemed inferior to the whiteness that the fashion system promotes as the best and the most popular— that which is definitively "American," "natural," and "classic." The *Look Book* uses these terms over and over as it specifies which appearances the company deems appropriate for its employees and which it does not. Acceptable looks include a "neatly combed, attractive, natural, classic hairstyle" and "simple and classic" jewelry (McBride 2005: 70). Stipulated as unacceptable are "fade" haircuts, shaved heads, and dreadlocks—all hairstyles associated with blackness (70). Thumb rings, gold chains, "dressy" watches with gold bands or diamonds, and large earrings for men and women are also grounds for denial of employment or disciplinary action, and again, all are modes of adornment with which black men in particular have been "overidentified or even stereotyped," from the television star and wrestler Mr. T to rap artists and athletes known for their flashy appearances. As McBride states, "Abercrombie codes for race and class without actually having to name it" (71) because these codes are masked in the *Look Book*'s seemingly neutral language of "style." Despite the ideological masking of Abercrombie & Fitch's racial politics behind claims about style and corporate identity, a parade of legal cases has been pursued against the company in recent years, including a successful suit filed in 2003 that argued that Abercrombie used the *Look Book* as a sort of how-to guide for enacting racially discriminatory employment practices at its North American retail stores.[12] The case did not just charge a few managers for exhibiting racial bias; rather, it was a full-scale indictment of the company's racist policies.

Abercrombie's exclusion of nonwhite style has had immediate material consequences for people seeking employment in its stores. But the rendering of blackness and other racial identities and modes of expression as being other than "natural" and "American" by Abercrombie and other fashion firms that promote and profit from whiteness also participates in the contouring of a broader social field in which nonwhite bodies and styles are perceived as less valuable to society and more threatening to the social order and are thus more readily available for other forms of social exclusion, exploitation, and even criminalization than populations recognized as white. This pattern of stereotyping and its exclusionary effects are evident when one looks at dress codes adopted by schools, municipalities, and other corporations across the United States in recent decades, codes that commonly target African Americans as well as Latinos, Chicanos, and other groups racialized as nonwhite. Although the civil rights movement and federal interventions had largely put a stop to the Jim Crow system of overt and legalized racial discrimination by the 1970s, dress codes have functioned in some of the same ways, limiting access to employment, education, public space, and private consumption by banning "inappropriate" and "nonconforming" styles of adornment and self-presentation, but without explicitly referencing "race" (Ponte 2009). One of the most common rules adopted by US public school districts and townships in recent years has to do with so-called droopy or saggy pants (see Cooper 2008; Kleinberg 2008; Peltier 2008; Associated Press 2005). Sociologists document the fears that baggy pants worn low on the hips by African American and Latino youths inspire in many teachers and school administrators, who consider this type of "gang-inspired" dress the external manifestation of an oppositional, aggressive, or violent personality (A. A. Ferguson 2000; Morris 2005). Corporations besides Abercrombie & Fitch have similarly banned braided hairstyles among their employees (Caldwell 1991; Turner 2000; Rosette and Dumas 2007; see also Mercer 1987, 1994). These regulations operate on much the same premise as the colonial strictures that were imposed as part of the Protestant missions in Southern Africa, where the adoption of an acceptable style was read as both contributing to and evidencing social and spiritual assimilation to a racial and civilizational ideal (Comaroff 1996: 24).

Contemporary dress codes work to categorize, subdue, and outright exclude racialized populations from full participation in society, but they are rationalized as being justified by a need to promote order and civility. When someone is expelled from school, not hired, or fired from a workplace for not meeting standards of dress, it seems like the person's own fault because he or she broke a clear set of rules.

Keeping African Americans and other racialized groups away from the Abercrombie trademark has been at the heart of the company's branding strategies and commercial success in the United States. Advertising campaigns, carefully crafted retail environments, and employee manuals have been important means of accomplishing this goal. As the brand's popularity has expanded worldwide over the past two decades, fueled by the company's investment in a multilingual online marketing and retail presence and hundreds of retail locations spread across Mexico, Canada, Europe, East and South Asia, Australia, and the Middle East (Abercrombie & Fitch 2014), the company has focused resources on antipiracy and anticounterfeiting campaigns as a means of regulating access to Abercrombie style. In 2005, the company appointed a former agent with the Federal Bureau of Investigation's Intellectual Property Rights Program to direct these efforts and, in 2006, launched the Abercrombie & Fitch Brand Protection team to "interact with investigators, customs officials, and law enforcement entities throughout the world" to root out and prosecute piracy and counterfeiting (Abercrombie & Fitch 2006). Abercrombie is also part of the International Anti-Counterfeiting Coalition (IACC), an organization that enlists attorneys, investigators, security firms, private associations, government agencies, and universities to research, prevent, police, and prosecute "counterfeiters and pirates" in an effort to keep its members "safe from illegal copying," as stated on the IACC website. The prominence of the trademarked Abercrombie & Fitch logos on the company's clothing designs enables Abercrombie, industry organizations such as the IACC, and local law enforcement to pursue and prosecute people who, in their attempts to reproduce the stylized aesthetic or design, the "look and feel," of a garment, also illegally copy the company's intellectual property. From the perspective of the fashion firm, this kind of policing is necessary in order to protect the brand. However, as I have argued, the brand does not lose its potency, popularity, or relevance as it circulates, and the people who buy knockoffs cannot actually afford the "real" thing and so would not be able to buy authorized goods if no pirated goods were available. These justifications for antipiracy enforcement simply do not hold up. Instead, antipiracy campaigns are ways to limit the access of poorer and marginalized populations to the company's trademarked clothing designs in expanding markets. Keeping Abercrombie "safe from illegal copying" means preventing the brand pollution that contact between the trademark and under-classed, racialized others might entail.

Part of why Abercrombie & Fitch is a popular clothing brand and its designs are copied around the world has to do with its corporate expansion into new retail markets. But the recognizability and popularity of the company's designs and trademarks in certain regions is also a by-product of how the company organizes its manufacturing operations. Abercrombie's clothing is made in contracted and subcontracted factories located mostly in Asia and Central America, where workers sew the trademarked logos onto sweatshirts, t-shirts, and sweaters every day. In Guatemala, *maquila* laborers who assemble clothing for export to the United States, Europe, and other markets are generally not paid enough to be able to afford the garments they stitch together. They are more likely to access these styles via informal markets supplied by the highland apparel trade, which is characterized by the modes of copying and appropriation that the fashion industry and international IP law label "piracy," or to purchase knockoffs imported to Guatemala from East Asia, where pirated copies of Abercrombie garments are made alongside authorized apparel. As noted in earlier chapters, apparel export factories also dump imperfect garments and overruns into domestic markets, a practice that further increases the visibility and relevance of brand-name clothing within local fashion scenes. Producers of pirated clothing often utilize materials such as tags, labels, and rolls of fabric that have been smuggled out of the export factories and sold to the proprietors of local clothing workshops. The practice of "piracy" and its sociological contours—the realities of where it happens and who participates—are inextricably linked to the concentration of apparel production in world regions where people cannot afford authorized goods, where the low wages paid by the industry ensure that that is the case, and where forms of exchange between authorized manufacturers and local markets add to the visibility of particular brands and even facilitate piracy production.

There are racial and gendered dimensions to the industry's globalization. The profit margins achieved by Abercrombie and other fashion firms depend on the undervalued labor of people whose social locations with respect to geography, gender, race, and ethnicity make them available for exploitation. The industry has worked this way for a long time, recruiting marginalized workers in an effort to minimize manufacturing costs. In the early days of industrialization in the US garment sector, for example, immigrant women were recruited as cheap labor for dangerous sweatshops (see, e.g., Greenwald 2005). As discussed in chapter 1, a major reason the industry has globalized its manufacturing operations since the 1960s, moving production from North America and Europe to Asia, Latin America, and sub-Saharan Africa, is the gains that have been made in workers rights, wages, and environmental protections in the Global North compared with the deep vulnerability of nonwhite people, and especially women and ethnic minority groups, in other world regions. The Guatemalan apparel export sector almost exclusively employs young, indigenous women, a segment of the highland population with few educational or employment options and limited access to worker protections, and one that the national elite and industry contractors and factory managers treat as fundamentally exploitable. These women earn meager wages and labor in unsafe and often humiliating conditions. Their vulnerability within Guatemalan society and the international, industrial hierarchy is the product of a long history of the racialized subordination of indigenous people and a patriarchal political and educational system that has generally excluded Maya women from the public sphere. These structures of discrimination come out of European colonialism, have persisted under the rule of *ladino* elites in Guatemala, and have been reinforced in recent decades by structural adjustment programs that mandate an international free trade system and export-oriented economies in "developing" countries. For countries such as Guatemala, "free trade" largely means making raw materials and labor cheaply available to corporations that are headquartered in "developed countries." The fashion industry's globalization has participated in and built on these inequalities, with the result being a profitable divide between privileged, white consumer classes in the Global North and marginalized, racialized, and gendered laborers in the Global South, who are expected to consume cheap finished goods that are distinctive in quality and desirability from the commodities they themselves make for export. This is the well-studied world-system model of international capitalist development (Wallerstein 1974; Wolf 1983). Trademark law propagates this system by enabling the criminalization and prosecution of groups who reproduce the popular and prestigious styles that they assemble for export but cannot afford to purchase via authorized channels. In these ways, antipiracy campaigns and enforcement efforts underwrite and perpetuate an international division of labor and consumption characterized by deep inequalities, ensure the maintenance of racial and ethnic divisions in terms of how people dress, and exclude whole swaths of the global population from the "look" of white style.

To conclude this section, I return for a moment to the discussion of originals and originality from earlier in the chapter. The way that Abercrombie describes its branding process in the *Look Book*—that it is crucial for the brand to be established in space and in practice as much as in the messages that the trademarked logo communicates—lines up remarkably well with how Maya people in highland Guatemala understand trademarks to function and how they distinguish between "originals" and "imitations" in fashion retail. Recall that Alberto Ixim did not interpret the GAP[PS] logo entirely as a "brand image" constituted elsewhere and communicated to consumers as a stable message with a fixed economic value or legal status. The mass marketing behind brands such as Gap or Abercrombie does matter for making the logos recognizable features of the fashion landscape, and it encourages certain associations between the logos and Americanness, whiteness, stylishness, and modernity. Alberto also evaluated the trademark and the clothing designs in terms of locally salient racial, ethnic, and class divides that designate some Guatemalan retail stores as nonindigenous spaces and endow those locations with higher status and value because of the racial subordination of Maya people and the privileges associated with *ladino* style, which is itself linked to connotations of whiteness and modernity and histories of colonialism and postcolonial nation-building. These contexts of experience and interpretation are not histories, associations, images, or values that can be owned by a fashion firm, even if the fashion system belongs to and has itself contributed in important ways to shaping the social and economic order and the racial dynamics that position people like Alberto on the underside of hegemonic divisions of race, ethnicity, privilege, and status. When Alberto said that the clothing sold at the GAP[PS] store was "original," he essentially meant that the store and the merchandise are associated with whiteness, part of a *ladino* sphere of consumption and belonging that is generally off limits to people like him. He did not mean that the apparel was legally or ontologically authentic in the sense that the multinational apparel firm Gap Inc. actually produced it. Nor did he mean that the presence of the GAP[PS] logo marked the clothing as necessarily authentic or original. The apparel was of better quality, higher-priced, and more socially and spatially exclusive than the "imitations" sold in the street markets of Guatemala City and in outdoor markets around the highlands. Alberto's interpretation of fashion logos and clothing designs as "originals" or "imitations" thus reveals how powerfully the concept of originality—perhaps in many geographical regions and ethnographic settings, and in no small part thanks to the logics of property and rights ensconced in IP law—has become linked to connotations of racial and gendered forms of exclusivity and structures of regulation and ownership over style.

INDIGENOUS BRANDS

The brand form lends itself to a range of marketing and political strategies, including the efforts of marginalized populations to assert their own creativity, authority, and rights (Coombe 1998). Partly in response to increasing foreign competition, including the overruns from *maquila* production and the knockoffs imported from East Asia, and partly in response to the recent criminalization of piracy, a set of business practices focused on the creation of unique brands and a moral discourse regarding the appropriate use of brand names are both evident in Tecpán's apparel trade. A few indigenous garment manufacturers have developed their own clothing labels based on Kaqchikel Maya terms such as *b'alam* (jaguar) and *kem* (woven textile).

The fact that the provisions, protections, and potential profits afforded by trademark law are available to Maya people in Guatemala might seem to contradict my argument regarding IP law's role in the promotion and maintenance of a racialized social order at national and international scales. If everyone has access to trademark law, it should be possible for Guatemalan Mayas to construct and protect their own privileged styles and derive profits from their own branding and legal strategies, regardless of the exclusionary practices of Abercrombie and other fashion firms. I found in my research, however, that structural inequalities make trademark ownership in highland Guatemala difficult, if not altogether out of reach, for most Maya people, mostly due to the financial investment required, but also because of the kinds of know-how and the rationalities and market logics that are fundamental to someone taking it upon himself or herself to own a trademark and craft and sell a brand. Becoming a trademark owner is a process of becoming a certain kind of person, one oriented toward the market, laws, the community, and competition in ways that depend on access to formal education and, perhaps, on the rejection of the neighborly ethics and modes of politics and community development that have been fundamental to the growth of Tecpán's apparel trade.

When I talked with Bernardo Kej, a twenty-five-year-old Maya man, in 2009, he was hoping to launch a brand of young men's fashion under the name Xarkar, which means "blue fish" in Kaqchikel. Its pronunciation reminded him of the English word "shark," and he wanted to use a shark for the logo. Bernardo developed the logo plus a tagline, marketing plan, financial profile, production flow charts, and design samples for a university business course. His father entered the garment business before the armed conflict and had done just well enough to help Bernardo attend weekend university courses in Guatemala City.

Bernardo wanted to do business under a brand name that highlighted his Kaqchikel identity. He was active in a local political party called Qatinamit, "Our Town," a name that referred to Tecpán's indigenous majority. He identified with an older generation of indigenous leaders who comprised the pan-Maya movement, a loose affiliation of activists and nongovernmental organizations that advocated for cultural rights and shaped national policy toward indigenous people during and after Guatemala's peace process (Fischer and Brown 1996). Using a Kaqchikel term as a brand name was a political move for Bernardo, who sincerely hoped his clothing line would encourage pride and affiliation among young indigenous men who might wear it. It was also a strategic business decision. Like other "ethnic entrepreneurs" (DeHart 2010) around the world, spurred by the growth of heritage and ethnicity industries, Bernardo wanted to commodify Maya identity to capitalize on what differentiated his clothing line from imported garments and clothing made by his neighbors. His pursuits reflect the current phase of global ethnic politics and identity-based enterprise: a neoliberal turn to capitalism as a vehicle of political as well as economic "empowerment" among historically disenfranchised and marginalized populations (John L. Comaroff and Jean Comaroff 2009: 15; Freeman 2007; DeHart 2010). This turn has been especially evident in postcolonies such as Guatemala, where the state has threatened much more than protected the indigenous population. Because of Guatemala's history of violence and contemporary policy failings, Bernardo was attempting to promote ethnic pride and imbue Maya identity with value and prestige in ways that depended on his own initiative and business acumen within a free market system rather than on indigenous people achieving political recognitions or a broad set of state guarantees to rights and services.

As Marilyn Strathern and Eric Hirsch (2004: 3) note, "ownership claims emerge within a world of owners." The possibility of trademarking a Maya term as a way of promoting identity politics and ethnic affiliation, for example, comes to seem reasonable and feasible in a context in which new regimes of ownership over physical and intellectual property are taking shape in other arenas as well. In Guatemala, land and resource rights are a sometimes violently contested political issue, involving Maya communities throughout the western highlands and northern lowlands in all kinds of activism, including the staging of large-scale protests and the organization of community forums and voting proceedings to foment and demonstrate opposition to mining, hydroelectric, and export agriculture projects funded by multinational corporations (Crystal et al. 2014; Urkidi 2011; Yagenova and Garcia 2009; Nolin and Stephens 2010; Fultz 2015). Maya communities have resisted these projects because they often involve the privatization of communal land holdings, exploitative labor practices, and the potential for environmental degradation and contamination. Indigenous people who might not otherwise talk about land and natural resources in terms of Western concepts of ownership and rights have moved toward such language in order to advance their political claims in ways that correspond to national and international legal framings and thus achieve recognition and protections. Indigenous leaders have posed claims to "heritage" and "culture" in terms of property and ownership for the same reasons (D. M. Nelson 1999: 24). For example, pan-Maya activists have opposed the Guatemalan state's commodification of indigenous dress and language for tourism promotions by claiming clothing and language as "cultural property" (Warren 1998). Although the discourse of "cultural property" objectifies indigenous identity and ways of life in accordance with the logics of Western property regimes over and against indigenous epistemologies and ontologies (Winthrop 2002), scholars and indigenous activists alike have tended to justify this approach in terms of strategic essentialism (Fischer 1999).

Other strategies adopted by indigenous activists in Guatemala have also shaped the political context in which Bernardo developed his business and branding plans. With a great deal of success, pan-Maya activists have encouraged indigenous people to use the term "Maya" rather than more local designations, such as the name of their town or the particular Mayan language they speak, as a source of identification (Fischer 2001: 247; D. M. Nelson 1999: 21). This method of consolidating ethnic identity in Guatemala into larger segmentations echoes similar processes in other postcolonial settings. As John L. Comaroff and Jean Comaroff (2009: 12) note, "ethnic incorporation rides on a process of homogenization and abstraction: *the* Zulu (or *the* Tswana or *the*

San), for all their internal divisions, become one. . . . This may not undermine ethnic identification. . . . To the contrary, it may underline its importance as an object of *both* possibility and political struggle." Performative labels such as "Maya" and *pueblo indígena* (indigenous people, or indigenous nation) encourage a sense of belonging and common purpose while simultaneously distilling a remarkable panoply of cultural, historical, linguistic, and geographical diversity into a lone signifier. With this strategy and commitment, cultural activists in Guatemala have been able to promote a rights-based agenda on national and international levels and garner significant financial and political support from international agencies. Besides the legal rights to custom, language, and culture written into the 1985 national constitution, gains include funding from the United Nations, European and North American governments, and international NGOs for the preservation and promotion of Mayan languages and scholarship and for the pursuit of community land and natural resource claims (Fischer 1996; Warren 1998; D. M. Nelson 1999).

Bernardo's attempt to capture indigeneity in the form of a brand was built on the foundations thus laid by a broad cultural rights movement. Indeed, Bernardo was not the first to use markers of Maya identity to craft a brand. Apart from the tourism industry's use of Maya symbolism, the Maya owned and operated publishing company Cholsamaj and bookstores Nawal Wuj and Nuk'samaj in Guatemala City are just a few examples of enterprises that use terms from Mayan languages in their company names and Classic Maya hieroglyphs in their logos. The proprietors of these businesses are affiliated with the pan-Maya movement, and their services—especially the dissemination of Mayan literature and scholarship and information on Maya culture—are integral to the constitution and promulgation of indigenous politics (see Billingsley 2013).

The kinds of ethno-branding that are part of cultural activism in Guatemala have various cultural and political implications. Pan-Maya activists have used Maya symbols and signs to rally a disparate indigenous population around common goals. Indigenous leaders have deployed a unified ethnic identity to political ends in their attempts to congeal a social movement amid conditions of discrimination and during a peace process that held a great deal of hope for indigenous Guatemalans. There is something limiting, however, about the ways that nation-states and international agencies demand that assertions of political rights and claims about suffering, trauma, dispossession, and harm be channeled into certain recognizable forms, whether ethnic

monikers that assimilate contemporary experience to labels that Western anthropologists have ascribed to ancient civilizations (e.g., "Maya")
or brand names that channel politics through the market system. Neoliberal economic programs enacted since the end of the armed conflict
in Guatemala, as explained in earlier chapters, are part of the context in
which the trademarking of identity that Bernardo has been involved in
has come to make sense for him and for others. A focus in national and
international development discourse on market-based solutions to
structural inequalities has been coupled in Guatemala with the disparaging of political protest as antithetical to ideals of national harmony,
peace, and reconciliation in the postwar period (Benson 2004). The
promotion of entrepreneurship as the appropriate answer to poverty
and the "free market" as the best and most efficient mechanism for distributing economic resources and achieving "development" is a key
message in Bernardo's university courses. And his earnest pursuit of
business success as a way to promote Maya culture resonates with the
political and economic program of neoliberal multiculturalism (Hale
2005) whereby the state recognizes and celebrates the positivity of cultural difference without addressing structural processes of marginalization propelled by the government and capitalist enterprise that render
indigenous people more likely to live in poverty and more vulnerable to
conditions of precarity and insecurity. These broad-scale dynamics of
the problematization of protest and the promotion of business often
leave indigenous people with little alternative than to pitch themselves
as both marketable commodities and market-savvy entrepreneurs.

Bernardo's business plans and branding strategy are also conditioned
by his adoption of a model of business ethics that privileges individual
ownership and originality and that involves a moral discourse against
piracy that sometimes pits him against his fellow apparel producers in
Tecpán. Rosemary Coombe (1998) argues that signs of social and cultural difference are transformed when used as trademarks. They are, in
effect, taken out of the cultural commons and returned to the public
sphere as "jealously guarded" signs of commercial distinction (Coombe
1996: 203; see also Brush 1993). Bernardo told me in interviews that, if
someone else were to use his brand, it would be unethical and illegal. It
would be *piratería* (piracy), he noted, employing a legal discourse consistent with the international IP regime rather than the more colloquial discourse about *copiones,* which is premised on a model of flexible, dynamic
copying and sharing, as discussed in chapter 2. When Bernardo organized
a group of Tecpán's garment manufacturers to attend informational

meetings in Guatemala City in 2006 on the new free trade rules instituted under DR-CAFTA, meetings where he hoped to hear about export opportunities for domestic clothing producers, he invited only those who were also on a path to state-regulated market participation, some of whom also attended university business classes. When the half-dozen men set up a production and marketing cooperative to vie for export contracts and secured a meeting with representatives from a North American apparel distributor, the US businessmen told the group that their clothing samples did not meet the requisite quality standards. The corporate representatives also poked fun at the group's members for naming the cooperative Koton, the Kaqchikel term for "sweater," which they reportedly interpreted as an ignorant misspelling of "cotton."

Bernardo and others told me that they felt stigmatized and embarrassed by this interaction. Their best efforts to conform to an ideal institutionalized in development discourse, be entrepreneurial, and take advantage of a globalizing marketplace were met with ridicule. The meeting confirmed for the group that DR-CAFTA was meant to benefit not their regional trade but only the already established, foreign-financed export sector. The interaction also stung of racism, as Bernardo explained. An important part of calling the cooperative Koton was to proudly display the men's Kaqchikel identity and make cultural difference a selling point in the negotiations, but the strategy had resulted instead in the group being negatively stereotyped as uneducated in ways that echoed the disparagement of indigenous people by *ladinos* in Guatemala.

Bernardo interpreted his experience with the cooperative in terms of the politics of race and geography that I have described as being part and parcel of the fashion industry—that is to say, he saw it as evidence of dynamics of discrimination and structural marginalization that make it unlikely for indigenous people to be recognized as legitimate participants or to find entrepreneurial success in the globalized fashion system. But he also blamed the failure on his fellow producers in ways that echoed the moral discourses promoted in international IP law and state-led campaigns that promote formalization. He complained to me about the rampant informality that he said characterized Tecpán's apparel trade, criticizing the cooperative members for not having the knowledge and skills necessary to manufacture an export-quality product, and especially citing the *piratas,* as he put it, for contributing to an overall lack of professionalism across the regional trade. He seemed to think that development chances were being foreclosed because of the flaws of his neighbors and not only or primarily because of large-scale policies and processes. His complaints reflected the complicated modes of evaluation and moralization that differently positioned producers in the apparel trade often take up in order to make sense of their individual situations, market dynamics, and the difficult effects of inequality. But Bernardo's attempts to set himself apart from other producers conformed to institutional mandates and development discourse in ways that stood out from most of my other informants because his university education had encouraged him to think of a relationship to the state, IP law, and international trade regimes in a much more positive light. He and a handful of other producers belong to a class of educated, relatively well-to-do young men in Tecpán who have come to view taking university classes, registering their businesses and brands with the state, paying taxes, planning their work according to technical principles in manufacturing and marketing sciences, and avoiding piracy as both business strategies and moral obligations, part of what it means to be a good businessman as well as a good citizen in an evolving context of regulation, moralization, and "development."

Bernardo's educational status and commitment to state-regulated production, scientific management techniques, and unique branding combines with his deep familial and personal commitment to indigenous politics in ways that echo Diane Nelson's (1999) portrait of indigenous activists as "Maya-hackers." She writes: "*Ladino* identity is defined as modern in terms of technology and lifeways. . . . [Any] indigenous person who speaks Spanish, has earned an academic degree, or holds a desk job has historically been redefined as *Ladino*." In the context of the pan-Maya movement, however, many indigenous people moved into cultural and political spaces traditionally carved out for *ladinos* but refused to relinquish their indigenous identity, as is the case with Bernardo. Nelson compares these activists to computer hackers, "who do not control the systems they work in but intimately understand their technologies and codes." She continues: "The Maya are appropriating so-called modern technologies and knowledges while refusing to be appropriated into the *Ladino* nation" (D. M. Nelson 1999: 249). Nelson's laudatory description of a previous generation of pan-Maya activists applies well to Bernardo and others of his generation and educational status who are engaged in branding as a political-professional pursuit. Bernardo has sought out participation in the systems and structures of higher education and formal enterprise while continuing to assert and promote indigenous identity and refusing to conform to national development models premised on the loss of identity, ethnic assimilation, or the pressures of "ethnic passing" (Warren

1998) that so often confront indigenous people who move in urban, educated, and professional social spheres in Guatemala. At the same time, however, he has adopted certain elements of performance, ethics, and livelihood that draw ethnicity close to an area of ambivalence. His business plans and branding strategy involve a mode of ethnic entrepreneurship wrapped up with the state and formal market system in ways that are not attainable for many Maya apparel producers because of the structural marginalization of indigenous Guatemalans. Most workshop owners, and certainly the general population of Maya people living in Tecpán, do not have access to university education. Bernardo's goals of formal market participation and international export contracting are not necessarily desirable from the perspective of most other Maya apparel producers, who often view the state and its regulatory apparatus with a great deal of suspicion, and who value concealment and secrecy above legal compliance (see chapter 1).

There are also important gender dimensions to Bernardo's entrepreneurship. In business classes, he learned a particular diagram of masculinity premised on technical knowledge and mastery, capitalist relationships to labor and the market, and identification with the project of national economic development. It is a model that is linked to the hegemonic masculinity that is part of *ladino* style in Guatemala and the gendered styles of other populations of "white" men across Latin America.[13] As noted above, garment manufacturing is a gendered form of work. Men are positioned as owners, managers, machine operators, and salespeople. Women sometimes perform tasks in the workshops that are considered easier or more delicate and contribute to the production process by hand embroidering or sewing adornments onto garments in their homes on a piece-rate basis. Bernardo's case draws attention to the ways that, in highland Guatemala, the social construction of the Maya man as a business owner with ties to the state and higher education and a role in political leadership may perpetuate longstanding gender divisions and inequities that help to structure the local trade and daily life in the region in general. Bernardo's business plans and branding strategy may also participate in a broader trend that anthropologists have documented in which the globalization and formalization of economic systems often fosters a widening of the gender gap, as men and women are recruited and incorporated into industrial and professional labor markets in uneven ways, with men's work generally rewarded with higher wages and greater prestige (Ong 1987; Freeman 2001).

As in other colonial contexts, sumptuary laws once required Maya men interacting with the Spanish to wear European-style attire—shoes, long pants, a collared shirt, and a hat (Carrillo Ramirez 1971). The public-private divide engendered by such laws means that indigenous men today are less likely than indigenous women to wear traditional clothing and women are less likely than men to speak Spanish. As discussed in this book's introduction, the state and private interests treat Maya women's *traje,* or traditional dress, as a static custom and form of cultural property, relying on a gendered indigenous style to distinguish Guatemala from other nations and market it to tourists. Figured as a remnant of the past, *traje* provides the historic depth necessary for the construction of a national identity (D. M. Nelson 2001: 321). At the same time, and often as a means of discrediting the work of Maya cultural activists, the *ladino* elite advance the belief that Maya people no longer exist in Guatemala, claiming that the Maya civilization was wiped out when the Spanish arrived or that racial admixture over the centuries has resulted in a racially and ethnically homogenous population and consequently that no one deserves the special treatment that the cultural rights protections demanded by the pan-Maya movement could confer (Fischer 1999). In this context, the *mujer maya* dressed in her *huipil* and *corte* has served as a "prosthetic" for indigenous activists attempting to construct a movement "from the stumps and wounded body images left by conquest and civil war," writes Diane Nelson (1999: 274). In other words, a stereotyped image of an unchanging, culturally distinct Maya woman serves as a visual aid for Maya men leading the cultural rights movement to call national and international attention to the persistence of indigenous communities (represented obviously and effectively by Maya women in traditional dress), in spite of centuries of violence and discrimination, and to rally political support for indigenous rights on the basis of cultural difference. Maya women dressed in *traje* trouble the notion that Guatemala is ethnically homogenous because their clothing evidences cultural difference in a visually impactful way. Furthermore, Nelson continues, indigenous male activists, the "Maya-hackers" like Bernardo, who move in *ladino* spaces and institutions and appropriate *ladino* forms of knowledge, "can be modern because Mayan women represent tradition." Without such a distinctive figure to lean on, without their personal and cultural and community-based relationships to women who wear traditional dress, associations that confirm their own Maya-ness, these men "would just be *Ladinos,* without a valid claim for a separate cultural existence." The point is that Bernardo, dressed as he often is in khaki pants and a (knockoff) Lacoste polo or neatly pressed button-down shirt, might easily be mistaken for *ladino* as he crosses the university campus or delivers clothing to retail stores in Guatemala City. His claims to cultural difference might be invalidated in the eyes of *ladinos* (or, in more subtle ways, debated by Maya people, as discussed in chapter 2) because of his educational attainment, relationship to state institutions and modern technologies of business and branding, and even professional aspirations. But Bernardo and other Maya-hackers can claim indigeneity because Maya women in their families and communities dress in *traje*, often do not speak Spanish, and maintain a set of cultural practices, including traditional weaving, that are utterly distinct from *ladino* style and immediately recognizable as Maya (C. A. Smith 1995). The social and economic value of Maya ethnic identity for political activism as well as commercial branding is thus contingent to some extent on a gendered and racialized styling of Maya women and a patriarchal portrait of them as tied to the past, to culture, and to tradition.

The gendered dynamics of indigeneity in Guatemala show up in how Bernardo planned to position his Xarkar brand within the marketplace. He told me that he wanted the brand to be about a new "masculine" style as well as indigenous identity. "Da un toque de originalidad a tu personalidad masculina" (Give your masculine personality a touch of originality) was one of the taglines he was considering during my fieldwork. The clothing line, he explained, would appeal to young men who understand the value of cultural difference. His ambitions indicated earnest desire for Maya men to express their indigeneity through fashion—to consume the jackets and sweaters that he produced under the Xarkar label as a way of sharing with Maya women in the "cultural responsibility" (Otzoy 1996: 147) of displaying ethnic difference through dress practices. His business plan incorporated lessons learned from the previous generation of indigenous leaders, who had attempted to develop a distinctly Maya fashion, a traditional look, for indigenous men in the 1990s. At that time, in a fitting move for Maya-hackers, several cultural activists from Tecpán designed and promoted a line of clothing that incorporated elements of women's *traje* into Western-styled men's fashion. These garments displayed signs of ethnic difference associated with the *mujer maya* in a form that simultaneously figured their wearers as modern and cosmopolitan. The best example of this trend was a dark-hued, casual, zipper-front jacket designed by a close friend of Bernardo's father and constructed of cotton cloth dyed in the style of a woman's *corte*. The cloth was woven in Totonicapán (a K'iche' Maya town) and trimmed with cotton cord from Tecpán (a Kaqchikel Maya town), and thus the garment symbolically joined together two prominent indigenous communities. The pan-Maya movement's male leaders wore the jackets proudly as a display of Maya identity in the early 1990s (R. M. Brown 1996: 174). Since its production and circulation was tightly controlled for several years, the jacket was initially "an unmistakable indicator of status within the movement" (Fischer 2001: 119). The jackets were eventually marketed to the general population, but they never gained widespread popularity.

Notably, this fashion pursuit did not involve the marketing and promotion of designs already on the men's traditional dress scene. The movement leaders did not adopt the colorful *traje* famously worn by men from Todos Santos Cuchumatán in the department of Huehuetenango or the brilliant shirts, pants, and belts donned by men from the lakeside villages of the department of Sololá. Nor did they adopt the traditional dress common to the oldest men in many towns throughout the highlands, including Tecpán, where a handful of elders complement their button-down shirts and felt hats with sandals, a wool *rodillera* (rectangular cloth wrapped around the hips), and loose-fitting, white cotton pants. Perhaps the fact that the *traje* of towns such as Todos Santos Cuchumatán have such powerful and localized geographical references made them seem less than ideal for a national movement that promoted a consolidated ethnic identity. Or perhaps the leaders felt they would not be taken seriously in such garb. Carol Hendrickson (1996: 162) has written that "the values manifested by the colorful, hand-woven shirts and the calf-length pants of some male *traje* . . . do not match those of, say, blue jeans and T-shirts or suits and ties. Men in *traje* are therefore seen as 'less' masculine, serious, and competent." Diane Nelson (2001: 344) notes that, when a newly elected or named national president has made the ritual pilgrimage to one of these towns and donned the local men's dress, people often "snort that he looks like a *payaso* (clown)."

Bernardo referenced the men's fashion designs developed by pan-Maya activists—the jackets and also some sweaters featuring Maya hieroglyphs—when we talked about his plans for the Xarkar brand. He explained that those styles did not catch on because they did not appeal to young people; they were considered *muy del pasado* (literally, "from the past," meaning that they were old-fashioned but also that the hieroglyphs and *corte* material referred to antiquity). In Bernardo's view, his designs are decidedly forward-looking. As is common to the local trade, he draws inspiration from his neighbors, online fashion retail sites, and the latest styles on sale in Guatemala City. The slogans he developed for the brand, including the one mentioned above, were more about the prospective consumer's personal image than a shared, ethnic identity rooted in the past and tradition. "Define tu estilo" (Define your own style); "Mejora tu imagen" (Improve your image); "Date un toque de originalidad" (Give yourself a touch of originality); "Tu eres original" (You're an original)—there is nothing particularly Maya about these taglines. The connection Bernardo hopes to make is subtle. His jackets, shirts, and sweaters are meant to appeal to what he sees as truly modern indigenous youth: fashionable men who know the value of cultural difference. The brand name, Xarkar, serves as a bit of indigenous flair—a splash of Kaqchikel cachet—an original yet also politically and ethnically minded inflection on hip, urban youth apparel. Bernardo said that the styles have to sell themselves. People will not wear something just because it has a Mayan logo, he explained. They first have to be drawn to the overall look of a garment, *ruwäch*. In this way, he represents a new generation of Maya-hackers who can wear all the trappings of *ladino* modernity—the nontraditional clothing and hip, modern styles— while keeping their indigenous identity close by, on the inside (in Bernardo's case literally sewn into the collar of his Xarkar sweater), a somewhat secret or latent pride revealed in a retail transaction or the purposeful flash of a tag.

Given the cultural politics surrounding indigenous women's dress, this branding strategy is a gendered approach to interpreting both modernity and indigenous activism. Men's relationships to the written word rather than the woven image, to Spanish rather than Mayan languages, to modern styles rather than traditional dress, to a branded ethnic identity rather than traditional heritage, and, in Tecpán, to their position as owners of garment workshops rather than as manual workers mean that fashion and business style mediate the changing relationship of Maya men to the state and civil society in ways that are largely unavailable to Maya women. These realities also speak to the ways that structural reorganizations of industries and economies—the turn to neoliberalism and entrepreneurial development and the push for formalization that is happening in Guatemala and in other "developing" countries—impacts local social dynamics and regional patterns and often involves an intensification of gendered and racialized divisions of labor and status.

Bernardo's business venture was made possible, in many ways, by the historical constitution of the highland garment industry as an *indigenous* trade. His father's early successes, the pride that generations of producers have taken in their work, and the form of community development that has undergirded the economic mobility of indigenous people in Tecpán are part of the story of how Bernardo has been able to access educational opportunities and develop a different kind of relationship to formal market structures, marketing science, and possibilities of IP law protections. His branding strategy foregrounds the political stakes of fashion and entrepreneurship by reconfiguring indigeneity as an important component of the making and marketing of style in Guatemala. But his story also evidences how a changing relationship to trademark law and brand ownership in places such as Guatemala involves a complicated process of social stratification, moralization, and the institutionalization of ethical commitments and community divisions along lines of class, race, ethnicity, and gender. Bernardo simultaneously challenges racialized stereotypes that circulate nationally and internationally about indigeneity, piracy, and informality that would caricature him as backward and premodern and participates in moralizing discourses about the business styles of his neighbors, whom he calls "pirates," and who, from his perspective, are low-quality businessmen, produce low-quality goods, and hold back the progressive advancement of the regional industry. His business plan also moves indigenous politics into the realm of market-based consumption and self-branding, calling on young Maya men to brand themselves and their ethnic identities and express indigenous affiliation through formal production and the consumption of logos such as Xarkar. Bernardo's branding strategy implies a kind of consumer citizenship (Lipsitz 2006) in which indigenous men are encouraged to affiliate themselves politically and claim social goods through private consumption in ways that may take away from the more collectivized spirit and framework of political mobilization that defined the pan-Maya movement in past decades and that continues to appeal to Bernardo as he pursues local party politics alongside his entrepreneurial training and work.[14]

The racial politics that undergird the international fashion system; the fact that successful fashion branding has so often been premised on the promotion of racial and national forms of belonging at the expense of and via the exclusion of colonized and marginalized groups; the ways that profit margins and business success in the industry have depended for so long on the exploitation of subordinated populations and divisions of labor and access to consumption along racial, gendered, and geographical lines; and the role international IP law plays in the maintenance and promotion of distinctions, inequalities, and the regulation of racialized style—all of this is key to understanding how and why trademark law matters for the globalized industry. These dynamics play out in highland Guatemala in the *maquila* system of apparel export manufacturing, which employs indigenous women to assemble branded clothing they cannot afford and are not supposed to consume anyway; in the novel ways in which Maya apparel producers create, copy, and appropriate within the local apparel industry, pursue livelihoods, and engage in political and economic struggles; and in the antipiracy campaigns that attempt to keep poor and indigenous Guatemalans away from white style, even though assimilation is often promoted and cultural and ethnic diversity are often denied or disparaged in discourses of national harmony and improvement. Bernardo's case illustrates how the many fault lines and divisions that structure and animate the globalized regulation of style play out in a local context when trademark law gets taken up as a means of promoting identity and affiliation, of trying to make a living, and of working to establish something new and different and as part of a politics of recognition and resistance. The results are multifaceted. They reflect the thorny implications of a prosthetic relationship of indigenous men to indigenous women and the entanglements of tradition and modernity in a postcolonial setting where Bernardo and others navigate a pan-Maya identity, local commitments to an industry that is indigenous, and the valorization of deracialized modern styles. Bernardo also navigates the privileging and promotion of neoliberal economic models of development and success. He confronts a difficult paradox when the tools afforded to him to negotiate the legacies of colonialism and systems of economic exploitation and longstanding marginalization are the very means by which racial and gendered patterns of subordination have been so effectually manicured and maintained in the global development industry. The models of competition, ethics, and moralization that he learns in the classroom and applies to the apparel trade, and the desire he puts forward to carve out a space of autonomy and ownership by using a logo that could possibly drive or support a movement, if only a movement of consumers, do not nullify or escape the ways that such a movement would be caught up in a context of both passing and identifying (of being Maya and being young, hip, and fashionable) or the necessities of having to figure out how these hybridities, which have been seen in the context of colonialism and postcolonial struggle as polluting and threatening, can assemble into forms linking personal gain and community development, and social distinction and political change.

CHAPTER 4

Fiscal and Moral Accountability

In a recent book, *Reckoning*, Diane Nelson (2009) points to the centrality of counting (recounting, accounting, fixing, and settling) to institutional, individual, and community-based attempts to come to terms with the uneasy "structure of feeling" (Williams 1977)—the sense that all is still not well—that pervades postwar Guatemala. International organizations and the state judiciary have audited the country's long internal armed conflict in various ways through truth commission reports, victim compensation programs, and human rights trials. Meanwhile, Guatemalan citizens are confronted with the deeply personal and sometimes public task of accounting for who they were during the war and who they are now that the war is officially over. Given that people were induced, if not forced, to hand their neighbors over to the military on suspicions of guerilla sympathy as part of the state's counterinsurgency campaigns, senses of "community" have often been experienced as two-faced and duplicitous in the highlands, a feeling that lingers in the aftermath of the war (McAllister and Nelson 2013). During the counterinsurgency, Maya people had to develop sophisticated ways of demonstrating to state agents their allegiance to the official "cause" of anticommunism while simultaneously affirming to neighbors and friends that they remained loyal and would not comply with state orders to turn in people who disagreed with or resisted the authoritarian military regime. Nelson (2009: 13) quotes one war survivor as saying, "I have two faces. One I show to the army, the other I show to my people." Nelson hones in on the uncomfortable and uncanny feeling among people in the highlands that they were duped by a state that claimed to want to protect them but actually sought their destruction, and sometimes duped by one another because of how state surveillance, threats of brutalization, and the experience of violence generated existential rifts between individuals and lasting social divisions within communities.

Many Guatemalans felt cheated and tricked again in May 2013, when the trial of former dictator and military general Efraín Ríos Montt, charged with genocide against indigenous Guatemalans and crimes against humanity, was broadcast live on television and on the web. Of course, we know that Ríos Montt was responsible for the bloodiest military campaigns during the armed conflict. The facts are plain and obvious. The trial promised, however, that this "truth" of the war would finally, formally, and conclusively be validated by the state and that some form of justice would be delivered. Days of testimony built on decades of difficult and dangerous work by indigenous community leaders, forensic anthropologists, and human rights activists and attorneys, all of whom worked to piece together evidence that could be used in the case. Although it seemed improbable that legal justice would actually be served in Guatemala, a country so deeply marked by impunity and disavowal, the guilty verdict did come. Headlines proclaimed justice, human rights advocates declared victory, and it all seemed too good to be true.

Unfortunately, it was. The Guatemalan Constitutional Court overturned the verdict ten days later. Legal maneuverings on the part of the defense attorneys, protests on the political right, and political and financial pressure from the country's business leaders were all that was needed to have the judgment thrown out.[1] Ríos Montt's conviction had marked a potential turning point in terms of the legal accountability of military and political leaders in the country, and it also amounted to an official affirmation that genocide against the Maya had occurred in Guatemala, a fact that the business and political elite consistently deny. As Lisa Laplante (2014: 625) explains, a narrative that precludes genocide allows the Guatemalan elite to frame the war "as a purely political conflict between two opponents [a capitalist state and communist subversives], without ever having to dig into the systematic nature of the government's human rights violations and the underlying racism that motivated this policy." She continues: "Given that most indigenous Guatemalans still suffer from racial discrimination, which, in turn, contributes to drastic socio-economic inequalities, the debate on how to characterize past atrocity has serious implications for the present." Ríos Montt's conviction threatened the social and economic order and the interests of people who had supported his political career during and after his dictatorship (he served in Congress from 1990 to 2004 and again from 2008 to 2012 and ran for president in 2003) and who continue to benefit from the politics of racial subordination in Guatemala. After the verdict was overturned, the attorney general who had prosecuted Ríos Montt was removed from office, and things returned to a disappointing and aggressively conservative normal, made even more difficult to accept by the embarrassment of failed hope. A phrase that I have heard over and over in my conversations with highland residents still rings in my head: *No hay control.* There is no control, no discipline, no responsibility, no one taking account, and no accounting in Guatemala.

The apparel producers from Tecpán whose lives this book traces employed this phrase as a general indictment of the "law and dis/order" (Jean Comaroff and John L. Comaroff 2006) that surrounds them. Laments about a lack of "control" circulated about everything, from national politics and widespread crime and "*delincuencia*" to the perils of highway travel and the vicissitudes of market prices. This is not to say, however, that *tecpanecos* were calling for stronger state surveillance or fiscal involvement. The *mano dura* (iron fist) approach to crime and violence promoted on the political right and characterized by tough rhetoric and the increased militarization of police and security forces does find some support in the highlands (Fischer and Benson 2006; Benson et al. 2008), but apparel producers who complained about a lack of control were also quick to recall that the state "control" exercised during the armed conflict resulted in more danger for them, not less, and calamitous human costs. As one manufacturer put it, "It was more dangerous [here] in the west because this was the area that was most affected [during the violence]. . . . There was more control here, and sometimes you ran into the army or sometimes the guerilla. At that time, it was a really unstable environment." As he went on to explain, this man experienced the conflict period as "unstable" because of the general threat posed by the army and the indiscriminate violence perpetrated against Maya people but also because of the particular forms of danger that affected indigenous people involved in the apparel trade. One of the army's methods of "control" was to stop and question people traveling on the highway, demand identification, and sometimes confiscate their goods (discussed in previous chapters). At best, one could expect to pay a bribe for passage; at worst, a soldier could discover one's name on a list of suspected *guerrilleros* or guerrilla sympathizers, leading to potential imprisonment or "disappearance."

For apparel producers, the need to have "two faces"—one turned toward the state and the other toward community members—conditions a complicated relationship to "control." Maya workshop owners' strategies of concealment and disclosure, the two value regimes described in chapter 1 that have structured the historical unfolding of the trade, have been honed in line with the need to carefully manage one's self-presentation, given the threats posed by the state during the conflict and the state's demands for formalization and legal compliance in the postwar period, and to avoid accusations of envy, individualism, ethnic betrayal, or unfair competition that might arise among neighbors and fellow producers, as discussed in chapter 2. Rhetorics of "control" partly speak to the arts of autosurveillance, concealment, personal (ethical and political) accounting, and self-audit that life in the highlands in general, and work in the apparel trade in particular, demands—the kinds of inwardly oriented disciplinary practices that help to ensure that one is not put in harm's way or available for blame. At the same time, these modes of control must be rendered externally visible to the state and to neighbors, a form of *presentación* (see chapter 3) that demonstrates one's submission to governance and formality and one's sense of responsibility to a production community where ethnic solidarity is important.[2] These dynamics of display and concealment, presentation and pretense, and show and suspicion, which are linked in rhetorics and practices of control, are readily apparent in how apparel producers manage and perform the task of business accounting. The management of budgets and paperwork, the setting and monitoring of prices, and the figuring of credits, debts, and costs are part of the routine, everyday work of running an apparel business. These practices are also key components of highland business style and are targeted for regulation in state surveillance programs and international development industry interventions, and they are a frequent topic of conversation among producers, who evaluate neighbors and competitors based on how their accounting routines and skills show up in the marketplace via pricing and profitability. As I demonstrate in this chapter, business accounting is an important aspect of the wider field of postwar audit and ethical accountability in highland Guatemala, where people work to define and demonstrate moral as well as financial responsibility to multiple audiences and at multiple scales.

Building on the work of critical accounting scholars and anthropologists of audit and finance, I draw on ethnographic evidence related to business accounting in the highland apparel trade to argue that the work of counting and accounting is about inciting change and regulating styles of business, market orientations, and modes of entrepreneurship as much as it is about documenting objective business and market data.[3] Accounting practices institutionalize norms regarding bureaucratic power, market participation, and state-citizen relations while also providing a numerological and narrative formulation through which people make sense of those norms and further evaluate themselves and their social and material relationships to each other, the state, and the economy (Maurer 2002; Law 2002; Power 1997).

In order to trace how these processes play out in the highland apparel trade, I begin the chapter with a close examination of the politics and practices surrounding receipts. A recent media campaign has urged consumers to "¡Pida su factura!" (Ask for your receipt!) when paying for goods or services in retail settings. The campaign, launched in 2009 by the state tax administration (Superintendencia de Administración Tributaria, or SAT), is but one attempt among many by the state to encourage economic formalization and extract wealth from the private sector through accounting and taxation in a country where total tax revenue as a percentage of GDP is lower than almost anywhere else in Latin America or the Caribbean (Cabrera et al. 2015). These attempts have been continually thwarted as people have refrained from using receipts to document market transactions, partly as a means of avoiding taxation, but also for other reasons, which I explore below. Workshop owners in the apparel trade are no different in their reluctance to issue receipts than people in other sectors of the Guatemalan economy whom the SAT views as problematically noncompliant. Rather than assume that such "noncompliance" is based in willful ignorance, straightforward criminality, or simple defiance (although resistance to state control and extraction is important here), I analyze the specifics of how and when producers use receipts and how this relates to the regulating style that shapes business practices among Maya workshop owners.

In later sections of the chapter, I connect my findings about the use of receipts to the broader arena of business accounting in highland Guatemala and to how apparel producers *hacer cuentas* (keep accounts) of their business dealings as well as their social positions within a community of producers, neighbors, creditors, and clients. While the state and development organizations mandate and try to cultivate a kind of professionalism premised on formal market participation and documented transactions, Maya apparel producers have their own debates about what constitutes "professional" business practice and accounting techniques. For them, professionalism is wrapped up with and evaluated in terms of a certain performance of masculinity, where managing budgets and setting prices in a professional manner depends on knowing one's place within a gendered labor hierarchy and assigning monetary value to one's time, labor, and managerial skill in a way that contrasts with how women who weave, for instance, set prices for their textiles, not counting their time as part of the value of the products they make and sell. The gendered dimensions of what it means to be a "professional" businessman in the apparel trade are an important part of how the politics of knowledge and numbers are unfolding in the highlands alongside international development discourse and state formalization programs that encourage people to adopt bureaucratic and technical logics of audit and fiscal and moral accountability.

DOCUMENTING CONTROL

The Guatemalan government's *¡Pida su factura!* campaign and broader efforts to construct a *cultura tributaria* (tax-paying culture) have aimed to generate tax revenue from precisely the kinds of enterprises described in this book. Receipts are accounting tools: simple, paper forms that register transactions and make them into a record that can be mobilized in various ways and to diverse ends. Agents of the state interact with receipts in terms of their evidentiary capacities. Receipts signify to tax administration officials that a transaction occurred. Anthropologists might approach receipts, therefore, by considering their representational capacities for saying something about or reporting on a fact, a real world event. But receipts, like the files Matthew Hull (2012) analyzed in his study of Pakistani state bureaucracy, do not only communicate objective data or information. Due to the way that receipts get taken up in bureaucratic public relations and in everyday business practice in the highland economy, they are in and of themselves *the transaction*. I mean this in two senses. First, as far as state agents are concerned, there is no market transaction if there is no receipt. That state agents (and everyone else) know very well that transactions occur without receipts thus mobilizes a great deal of suspicion about "informality" and presents the forensic problem that the *¡Pida su factura!* campaign seeks to redress via a totalizing gaze that can see all of the economy in action and measure it. Second, the receipt is itself a certain kind or category of transaction in the sense that the receipt constitutes a relationship to the state and its bureaucratic apparatus that would not otherwise exist. Receipts accede to authority and concede a part of one's business and finances to the state, involving the market participant in the system of taxation and governance. The push for the use of receipts asks citizens to account for themselves and their habits—to monitor themselves ("Did I forget to ask for a receipt?") in such a way that ritualizes acknowledgment of the state's sovereign capacity and right to tax citizens and that projects state-citizen relations into the future, to a time when the state will ask for what it is due, and conjures an imagined horizon of a more developed, formalized, rationalized, and modern national economy.

The SAT's elaborate and expensive campaign to encourage fiscal compliance has included information sessions for business owners and consumers regarding their tax obligations, brochures distributed to foreign travelers on arrival at the international airport, online educational materials that explain business and tax law, and stickers distributed to retailers around the country that remind the consumers who patronize them to ask for a receipt. The agency has also produced a children's television series that "promotes citizenship values in childhood through the adventures of a group of animals that live in the jungles of Petén [a tropical region of northern Guatemala] and decide to found an ecological park" (Superintendencia de Administración Tributaria 2014b). Each episode is hosted by Simón Tax, a character whose given name, Simón, is also slang for "yeah" in Mexican and Guatemalan Spanish, and who is the cartoon face of the Cultura Tributaria initiative on the SAT's Facebook page and in printed materials. The inclusion of an educational component addressed to children fits with the state's framing of tax evasion as a problem of culture and bad habits, with blame for the country's fiscal shortfalls placed on an uneducated populace that does not understand the importance of formality and taxation. As I noted in chapter 1, this framing overlooks the fact that some citizens might not pay taxes because it does not make sense to them to give money to a state that has such a horrific history of violence, terror, and corruption. The cartoon series encourages children to see taxation as a routine part of citizenship, one linked with other modern, progressive ideals, including entrepreneurship, environmentalism, and stewardship over natural resources and national patrimony. These links are forged via the animals' efforts to found an ecological park in Petén, a rain-forested province that is home to tremendous biodiversity and the world-renowned Classic Maya archaeological site Tikal, the country's most popular tourist destination, the gigantic stone pyramids of which serve as a powerful symbol of the nation's indigenous past and cultural richness and are a source of nationalist pride. What the cartoon series ignores and elides are the politics of capitalist exploitation and government corruption that actually surround the Petén region, where state-led development initiatives, turf wars being fought by drug cartels, and the interests of multinational corporations in mining, logging, and intensive agriculture all contribute to resource depletion and environmental degradation and threaten the lives and livelihoods of Q'eqchi' Maya and other populations that reside in the province. The story is, of course, much more complicated and the state and capitalist enterprise much more deeply imbricated than the cartoon series, which frames environmental stewardship as a cultural value best realized through formal market participation, lets on.

A set of television ads round out the SAT's *¡Pida su factura!* campaign, each ad portraying a commercial setting where the receipt functions as the climax of the economic transaction. In a twenty-second spot titled "Gasolinera," a gas station attendant prematurely announces that a much lighter-skinned, attractive woman behind the steering wheel of a late-model SUV has been *servida* (served). Her initial word of thanks is followed by an expectant look as she wonders why he is taking so long with her receipt. A voice-over accompanies his goofy smile and enraptured stare, revealing that the source of his distraction is not the customer's fine physical features and looks, as the camera initially seems to indicate, but rather her sleek automobile: "¡Qué camionetona! Pero cuánto hará por galón?" (What a truck! But I wonder how many [kilometers] to the gallon it gets?) The slippage between the woman's physical appearance and the Jeep's captivating body brings the *factura* problem into comic relief. The joke plays on stereotypes about the hypersexuality of underclass men and their hypermasculine obsessions with pretty women and powerful cars, setting up a scenario where questions of economic inefficiency related to gasoline consumption are also about the inefficiencies of informal economic activity and the problematic culture of unprofessional, racialized service workers. Business owners and their bumbling employees, the story goes, are reluctant to provide receipts, and their habits are rooted in cultures of ignorance, distraction, and perhaps envy. Service workers like the hapless gas station attendant, part of the lower rungs of a "developing" economy, are blamed for slowing down the market and hindering movement and progress and are pressed to change themselves into professional, responsible members of society who are not distracted by things they cannot have. At the same time, the ad urges consumers, represented as white, affluent, and objects of social aspiration (i.e., role models), to demand proper business behavior. "Don't wait. Ask for your receipt!" the ad prompts the impatient driver and the public. Consumers are encouraged to rise above the informality and unprofessionalism that characterize the retail environment and take responsibility for the economy by insisting on documentation.

The campaign's messages about consumer agency and responsibility resonate with how Maya apparel producers and other indigenous business owners in Tecpán talked about *facturas*. I spent an hour in early 2009 talking with the Kaqchikel Maya proprietor of a successful restaurant located in the town center. The owner's two daughters were regulars at the English classes I offered at the public library, and I stopped in occasionally to get a bite to eat and the word on the local business climate. One day, I asked him about taxes, noting the *¡Pida su factura!* sticker affixed to the restaurant's front door:

> The vendors in the streets, they don't pay taxes, and the SAT doesn't monitor [*control*] them. The only thing they pay is the fee charged by the municipal government, which is five quetzales. The vendors in the market, the ones who set up everyday and sell secondhand clothes and sandwiches [*shucos*] and all that, they pay 150 [quetzales] for the town's permission. That's what they pay, but they don't pay anything to the SAT. The businesses that are established, they pay taxes to the SAT. They have to use receipts and be in total compliance with the law, either as a small enterprise or large [*contribuyente pequeño o grande*, the legal terms that designate differential tax rates]. But it's up to the person who owns the business. In my case, I have this business and the one on the corner and a bakery down the road . . . and I have three receipt books, one for each business. And that's how it is.

I asked him how long he had been in business and how he was able to register with the SAT, a process he explained in great detail. He then added: "Here in Guatemala, anybody can issue a receipt. Most people don't ask for them, honestly. [Business owners] don't make them openly available when they sell something, so you have businesses that don't always give them; only if the customer asks them for one. So in restaurants they don't always give receipts, and the same all around town, they rarely give them. [Consumers] don't ask for them."

His comments were about the role of the consumer but also about the differences in state levels of *control*—the monitoring activities carried out by state agents and the potential for state interference that make evasion and concealment more or less difficult for differently positioned business owners operating larger or smaller businesses. The distribution of receipts is also predicated on economic and moral reasoning that has to do with different categories of consumers and transactions. Time spent in the notions and thread shop of another businessman in Tecpán revealed local patterns of record keeping premised on regular interaction and implicit understandings about who needs receipts and who does not. When I spoke with the shop owner about receipts, he told me, "If someone asks for one, we give it to them." As I hung around the shop making conversation with him and his wife and playing games with his youngest children, I noticed that *no one* asked for a receipt when purchasing zippers, buttons, or spools of thread. Most people who stopped in were owners of small apparel workshops, looking for supplies, men whom I recognized from my surveys and interactions. Occasionally, an out-of-towner who was in Tecpán for market day would come in to pick up something on his way home to a neighboring town or hamlet, making conversation about the heavy traffic on Tecpán's narrow streets. Receipts did not get mentioned during these transactions. In fact, the owner issued receipts only to the larger workshops that I knew operated with business licenses and that employed accountants to assist them with their trimestral and quarterly tax payments. These workshop owners rarely came to the shop in person but rather sent low-level employees to pick up supplies. The employees made no mention of receipts during the ordering and payment process, but the shop owner and his wife knew to issue receipts to them. The issuing of receipts had to do with the size and formal organization of the particular customer's business. On the top sheet of a thick pad of receipt forms, the supplies distributor would scribble the date and registered business name and then enter the items and quantities ordered on the ledger lines with accompanying prices, totaling everything at the bottom. He left the line for the business's tax identification number (Número de Identificación Tributaria, or NIT) blank, presumably since the employee did not know it and the workshop owner or his accountant could fill it in later. The top copy went with the workshop employee, and the store's owner flipped the carbon transfer paper and carbon copy over to reveal the next clean sheet.

When receipts are issued in the apparel trade, they usually end up in the hands of accountants who have been hired by businesses and workshops to sort the pieces of paper and determine the amount of taxes owed each tax period. There is one accounting office in Tecpán that advertises such services on its painted façade, but there are other people who work as accountants for business owners around town as well. A high school diploma in accounting is the basic requirement for working in that profession, and although high school education is out of reach for most Guatemalans, a number of apparel-manufacturing families have accountants among their kin or associates. While accounting services are integral to the functioning of more formalized workshops in the apparel trade, the profession of accounting is also more generally seen in terms of economic achievement and livelihood related to the development industry. People in Tecpán talk about accounting as a sensible degree for young *tecpanecos* to obtain, not so much because the regional apparel trade would provide aspiring accountants with work but because the manifold NGOs operating in the highlands hire local accountants to assist with their bookkeeping and reporting, especially as these organizations open up local offices, integrate themselves into communities around the highlands, and come to depend on local knowledge, language skills, technical know-how, and personal relationships with residents for their daily functioning.

As noted above, business owners around town used the Spanish term *control* to describe the state's monitoring of business activities and the use of receipts. They also described the work of accountants as a kind of *control* exercised over paper and numbers. The restaurant owner introduced above, for example, had this to say about his accountant:

> Those who have accounting businesses, they're the ones that have control over and manage [*llevan control*] the receipts and all of that. You have to give them the receipts so that they can total your sales receipts, your purchase receipts. . . . That's what they do. They add it up and that's how you know how much you have to pay [in taxes]. A lot of people don't pay anything. And the taxes change, too, and it's all according to a percentage that you're supposed to pay.

His use of the word *control* to specify the work of counting and accounting signals both the managerial responsibility and regulatory role that accountants have over financial matters and the responsibilities accountants have that are related to managing the state-citizen relationship. Apparel producers who operated relatively formal workshops indicated to me that accountants need some receipts for every tax period, although not every transaction is being documented and much of the business thus happens off the books. Without some receipts, however, accountants would have no way to demonstrate a workshop's legitimacy to state agents and protect it from audits and accompanying problems. The practice of issuing receipts for some transactions but not all—either only when a customer asks for one or when a pattern of documentation has been established as part of an ongoing business relationship, as in the case of suppliers who routinely issue receipts to larger-scale producers—ensures that enough receipts circulate to protect registered businesses from state interference but also that tax payments will stay as low as possible. Thus, this is an economic sector in which control is negotiated by maintaining a measured acknowledgment of the power of state extraction and a modicum of formal business style while also limiting the extent of what is being reported, as a means of minimizing extraction. As the owner of the notions and thread shop stated, "The taxes are high, and since our profits are so small—we make a few quetzales here and nothing more—we just give receipts to those who want them." This logic of issuing receipts only to those who ask for them fits with a focus on the consumer as the encouraged and empowered agent of formalization in the state's *¡Pida su factura!* campaign, even though these apparel producers could offer receipts for all transactions and adopt the kind of business ethics that the campaign invests with meaning and value—that is to say the ethics of professionalism and responsibility that the "Gasolinera" ad juxtaposes with the laziness and distraction of the gas station attendant. The reason that they do not do so is because they are not audited, there are not extensive risks involved in evading these areas of law and regulation, and they operate in a context of state mistrust coupled with slim profit margins and minimal socioeconomic opportunity.

Not always issuing receipts also makes moral sense to business owners because it is seen as a way of protecting the purses of one's clients. The owner of one of the largest apparel workshops in Tecpán told me that receipts are helpful to some and harmful to others, so business people have to take into account the economic situation of their customers when determining whether or not paper has a role in a given transaction. Eduardo Campos, about forty years old, was unique insofar as his large-scale manufacturing business was not inherited. He founded the business in the mid-1990s, after selling off a parcel of family-owned land, and has focused his efforts on the school uniform market. In 2009, he owned two multistory buildings on the outskirts of town, each of them housing about twenty employees working at sewing machines and industrial cutting and ironing equipment, and one of them also equipped with a set of computerized embroidery machines used primarily for emblazoning school insignia on sweaters, t-shirts, and polo shirts, although Eduardo also fills orders from other apparel producers for embroidering popular brand names and sports team logos on clothing they make. Young men ran the embroidery machines, their workspace decorated with pinups from the national tabloid newspapers and photos of Ferraris and Corvettes. A mix of teenage and twenty-something men and women operated the sewing, cutting, and ironing stations, which were free of adornment and organized into rows of small tables with hard wooden chairs. One of the buildings seemed unfinished. The concrete stairs leading from the embroidery machines on the lower level to the sewing stations above lacked a railing, and plastic sheets were draped over the upstairs windows in a halfhearted attempt to keep out mountain breezes and dust from the unpaved road below.

Receipts are an essential and strategic technology in Eduardo's particular line of work. Public and private schools alike need receipts to document expenses and substantiate funding. Eduardo often contracts directly with school principals or with the teacher appointed to the task of securing uniforms for the school year, which begins in January in Guatemala. It would be impossible for him to secure uniform contracts if he did not issue receipts to the school administrators or teachers when he delivered their orders. Sometimes, Eduardo explained to me, the school administrators do not want to get involved in contracting for uniforms, so they put a committee of parents in charge of the task. This committee then engages a workshop owner to make the uniforms and informs the families of the schoolchildren that they can buy the uniforms directly from the specified vendor. Eduardo noted to me that this system allows both the school and the parents committee to "wash their hands" of the responsibility of documenting the uniform purchases and sales, as it is the individual families who buy the uniforms. "All of this [the uniform business] has to have legal invoicing [*facturación*]," he said, "and if it's found that [the parents committee] doesn't have receipts, well, then they have legal problems, and no one wants that." Private schools, which are under the watch of the SAT and the NGOs that fund them, that sell uniforms without issuing receipts can be fined or shut down, and the administrators of public schools that engage in this practice could get in trouble with the Ministry of Education and possibly lose their jobs, Eduardo speculated. A parents committee might not want to issue receipts to individual families, however, because, Eduardo continued, "The situation is that people who have limited resources, who are poor, receipts don't do anything for them. . . . So most people in the highlands don't ask for a receipt. We're talking about maybe 70 percent who don't ask for receipts and 30 percent who do.

But, here, we issue receipts to anyone who asks. We don't go around refusing to give receipts." When a school, parents committee, or workshop owner issues a receipt to a poor parent purchasing a school uniform for his or her child—and the majority of the parents in highland Guatemala are poor, Eduardo points out—it requires that a value-added tax be included in the transaction cost, such that not issuing a receipt saves the parent money. They do not have to pay the tax because there is no receipt. And whereas a school administrator or parents committee would have to issue a receipt to each individual parent in order to avoid the risk of getting the school in trouble with the SAT, private funders, or the Ministry of Education, Eduardo has some degree of flexibility when deciding whether to document a particular transaction. Like other large-scale workshop owners, he needs to have enough receipts on hand to satisfy SAT agents who could show up at any time to perform an audit, but he can forego receipts when it benefits a poor client or consumer.

Eduardo's explication of how and when receipts are used in the school uniform trade and the other examples given above demonstrate that there is more to taxation, formalization, and the issuing or withholding of receipts than the degree to which a business person is or is not "professional" in his dealings. Professionalism, as understood among business owners in Tecpán, more interestingly and complexly rests on knowing whom receipts will help and whom they might hurt. In other words, it involves moral and socioeconomic considerations as well as considerations of the law. The reluctance to issue receipts is not just about getting away with not paying taxes but also about protecting the pocketbooks of small businesses and individual consumers in a context where most people are poor and the potential benefits of pooled tax revenues in terms of public investment in infrastructure and education—the logic behind why citizens are obligated to pay taxes to the state—are not obvious to indigenous people, who have little faith in the state given a history of violence and corruption and the realities of lacking state services and resources in their communities. When citizens see a dearth of public schools, healthcare services, and other public institutions, taxation seems like a purely extractive practice that does not deliver them any benefits. Maintaining flexibility and a degree of discretion in relation to recordkeeping and reporting—that is to say, not giving the trade over entirely to the demands of the state—allows considerations other than bureaucratic compliance to shape market interactions and protects a sense of community that apparel producers and others in

Tecpán value, because in protecting small businesses and poor clients and consumers, producers are benefitting these groups in ways that the state does not.

KEEPING ACCOUNTS

At the level of state government, receipts are a medium through which fiscal responsibility, enforcement obligations, and police authority are configured. The government's media campaign casts a shadow over business owners and service workers who do not automatically issue receipts and enlists citizens as fiscal enforcers and moral reformers. Delegating fiduciary responsibility to consumers—a liberal solution to the problem of limited state resources for business oversight and tax collection—also bypasses the issue of corruption in law enforcement and other state institutions. The state mobilizes culturalist discourses of unprofessionalism and cultural backwardness and itinerancy to legitimize state sovereignty over economic practices and promote hegemonic development industry logics related to formalization (Roitman 2005) and focus critical attention on the point of sale—that is, the producer-consumer relationship—rather than on the state itself, the composition of the society or economy, or the state and development industry's role in structuring the economy in particular directions that have produced a situation of deep inequality. These deflections of attention and rerouting of responsibility away from the state became untenable in April 2015, when an investigation led by the International Commission Against Impunity in Guatemala (CICIG), an agency established by the United Nations in 2006 to facilitate Guatemalan criminal prosecutions and encourage public trust in the country's judicial system, exposed a customs fraud ring that initially implicated senior officials and various managers at the SAT as well as Vice President Roxanna Baldetti and her top aides, all of whom were arrested on fraud and conspiracy charges. Massive popular protests in the wake of the arrests eventually led to the resignation of President Otto Pérez Molina, who was moved from the presidential palace to the jailhouse in early September 2015, where he was detained until the full hearing on his involvement in the multimillion-dollar fraud case could be concluded. It is too soon at the time of this writing to know whether CICIG's investigations and the pending prosecutions of state officials will be enough to curb institutionalized corruption in Guatemala. However, as other anthropologists have pointed out (Herzfeld 1992; Strathern 2000), even if the crackdown on corruption is successful, the idiom of audit—through which the state-citizen relationship is articulated in the modern nation-state—allows governments to continuously defer and evade responsibility to their citizens while, at the same time, calling citizens to account.

Audit is a form of risk management (Shore 2008). In one formulation, this means that accounting and evaluation are tools through which states and other organizations manage the dangers (Douglas 1992) associated with their modern institutional structures. These dangers—which include corruption, crime, and abuse of power—are said to exceed or escape informal trust relations and thus necessitate strict, standardized, bureaucratic oversight involving reporting, auditing, and accounting (Power 1994: 11; Beck et al. 1994). In another formulation, audit is said to manage risk by institutionalizing techniques of self-discipline among those subjected to audit, since these individuals internalize the bureaucratic performance measures as actually saying something about their own moral and professional worth. People come to consider themselves as "auditees" (Shore 2008: 281) and hold themselves and others to account through a process of subject formation, and this changes how people see and monitor themselves—how they behave and interact—in contexts of bureaucracy and surveillance (Foucault 1990; Strathern 2000). In Guatemala, both of these explanations of the functions of audit hold true to varying degrees. Citizens and activist groups that advocate state accountability and transparency, pushing for criminal investigations, audits, and open access to state documents and reporting, point to ongoing corruption and the government's gross violations of human rights, past and present, to argue for the need for further and intensive oversight and auditing. State agencies, including the SAT, publicize their commitment to transparency and make an overwhelming volume of documents and reports available on their websites and in their offices as a way of performing accountability and cultivating trust. As Rachel Dotson (2014) demonstrates in her study of an antipoverty initiative funded by the Guatemalan government, transparency discourse can also have the effect of focusing bureaucratic attention on the act of reporting while little regard is paid to the actual, material impacts of a program or project. The processes of quantifying performance, conforming to measurable standards, and publishing results become goals in and of themselves, while individual citizens who are the recipients of funding or support from state and NGO programs are rendered susceptible to increasing suspicion and surveillance in the name of improved, more precise measurement and reporting, even in the absence of clear material benefits to those individuals themselves (Dotson 2014).

Managing risk is also about managing blame (Douglas 1992). Audit may distribute blame across organizations or lay it at the feet of a single scapegoat, but the question of who is responsible for an outcome and what kind of response is thus merited is integral to audit's structure and function. In the highland apparel trade, the risk of being audited by state agents powerfully contours producers' relationships to receipts, but not in the ways that state agents might expect. As we have seen, the possibility of audit does not push all producers to adopt formal accounting practices, and this is not simply or solely related to lax enforcement. Rather, apparel producers in Tecpán assess the risk of audit and legal penalties in relation to other commitments that matter to them, including the moral value of protecting other producers, clients, and poor customers from what they perceive to be unwarranted extraction by the state. When a workshop owner does find himself the subject of a SAT investigation, a second-order forensics of blame is also triggered as he tries to determine how and why he was targeted when others were not. Producers understand that the SAT tends to target larger businesses with more visible market presence, but this is not always a satisfactory explanation since not all large workshops are consistently audited. Some producers thus look to community-level social dynamics in order to piece together the full story.

As we conversed in his office, Moisés Guzman assured me that his business was completely formal and legal. "I run a big business," he explained. "I have my accountant and my business license, and everything, everything, I have is declared with the SAT. Including my cars. Everything is there because I did a physical inventory, and I had to put everything in there, how much it cost, and all of that." Like at the all-male workspace of Eduardo Campos's embroidery shop, the walls of Moisés's office were plastered with photos of fancy sports cars, framed for safekeeping, and a few soccer posters. A picture of him with his wife and two children sat on his polished wooden desk, and binders that held several years of invoices made a pile in the corner. Moisés was frequent fodder for the local rumor mill. With his two-story home, two late-model cars (one of which was a shiny black SUV), and "fancy" way of dressing, his peers considered him to be suspiciously *medio-ladino* (see chapter 2). His office was inside his spacious house, and his workshop occupied the entire first floor and a large building in back. His family lived upstairs. His employees ran knitting, sewing, and embroidery machines, and he worked primarily on a contract basis with schools, local and national sports teams, and government agencies.

Moisés, like many producers with whom I spoke about accounting practices, had varied explanations for why he documented his sales and paid taxes. He moved fluidly among these rationales during my inter-view with him. He communicated a sense of pride in the professional-ism with which he manages the operation and called my attention to the workshop's size and scale of production, noting that "big businesses" like his have to pay taxes. Before explaining why, he changed direction, stating that he pays taxes because "it's the law." If not for the threat of legal action against his "big business," he contended, he would avoid taxes, just as most other producers do:

> Because it would be better for me to not pay taxes, not pay the accountant, and not have to declare all of my property. . . . Obviously, it's expensive [to pay taxes], and that's why people don't apply for business licenses. I know a lot of workshops that don't have a license because you have to pay an accountant to do your accounting, your paperwork, and it's not just the accountant. The accountant doesn't really charge that much. He gets two hundred or three hundred quetzales. But you have to use receipts. I mean, when you register with the SAT, you're then obligated to use receipts. . . . For all of your sales, you have to give [the client or customer] a receipt, but with every receipt, you're paying taxes. I buy something, I'm paying the IVA [*impuesto al valor agregado,* or value-added tax, which is supposed to be added to every sales transaction and paid by the consumer], and when I sell, I have to pay taxes at the end of the month. And this is what people don't like.

Moisés explained that there are clear, financial reasons for why many producers choose not to register their businesses, hire accountants, or pay taxes. With the next breath, he shifted the conversation again, this time from the practical pursuit of profit to the metaphysics of religion and society. He claimed that, while others didn't like paying taxes, he didn't mind:

> First, God has blessed us with a big workshop. If the SAT comes here and asks for my business license . . . because a lot of people are jealous [*envidi-osa*], and one time, they sent the SAT after me. I don't have a sign out front or anything. But all of a sudden, they knocked on my door, he [one of the agents] had my name [and said], "Look, they told me that you have a big business here." "Come on in," I said. "Can we see your business license?" So I got my papers and called the accountant, and he had everything. "Oh, okay," they told me. But somebody sent them.

In this conversation, Moisés partly defined his relationship to the state in terms of the antagonism he has experienced within his own production community. Apparel producers are suspicious of Moisés, interpreting his business success as ethnic and community betrayal and his class status as a threat to regional solidarities. It is interesting to note that Moisés did not counter local suspicions about his success with diatribes on hard work and perseverance. He works hard, but so do other manufacturers who do not have fancy cars to show for it. But Moisés explained that he is "blessed," layering the fervor of neo-Pentecostal Christianity onto the moral cosmology of the regional economy. "It's good to pay [taxes]," he continued. "It's good because the Bible says that Jesus paid his taxes. . . . He paid his taxes, and the Bible says that you have to contribute to the state." Moisés is a prominent member of Tecpán's growing Evangelical Protestant community. It is difficult to ascertain what percentage of the town's workshop owners are similarly religiously inclined. Older manufacturers and those whose families started in the trade before the 1990s tend to identify as Catholic, but the younger generation across Guatemala is defined in part by the ascendance of Protestantism, generally of the fundamental and neo-Pentecostal variety (O'Neill 2009; Garrard-Burnett 1998). A few anthropologists have attempted to delineate distinctive economic values in the highlands according to religious affiliation (Goldín and Metz 1991; Goldín 1992). I did not survey broadly on this question, and I did not encounter obvious patterns that linked either business style or economic ideology to religious belief. Moisés's direct invocation of the Bible may typify a certain Evangelical relationship to scripture, and he enjoyed telling me about the periodic visits to his home and his church of an Assembly of God pastor from the Midwestern United States, the kind of international partnership that has underwritten Guatemala's religious transformation. He placed a great deal of emphasis on his church's philanthropic outreach and missionizing to poor highland families. He expressed what might be called a "prosperity gospel" outlook on faith and business, a trend in transnational Protestantism that interprets financial success as a blessing received in return for one's faithfulness to God (Maxwell 1998). Moisés was not alone, however, among Protestants, Catholics, or those practicing Maya spirituality in grounding economic actions in the moral obligations of his faith and attributing positive economic outcomes to a spiritual force. Where economists might perceive the work of the metaphorical invisible hand, local business owners might see exploitation and the evil eye or the hand of God distributing spiritual and material blessings.

Moisés also diagnosed the financial audit of his apparel business that SAT agents carried out, which policy analysts might simply consider to have been an example of effective enforcement, as a symptom of widespread envy, that ubiquitous discourse that regulates economic and social life in the apparel trade in important ways (see chapter 2). His interpretation of how he came to be audited adds a layer of complexity to the commentary that he and other workshop owners commonly relayed to me regarding the need for "big businesses" to register with the state and issue receipts in order to avoid being audited and fined by a vigilant state. Moisés and other business owners recognize that having a large-scale operation with a visible market presence can put one at greater risk for state surveillance and intervention. At the same time, these men know that SAT agents do not know where most of the workshops are located. After all, Moisés does not have a sign out front that would make state agents aware of his business. The real reason that SAT agents knocked on his door that day, in his estimation, was thus that someone sent the agents to investigate him. Moisés sensed that he was at perpetual risk of such an investigation because having a "big business" not only makes one's enterprise more visible to state agents but also makes one a more likely target of local suspicions, envious stares, and, possibly, plots by neighbors to subject one's business to threatening forms of state *control* that could result in damaging fines or perhaps even jail time. A high degree of business success in the highlands often translates into moral insecurity, but not because of the competence of the state or the efficiencies of its bureaucratic apparatus. In Moisés's view, legal insecurity was a side effect of social relations organized by envy.

INSIDE THE NUMBERS

Although I found that Maya business owners did not generally avoid, withhold, or issue receipts for the reasons that the *¡Pida su factura!* campaign imagined, some apparel producers did talk to me about accounting practices in moral terms that resonated with the government's discourse around unprofessionalism. Here, then, I consider how accounting fits into the moral economy and changing milieu of gender and professionalism that is partly described in previous chapters. Receipts are part of a larger constellation of accounting techniques and practices that some apparel producers use to evaluate the business styles of their neighboring competitors. How a producer keeps records, figures profits, and sets prices—all of the counting and accounting work that is part of business ownership in the apparel trade—is understood by some manufacturers to demonstrate a person's moral sensibilities and their value to the project of community development, as well as their relationship to an emergent sense of entrepreneurial masculinity. Discussions I had with producers about the use of receipts in the trade often led to more extended conversations about accounting practices that were "accounts" and acts of "accounting" in and of themselves (Maurer 2002), offering insight into the politics of knowledge in Guatemala and the gendering of entrepreneurship in international development.

Maya manufacturers had a particular vocabulary for talking about their methods for determining prices and production levels and keeping accounts. Most producers I spoke with talked about doing *investigaciones* (research) or *estudios* (studies) to understand the market and make informed decisions about what products to offer and at what prices. Many noted that operating a workshop requires *análisis* (analysis) of the competition and consumer tastes. This research and analysis, they explained, involves watching what others are doing, taking careful notice of trends, listening to the comments of wholesalers about what consumers are asking for, and learning from one's mistakes. Manufacturers characterized their method of investigation as "empirical," based on experience. They emphasized that, in the apparel trade, one finds out what works and what does not by trial and error. "We don't have schools to learn how to make clothing," commented a small-scale manufacturer whose workshop sits on the outskirts of town. "Maybe in Italy or Spain they have institutes just for learning about the textile industry. But, here, we do things empirically." His talk about empirical knowledge had the tone of a defensive commentary on the perseverance and aptitude of small producers. As noted, indigenous people have largely been denied access to formal educational institutions in Guatemala. With similarities to the artisanal context Michael Herzfeld (2004) studied in Crete, Maya manufacturers made it clear to me that academic instruction would be a poor mode of preparation for the highland marketplaces where most of them earn their livings and where interpersonal skills and reputation are understood to be what really matter, even if, as explored in chapter 3 and discussed further below, access to higher education is part of how certain producers are positioning themselves in terms of claims about professionalism and modernity.

One skill that producers claimed to learn empirically was how to *hacer sus cuentas,* which means to keep accounts, to do one's accounting, or to do the math. The phrase was used to talk about the ability to figure how much it costs to produce a particular garment in order to determine a price point for it that would yield a reasonable profit. Producers explained to me that there are relatively fixed costs for electricity, cell phones, labor, and transportation and variable costs for yarn, thread, fabric, and notions associated with garment manufacturing. There is also the cost of machinery and its depreciation and the upkeep of buildings to consider. Some manufacturers also put aside savings for future capital investment. Any and all of these costs figure into how much a garment costs to produce. Many manufacturers alleged that their neighbors—and especially the owners of smaller workshops and more rural workshops—either did not know how to figure costs accurately or simply did not bother with this aspect of accounting. The owners of small, rural workshops got cast as less knowledgeable and less skilled along a continuum of professionalism that encoded class and cultural distinction. But stereotypes about the "city" and the "country" (Williams 1977) that are pervasive cultural frames in Guatemala (O'Neill and Thomas 2011) also revealed sympathetic affective relations among manufacturers who have understood their trade as a form of community in and of itself.

Florencio Pérez raised the issue of *cuentas* as we made the predawn drive to San Francisco El Alto in his microbus. His family had been selling sweaters in the western highland wholesale market twice per week for more than thirty years. His father and brother met us there, helped set up the wooden table and its tarpaulin roof, spread out the week's selection of men's and children's designs, and spent the rest of the day drinking coffee and *atol,* chatting with other producers, and haggling with potential buyers. The printed labels inside the sweaters' collars bore the family surname, a practice Florencio's father instituted in the late 1970s. The basic look of their wares—dark, deep hues of blue, grey, maroon, and brown woven into geometric patterns that circled the bodice and sleeves—had not changed in two years, Florencio told me. But the sweaters had been selling relatively well and were immediately recognizable to their clients as decent quality goods from the Pérez workshop in Tecpán.

The Pérez family members worked as *mayoristas* (wholesalers) in San Francisco, selling their sweaters by the dozen to *minoristas,* the people who work as vendors in consumer markets around the highlands where they sell the sweaters to individual clients. Most apparel producers from Tecpán do not work as wholesalers. They generally focus on manufacturing and travel to the markets in San Francisco (open on Wednesday, Thursday, and Friday) and other trading centers around the highlands to market their goods to the wholesalers who set up tables there. After the producers make their rounds early in the morning, showing off their latest designs, negotiating prices, and dropping off orders, *minoristas* arrive to browse the latest offerings on display at the wholesalers' tables and make their purchases.

I asked Florencio about the use of receipts in the wholesale market, a question that he brushed aside as irrelevant. Having your receipt book with you on the highway is important, he noted, because of police stops, but sales in the market are recorded in a notebook, not on printed invoices. Indeed, each of the producers I traveled with to highland markets used a hardbound notebook, the kind available at school supply and photocopy shops in Guatemala, to make a careful record of wholesale transactions. Wholesalers take a producer's goods on consignment. As manufacturers pass from table to table once a week to offer their products to the wholesalers, they also collect the debts owed to them according to how much of the previous week's (or month's) product the wholesalers have been able to sell to the *minoristas*. Producers use the notebooks to keep track of the wholesalers' debts to them; they write down the value of the goods consigned and the amount of each payment received and usually ask the wholesaler to initial beside the new outstanding balance. This "formal" accounting system produces a reliable transaction record, but it has no legal weight. If a wholesaler refuses to pay his or her debt to a producer (or alternatively return unsold goods, which is, in any case, a much less desirable outcome, financially as well as morally and emotionally, for producers since it means their styles did not sell), there is little that he can do except to continue to request payment and refuse to consign any additional products to that wholesaler. Spreading the word about a wholesaler's unsavory practices or refusal to pay within a reasonable amount of time, or at all, can either work to a producer's benefit or backfire, insofar as the producer's inability to collect his debts might be taken as evidence of his lack of business acumen rather than of the wholesaler's untrustworthiness.

Florencio mentioned the ubiquitous notebooks and then the problems he perceived with what gets recorded in them. Wholesalers aim to obtain garments at the lowest possible price; that's the nature of their business, he explained. But producers have to know what their lowest price is and not go below it just to move product. "We have maintained our prices at a level that we can sustain," he continued, "but other people lower their prices just to be able to sell. Not many people maintain their prices. There are even products out there selling at half of what we charge for what we make." I wondered aloud how his family was able to compete with other workshops given that other producers sell clothing for much less. He replied that it was impossible and then walked me through some of the details of setting prices:

> The thing is that there are small workshops, kind of like ours, and we work as a family too, but we take out salaries for ourselves. Other people just work for the profits they earn. So let's say they make eight quetzales per dozen [sweaters], and let's say that they sell twenty dozen per day when they go out to sell. With whatever they earn, that's 160 quetzales, and they settle for that [*están conformes*]. But we pay laborers, and we take out salaries to keep ourselves up. We did the math [*hicimos las cuentas*] with one man from Xepac [a hamlet with several dozen clothing workshops] who was making six quetzales per dozen, and it's not that he was dealing in huge quantities, it's just that he wasn't figuring out how much it really cost him.

The "real cost" of business has a material referent for Florencio. He and his father and brother set the prices for their sweaters at a certain level to ensure that they are covering fixed and variable input costs, making enough to reinvest in production, and able draw a salary each week from their workshop, paying themselves for management and labor at a rate that they consider sufficient to make ends meet for their households. In contrast, Florencio indicated, the man from Xepac was selling at much lower prices because he was not including the price of his own labor or salary in the cost of production. In Florencio's estimation, that is not a sensible way to do business because six quetzales (less than US$1) in "profits" per dozen sweaters is not actually enough to buy more inputs for ongoing production and support basic household needs. The implication is that the man from Xepac probably believes that he is making money because he has cash in his pocket each week after selling a few dozen garments, but he is really losing money over the long term and doing business in a way that is not sustainable for his household or his workshop. Florencio's talk about "real cost" opened up a significant gap between his business style, on the one hand, and that of a workshop situated far from the town limits, on the other hand. In hamlets such as Xepac, he continued, producers operate *fábricas domésticas* (domestic workshops), a phrase that juxtaposes "domestic" operations with more "industrial" ones, like Florencio's. "Domestic" has many connotations in this context. Florencio explicitly defined domestic workshops as those that employ family members rather than non-kin wage laborers, insisting that, even though he and his father and brother work "as a family," they get paid. The belief that rural workshops charge less for their products because they use the household labor of husbands, wives, and children and do not treat their own or their family members' time as a commodity, therefore failing to consider the "real cost," was expressed to me by many workshop owners in Tecpán's urban core. The wherewithal to count one's time as productive, recognize its value, and charge a premium for it counts in some producers' calculations as a sign of professionalism (materialized across the market through pricing) and a symbol of belonging to a more modernized, urban space and a production space—a factory—that is not tacitly gendered in terms of a domestic sphere.

The gendered connotations of paid labor are indeed evident in Florencio's claims about domestic and industrial production. It is not simply that women are associated with domestic space in Guatemala, as they are elsewhere, but that not counting one's time is understood in the highlands as a feminine way of interacting with the market. Men and women who work as *minoristas* selling traditional clothing in highland markets remarked to me that the financial ignorance of rural, female weavers who do not count the months of ten-hour days they invest in a *huipil* as part of the garment's value enables the vendors to pay them much less than they "really" deserve or even need to live. It is revealing that in the gendered, oral history of Tecpán's apparel trade, different types of machinery are coded as either "domestic" or "industrial," reflecting not only changing technologies but also a divide between the country and the city. Until at least the 1960s, rural women used knitting machines to make clothing for their families. Those machines are now read as simple technologies because they required manual labor, whereas later models were electric and then computerized. The apparel trade, or as many producers term it, the *industria textil* (textile industry), was born of male ingenuity when the latent potential of these "domestic" machines was harnessed by male operators and reoriented toward mass-market production. This transformation took place in the hamlets but then moved to the town center for reasons discussed in chapter 1. Some male producers therefore seem to occupy the liminal position of participating in an "industry" in ways that still situate them in the feminized, rural space of "domestic" work. They occupy the margins of intelligibility, being located in rural areas that seem to urban producers to be fundamentally different from Tecpán's urban core (i.e., traditional versus modern) and work according to feminine logics that defy rationalized modes of accounting and challenge the viability of the apparel trade for all producers by driving down prices across the marketplace.

Florencio was not finished discussing the problem of bad math. "It's hard to explain [real costs] to people in the hamlets," he bemoaned.

"There's another man from Xepac who brought huge bundles to sell in San Francisco. After a while, I heard that he had stopped selling. [Later, he started back up again, but to do so] he had to sell a cow to buy more thread. But he never raised his prices. He kept them just the same. Once he went through the value of the cow, he had to stop again. This is what happens, and it affects the market, affects it tremendously." I asked him if these people knew that they were losing money. "No, they don't know," he replied.

He told me that another man was selling hats at low, low prices, and when Florencio asked him how much he was making per dozen, the man replied that *había hecho sus cuentas* (he had done the math), a phrase intended to assure Florencio that he was indeed earning money on his sales. Florencio grabbed his calculator, and they ran the figures together, only to discover that the man was losing twenty-five centavos per dozen hats. "I have no idea what that man does now," he concluded, assuring me that the man could not possibly be sustaining a workshop.

Talk in the highland apparel trade about how people do or do not *hacer sus cuentas* sounds a lot like colonialist accusations about the irrationality of peasant and protocapitalist economies and current instantiations of such thinking in technocratic politics and development discourse. For example, the manager of a commercial microcredit organization with offices around the highlands explained to me that getting his clients to "keep their books" is essential to his organization's mission. The microfinance model promoted by Muhammed Yunus and exemplified by his Grameen Bank in Bangladesh—which has come to define a dominant approach in global development—rests on the notion that the provision of financial products and services, especially microcredit (relatively small cash loans that typically do not require collateral), to underserved poor people has the potential to unlock their entrepreneurial spirit and untapped skills and thus allow them to lift themselves out of poverty through participation in small-scale enterprise. The Guatemalan microcredit organization that employed the manager I interviewed followed the Grameen model of loaning money to groups (rather than individuals), and especially groups of women, who, in Guatemala and on a global scale, have more limited access to banking and financial services than men. I initially got to know this manager over family dinners with his brother, a Maya apparel producer in Tecpán, and then set up a meeting at his office to learn more about microcredit.

During our interview, he talked about the "informality" of highland enterprise. "When a business is formal," he explained, "it has receipts [*facturas*], a business license, and declares its earnings with the SAT. But here, it's not like that. There are a lot of businesses that are like, they sell oranges, they buy them, they sell them, without even keeping their accounting books. They don't have the documents to grow a business." From his perspective, documents do not just record business activities; they also permit business itself. If women who sell oranges, chickens, or homemade bread do not keep accounts, they have no way of knowing if they are seeing profits or losses and no way to separate out household expenditures from business ones. They are apt to spend all of their money on "consumption," he continued, "to buy some clothes maybe, and then they're left once again with no capital."

Regardless of the fact that that many of his clients are illiterate, he blamed this perpetual lack of capital and surplus among highland households on a problematic financial culture, saying that the women refuse to change their habits and count, or become accountable, because they are tied to custom. The mandatory *capacitaciones* (educational workshops) that his office ran for each client group aimed to reorient them away from custom and toward impersonal market calculations about what they should sell, how they should market it, and how to tell if their businesses were doing well or needed to change. In the microfinancial world, such entrepreneurship training programs are seen as progressive efforts to address lack of business knowledge as a root cause of poverty, improve business performance, and increase client retention rates (Karlan and Valdivia 2011).

According to the training sessions that women's groups attend in highland Guatemala, calculators, pencils, and notebooks are the tools of economic success. These instruments are also integral to the process of transforming the women into proper market actors and converting the highland region into a business environment that "works" according to the standards of the international development industry. As Michel Callon (1998: 46) notes, "the extension of a certain form of organized market, an extension which ensures the domination of agents who calculate according to the prevailing rules of that particular market, always corresponds to the imposition of certain calculating tools." The microcredit manager in Tecpán explained to me that the goal of the workshops is to get the women to write things down. In turn, it is his hope that these acts of inscription prompt the women to think and act in ways that demonstrate concern for their children and for the future:

[The women] do things just to do them, because "that's how it's done." Another thing we see is that they are always thinking about what they're going to eat today—no matter the past, no matter what will happen in five years, what's going to come of their children, where they're going to live. But sometimes people only see what is in front of them today, and tomorrow they will work another day, and they keep up that routine. We try to pull them out of that a little bit so that they'll think more about the future.

The implication here is that poor women lack a "future orientation," as behavioral economists and psychologists have termed it, and thus have an improper orientation toward or underdeveloped ability to assess long-term versus short-term needs, desires, risks, and benefits (Camerer et al. 2004; Raynor 1969; Trommsdorff 1983; Nurmi 2005).[4] The act of inscription and the use of "calculating tools" are presumed to impel a new disposition and cognitive, behavioral, and affective relationship to the family, the market, and the state in ways that will permit the women themselves to become part of what counts—that is, to be among those who can be figured into GDP calculations and other measures of the national economy and indicators of development success—and what can, in the future imagined by economists and other development experts, be engaged, managed, and counted on for returns to capital and to national coffers.

The microcredit manager rounded out his assessment of the organization's clientele with what I took as a rather sympathetic turn of phrase: "Siempre se les hace mucha conciencia, pero a veces la necesidad es mucho más fuerte que la conciencia" (We always make them really aware [of the importance of planning], but sometimes necessity is a lot stronger than awareness). He used *conciencia* to refer to the specific information that the organization tries to impart to women about investing in their futures and the futures of their families. But the word carries significant moral and philosophical weight in Spanish, as it can also mean "conscience," "consciousness," and "awareness"—not just of facts or information but also the existential awareness of oneself as a subject. The juxtaposition of "necessity" with *conciencia* suggests that the women are engaged in a prototypical "bare life" struggle between the immediate pressures of survival and a set of higher order objectives promoted via the "emancipatory" politics of development (Comaroff 2007: 207; Agamben 1998; Biehl 2007). The manager tacitly acknowledged with this phrase that concerns over what to eat might actually have to come first for his impoverished clients and that the business knowledge that he and his team impart in training sessions and workshops is indeed and understandably secondary in importance for women whose daily struggles include thinking about and planning for basic subsistence. At the same time, the contrast he drew between *conciencia* and the immediate necessities that concern his clients seemed to discount the kinds of planning, awareness, and knowledge that poor women do, of course, actively engage in and draw on as part of their everyday lives, as well as the significance of that daily struggle for their families and futures. Indigenous women I got to know in Tecpán managed a complicated array of market activities—selling oranges, tending chickens, weaving and selling textiles, and taking out microfinance loans—in order to piece together a livelihood for their families with the explicit goal of ensuring that their children could attend school and not face the tremendous obstacles of illiteracy and poverty they themselves faced. These obstacles are rooted in the structural and endemic forms of inequality that disproportionately affect indigenous people in Guatemala and that have made Maya women particularly good candidates for microloans and other "development" interventions.

Complaints about rural apparel producers who do not (or do not know how to) *hacer sus cuentas* were also circumscribed with sympathetic addenda by Florencio and other urban manufacturers. Florencio often expressed great respect for those of his father's generation who had come from the hamlets to Tecpán to grow their businesses. He chuckled as he told me about the man who sold one cow after another to buy thread but never raised his prices. The story conjured a comical image for me of an old man treading the rural path from his home to market, an old, brown cow tethered close behind. For sure, there was frustration in the voices of garment producers when they talked about people who, however unwittingly, drive market prices below production costs, but there was also hilarity, incredulity, and empathy for these people, whom they understand as both part of and marginal to their own enterprises and communities. "How are they going to figure their costs?" asked a middle-aged producer with a few college courses in business administration under his belt. The rhetorical question followed a long explanation of the costs associated with sweater production and a series of comments on the fact that many people in the industry do not pay themselves or family members a salary. "People barely know how to read and write," he explained. "I've bought yarn before, and when it was time to get the receipt—and we're talking about people selling *to me*, the sellers—they don't know how to fill out the paperwork." The implication is that people who are in the business of selling inputs to garment manufacturers—people who own big stores situated in the center of town that supply yarn, sewing notions, and rolls of textiles to workshop owners—are higher up on the supply chain, presumably more urban and educated, and thus come ahead of him and other small-scale manufacturers in a chain of accounting and financial responsibility. If those input suppliers do not know how to complete the basic tasks associated with keeping accounts and documenting transactions, he reasoned, there could be no expectation that small-time, rural apparel manufacturers would be able to figure costs and work with receipts.

Apparel producers in Tecpán also diverted blame from their neighbors and more rural manufacturers when they cited wholesalers for instigating price-based competition through deceit. In response to a question about regional market competition, the owner of a midsized workshop explained to me how *mayoristas* in San Francisco El Alto, Cobán, Guatemala City, and other hubs in the garment trade pressure desperate manufacturers into lowering their prices. "Basically, it's the [wholesaler] who's in charge," he reasoned, explaining that the wholesalers are very clever and that they often tell apparel producers that someone else is selling to them at a lower price. The workshop owner may negotiate with the wholesaler a bit but will ultimately lower his price per dozen to make a sale that day. The next apparel producer who comes along will hear from the same wholesaler about the new, lower price on sweaters, and he will then have to decide whether to lower his prices or return home with a bag full of unsold merchandise. "That's why there are sweaters selling in San Francisco for thirty quetzales," he declared, adding that the people manufacturing those sweaters must be selling them for a meager fifty centavos above the cost of production. Perhaps some manufacturers can "get by" on those kinds of returns, he conceded, but he does not consider it to be a profit at all:

> The advantage [those manufacturers] have is that they pay their workers less, they don't have their own cars, pay taxes, report earnings, or use receipts. They don't have a landline [home or office telephone], buy computers, or new cell phones. The less they spend, the better. As long as they have food on the table, they're happy, everything's okay. Each person thinks about himself and does what he can do. But the problem is that the wholesaler always wants to make more money, so it affects all of us. It's normal, really. It's just the market.

What he described as the "advantage" that rural workshop owners have is the kind of *conformismo* that elicited both incredulity and sympathy from larger, urban producers. The term *conformismo*, often used by Tecpán's residents in conversations I had with them about rural life, indicated the willingness of poor, rural people to settle or make due with very little. Far from the "poor but happy" narrative evidenced in so many tourist and volunteer accounts of Third World travel (Crossley 2012), when apparel producers talked about *conformismo,* they were indicting the "individualism" of other producers, expressing frustration at people in their trade who think only about themselves. By concentrating on putting food on the table rather than covering the "real costs" of production and by settling for whatever wholesalers offer to pay rather than holding out for a price figured according to solid accounting techniques, rural producers were seen as lowering prices for everyone and forcing a race to the bottom across the industry. Urban, more educated producers thus faulted more rural producers for not thoughtfully and actively taking advantage of business opportunities to contribute to community-level collective development.

Although urban apparel producers blame small producers in marginal, rural areas for having conformist dispositions, they also extend some sympathy and understanding to these individuals insofar as the large producers are critical of the wholesalers and express a degree of affinity with the rural producers. They belong to the same industry after all, and it is an industry that has developed out of a shared history and ethnic community. The producer's comments cited above indicate a somewhat uneasy relationship to the capitalist marketplace, where urban and rural producers alike must make a living. On the one hand, he implies that spirited market participation and skillful management on the part of apparel producers could lift everyone up, a kind of "rising tide lifts all ships" understanding of business that is also a progress narrative about professionalization and consumer modernities, since rural producers are figured as people who settle for less because they do not use receipts or buy computers or the latest cell phones. On the other hand, "the market" impels just the kind of selfishness and individualism that ultimately threatens the apparel trade and community solidarity. *Mayoristas* embody the latter tendency. In conversations I had with manufacturers, they consistently characterized wholesalers as greedy, conniving, and savvy and blamed them for selfish market dealings in a way that they did not blame small-time, rural manufacturers. After all, if rural people think only of themselves, who can blame them? They are illiterate and so are unable to keep accounts, the story goes, and they need to sell in order to eat. It is the *mayoristas* who trick them into lowering their prices and foregoing reasonable profits. It is at this juncture, between a view of the market as inciting selfishness and a critical apprehension of "necessity" and "conformity," that urban producers who are better positioned and see themselves as more modern make claims about the importance of collective development and take distance from their rural neighbors and associates.

Another manufacturer helped to clarify for me how "the market" yields such intensive profit-seeking behavior among *mayoristas,* while producers will settle for next to nothing. It is, an anthropologist might say, a matter of structural position. This man talked about the fact that wholesalers have access to multiple producers with similar manufacturing capabilities, such that they are able to play producers off of one another. He said that wholesalers do not have to be honest with producers because producers do not have full knowledge of each other's transactions. That fact does not necessarily lead producers in Tecpán or me to agree with some economists that "imperfect information" is a cause of market inefficiency or socioeconomic inequality (Akerlof 1970; Stiglitz 1979; Rothschild and Stiglitz 1976), as if a perfect market could be achieved that would not result in such imbalances. To say that garment producers do not know the content of every market transaction in their trade is not a call for greater transparency, monitoring, or more efficient communication among producers, although highland garment manufacturers have made (unsuccessful) attempts to coordinate pricing in order to forestall discounting (see chapter 2). The fact that wholesalers have different information than producers matters to workshop owners simply because it helps to explain the differential influence on pricing that they perceive themselves as having in relation to wholesalers, a kind of inequality that they understand as fundamental to the market system rather than as a symptom of market imperfection.

From producers' perspectives, another structural factor that benefits wholesalers is that they operate relatively low-overhead, low-risk businesses. The same manufacturer pointed out that producers have to absorb costs that wholesalers will never incur:

> If I set a price for a sweatshirt I'm selling, and I'm making eight quetzales per sweatshirt, but overnight the cost of fabric goes up or there's some other setback—I get in an accident in my car, or a machine breaks—then I'm not making eight quetzales, I'm making six. If you're a *mayorista,* if you buy finished products to resell them, it's just a matter of buying and selling. Maybe you incur a loss if the product doesn't sell, but you just have to worry about buying things that are going to sell. All of your costs are fixed, and there's no other risk.

Talk about who does or does not *hacer cuentas* in the highland apparel trade is a complex idiom. These conversations are an expression of concern about the viability of an industry, a discourse about the cartography of class and educational status in Guatemala, a sensitive appeal to community and collective values, and a calculated complaint about how pricing works in a market economy. Apparel producers spoke about accounting from an uncomfortable location of residing in a society in which there is a perceived lack of "control," rampant impunity and physical and economic insecurity, and a history of violence, while their own commentaries about risk and blame sometimes mimicked colonial codes, brushing up against historical memory and contemporary experiences of discrimination and development that they would perhaps rather not propagate and that they would critique in other moments and in other ways. But questions of scale, place, price, and affiliation are thorny and demanded of these men a nuanced voice that articulated the uneven effects of capitalism alongside the enduring significance of socialized forms of fiscal and moral accountability.

SYSTEMATIZATION

For most apparel producers who *hacer cuentas* (keep the books and do the math), accounting work was routine, mundane, and unexciting. It was a drag to pay bills and pay taxes, write and request receipts, and keep track of employee hours and productivity. For example, Florencio complained to me about all the "little papers" he has to keep track of in order to *controlar* (control, manage) his labor costs. Every Monday, he gave each worker a piece of paper with the days of the week listed across the top. The employees were to record the hours they worked each day in the appropriate columns, and Florencio added up the hours each Saturday afternoon and paid the men accordingly. He was away from the workshop three or four days a week—buying inputs, selling merchandise, and collecting debts—and so relied on the employees' production levels as verification of the self-reported hours. There was also an employee who he was grooming to one day become a workshop owner in the apparel trade, and Florencio entrusted the young man to ensure that everything added up while he was away, a fact that illuminates the regulatory nature of apprenticeship in the industry. If the little papers and other "internal controls" (as he termed it) were a bother, Florencio also found them to be useful tools for business planning. He looked back at production and sales records often to make decisions about what products and designs to manufacture. "When you keep records . . . it makes things easier and also better," he concluded.

If anyone in the apparel trade demonstrated genuine enthusiasm for accounting, it was Bernardo Kej. In chapter 3, I described Bernardo's efforts to craft a unique brand out of his Kaqchikel Maya heritage using the latest marketing knowledge obtained from his university courses in business management. The brand was called Xarkar. Bernardo hoped to implement his branding strategy and marketing plans in the workshop that he and his father and brothers operated together. Apart from branding, the business plan he had been working on involved establishing new roles for Bernardo and his brothers within the organization, hiring and training new employees, and completely formalizing the workshop in line with state regulation. From his perspective, formalization was not just about using receipts, reporting sales, and paying taxes; it was also about accounting style. He wanted to manage the workshop's accounting in a "systematized" manner, using computer software to organize data and run reports in ways that made sense in light of his business education. Bernardo talked about this with me as an explicit move away from the "empirical" way of doing things that had long characterized the workshop's operations.

Although Bernardo's coursework inspired him to see his father's earlier, but defining, business style as antiquated and insufficient, the transformation he wanted to implement was also brought about by his everyday interactions with the material culture of state-regulated and techno-scientific accounting practice. More specifically, it was the materialization of accounting techniques via software programs that animated Bernardo, maintained his enthusiasm, and held out the promise of something new and better. Bernardo and I often talked in his father's workshop. One afternoon, we met for coffee at a *comedor* (eatery) in the center of town. He had finished his business plan just a few weeks before and was thrilled to share the details with me. After a half hour or so of talking about the plan, he insisted that I could not fully appreciate his vision unless we went to his house to review the project on his desktop computer screen. The machine was loaded with Microsoft Office products, some of them pirated copies bought on CD-ROM in local markets, and some of them free trials that he had downloaded from the Internet. At some point in his business studies at the university, he told me, he had come across the resume of the owner of a big company, and included in that man's list of qualifications was his mastery of Microsoft Project and Microsoft Visio. Bernardo immediately sought out the programs, read the online manuals, and developed his own business software expertise. He showed me a map he generated using Visio that illustrated the various phases of implementation for each business goal. He pointed to the dark blue rectangle in the far right of the screen, explaining that it was representative of the space and time when "it will be a profitable business, legally and organizationally formalized, focused on specific markets, with a marketing image." He continued, "If you have a formal business, it fills you with pride to say that you're part of it and that you're a business owner."

I asked Bernardo why he thought other apparel producers around town did not also "formalize" their operations, a process he had defined in terms of legal compliance with state regulations, including intellectual property law, but also the thoughtful, rationalized organization of work. He explained that it was difficult:

> I developed this project over three months, starting on it at seven in the morning. Before I knew it, it was one in the afternoon. I'd have lunch, wash the dishes, and that's it. By quarter to two, I was back at work. When I'd hear [my wife] at the door, it was already seven thirty. And the same the next day and the next. So, in the first place, there's the training. In the second place, one needs time, and when you are running a business, you can't make this kind of work a priority because you have to oversee the employees and figure out where to sell and keep everything going. You get used to doing things a certain way. So the time that I had enabled me to develop all of this.

The project had become an obsession over those three months, and his focus was trained on the visualization of his ideas as much as on the ideas themselves. After all, spreadsheets, maps, and flowcharts are design projects—aesthetic creations that demand the selection of color, shading, arrow shape, line width, font, and the appropriate spatial organization of data points. Each software program affords a particular kind of engagement with information, modeled in the instruction manual and elaborated across hours and hours of moving and clicking a mouse. Bernardo explained how it began:

> When I started the project and had the project in mind, I didn't know where to start. So I started with this chart. The first thing I did was a situational analysis of the current business, the business philosophy, where we were with our goals and objectives, including a general history of the company. I organized everything into an organogram of our organizational structure and then did a study of the market segment and its structure. We didn't have any of that: no sales analysis, product analysis, product description, analysis of the market cycle, consumer profile . . .

The list of what they did not have when he first undertook the project, and thus what Bernardo set himself the task of making, went on and on.

The components were gleaned from marketing textbooks and course notes. He had learned about organograms—a business education term for a chart that illustrates a company's organizational structure (reporting hierarchy, distribution of departments, titles, and responsibilities, and other relevant features)—in his classes, but he developed intimate familiarity with them by manipulating the lines and text boxes that are the bread and butter of the Microsoft Office suite. And, indeed, it was the technological interface—the digitized chart—that Bernardo felt had enabled him to move the project forward.

Bernardo's involvement with the material culture of "business" (I call attention here to the sense of "business" invoked earlier in this chapter by the microcredit agency manager, who implied that business does not exist apart from a formal accounting apparatus and technologies of inscription, accounting, planning, design, and management) shaped his experience of his family's workshop and his relationship to the highland apparel trade. Bernardo perceived moral distance between himself and the "pirates" who interact with computer technologies to "steal other people's brands," as he put it, rather than to "systematize" their businesses in line with technical-legal models of professionalism, a moral diagnosis that reflected the university training he had received as well as the material practices and aesthetic sensibilities in which he had immersed himself during the months he spent working on his project. "Ideas are material actions," writes Louis Althusser (1971: 168–169), "inserted into material practices governed by material rituals which are themselves defined by the material ideological apparatus from which derive the ideas of the subject." Receipts, notebooks, organograms, and spreadsheets are not self-evident tools of business administration. Their utility is not obvious to most business owners in highland Guatemala, and, regardless of this fact, they are not best understood as "passive tools" (Law 2002: 27) or "objects" (Law and Mol 1995) that some people use and some people do not. Rather, they are important "sociotechnologies" (Law 2002: 28) that become enmeshed with the very movement of people in a social field and produce effects in the organization of the practical world. These are technologies that, in the hands of Bernardo, are being used to contest aspects of the highland marketplace and engage in ongoing moral-economic struggles over the meaning, practice, and effects of enterprise in the highland region. They are artifacts of international development apparatuses premised on formal market participation, and they work alongside the Guatemalan state and higher education institutions to promote a professional style that systematizes, simplifies, quantifies, and sees new possibilities (Law 2002: 27–29). And across diverse contexts—from national media campaigns to the daily routines of highland manufacturers—they show up as techniques of regulation, discipline, and subject formation that structure economic life, market knowledge, and moral reasoning.

Max Weber's classic treatise, *The Theory of Social and Economic Organization,* includes extended discussions of the organizational effects of capitalist accounting. For him, money was the most basic accounting technique: "Accounting in terms of money . . . is thus the specific means of rational, economic provision" (Weber 1947: 186). Money provided the means for calculating, budgeting, and tracking the relationships between means and ends and between the present and future. He further emphasized, in ways similar to the microfinance manager introduced above, that an orientation toward capitalist accounting (and not just the search for profit) is what comprises an "enterprise" in capitalist society, although the presence of this orientation does not necessarily imply that the accounting is "in fact rationally carried out according to rational principles" (197). For Weber, a commitment to accounting also involved an estimation of the future potential of a market system (in the form of profit), and it was that focus on future potential that, in sociological terms, differentiated capitalism and its entrepreneurs from other sorts of market pursuits and market actors. Accounting, in other words, was a key mechanism in the orientation of capitalist entrepreneurs toward profit as an "ideal" and thus part of what constituted them as an ideal type with a particular moral purview and historical role in social organization.

Bernardo's ideals bumped up against his father's business style in ways that were sometimes uncomfortable for the young entrepreneur. He kept his business plan a secret from his father and brothers until it was perfected, at which point, several weeks after my visit to his home, he made a carefully prepared, digitally illustrated presentation to his male family members. The concealment up to that point was strategic. His father and older brother had been the primary decision-makers in the workshop, in keeping with local norms privileging birth order, age, and experience. He had not wanted to alarm his family prematurely about the new leadership and management role he envisioned for himself. Over dinner a few days after the presentation, I asked him how it had been received. "For my dad, at least, it hit him hard," he replied. "It was a lot for him—all that we needed to do, all of the changes. And what happens is that, since we're not accustomed to this way of thinking, my dad says to me, 'But how are we going to do this?' That's the question." In anticipation of his father's uneasiness about the changes, Bernardo had used Microsoft Visio to break the plan into discrete graphic phases that he felt would be more easily digestible. To forestall questions about the plan's financing, he had already secured a line of credit in his own name at one of the banks in town (although the loan depended as much on his wife's steady work at a government office in Guatemala City as the soundness of his plan). In spite of the fact that the presentation met with less resistance than he had feared, and he hoped to begin working toward the new business goals with his family's support, Bernardo expressed uneasiness about having challenged his father's business style so directly and incontrovertibly.

As we ate our dinner of beans and chorizo sausages and tortillas, he moved from telling me about his father's response to the presentation he had made to complaining about the fact that many of his professors had no real-world experience. They teach theories and tell the students how to run a business, he protested, but have never owned or managed a firm themselves. He picked up the refrains about empirical knowledge and the importance of understanding local markets that are central to how many apparel producers characterize their business style, refrains that are part of the longstanding heritage of the industry in the highlands and definitive of the older model of enterprise to which his father belongs. He expressed resentment toward the upper-class *ladino* men with whom he comes into contact in classrooms and on campus, who claim to know how to do things better than, say, Bernardo's father and other family members who had struggled and succeeded in building the apparel trade. But he maintained that work has to be "systematized" and insisted that the theories expounded in textbooks and classroom lectures about how that should be done are only useful when they are tested "empirically" and tailored to the specific contexts of production, marketing, and management in which he and his family worked.

After three months in front of a computer screen and in the wake of an intense and challenging conversation with his father and brothers, Bernardo was attempting to suture the divergent "calculative agencies" (Callon 1998) wrought through the methods and materials of "empirical analysis," on the one hand, and business education, on the other. His actions and comments draw attention again to the moral significance of business style. The ideals that he had come to espouse and the ideal type that he had come to embody through immersion in the techniques and technologies of accounting were not easily reconcilable to other commitments that also pulled at him, commitments to ways of knowing and doing that he associated with his family and the indigenous community that his business plans and branding strategies were ultimately intended to promote and support. State programs and development industry discourses that mandate and encourage systematized accounting, documentation, and formalization and denigrate business owners, workers, and consumers for their failure to get on board with progress and professionalism overlook the regulating styles that already condition and "control" market participation in the highland apparel trade, the moral stakes of market reorientation for people who are part of a longstanding business community, and the conditions of widespread economic as well as physical insecurity for which the state and international development industry are partly responsible from the perspective of many Maya businessmen. I turn to these contemporary conditions of crime and violence in the next chapter.

CHAPTER 5

Making the Highlands Safe for Business

On 10 May 2009, Rodrigo Rosenberg, a prominent attorney in Guatemala City, was shot in the head and killed while riding his bike. Days before his murder, Rosenberg video-taped an 18-minute message, subsequently circulated widely in Guatemala and internationally, in which he stated that should he be killed in the near future, the intellectual authors of the crime would be standing president Álvaro Colom and his wife, Sandra Torres. Their motive would be retribution, specifically for Rosenberg's representation of another recently murdered member of the Guatemala City elite, the business-man Khalil Musa. In the videotape, Rosenberg states that Musa was murdered because of the information he was about to release, which clearly showed the president's links to organized crime and drug trafficking. Rosenberg said he made the recording because he feared that Colom and his associates would not stop at killing Khalil Musa. (Smith and Offit 2010: 1)

When reports about Rosenberg's murder and his taped allegations sur-faced in Guatemala, headlining national newspapers and television news, people in Tecpán were alarmed. But they were far from shocked. One of my close informants, a middle-aged man who worked for a health-related NGO, told me he was certain that the president was to blame. Every politician is corrupt, he reasoned, so why should the coun-try expect anything different from Colom? Hadn't former president Portillo stolen all the money from the federal treasury and run off to Mexico just a few years before? Just like the others, he said, Colom would do anything—even order assassinations—to further his personal agenda and fill his bank account. What most concerned my interlocutor was not whether a government official was involved in corruption and other criminal dealings but rather how the *narcos* (short for *narcotraficantes,* or drug traffickers) the president had been linked to in Rosenberg's video would react to the scandal. Either the *narcos* would see it as an opportunity to step up the level of violence in the capital region, he told me, or the president would tell them to back off for a few weeks to let things cool down. He cautioned me about traveling on public buses or going to Guatemala City until we knew how the *narcos* and the *maras* (gangs) were responding. When I asked if he thought the president or anyone else would be held accountable for the crime, he said wryly, "There will be an investigation. But they will not find anything. You know, that's the way it is in Guatemala."

In the aftermath of his murder, Rosenberg's allegations played ceaselessly on television news stations and websites such as YouTube, where the video was quickly subtitled in English and racked up hundreds of thousands of views from Guatemala and around the world. A cadre of Guatemalan citizens, mobilized by Colom's right-wing opponents, began demonstrating in the capital's public plazas, calling for the president's immediate resignation and a full investigation into his alleged crimes. Less a plea for justice amid rising insecurities and more an opportunistic political move, the right was deploying Rosenberg's recorded message to unsettle public confidence in the Colom administration.

And yet life in Guatemala continued much as before. The lawyer's taped accusation soon ceased to circulate in the press, and the incident stopped being a main topic of public discussion. Convinced of Colom's ties to criminal organizations and probably also his responsibility for Rosenberg's murder, *tecpanecos* took the video as evidence of what they already knew about their country; namely, that people in power are corrupt (that's how they got there, many say). There were also sentiments, perhaps more troubling for those with high hopes for the postwar judicial reform process, that justice is a fiction and that the law is merely an instrument in the power struggles of the country's elite.

As the Rosenberg case faded from the headlines, the International Commission Against Impunity in Guatemala (CICIG) was undertaking a full-scale investigation into the attorney's death, which revealed a number of twists and turns. The video made by Rosenberg blamed his murder and that of Khalil Musa on the entanglements of President Colom and First Lady Sandra Torres with drug traffickers and the couple's desire to cover up those ties. The facts, however, did not fit this narrative. It turned out that Rosenberg had realized that Colom and Torres would never be prosecuted for what he believed to be their role in the death of Musa, who was not only Rosenberg's former client but also the father of his lover. This perceived injustice had been too much for Rosenberg to bear. Distraught by the loss of Musa and his powerlessness to make things right, Rosenberg planned his own death. He hired a hitman to shoot him during his regular morning bicycle ride and recorded the video message in hopes that it would bring down the Colom administration. CICIG investigators stumbled upon the melodramatic plot when they found a cell phone receipt in the possession of Rosenberg's bodyguard. When buying the phone that Rosenberg used to make calls to the gunman, it seems the bodyguard had remembered to ask for a receipt, complying with the ¡Pida su factura! campaign initiated by the Colom administration (described in chapter 4).

Fascinating and distressing, this episode speaks to the visceral threat of disguise and trickery that Guatemalans face when parsing out the situation of rampant crime, violence, and insecurity in their country. In one moment, the Rosenberg case appeared to confirm what people already knew or should have assumed about the drug war and government corruption, and in the next, it collapsed into a story of love, personal loss, and public deception to rival the best telenovelas. Was the lawyer a courageous crusader against injustice and impunity or a hapless fool who was tragically responsible for his own demise? Although the tale had been fabricated, the narrative Rosenberg had spun about the problem of drugs and the influence of drug traffickers on the political system as part of a general picture of official corruption resonated with Guatemalans and, for the political right in any case, served to confirm the untrustworthiness of Colom's center-left administration. Rosenberg had produced a pure and effectual simulacrum, a copy of the perpetual insecurity and lawlessness that people already believed they were living with. He was not "faking it"; rather, he had taken on the "symptoms" (Baudrillard 1994: 3) of widespread mistrust and disillusionment that already animated life in Guatemala and made them part of a fantastical story. There was, in fact, nothing "real" for Rosenberg to expose about the government and, similarly, no set of "facts" that the CICIG investigation could have revealed, despite the implicit hope that CICIG holds for setting the country on the right path. "The denunciation of scandal is always an homage to the law," wrote Jean Baudrillard (1994: 14). But despite the best attempts of CICIG to expose

Rosenberg for what he was (a kind of trickster) and what he had done, and thereby demonstrate the fact-finding powers of an *uncorrupt* judicial system and revive the "moral order" (Baudrillard 1994: 15) of law and justice, people were unconvinced. There was always already an excess of belief in what people knew to be true. There was only a hyperreality of crime and deception that confirmed for Guatemalans and others around the world that Guatemala is a "failed state" embroiled in a corrupt and corrupting "drug war."

Simulation and slippage—the power of the copy and threat of the fake—animate everyday experiences of crime and perspectives on law and security in highland Guatemala. Law and order seem empty and fraudulent. The state seems like a fake. Maya apparel producers and other men and women in the central highlands commonly perceive crime and violence as intractable parts of daily life, evidence of the normal functioning of a system of governance that they perceive as intrinsically corrupt and permanently scandalous. Their lives are wracked by what medical anthropologists call "everyday violence" (Scheper-Hughes 1993) and "social suffering" (Kleinman et al. 1997), the ordinary and routinized experiences of insecurity that are part and parcel of living in poverty, lacking basic public services, contending with discrimination and subordination, and surviving the brutality of warfare. And yet, in spite of critical sensibilities about the state and the law, everyday conversation in the highlands is rife with narratives of blame and accountability that figure particular people and communities, rather than structural processes, as responsible in varying degrees for conditions of insecurity. Maya apparel producers often assess the law, the state, and crime and corruption in terms of immoralities, both personal and political, in ways that hold up some other reality (e.g., a promise of an uncorrupt state, a working judiciary, a town free of criminals) as possible and that sometimes focus blame on people they perceive as others and outsiders to their communities.

This chapter delves into the contemporary politics and practices of law and security in highland Guatemala and, especially, the ways that indigenous people attempt to manage criminality and the effects of crime in their daily lives. As I have noted in previous chapters, violent crime rates have been on the rise in Guatemala in recent years, and Maya apparel producers who own small-scale garment workshops in Tecpán and nearby towns and hamlets now routinely contend with theft, assault, and extortion. My focus on violence and security in this chapter is motivated, then, by the prevalance of concern among my informants with these issues, the fact that talk of crime and historical and contemporary forms of violence are such a big part of daily life in Guatemala. These themes also occupy a significant slice of the anthopological literature on the region. Ethnographers chronicled the violence of the armed conflict as it unfolded (e.g., Richards 1985; Carmack 1988; Manz 1988; C. A. Smith 1990) and, in its aftermath, have examined how the experience of war, memories of state violence, and new forms of insecurity continue to shape everyday experience in indigenous communities (see, e.g., Manz 2005; Sanford 2003; Green 1999; Little and Smith 2009; D. M. Nelson 2009; Smith and Offit 2010; O'Neill and Thomas 2011; McAllister and Nelson 2013). My goal in this chapter is to contribute to these discussions by situating the regulating styles that structure the highland apparel trade and the relationships of Maya workshop owners to IP law and state programs of economic formalization—the subjects and themes explored in previous chapters—within the broader context of how indigenous Guatemalans are drawing on and contesting the language of rights and rule of law in their efforts to make sense of widespread insecurity and to formulate practical responses. My analysis brings together conversations in legal anthropology about rights, law, and the state with work in medical and economic anthropology on how people respond to chronic poverty and marginalization in the world system.

Apparel workshop owners—who are themselves figured as illegal actors in national and international IP law enforcement initiatives and antipiracy campaigns—have responded to crime and insecurity by participating in neighborhood security committees that patrol the streets at night and by assuming law enforcement responsibilites that might otherwise be the domain of state authorities. In a context in which the state is not to be trusted, politicians and police are believed to be corrupt, inept, and biased against indigenous people, and criminal impunity is the norm, people in the highlands have become entrepreneurial not just by developing business ventures and copying global brands but also by providing their own forms of security. Neighborhood committees that sometimes take aggressive action against suspected criminals and gang members participate in what Jennifer Burrell (2010: 93) calls a "do-it-yourself ethos," which largely defines civilian responses to theft and assault in indigenous communities.

Some anthropologists, legal scholars, and policy analysts frame these security activities as "indigenous law," defined as an approach to justice rooted in native values and traditional life ways. Indigenous law is often juxtaposed in the anthropological literature with state law and authority, and this framing has been useful for some Maya activists and community leaders who promote local control over judicial matters. But the characterization of "do-it-yourself" security in the highlands as rooted in an ethnic tradition and identity also leads national media, international agencies, and some sectors of the Guatemalan public to disparage such practices as backward and primitive in comparison to the national and international rule of law. Enterprising forms of security get characterized as an impediment to the extension of legitimate and official modes of law enforcement and judicial authority in much the same way as the enterprising forms of industry in which Maya apparel producers are involved get blamed as "piracy" and theft in relation to international IP law. Yet neither of these forms of entrepreneurship is best understood as culturally determined or locally isolated. Both the apparel trade and community-level security initiatives are examples of people contending and coping with limited life chances and limited opportunity. Business and security practices taken up by Maya people in the highlands resemble how people in other places around the world become enterprising when faced with ineffectual state governance and dire life conditions— for example, healthcare providers in Botswana "improvise" medicine (Livingston 2012), and indigenous peoples seeking livelihoods, recognition, and rights in neoliberal economies engage in "ethnic entreprenuership" (John L. Comaroff and Jean Comaroff 2009; DeHart 2010). But if these entreprenuerial activities are not fully explained by local ties and values, they are not adequately described by models in neoclassical economics of the maximizing and self-interested subject—the kind of market actor that neoliberal development and governance projects both presume and seek to cultivate—either. The forms of enterprise that I have documented so far in this book and that I describe in this chapter reflect the embeddedness of improvising responses, tactics, and strategies in social histories and the transformations and dangers of moral worlds. "Making do" (Pine 2012) in a world of structural insecurity and everyday violence is wrapped up with cultural politics, histories and experiences of suffering at the hands of the state and other institutions, complex relationships to and expectations of justice and the law, and a fundamental "will to live" (Biehl 2007) that is perhaps less about maximizing market opportunities and more about carving out meaning, autonomy, and a sense of community while sometimes struggling to survive.

In the case studies I present below, I find that Maya people actively debate the politics and implications of their own enterprising efforts to make their neighborhoods and towns "safe for business," as some apparel manufacturers phrased it in our conversations. Talk about crime and security among Tecpán residents revealed meaningful contestations over the proper response to crime, the root causes of violence, and the broader role of the state and legal rights in highland Guatemala and about the importance of security for the kind of community development that is valued in the apparel trade and that, as discussed in previous chapters, is premised on the growth and expansion of business opportunities for indigenous people. Tracing these debates is useful for understanding how the community-based forms of security and development in which Maya people participate in Tecpán are informed by locally held values and commitments to particular social relationships and formations but are also forged in a context of structural insecurity that is a result of long-term national and transnational processes of marginalization, warfare, racial subordination, and geopolitical entanglement.

THE SECURITY APPARATUS

Julio Toc was raised in the 1970s in a rural *aldea* (hamlet) outside of Tecpán. He and his eight brothers and sisters toiled in the family's cornfields and tended the cattle alongside their parents. Julio told me that his father worked hard because "that's part of indigenous custom." His father also wanted to earn enough in farming to pay for his children's educations, to help them achieve "something better" (cf. Fischer and Benson 2006). Julio attended Catholic school in Tecpán until 1980. That year, he turned fifteen and joined the Partido Guatemalteco del Trabajo (PGT, or Guatemalan Labor Party), a communist organization that supported guerrilla action against the militarized state during the internal armed conflict.[1] Having been born "in the midst of a conflict that defined the country's politics," explained Julio, it was "necessary to be involved in political life." For the next three years, he fought alongside other *guerrilleros* (guerrilla fighters) in the mountains, returning to Tecpán intermittently and, eventually, marrying a young woman from the town center. In 1983, military forces kidnapped three of his close family members. At that moment, he told me, he and his wife had to make a decision: get out of town or stay in Tecpán to likely be killed. They fled to Guatemala City, where he continued to support the PGT in less conspicuous ways. When democratic elections were held in 1985, after decades of military dictatorships, he and his wife moved back westward, but only as far as Chimaltenango, a city located roughly midway between Guatemala City and Tecpán. His wife still did not feel safe returning home to Tecpán.

In Chimaltenango, he found employment with nongovernmental organizations funded by foreign aid that focused on delivering food and agricultural inputs (seed and fertilizer) to rural farmers. After a few years, he explained, he was terribly dissatisfied with the work. He earned less than he wanted and believed that, although the "humanitarian assistance" the organizations offered mostly to indigenous families was necessary in the conflict's immediate aftermath, it had quickly devolved into a system of "dependence" and "submission" that encouraged aid recipients not to work. These are the personal opinions he developed about how changing livelihoods and ways of life were taking shape in the years after the war and in the midst of a large influx of international aid. In 1990, he put together three thousand quetzales (about US$750 at that time) in savings and family loans and started an apparel business. When I met Julio in 2009, he owned a three-story home that doubled as a garment workshop, employed a dozen young men at sewing machines, and had cornered the school uniform market in a large department of western Guatemala, delivering thousands of polo shirts, pants, vests, and sweaters to public and private schools at the start of each academic year.

Julio's transition from guerilla fighter to apparel trade entrepreneur traces Guatemala's broad shift in recent history from being a country defined by warfare and state-led violence to becoming a country powerfully shaped by neoliberal politics and policy and the international development industry. Julio's political commitments both have and have not changed over his lifetime and in the midst of this wider transformation in Guatemalan society. Julio was not unique among Maya apparel producers in terms of his support for leftist groups or involvement in guerrilla fighting during the internal armed conflict, and it was common for my informants who belonged to his generation to have been similarly exiled from their homes in the late 1970s and early '80s, during the bloodiest years of counterinsurgency warfare and genocide. As discussed in previous chapters, the military's targeting of indigenous people, including garment workshop owners, did not depend on the actual involvement of these people with groups considered to be subversive, and the vast majority of Maya people who were killed, disappeared, or exiled during the conflict had no ties to communism and were not guerrilla fighters (Comisión para el Esclarecimiento Histórico 1999). Julio's personal story illustrates, however, how entrepreneurship in the apparel trade and the more generalized do-it-yourself ethos referenced above that is part of how highland communities approach contemporary conditions of crime and violence have emerged in relation to widespread mistrust of the state and deep-seated cynicism about state and transnational discourses of law and order, as well as disdain for past and ongoing international interventions in Guatemalan politics and the regional economy.

When I visited Julio's family and toured his apparel workshop, I also inquired about any lingering political involvements in his life, given that politics and political struggle constituted such an important part of his youth. Dressed in grey tailored slacks and a long-sleeved, button-down shirt, with a pair of glasses hung from his open collar, he insisted that he wanted no part in political life. He then added, "We aren't going to be apolitical either. The worst sin in life is to be apolitical. But we have to choose our politics, because it wouldn't be right for me to involve myself in political life as it is now. Really, it's disgusting. The politicians are the ones who are killing our people with hunger and stealing our taxes. . . . Everything is completely corrupted." He went on to criticize the wave of popular political movements that had received a great deal of national attention that year. Political parties, trade unions, and peasant organizations had initiated roadblocks and strikes in protest of mining projects and tax increases. Julio complained that the organizers put people in the position of losing their lives for the movement without guaranteeing that their children would be looked after. There remains in Guatemala a serious threat of being killed for involvement in leftist political organizing and protest, and he knew all too well from personal experience the dangers posed by political participation. "I have to provide for my kids," he insisted, and emphasized that his responsibilities were different now than they had been during the armed conflict. The politics and economics of the current movements were also a sticking point for him:

> Take the case of the [organized efforts to block construction of the] cement works in San Juan Sacatepéquez.[2] Now that there have been deaths [of protestors, who were slain by armed cement company workers], I've changed my political position. I look at the people, indigenous people, who direct these marches. I look at the commercial point of view. Half the world is complaining that there are no jobs. "I need a job!" they say. Yeah, but you refuse to allow them to build a cement plant in San Juan.

I asked him if the concerns about environmental contamination that activists were raising about the project were valid, to which he replied: "If we really want to conserve the environment, and if it's going to contaminate it, then let's plant trees or whatever needs to be done to save the environment. But we just hold [the project] up from the very beginning. Those are the politics that the NGOs use to slow down a country's development."

Julio's politics had changed, to say the least. He went from supporting the leftist opposition to authoritarianism in Guatemala to very much advocating development projects that reflect a hegemonic capitalist model and a particular relationship to activism and environmentalism. And along the way, he came to use rhetorics of dependency and submission to criticize the ways in which humanitarian assistance functions. However, he also quoted Marx fluidly in our conversations, albeit principally to explain his own positioning in the apparel trade—how, "in the capitalist system," there is a necessary division between labor and management. "The most difficult part is sales; operating a machine is easy," he noted. Perhaps his personal transformation stems from the material, technological, and ideological context of his own formation as an economizing and entrepreneurial person. Julio went back to school in the late 1980s and earned a high school degree in accounting. He spoke confidently about his ability to *hacer cuentas* and set prices using calculations of the equilibrium point between supply and demand, reflecting the intensifying, masculinizing discourses about professionalism, modernity, and accounting discussed in chapter 4 as redefining models of business sense and moral personhood in the highland apparel trade.

Or maybe Julio's politics have not changed in ways that are terribly dramatic, aside from the responsibilities he has now to his family. Guerrilla fighters joined the armed conflict for many reasons, not all of them in line with academic interpretations of Marx or international anticapitalist movements. Various injustices drove Julio to take up arms against Guatemala's dictatorial regimes in the early 1980s, a result of his critical interpretation not only of Guatemala's economic system but also of the country's political history. During our conversations, he linked his prior involvement in the PGT to his absolute outrage over the violent intervention of the United States in Guatemalan politics in 1954, when the Central Intelligence Agency orchestrated a coup d'état that overthrew democratically elected center-leftists. That coup sparked the war, and, for Julio, it marked a breaking point in Guatemala's history. He explained his guerrilla activities as a means of combatting foreign interventionism and securing self-determination for the Guatemalan people.

Indeed, Julio's longstanding disdain for the US government shaped our interactions during my fieldwork. He was noticeably cold toward me when his *compadre* (coparent), a close friend for whose son Julio acted as godfather, introduced us at a family gathering. He seemed to relax when I did not disagree with his diatribes about the basic human costs and negative ramifications of US foreign policy over the years. At subsequent meetings with Julio, he welcomed my queries and observations about the apparel trade but would inevitably bring the conversation back to US politics. This topic struck a chord with him, as it did for more than a few of my informants who often wanted to talk with me about US foreign relations with Latin America, the overwhelming economic power and political influence of US-based corporations vis-à-vis international trade, the national elections that took place in the United States during my fieldwork, and the rhetorics of "underdevelopment" and "backwardness" that characterize how indigenous Guatemalans perceive themselves to be understood in the eyes of US officials, NGO employees, volunteers, and development workers.

Julio was always keen to speak with me about what he framed as the problems of US neocolonial power. During one visit to his workshop, he asked for my thoughts on George W. Bush's presidential administration, which had ended earlier that year. I told him that I disagreed with the US invasions of Iraq and Afghanistan, to which he responded, "Speaking of Iraq, what do you think about the terminology that the [US] government officials use about other countries, about 'acts of terrorism.' Is it true or not?"

"That there is terrorism in those countries?" I asked for clarification.

"Yes, what do you think about that?"

I offered a few comments on the term's political utility for rallying public support for warfare, to which he added:

> It's easy for them [US government officials] to say that we should apply that word, "terrorism," to the whole world, to say that Afghanistan and Iraq are terrorist countries, because, look, if you try to invade my house, am I then a terrorist for trying to defend my house? It's crazy; I can't get my head around it. Because you defend your country, they call you a terrorist. I don't accept it, and I will never understand it. They have another election, and [Bush] wins, and it's just what I'm telling you. . . . He carried out a massacre [of civilians by invading Iraq and Afghanistan], and he is still in power. . . . Why don't the North American people think? What is going on in the world?

He spoke frustratedly about what he perceived as the US electorate's lack of critical awareness and the willingness of many North Americans to support politicians and governments that are bent on what seems to him to be a form of doublespeak and hypocrisy about the promotion of democracy and freedom, on the one hand, and the "massacre," as he termed it, of US military invasion, on the other hand. I also got the sense that our conversation about words and war had a lot to do with Julio's experience of Guatemalan politics. I suggested that the term "terrorist" has similarities to how the terms *guerrilla* and *comunista* have been deployed in Guatemala, which he affirmed. These are words that are used to make whole groups into enemies and legitimize punitive and militaristic measures, he explained to me. And although there was talk of "hope" and "change" in the air in the United States because of Barack Obama's election, Julio quipped, he was not so easily fooled. "They went to war in Afghanistan, and no one can change that. That policy is going to continue. It's just what happened with us in Guatemala. We've had fifty years of the North American political invasion."

Although, at first blush, when one considers Julio's role as a minor capitalist and his resentments about populist and environmental activism in Guatemala when the country is facing a lack of jobs, it seems that Julio's politics have shifted from the left of the spectrum to the right, one thing that has actually remained constant is his powerful indictment of Guatemala's subordinate position in the world economic and geopolitical order and the central role of the United States in shaping conditions of social suffering in his part of the world. The oral history and political commentary that Julio shared with me brings to light the metonymical slippage from *guerrillero* to *terrorista* that defines, in many ways, how a transnational security apparatus sustains itself today in Latin America and beyond. Michel Foucault (1977, 2010) used the concept of the "security apparatus" to describe how a set of institutions, narratives, techniques, and technologies of surveillance and regulation function to effectively extend the reach of capitalist market systems and bureaucratic forms of authority across societies, and how the effectiveness of these instruments depends on a process of classifying some people as proper, law-abiding citizens and others as problematic and delinquent, in need of continual surveillance, intensive regulatory attention, forms of discipline, and sometimes violent punishment. The transnational security apparatus that implicates North America and Western Europe in the kinds of political and military interventionism that Julio decried has, for a long time, coupled the positive promotion of democracy, freedom, and entrepreneurship with the criminalization and penalization of styles, dispositions, and behaviors that come to be perceived as dangerous vis-à-vis national and international projects of modernization and development. These interventions have unfolded across a series of successive, transnational campaigns. The Cold War, the War on Drugs, and the War on Terror have each had their own populations of people designated and targeted as subversive, delinquent, abnormal, and threatening. During the Cold War, the US government and the Guatemalan state targeted people like Julio, holding up communism as an internal threat to the security and prosperity of the Guatemalan nation and the stability of the wider Central American region. Communism was figured as a form of domestic betrayal in which indigenous people were particularly likely to be inculcated and involved, a type of subversion that had to be carefully detected and rooted out from within Guatemalan society (see Grandin 2004; Schirmer 1988). In the two decades since the signing of the 1996 peace accords that officially ended the conflict in Guatemala, international agencies, state officials, and national media have identified a new internal threat: street gangs and drug traffickers. Official narratives lay the blame for rising violent crime rates on the presence of gangs, the problem of drugs, and a national epidemic of youth delinquency. While transnational gangs and the drug trade are empirical and real and their effects wide-ranging in Guatemala, the tendency of the transnational security apparatus to diagnose these problems in terms of bad actors (e.g., gang members, *narcos*, and troubled youth) who are said to exemplify and promote a culture of violence takes away from an understanding of how the processes of militarization and criminalization that define the hemispheric War on Drugs, the structural conditions of poverty and inequality that are the result of colonial and neocolonial forms of rule and modes of resource extraction and distribution, and the lack of economic and educational opportunity linked to the racialized subordination of indigenous people in Guatemala are all factors that contribute to a context in which gang membership, engagements in informal economic activity, inducements to criminalized activities, violence, or drug use or other diacritics of pathologized anticitizenship might take hold and thrive.

Julio described how, in his view, Cold War interventionism has also given way to and found renewed energy, meaning, and justification in the War on Terror. In the above quote, he decried the politics of blame through which entire countries and national populations are designated as "terrorists," even if their armed mobilization is, as he sympathetically put it, an attempt to defend their homes from invasion. An evolving security apparatus perpetually targets and victimizes peripheral places (e.g., Guatemala, Iraq, and Afghanistan), he argued, even if the terminology and rhetoric shifts, and even if the exact mechanisms of control and engagement evolve, too. Considering his vehement critique of US interventionism and the modes of subordination and warfare that the security apparatus elaborates, it perhaps seems contradictory that Julio has embraced a vocal pride in nationalism and defense of his homeland as well as an entrepreneurial ethic that resonates with a neoliberal program that has been part and parcel of what the US government and broader development industry have sought to promote in Guatemala and around the world. His personal story and political commentaries, however, help to situate business ownership and capitalist activities in highland Guatemala as something other than a new phase of neoliberal realignment vis-à-vis the state and market system. His commitment to entrepreneurship—to a "do-it-yourself" program—and his concerns about humanitarian aid and impediments to economic development can be seen as being part of a longer political and economic struggle against dependency and interventionism that he understands himself as having been involved in—a struggle linked to a vision of Guatemala as a country that he believes held some promise for indigenous people during the democratic period that the coup brought to an end, to anti–North American sentiments, and to disregard for a US brand of politics, regulation, and subordination that has largely shaped how his country's government has engaged its citizens since the coup. His politics are not so much left or right, perhaps, as they are dead set against a longstanding and evolving project of security and interventionism that marginalizes people like him through labels and mechanisms and that makes him feel like his life chances are being manipulated and managed from afar and for nefarious or unfair gain.

But Julio's personal story suggests that yet another category should be added to the list of actors in this security narrative and framework alongside the guerrilla fighter, the drug trafficker, and the terrorist: the *pirata* (pirate). Julio started in the apparel trade by manufacturing and screen-printing children's t-shirts adorned with "the famous Power Rangers," as he put it. Quality did not matter in that market sector, he insisted. All that mattered was the screen-printed design. At one point, he tried to market t-shirts that displayed what he termed "indigenous designs," based on Classic Maya hieroglyphs, but they did not sell. So he stayed with Power Rangers, Winnie the Pooh, and Mickey Mouse. He was good at selling t-shirts, but he found that the market for children's clothing was unpredictable in its highs and lows. Eventually, he switched to manufacturing school uniforms, and he now occupies a big part of the regional market in that sector.

It is no accident that pirates—the people who copy trademarked brand names and popular cartoon characters, reproduce copyrighted music and movies, circulate illegally downloaded business software, and hawk photocopied textbooks on the margins of university campuses—are called "terrorists" in government reports, journalistic accounts, and industry association press releases. Kavita Philip (2005: 200–201) recounts, for example, the narratives spun by law enforcement agencies about connections between IP piracy and international terrorist organizations (including Al Qaeda) and quotes a story in the *New York Times Magazine* that compared the threat posed by piracy to "weapons of mass destruction." These might seem like exaggerated associations or egregious word choices. Intellectual property pirates are not killing people or terrorizing civilians or societies. They do not work with political demands and do not usually articulate a politics of opposition. They are not driven by the ideologies that often define groups labeled "terrorists." However, they are said to lack "Western values," as discussed in previous chapters, and are lumped together as "collectivists," disparagingly compared to the idealized, economizing individual of the development industry in ways that hearken back to Cold War divisions between (collectivist) communism and (individualist) capitalism. The moralization against them reflects processes by which other disparaged figures—such as delinquents, drug dealers, and drug traffickers—are framed in the War on Drugs. That is to say that they are portrayed as threats to national economic development and public morality. Rhetorical linkages between "piracy" and "terrorism" occur in a context where the labeling of these people as "pirates" is already hyperbolic and where strategic practices of naming have been an important part of how IP rights have been justified and how the violation of these rights has been vilified as both immoral and unlawful (Johns 2010). The implication of these linkages is that pirates terrorize—or rather "dilute," as discussed in chapter 3—corporations and their brands and that they use profits derived from piracy to fund other criminal activities as well. But Julio did not characterize his participation in the copying of trademarks as an act of mobilization and resistance akin to his participation in Guatemala's armed conflict. The very idea of him equating brand piracy either with his past involvement in communist organizations and guerrilla fighting or with forms of violence labeled "terrorism" seems absurd. One involves selling garments that feature cartoon characters; the other involves killing people. Why does the false equivalency between pirates and terrorists persist, then, and how does it reflect a convergence of contemporary security agendas and international efforts to promote the rule of law in the fashion industry and in economic globalization more generally?

RIGHTS TALK

Political scientist Rachel Sieder (2003: 141) has written that "any analysis of attempts to promote the rule of law must examine what 'law', 'rights' and 'justice' mean for different actors in different places and to [*sic*] analyse the interplay between broader dynamics of internationally promoted judicial reform and national specificities." Indeed, anthropologists find that internationally promoted rights discourses transform and get taken up in various ways and to diverse ends as they move across contexts (Merry 2001; Goodale 2009; Tsing 2004). Terms such as "rights" and "justice" have multiple and layered meanings for Guatemalan Mayas. As one Maya cultural activist from Tecpán commented to me, "No one talked about 'rights' when we first started [building a social movement in the 1970s], but now we know that's what we were seeking." The language of cultural rights and indigenous rights became central to the Guatemalan peace process of the late 1980s and early '90s, as Maya activists and international organizations such as the United Nations pushed the Guatemalan government to institutionalize legal protections for the country's indigenous majority. Women's rights are another aspect of international rights discourse that has been promoted in the highlands through the efforts of various development agencies and NGOs that sponsor training workshops that encourage women to understand themselves as rights-bearing citizens who are authorized to make demands on the state. Women's rights provide a new vernacular in which women often negotiate and make sense of their roles in the family and civic life. Women in Tecpán invoke the term "women's rights" to parse out everything from proper courting behavior to reproductive health issues to the privileges and responsibilities of citizenship. In a country where "domestic violence is rampant" (Preston 2014), where the Catholic Church dominates conversations about family planning and women's health, and where issues of gender discrimination have so often been obscured and suppressed even within the indigenous rights movement (Warren 1998), the proliferation of talk about women's rights could be seen as an important step in the promotion of gender equality.

In this section, I discuss a particular case of violent crime in Tecpán where the language of "women's rights" surfaced in ways that reveal that the meaning of "rights" is open to disputation and interpretation in the highlands as people put rights-based appeals into action and negotiate tensions, conflicts, and disparate perspectives on the role of state law in everyday life. The term "rights" is sometimes invoked in the

highlands as a means of advancing political claims and furthering community interests, as in the context of Maya cultural activism and the
peace process. The concept can also be a valuable resource for people
seeking more localized forms of recognition and response, as in the case
I present below. I go on to also discuss situations in which the language
of rights, and especially "human rights," meets with a great deal of
resistance, where the need for security and a desire for peaceful streets
and swift justice can seem to highland residents to trump the rights of
accused criminals. This tension between rights and security, which has
been explored fruitfully by other scholars as well (Burrell 2010; Ekern
2008), is important for understanding the complex ways that the "rule
of law" comes to matter for people in the highlands.

Before the Rosenberg case hit the headlines, early in 2009, a lawyer
was shot to death in the street outside his office in Tecpán. According to
witnesses, the lawyer had just unlocked his office door to begin the business day when a black sedan, a grey pickup truck, and a motorcycle all
pulled up behind him. The driver of the motorcycle fired several shots.
Then, all three vehicles sped away, leaving their victim lying in the busy
street. A volunteer fireman attempted first aid, but there was little he
could do to save the man's life.

Rumor and gossip about the shooting—and the lawyer—spread
quickly around town. Just a few hours after the murder, there was a
general consensus among people with whom I spoke that the lawyer
had been working on cases that involved "very bad and very dangerous
people," as one middle-aged woman who ran a *tienda* (small store) near
where the shooting occurred explained to me. "If you're going to be
involved with the law, it is better to take light cases [*casos livianos*],"
she said. "He was in for more than he could handle." In other words,
he was known to have taken on cases that involved *narcos* (drug traffickers), and these cases were presumed to be dangerous from the start.
It was little wonder, in her estimation, that he had ended up dead after
having entangled himself in the drug war. In her explanation and those
of many others, there was little talk of legal justice for the dead man and
his family. Blame, in fact, seemed to fall on the shoulders of the victim
rather than the *narcos* who were presumed to have assassinated him.
"He should have known better" was a common refrain. Such accusations implied that the lawyer, a Kaqchikel Maya man who formed part
of a small cohort of indigenous professionals in town, had acted irra-
tionally or irresponsibly in his business dealings, getting involved in
dangerous legal cases and with problematic clients out of ambition or

greed. The discourse of *envidia*—the moral rhetorics of envy, individualism, and personal economic gain introduced in chapter 2—was not far beneath the surface of such talk.

A few days after the shooting, I had lunch at a local *comedor* with a woman who worked at the government health clinic in Tecpán. She complained that the lawyer's body had been left in the street for six or seven hours before authorities took it away to the morgue in Chimaltenango. "This is the problem in Guatemala," she told me. "The government services don't work. It always takes so long to get anything done." For me, the prolonged and delayed response of officials may have resonated as part of "the problem in Guatemala" or part of a personal way of apprehending the morbid nature of the event, but the assassination of the lawyer seemed, at the time, to be a much more pressing issue than government inefficiencies and inadequate services. Since 2008, the annual number of homicides in Guatemala has equaled or exceeded the average number of intentional deaths per year during the armed conflict (United Nations Office on Drugs and Crime 2013; Comisión para el Esclarecimiento Histórico 1999). Under the courageous leadership of Claudia Paz y Paz, who served as Guatemala's attorney general from 2010 to 2014, the impunity rate for homicides fell from 97 percent to 70 percent, a statistic that still leaves most Guatemalans convinced that justice is not being served for violent crimes in their country. In the last three national elections, right-wing parties promising a *mano dura* (iron fist) approach to security garnered widespread support. Internationally assisted processes of institutional reform in the judiciary and anticorruption campaigns in the police ranks and court system have yielded a handful of prosecutions of high-profile military officials responsible for war crimes (including the ultimately overturned decision against General Efraín Ríos Montt discussed in chapter 4), but few other tangible results for the Guatemalan people. Even the September 2015 resignation of President Otto Pérez Molina and arrests of many top officials in his administration over customs fraud allegations—which international news media quickly hailed as a great success in the fight against corruption in Latin America (Watson 2015; Lakhani 2015; Ahmed and Malkin 2015)—has been met thus far with measured optimism in Tecpán. As noted with regard to how people in Tecpán interpreted the Rosenberg case, many Guatemalans consider crime and violence to be deeply entrenched in daily life, as if it were a natural part of how the country functions. This helps to explain why state inefficiencies—and not the fact that a murder had occurred in broad daylight on a busy street—seemed to occupy a central place in the narratives that came to surround the death of the lawyer from Tecpán. In the realm of national politics, more violence—the "iron fist" militaristic approach to rooting out the *narcos* and street gangs that have overwhelmed Guatemala City in recent years—has seemed to some to be the only sensible response, and right-wing political parties have become popular in promising such amelioration.

A rising violent crime rate is symptomatic of the legacy of the long armed conflict, the conditions of deep inequality and marginalization that partially drive gang participation, and the intensifying turf war being fought in Central America among drug cartels. Guatemala has been labeled a "narco-state" by international media, and hundreds of tons of cocaine now move through the country each year; over US$10 billion worth of illicit drugs were seized inside Guatemala's borders between 2007 and 2011 (López 2010; BBC News 2011). Increased policing and legal pressure from the Mexican government on drug cartels in that country in the 2000s—compelled and largely financed by the US government as part of the War on Drugs—only pushed the powerful cartels south into Guatemala (Beaubien 2011). Los Zetas and other Mexican gangs have heavily recruited ex-soldiers and special operations forces from the Guatemalan army into their ranks and, for protection, insinuated themselves into Guatemala's political and economic networks (López 2010). Citing the epidemics of drug trafficking and gang violence, Pérez Molina—a former army general and director of military intelligence elected to the Guatemalan presidency in 2011 on an "iron fist," tough-on-crime platform—surprised many observers in 2012 when he expressed disdain for the War on Drugs and began floating the idea of legalizing marijuana.

My fieldwork took place just as people in the highlands were becoming concerned with the impact of drug trafficking on Guatemalan society. Talk about *maras,* an amorphous term used in the highlands to refer to both the transnational gangs that control parts of the capital and the "delinquent youth" who stay out too late in the streets (Thomas et al. 2011; Burrell 2010), was being supplemented with talk about *narcos,* and today, locals converse about a generally dangerous masculinity composed of gangs, drug traffickers, and delinquents. The abovementioned lawyer's death, allegedly at the hands of drug runners, confirmed the suspicions of many *tecpanecos* that violence associated with the drug war was ubiquitous and quickly becoming their problem. I knew the family of the lawyer well, and they invited me to visit them for the *novena* (a Catholic ceremony of mourning, prayer, and remembrance) nine days after his death. I sat with his widow as she wrung her hands and, between fits of tears, struggled to get out a few sentences in Kaqchikel Maya, explaining to her mother and four sisters the predicament facing her. She was troubled by all the rumors circulating in Tecpán that blamed her husband for his own demise because his work involved contact with drug and street gangs. Since the shooting, she had met with judges in Chimaltenango and state prosecutors from the attorney general's office, and she urged them to advance the investigation and track down those responsible for the murder. She had solicited state protection for herself and her children in case the perpetrators were not finished. Officials had coarsely advised her to pack up her family and leave Tecpán if she wanted to feel safer. The widow was deeply angered by the government officials' unsympathetic attitudes and unwillingness to help her. She expressed doubt that the people who killed her husband would be caught.

As she talked, we heard a sound like a gunshot from the street, and the household domestic worker ran outside to check on the widow's children. She returned to report that the noise was evidently a firecracker—not surprising given the ubiquity of pyrotechnics in town. Fireworks are exploded to celebrate birthdays, religious holidays, weddings, and baptisms, so it is not uncommon to hear them throughout the night in Tecpán. However, there is frequent speculation among neighbors as to whether or not there are gunshots intermingled with the explosions, and people are constantly scanning the sensory landscape for evidence of delinquent youth and gang members. Hearing the young domestic worker's report brought the mourning family a moment's relief, but the incident had also reminded the widow and her sisters just how fearful they felt. The women embraced in a flood of tears. Their mother insisted that we all take a drink of *cuxa,* a locally distilled cane liquor, to relieve our sadness and ward off *susto,* a dangerous illness brought on by fright. The outpouring of emotion at that moment reflected a common form of embodiment among Maya women that I witnessed in other contexts of trauma and grief, where the embraces, crying, and comforting were means of expressing intimacy and creating a material space of mourning and social suffering. Among these women, who were so distraught over the loss of their husband and brother-in-law, affective attachment and collective sentimentality also served as a defensive and protective stance against the discourses of blame and accusation that were circling around them. Gossip about what the lawyer had done wrong and allegations about how envy and individualism had consumed him in ways that compelled him to put himself in harm's way were threatening to the widow and her family, as the rumors implicated her and perhaps also her children in a breach of community solidarity and implied their embroilment in a malicious politics of jealousy and greed, not to mention their entanglements with danger, drugs, and delinquency. The embraces between the widow and her sisters were a form of comfort in the face of the state's refusal to provide support and safety, too. The widow's request for a safe haven for herself and her family had been an appeal to the state and the law to recognize the responsibilities shared across a range of actors and institutions for her particular condition of insecurity and grief—that is, the ways that the hemispheric War on Drugs and the failures of state police and the state judiciary to prevent and punish violent crime contributed to her husband's death. She was angered that both official and local discourses of blame and responsibility that cite individual, bad actors for conditions of widespread violence had made her case into a singular fight for justice rather than a socialized experience of endemic insecurity and chronic, systemic dysfunction.

As the widow's mother portioned out the liquor for each of us to drink, one of the sisters, a trained midwife and nurse, commiserated with her sibling by decrying the state officials' response to her sister's request for protection as *una discriminación* (a discrimination). She cited information she had received at a workshop funded by a foreign NGO on the topic of *los derechos de la mujer* (women's rights) to explain that women have the right to live where they want to live and to decide what to do with their families. This sister—dressed in a simple cotton blouse and navy-blue, knee-length skirt, unlike her mother and sisters who donned the colorful, handwoven *huipiles* and *cortes* of Tecpán and nearby towns—urged that it was not right for the men at the government prosecutor's office to deny her sister police protection and to tell her that she had to flee town if she felt unsafe. Even if the widow could not prove that her family was in imminent physical danger, the sister continued, she deserved assistance because she was in danger of a psychological and emotional collapse due to the trauma of losing her husband. The room circulated with different appeals about assistance, support, violence, and forms of discrimination and marginalization that the women felt they were particularly susceptible to given their subordinate position within a gendered hierarchy of authority that existed within state institutions and their own community. The women's talk of rights within this socialized scene of grief—led by a sister who figured herself as a modern, educated, healthcare professional with training from an international agency—was an attempt to retrieve the reality of death from the rhetorics of blame and envy that circulated locally and to articulate a vision of gendered empowerment both in the context of masculinized delinquency and over and against the individualization of suffering, victimhood, and responsibility that they sensed had animated the responses of the state agents and their neighbors. This case illustrates that the language of rights is only one part of how people make sense of conditions of marginalization and insecurity that are often difficult and overwhelming. Their responses also involve cultural frames of loss and support and forms of kinship, affect, and ritualized sentiment and mourning. The invocation of women's rights by the widow's sister was not a simple appeal to the state for better or greater security. Rather, it was a complicated commentary on how the kind of security that the state provides—premised on the rule of law and an understanding of crime as an individual act requiring a narrow official response and of victimhood as an individual experience that does not merit the state's attention—is insufficient in the face of social suffering. She was arguing that these women, as women (and not just as Maya women), have a right to home and safety, and thus her appeal defined this scene of mourning and embodiment as a site of political and legal disputations and layered social belonging and longing.

At other times, and in other cases, anthropologists have found that talk of rights is perceived in Maya communities as threatening to the very forms of community solidarity and shared responsibility that the widow and her family sought to recuperate in their mourning. "Rights" are not always or even generally considered in a positive light in Guatemala. For example, children's rights were a topic of popular discussion during my fieldwork, in part because of one international NGO's highly visible campaign that included rather vague messaging about *los derechos del niño* (the rights of the child) on signs along the Pan-American Highway. A few primary school teachers in Tecpán complained to me that they could no longer discipline the children in their classrooms because of all the attention to children's rights and parents' rights. One explained that a colleague had physically disciplined a fourth grader after the child bit her arm. When she called the child's parents in for a meeting to discuss the incident, the parents complained that the teacher had no "right" to hit their child and that they could report her to the authorities for abuse. To the teacher recounting this story, the case served as evidence that "things are getting really bad with everyone having so many rights."

The term "rights" often takes on a decidedly negative valence in Guatemalan media and everyday conversation. "Human rights," in particular, are conceptualized by many Guatemalans as stumbling blocks to justice, a set of protections that seem to apply to "delinquents" more than to law-abiding citizens and to impede the prosecution and punishment of criminals. An older apparel manufacturer from Tecpán expressed such concerns as we talked about the dangers of selling goods in Guatemala City's wholesale markets. With more than 20 percent of the national population living in the capital region, Guatemala City is an important center of commercial life. Rising crime rates discourage many producers from selling there, however, and this is especially true for smaller-scale workshop owners, who do not have the provisional safety of their own automobiles for traveling back and forth and making deliveries (Thomas 2009). This particular workshop owner explained the situation in the capital region as follows:

> Guatemala City is tough right now, even worse than before. Now the thieves are taking over. And the government doesn't do anything. They let them go. Because it's like this: human rights are helping them. There's no law. There's nothing. The police grab them, but what for? They take them in [to jail], but there are others walking out at the same moment. Now [criminals] are killing people in Guatemala City every day, and no one is doing anything, as if [the victims] were animals.

When he commented, "human rights are helping them," he meant that the application of evidentiary rules, due process guarantees, and other basic principles of the rule of law can sometimes result in suspected criminals being released. He blamed "rights" for the legal protections the justice system affords to accused thieves and murderers, when, in his estimation, people involved in crimes should simply be locked up. His position, shared by many highland residents, is made all the more convincing to people by the low conviction rates and short prison terms that characterize Guatemala's criminal justice system. In this ethnographic setting, they view due process as an unfair privilege granted to people who are "known" criminals but are released in spite of the fact that they were caught *con las manos en la masa* (literally, "with their hands in the dough"). Such complaints were part of the aforementioned context of the lawyer who was murdered, in which the fact that he legally represented drug runners and gang members—that is, he defended the "rights" of criminals—made him seem guilty and perhaps even deserving of his fate. He was seen to be protecting people who, according to a certain local view of things, had forsaken their rights by becoming criminals. This understanding of "rights" obviously does not mesh with the meaning and application of legal rights in international judicial reform agendas and human rights campaigns. But it is one way that people in Guatemala respond when they witness endemic impunity and the prevalence of criminality and violence: they insist that justice be swift and that the law be more decisive.

The condemnatory attitude toward "human rights" in Guatemala has been analyzed by some scholars in terms of a contrast between the globalized rights framework and the forms of justice meted out by local communities said to practice "indigenous" or "customary" law (Sieder 1996, 2011; Esquít and García 1998; Mayén 1995; Ochoa García 2002; Godoy 2006). In Guatemala, the term "indigenous law" often refers to the conflict resolution procedures undertaken by Maya leaders, which are grounded in principles of indigenous self-rule, communal obligation, reciprocity, and a respect for the sacred (Ekern 2008). In some municipalities, including the western highland town of Totonicapán, indigenous law has been institutionalized in the form of an indigenous council that works in parallel with the elected mayor and municipal authorities. Leaders of indigenous councils have sometimes contrasted the values and principles on which their authority lies with the values and principles ensconced in human rights frameworks. As Stener Ekern (2008: 126) writes, "Many Mayas find the work of human rights activists—governmental or nongovernmental—to actually reproduce and even to further state power in their communities and therefore conclude that, at least locally, human rights are out of place." He gives the example of a dispute over logging activities on communally held land in Totonicapán. When the indigenous council leaders cut off the water supply to a group of residents who refused to discontinue their overharvesting of timber, the affected residents filed complaints about a human rights violation with the United Nations peacekeeping mission in Guatemala, the national Human Rights Ombudsman, and the Office of the Prosecutor (Ministerio Público). International and state authorities eventually sided with the residents engaged in the logging activities and ordered the immediate reopening of the water supply. In the aftermath of the decision, community leaders complained that "human rights favor the guilty" and expressed concern that judicial emphasis on human rights comes at the expense of a more locally salient emphasis on community obligations (Ekern 2008: 136).

Based on this and other cases, Ekern has interpreted indigenous people's concerns about human rights as evidence of a suspicious attitude toward the state, conditioned by histories of state violence and discrimination. Indigenous people are not the only ones in Guatemala to critique human rights, however, nor are the critiques necessarily rooted in "indigenous law." Mayas in Tecpán, for example, did express concern to me that *derecho kaxlan* (state or international law, as opposed to *derecho Maya*, or Mayan law) poses a threat to community stability, but similar critiques have been voiced by diverse populations throughout Latin America and the Caribbean (Scheper-Hughes 1993; Tate 2007; Pitarch et al. 2008; Goldstein et al. 2009; Smulovitz 2003). As Daniel Goldstein (2007) has argued, collective stances against "human rights" are neither always attributable to "culture"—an alternative and local cosmology, for example—nor evidence of romantic resistance movements among indigenous citizens or the poor. Rather, attention to human rights seems, for many Latin Americans, to directly contradict the discourses of security and "talk of crime" (Caldeira 2001) that state officials and institutions instigate and exploit to further national political campaigns and international development agendas because rights often seem to protect the very people who are said to be the targets of securitization and "iron fist" politics. The historically evolving transnational security apparatus, described above, involves talk about gangs, *narcos*, terrorists, and pirates as global threats and national problems, and although human rights discourse does not stand apart from this apparatus (the need to promote, disseminate, and defend human rights is often part and parcel of how security interventions are justified), there is sometimes a perceived disconnect between tough "security talk" (Goldstein 2007) that points a finger at particular individuals and groups who must be punished for the good of society and "rights" that seem to prevent these people from being held accountable. This seeming contradiction is at the heart of why many Latin Americans and others around the world see "security" and "rights" as mutually exclusive, however compatible and intertwined these concepts might be or seem from the perspective of the Global North (Goldstein 2012).

There is another layer to this relationship between security and rights, which shows up in how the widow's sister invoked "women's rights" following the shooting death of the lawyer in Tecpán. Her invocation was indicative of the hope and promise with which national and international authorities, development workers, activists, and advocates have surrounded the concept of rights in their educational and promotional efforts, which are often targeted at women and indigenous people, conceived of by the development industry as groups that are

particularly vulnerable to rights violations and therefore in need of protections, guarantees, and supports. International agencies, NGOs, and
development programs advise members of these groups that rights-
based demands are an appropriate and effective way to overcome the
difficulties they face as members of a marginalized class, putting the
onus on them as groups or individuals who already face discrimination
to stand up for themselves and voice demands and encouraging a claiming of rights, a "do-it-yourself" approach to justice and citizenship. In
some ways, this strategy lets the state and the international development industry—entangled as they are in the conditions of precarious-
ness and insecurity that provoke a need for protections, guarantees, and
supports in the first place—off the hook, relieving them of the responsibility for proactively ensuring forms of social security and equality (cf.
Burrell 2010; Hale 2007). Marginalized groups are burdened with the
need to confront situations of precarity and insecurity in terms of an
individualizing and narrowing appeal to legal rights. The flipside of this
process of promoting rights as a resource for marginalized groups is
that suspected criminals who claim or benefit from rights seem to many
people to be unfairly and illegitimately claiming their own status of
marginalization or victimhood and demanding protections based on
that status. Given the tough "security talk" about bad actors and delinquency discussed above, the idea that criminals might themselves be
victimized in some way, that crime and criminality might be related to
structural processes of marginalization, institutional failings, and social
and economic inequalities, and thus that people suspected of criminal
activity might indeed be in need of rights-based protections seems out of
place, if not utterly absurd, to many people in Guatemala. In the context of tough talk about national security and the problem of delinquency in a place that is considered a "narco-state" or "failed state,"
and amid the globalization of neoliberalism, with its emphasis on enterprise and a "do-it-yourself" ethos, as the reigning framework of political economy, rights come to seem like both part of the problem (i.e., a
stumbling block to effectively dealing with insecurity) and a solution to
that problem (i.e., the only way to contend with social suffering and
contest a lack of safety).

LOCATING INDIGENOUS LAW

Despite their suspicious attitudes toward both human rights and state
institutions, Maya people in Tecpán have not uncritically embraced a

program of "indigenous law." Many do not see it as a welcome alternative. In popular discourse throughout Guatemala, indigenous law is often equated with lynching and other acts of violence carried out by citizens against suspected criminals. A news story in Guatemala's *Prensa Libre* (Castillo et al. 2011), for example, quotes a representative of the President's Commission on Human Rights recounting a lynching incident in the majority-indigenous department of Huehuetenango in terms of people there "quenching their thirst for justice" (my translation). There were at least five hundred cases of lynching in Guatemala between 1996 and 2002, and these incidents have been a favorite topic of the national media, exploited in colorful images of burning cars and beaten bodies.

The violence sometimes carried out by highland residents in the immediate aftermath of a suspected thief's capture tends to overshadow, in the popular imagination, other manifestations of "indigenous law," which include processes of fact-finding and conflict resolution carried out by Maya community leaders apart from state proceedings and according to specific sets of values.[3] Social scientists tend to frame the incidence of lynching in Guatemala as an inevitable outcome of the internal armed conflict, brought about by the enduring social and psychological trauma the conflict caused and the militarization of daily life it impelled through institutions such as the military's Civil Self-Defense Patrols (Patrullas de Autodefensa Civil, or PACs), which mandated that highland residents patrol their communities' streets at night and hand over anyone suspected of subversive activity to the state. PACs sometimes carried out acts of brutalization and violence against their neighbors. Researchers also point to the social and economic conditions of the postwar period—which include widespread inequality, chronic poverty, a lack of access to formal judicial institutions, and endemic criminal inpunity—as lying at the root of lynchings in the country (see Godoy 2002, 2006; Fernández García 2004; Handy 2004; Adams and Bastos 2003; and Kobrak and Gutiérrez 2001). Lynching and other forms of collective violence have been associated in much of this literature and in the Guatemalan media with indigenous people and the rural regions they inhabit. Yet 53 percent of lynchings and attempted lynchings reported in 2008 occurred in urban areas, mostly in the capital department of Guatemala (Camus 2011: 65), where the majority of people do not identify as indigenous, and where, as I noted previously, nonindigenous *ladinos* often deny the presence of an indigenous population altogether.

In Tecpán, Maya people described to me that there was a fine line between indigenous law and the "dangerous" tendencies in many highland towns toward violent reprisals against suspected gang members and criminals. Miguel Cumez, a thirty-five-year-old garment manufacturer who I often accompanied when he traveled to sell his products in market towns around the highlands, described what he called *el castigo Maya* (Mayan punishment), in starkly negative terms:

> It's not that the Mayas were always like this. Mayan punishment is what the indigenous people do over there in Sololá and El Quiché. The indigenous municipalities have it as a kind of rule that, when a person is captured, they tie him up and put him in the center of the plaza, and, in a public display, they whip him. . . . They punish him, take his clothes off, and beat him. In Tecpán, we're not capable of that kind of thing. We say that those people are backwards [*atrasadas*]."

With a sly nod toward my potentially exoticizing anthropological studies or *gringa* gaze (or both), he added, "Like cannibals." I pointed out that no one was being eaten. He laughed and continued:

> Well, we say they're backwards. I mean, not moderate. And they don't go along with our principles, our religious principles here in Tecpán. For us, our religion doesn't permit us to act like that, and our customs don't allow it either. Over there in Sololá, they still have a lot of respect for their ancestors, really. So the custom from long ago, before there were any police, was immediate punishment. In El Quiché, the immediate punishment is to set the criminals on fire.

Miguel pointed to his Catholic faith as providing a source of principles to use for dealing with questions of justice and punishment. He also contrasted the "customs" in Tecpán with those of people in Sololá and El Quiché, two departments with indigenous majority populations located further to the west in Guatemala and associated, in his mind, with more firmly rooted traditions and less modern ways of life. The perceived loss of traditional values in Tecpán, which apparel producers, including Miguel, often lamented and associated with the move away from subsistence farming and toward commerce and industry, took on a positive valence in Miguel's commentary on "Mayan punishment." His ambivalence about tradition reflects the historical layering of diverse meanings of indigeneity in Guatemala. On one hand, there is the long-standing "Indian problem": the idea that Maya people—poor, uneducated, mired in tradition, and inferior in every way to *ladinos*—pose an obstacle to the state's social modernization and economic development

(Handy 1989). This "problem" has been addressed in various ways according to shifting security agendas, discourses, and institutional formations, from the assimilationist projects understaken by the state during the nineteenth century liberal period to the genocidal violence of the armed conflict. On the other hand, indigeneity has emerged in the postwar context as an objectified identity that holds significant political, legal, and symbolic capital vis-à-vis international law and neoliberal modes of publicity and promotion, including branding (see chapter 3).

Edward F. Fischer (2001: 51) writes that, since colonial times, Tecpán has been "on the border between the Indian and Spanish worlds" of Guatemalan society, as it was situated close enough to the Spanish- and later *ladino*-dominated capital region to facilitate access and exchange while also serving as a gateway to the indigenous west. The departments of Sololá and El Quiché, which border Tecpán's municipal boundaries, are part of the western ethnoscape, conceptualized as more indigenous, more rural, more remote, and more closely linked to tradition in the national spatial imaginary. "Spatial imaginary" is a term used by Ghassan Hage (1996) to emphasize how particular kinds of space, such as the nation or the city, are thought to have particular qualities and how senses of community and belonging are often mapped onto geographical space. As part of the Guatemalan national spatial imaginary, anything outside of Guatemala City is referred to as *El Interior* (the interior) by capital-city *ladinos,* despite the fact that the capital sits near the geographical center of the country. The term connotes, therefore, the kind of colonial geography that associates modernity with the colonized coast and indigeneity and "the primitive" with the uncharted, inner regions of the continent and with the colonial subject (Said 2008).

In Miguel's discussion, spatial distinctions took on temporal dimensions as well. He said that "the Maya," among whom he counts himself, "weren't always like that," and yet he situated practices of community justice as part of a shared past, a time before modernity, "before there were any police." He diagnosed lynching as a symptom of both the contemporary problems of insecurity in Guatemalan society and the backwardness or backward-looking tendencies of certain constituencies or groups of Mayas who have not adapted their customs to modern times or transitioned from the ways of "their ancestors" to the norms imposed by institutionalized religion and state law, thereby rendering issues of law and custom a matter of assimilation and hybridity. His commentary speaks to a cultural politics, the interesting position that *tecpanecos* straddle between neocolonial stereotyping and the revaluation of indigeneity since the end of the armed conflict, as indigenous people in Guatemala have come to occupy social locations and rhetorics of hybridity in which they are able to claim indigenous identity at the same time as they take distance from cultural forms, practices, stereotypes, and physical spaces that are overdetermined as indigenous, backward, lawless, and even immoral.

But other garment manufacturers in Tecpán with whom I spoke idealized "immediate punishment." They characterized what they termed "community justice" as the answer to the kinds of insecurity that threaten commerce, and the social order more generally, even if they also expressed ambivalence about whether beating up suspected criminals is an appropriate way for people to behave. Miguel himself has been involved in a neighborhood security committee organized to investigate suspicious activity and "prevent crime," as he explained to me. In at least three of Tecpán's four central barrios, men have organized into such groups and regularly *hacer rondas* (patrol the streets) after nightfall. Neighborhood watch associations are common to many parts of the world (Low 2003; Caldeira 2001). In highland Guatemala, however, *rondas* call to mind the history of the PACs, which were organized by the military after its scorched-earth campaign had weakened the guerrilla movement. *Patrulleros* (patrollers) in towns across the highlands were charged with surveilling and reporting on their neighbors to military commanders; they were required to follow orders, which included, at times, carrying out disappearances and murders; and they were sometimes mobilized as unpaid labor on state-led development projects (Schirmer 1988: 91). Miguel and other *tecpanecos* insisted to me that the neighborhood watch organizations they were forming during my fieldwork were utterly distinct from the PACs and disconnected from that history. They pointed to the fact that people had no choice but to serve as *patrulleros* during the conflict and that the military was in charge of those organizations, providing training, arms, and enforcing participation. *Patrulleros* were not protecting their communities back then, insisted Miguel, but rather following orders. The PACs also provided the opportunity for people, especially the *comisionados* (individuals selected by the military commanders to serve as local leaders), to accuse local rivals of subversive actions and thereby subject them to violence.[4] The new watchgroups formed by Miguel and men like him are different. They have, at least theoretically, a biopolitical bent toward fostering life, welfare, and—especially—market activity rather than enacting austerity or extending state-sponsored violence. As Miguel and others explained to me, neighborhood security committees are voluntary, democratic, and unarmed. At the same time, these associations have been, in part, an attempt to regain feelings of security and "control" (see chapter 4) associated with the conflict era's empty streets and narrativized by some *tecpanecos* in terms of cohesive families, obedient youth, and organized communities. The formation of these watchgroups must be seen in the context of the rise of right-wing support even among Maya men and women, who have historically been terrorized by state militarism, as a response to the much-publicized and rumored problems of delinquency and drugs, and the realities of widepread crime, extortion, and violence. Highland residents sometimes expressed nostalgia for the 1980s, when, as they commented to me, heavy-handed political administrations kept the streets clear and the civilian crime level low. This was a common reason cited by some Maya men and women for their support, for example, for former dictator Efraín Ríos Montt's presidential bid in 2003 and was a regularly preferred explanation for the popularity of former general Otto Pérez Molina in the 2007 and 2011 elections (Benson et al. 2008).

In 2009, groups of men in Tecpán gathered to physically punish suspected theives on at least two occasions. In one incident, violence was directed toward a young man accused of stealing meat from a butcher shop. In the other, a group of young men accused of breaking into a home on the edge of town were bound, beaten, and doused with gasoline. "No one dared" light them on fire, as one Tecpán resident explained to me, because "if you commit that crime, it doesn't matter if the thief is guilty. Killing someone is a major offense, and that's a problem that it's better to just avoid." Human rights and the rule of law figured as obstacles to swift justice in this resident's account. Other *tecpanecos* with whom I spoke about these two cases—even people who were standing by while the young men were tied up and beaten—expressed concern about the ethics of the harsh treatment the suspected thieves received at the hands of community members. Miguel asserted that the desire to beat a criminal is "normal . . . because, what else can you do? If you don't stand up for yourself, people will take advantage of you." He referred to the beating that the accused meat thief received as "an act of self-defense," a turn of phrase that put the wartime PACs and current modes of vigilance in uncomfortably close proximity. He then changed his tone and distanced himself from the occurrence by noting that the town resident who had taken the lead in meting out the punishment was a former *comisionado,* a *ladino* man who had been trained by the army as a PAC leader, implying that the man's involvement with the state during the armed conflict partly helped to explain the severity of the man's actions, a stretched temporality of violence. Miguel told me that everyone at the scene felt the man doing the punishing was taking things too far by abusing the boy, and Miguel lamented the fact that no one dared to speak out against the man or even resist his orders to tie up the suspect and hold him still while the ex-*comisionado* pummeled his face and abdomen. If ethical debate and sorrow surrounded such episodes, so too did a history of violence carried out in the name of law and order, and this episode reflects the extent to which broad histories and circumstances of violence and insecurity can foster a dangerous "moral world" that induces brutalization and encourages the use of collectivized violence to obtain various ends (Kleinman 1999).

Community justice is a potentially dangerous enterprising mode of security practice and law enforcement in Tecpán, but it is not the outcome of an automatic process, the inevitable unfolding of indigenous custom and tradition, or a rote response to the state's inadequacies in terms of providing reliable police protection or criminal justice. The fact that military and police no longer exercise the authoritarian modes of surveillance, control, and violence in Maya communities that they did during the armed conflict and that the extension of the democratic state into the highlands has been somewhat constrained and conditioned by a neoliberal program of fiscal austerity and limited government is part of the picture of community-level security. There is a political economy to this violence. There is also a historical and anthropological explanation related to the formation of dangerous moral worlds. The fact that people in the highlands express a generalized mistrust of the state and its law enforcement and judicial capacities factors into their involvement in neighborhood security committees. These practices are also an emergent form of action—sometimes violent action—in the context of a society that is itself wracked by violence and shot through with felt senses of insecurity, and they constitute a response that is not unique to the Maya highlands but that shows up in the capital city and many other parts of the world as well. What is more, the abstract or theoretical problematization of community security practices as not being in line with an idealized rule of law fails to account for the ways that militarized and heavy-handed security is promoted on a national level by the political right and on an international level by a security apparatus that blames delinquent populations for all kinds of problems and makes them available for targeted surveillance, development interventions, reform efforts, and violence. Maya men and women are caught up in existential scenarios and moral conundrums in which violence sometimes comes to seem legitimate and reasonable but is also actively debated and problematized among people who have differing perspectives on the ethics of community and the politics of the iron fist.

LIVING OFF OF OTHERS

Even as Maya people in Tecpán confront and attempt to address felt insecurities related to crime in their town, many residents made a point of communicating to me that Tecpán is not, in and of itself, a source of crime and criminality. Amidst national narratives that associate the indigenous highlands with backwardness and forms of lawlessness and violence related to lynching and other supposed signs and scenes of primitiveness, many people in Tecpán not only distance themselves from "indigenous law" and its connotations but also narrate the crime with which they contend as the result of distant processes and conditions that are decidedly separate and distinct from the modern, ordered, and enterpreneurial context that they say describes their community. Apparel producers in particular emphasized to me that their local industry is a form of enterprise and development that keeps people busy with work and engaged in positive social and market relations, leaving little time or space for delinquency to take hold and thrive within the town limits. The stories they told me about the origins and causes of crime had a lot to do with spatial imaginaries and processes of scale-making. Anna Tsing (2004) developed the concept of "scale-making" to call attention to scale as a social construct rather than a fixed category of analysis or attribute. She describes, for instance, how "global" rights and development agendas and social movements emerge out of practical engagements on the part of people acting in specific places to extend projects and ideas across space and inflect them with a universal character by arguing and advocating for their broad relevance and applicability. The same can be said for how situations, problems, and practices come to take on the quality of being "local"—that is, rooted in a particular place and set of geographically bounded conditions. In Guatemala, the perception of crime as originating in and deriving from specific contexts and processes happens through cultural dynamics of definition, interpretation, and representation. For example, in the stories that apparel producers told me, crime was scaled and spatialized in ways that pushed back against portrayals of delinquency as a generalized condition in the highlands that is endemic to all indigenous communities. Their stories focused blame on particular individuals and groups said to reside outside of Tecpán, scaling delinquency and defining the scope of responsibility in a way that perhaps motivated against a more holistic, anthropological understanding of insecurity, crime, and "everyday violence" as the result of broad institutional and structural processes.

The stories apparel producers told me about space, scale, and security often turned on associations between different kinds of economic relationships and forms of work and different kinds of places in Guatemala. For example, an older workshop owner explained rising crime rates in the center of town as follows:

> There used to be a plantation [*finca*] outside of town. The man who owned it had plantations on the coast, too. Our whole *raza* [race, people] went to work on the coast, worked for many years. One day, this man says, "Leave." "But we've given a large part of our lives, so give us somewhere to live." "Okay, I will," he says. So he divided up the plantation, and I don't know if he gave it to them or sold it to them, but everyone who was working on the coast came here to that land. They made it into a *colonia* [peripheral residential development]. So those people have all the bad habits from over there [*de por allá*, meaning "from the coastal region"], and that's why they turned into gang members [*mareros*]. They love to assault people and steal. That's another way of life, but they're indigenous people, just like us.

The *colonia* to which he referred, known as La Giralda, has grown over the last two decades to include a couple hundred homes constructed of cement block, wood, and sheet metal, which lie mostly along dirt paths that cut through fields that stretch toward the mountain range on Tecpán's northern edge. Recall the photograph of a garment workshop in La Giralda (figure 9) featured in chapter 2, which showed dusty concrete floors and cracked wooden walls, as compared to some workshops in the center of Tecpán that have neatly tiled floors, painted concrete-block walls, and sealed windows. The cheap construction of homes and workshops in La Giralda and anecdotal evidence I collected that revealed much lower land values in the neighborhood as compared to the town center suggest that residents of La Giralda have a lower socioeconomic status than those who live in other parts of the town, and the unpaved roads and peripheral location of the *colonia* certainly led many residents of Tecpán's central barrios to interpret La Giralda as a place where poverty and danger were intertwined. People living in the center of town often cautioned me against visiting the several dozen garment workshops scattered among houses in the *colonia* or even walking along the street leading to the development. The general consensus among *tecpanecos* who did not live there was that La Giralda was overrun with gang activity. The older manufacturer who recounted to me the story of the founding of the *colonia* continued by offering an explanation for why its inhabitants had turned to crime and violence:

> Things are different on the coast. The system of work is different. There, you get up early, and because of the heat, by eight or nine o'clock in the morning, all you can do is rest. So they pass the whole day doing nothing. Well, all of a sudden, they're getting into trouble every day. It's like that sometimes when you have free time. It's just what comes to you to do, what is not correct. So this was about fifteen years ago, and it started to cause problems. The kids were drinking, doing drugs, hanging out in the streets, robbing people. I think the problems we have today are rooted in that. The seed was planted years ago. Now it's a way of life for the kids: hanging out, wearing black, and messing around [*fregar*] on the weekends.

In this man's narrative, problems and problematic social types, who are recognizable in dress and behavior, come from some other place, one outside of Tecpán's social and geographic boundaries (cf. Burrell 2010; Goldín 2001). Delinquency is understood in terms of spatial and social disjunctures between the highlands and the coast and between the rhythms of work in each setting. Importantly, work has been identified as a principal causative agent in the illness models that many Maya people in Guatemala share (Cosminsky 1977). The harsh conditions of plantation labor (as opposed to *milpa*, or subsistence, agriculture in the highlands) make one especially vulnerable to sickness, some have said, given that the hot, humid climate, distinctive plant and animal life, and difference in diet on the coast all compound the effects of the work itself, leaving a person's natural and metaphysical defenses against disease and disability dangerously weak (McCreery 1994; Offit 2011). Given the complex relationship between psychophysical factors, emotional states, and moral actions that researchers have identified as central to illness models in Guatemala as elsewhere, it is not surprising that conditions believed to produce physical illness are also invoked to explain the purported moral defenciencies of these migrant workers (Cosminsky 1977). Illness is commonly explained by Maya men and women as a punishment for "angry living" (Brintnall 1979). There are interesting similarites here to how *ladino* residents of Guatemala City explain crime and violence in urban neighborhoods. As Manuela Camus (2011) notes, nonindigenous people living in the capital commonly say that Maya men and women who move to the city from the countryside become corrupted not only by encountering *delincuentes* (delinquent youth), who prey on their naiveté, but also by becoming unmoored from the moral and social structures of agrarian life. They "get lost" in the unfamiliar terrain of the city (Camus 2011: 59). The cultural importance of place as a determinant of identity, morality, and health and the close association between forms of work and ways of life evident across the ethnographic literature on Guatemala come together in these tropes of spatial displacement, disorientation, and corruption.

Part of the story of plantation labor in Guatemala is the harsh work conditions and pestilent climate of the coast. The older manufacturer's story recounted above also cited an abundance of "free time" as a major factor in shaping the morality of people who were once migrant laborers and now reside in La Giralda. This was a common theme in explanations of contemporary crime in Tecpán. Another garment producer relayed concerns about how La Giralda is full of delinquent youth and then commented to me, "This is why there is so much violence, robberies, extortion, bribes, all of that: because [the delinquents and the criminals] want to have things, but they can't have them, not because there is no work, but because they want things to come easy." These men's narrative explications of how crime came to Tecpán or how crime in Tecpán can be explained turn on the idea that people can be corrupted through a process of being displaced from their native lands and then returning to those lands, a narrative that links to broader idioms of migration, corruption, and urban criminality in Guatemala as well as to cultural models of affliction, illness, and moral depravation. Their stories also reveal the ways that criminal activity threatens a social and spatial imaginary that many apparel manufacturers hold dear, one that links Tecpán's urban core and the rhythms of work and industry that define the history of the apparel trade with safety and security, diligence and earnestness, and a sense of ethnic and gendered solidarity and community-level economic development. This is more than just a way of interpreting crime, of making it into a certain kind of scalar process linked to movement and mobility and the outside. It is also an expression of pride and the importance of self-reliance, business ownership, an entrepreneurial ethic, and a commitment to a progress model of local development achieved through steadfast industriousness. These tropes are salient in a place where labor migration, uprootedness, exploitative relations of economic dependency, and harsh work conditions have actually been the norm for many people and their families, and where, in the broad social imaginaries that swirl about in Guatemala, these histories of manual labor, rurality, and capitalist subjugation are also used by nonindigenous people to locate and disparage the indigenous population.

In a third story that was recounted to me about La Giralda as a place of criminality and a source of crime affecting Tecpán's urban core, a garment workshop owner commented to me that the former laborers who had been granted land were not the only ones involved in criminal activity. He also expressed concern about the other side of the division of plantation labor: the rich man's family. He explained that there was a *finca* nearby owned by a man who provided work for indigenous people in the area. However, "his children just watched. We watched those people [the family], and how they have all grown up. They make all kinds of trouble. They live disordered lives." He paused and then added, "People just want to live off of others, off of the people" (Quieren vivir de la gente). He suggested that the wealthy land owner's heirs, who ended up living alongside the former migrant laborers in the *colonia,* had themselves fallen into lives of crime and chaos and went on to link the family to gang activity. He associated the "disordered lives" of the rich man's children with conditions of inequality arising from a history of labor exploitation and the accumulation of land and capital, suggesting that the decadence and laziness that is part of plantation ownership leads to delinquency and degeneration. Wealth figures as a generalized metaphor for easy living and a lack of work ethic and as an explanation for social deviance, since the man's family was said to have adopted a way of life premised on "living off of others," which may describe both the process through which people who own the means of production— the land owner and his heirs, in this case—were able to exploit the labor of indigenous workers and accumulate wealth, and the specific forms of criminality—linked to idleness, greed, and a lack of industry—in which the descendents living within a vague present are said to be involved. As a commentary on the dynamics of capitalism and the potential moral dangers and pitfalls of greed and excess, this man's explication of one family's involvement in crime has a lot in common with the discourses of envy and individualism that apparel producers in Tecpán draw on to condemn unfair competition and socioeconomic stratification within their trade (see chapter 2), where producers understand a bad moral disposition, rooted in jealousy and greed, to be threatening to social stability and community solidarity, not necessarily because it leads to illegal activity but because it inspires unethical business practices and unusual wealth accumulation. This story, like the others told about La

Giralda, thus characterized certain forms of work and ways of doing business as part of the problem of crime, with the apparel trade standing apart as an industry in which people develop a different set of values and a relationship to capital, labor, and community that motivates against unfair gain, laziness, and deviance.

This evaluation of the apparel trade as a site of morality and an antidote to delinquency was made even more plain in the way that yet another apparel producer characterized the problem of crime and its relationship to the plantation system. He recounted the basic tale about how indigenous people had moved to the coast to work and then come back and resettled in La Giralda, adding the following commentary: "People from the coast are really bad, they come here to make trouble, and then other people get blamed. But the reality is that people here are by and large hardworking and kind; we all have our own businesses. We're businessmen [*comerciantes*], and so it doesn't make sense for us to be mean. We live off of other people [*vivimos de la gente*], and you know yourself that Tecpán is very tranquil." As part of his telling of the story of plantations, the coast, migration, and Tecpán, this manufacturer used the same phrase, "living off of others," that was used by the man quoted above to disparage the exploitative practices of a wealthy land owner and the consequences of capital accumulation for successive generations, yet he invoked the phrase to positively explain how deeply his business and those of his fellow garment producers depend on the cultivation of "kind," respectful, and thoroughly professional relationships to clients and customers. In both uses of the phrase, "living off of others" refers to capitalist market relations and serves as an acknowledgement of the social tensions and potential moral hazards that often accompany profit-seeking behavior. Making a living by extracting value from a production and marketing process, this man figures, demands a regulating style that promotes the collective organization of a safe and secure market environment where clients feel they can trust manufacturers and where collective gains are being made. In his estimation, the apparel trade motivates against meanness at the level of individual interactions and conditions a peaceful, "tranquil" way of life.

The man's criticism of people from the coast was also a defensive posture against potential allegations that *tecpanecos* themselves might be responsible for crime and violence or that their businesses involve elements of concealment, secrecy, aggression, or hostility. In complaining that the wrong people sometimes get blamed for insecurity and then asserting that he and other businessmen could never be the real culprits of such "trouble," he expressed concern about the possibility of misrecognition, a concern that other residents of Tecpán, the state, law enforcement agents, and national media are mistaking people who rightfully belong to the town and its entrepreneurial trade for criminals, businessmen for pirates, and pirates for delinquents. His commentary and those of the other manufacturers quoted above—who all linked crime, the coast, migration, capitalist enterprise, and various strategies and degrees of accumulation—participated in a process of scale-making in which crime was made into an outsider problem related to influx and interconnections. These commentaries were about managing the scope and scale of blame for crime and violence in a context where security discourses that have been scaled up to national and international levels allege that particular groups and individuals, such as indigenous people and brand pirates, are indeed responsible for insecurity and moral disarray. The claims made by apparel producers about stereotyped bad actors, such as those who live in La Giralda, and the need to speak about, monitor, or punish them are linked to the careful surveillance of outsiders and unfamiliar faces in Tecpán, the organization of neighborhood watch groups, and a somewhat defensive rhetorical and affective stance among highland residents who want to put forth a model of a moral community and thriving industry in the face of accusations that might implicate them as part of a security problem.

Talk about delinquency and crime in Tecpán as a moral crisis happens amid experiences of danger and challenges to safety. Garment manufacturers regularly contend with extortion and threats of violence. In 2009, Julio Toc was paying regular *impuestos* (taxes, bribes) to extortionists. He first received payment demands accompanied by threats against his family in 2001. He recounted to me that one of his employees, who was later discovered to be a "very dangerous" individual involved in numerous kidnappings and killings, had shared information about Julio's business with his criminal associates. "Fortunately, we were able to get to the bottom of things, and the police arrested him," Julio explained. "It was a real threat and a truly difficult situation for us." Since then, however, other people (not employees) have made similar demands on a regular basis. Julio figured that it was not worth risking his or a family member's life to find out if the threats were credible, so he was paying about five hundred quetzales per month in exchange for safety. "It's hard to raise a family here," he told me. "We stay inside. We don't want to run the risk, because they surveil us [*porque controlan*], they know our names, and say, 'Pay up, or I'll kill your family.'"

It is generally considered better to be safe than sorry, yet apparel producers with whom I spoke sometimes interpreted forms of *delincuencia* they observed in their town as copies of the "real" crime that plagues the capital city. They had the sense that many young *tecpaneco* men merely imitate the delinquency they see portrayed in media, adopting dress practices and a bodily hexis associated with criminality in order to participate in a rough-and-tumble, masculine style. These men may engage in petty criminal activity due to pressure from peers, but their true identity, the story goes, is distinct from the "real" gang members and drug traffickers who are assumed to reside in Guatemala City. A young manufacturer who said he knew a few of the supposed *delincuentes* who hung around the corners in their baggy jeans said to me:

> There are some kids here who don't have any power, who just imitate others but don't do anything. They are kids who imitate, they do drugs and all that, but they don't kill anyone. Sometimes they come after a person and extort money from them, from people who come from the *aldeas* [hamlets]. They came after my brother once, and he told me, so I went with him and told them to back off. Maybe they tried to get money from people here [in the urban center], but the people didn't let them, so they've started up with people from the *aldeas*.

He implied that people from the hamlets are more naïve about youthful pranks and perhaps less able to discern between the "original" criminals and the "imitations" and so therefore give in to demands for money more easily than residents of the town center.

In other stories I was told about experiences of crime and violence, this ability to distinguish between real and fake threats was portrayed as an important dimension of how people contend with insecurity and pursue security and survival strategies. The owner of a long-established and well-known workshop that specialized in men's sweaters recounted that he had received a phone call from a man demanding a thousand quetzales. "It was extortion," he told me, "and because I didn't know any better—one gets confused and doesn't know how to handle things—I paid them." He went on to describe how, after additional phone calls and payments, he began to sense that the threats the caller was making against him and his family were not real and ventured to gamble on that feeling:

> They called again and told me the same story over and over, a story about how they are with an organized crime ring, that they know me, they know when I come in and when I go out, they know my family, . . . and they need this amount of money. So they start to tell me this same story over again, and

I reacted. I said, "Look, you're screwing with me. Why are you asking for money again?" And I had the receipt from the bank where they told me to deposit the money, and there was a name on the receipt. So I told them, "I know who *you* are. I have proof against *you,* so now I'm going to screw with you. Go fuck yourself!" And *pum!* [He mimes the action of slamming down a telephone receiver.] And that was it. That was three months ago.

Based on the fact that the caller seemed not to remember his own story, and emboldened by having what he believed to be the extortionist's name on the receipts for the bank deposits, the producer refused to deliver another payment.

I asked him how someone could act like a dangerous criminal but not actually pose a threat. He replied that he figured the people were calling him from jail, where they had picked up the idea from "real gang members." It is common for extortion rings to be run from Guatemala's prisons (O'Neill 2010), and this fact circulates among manufacturers as they confront threats and decide how to deal with them. This man determined that, if the people were calling from jail, they could not likely carry out the threats made against him and his family. Even so, when I asked why he had not turned the receipts over to the police, he replied that escalating the matter to an official accusation could transform it "into something real." His mistrust of the police and the criminal justice system led him to assume that if he "informed" on the extortionists, they would surely evade prosecution, and his act of aggression against them would be reason for them to actually come after him and inflict real harm. He viewed engagement with the formal legal system not as a security strategy but as a medium for the transubstantiation of an impotent copy into a reality that would be capable of causing genuine harm. He sensed that legal action would have put him into contact with criminals in a way that was truly threatening. It would have moved the delinquent from the distant confines of jail into a formalized relationship of accusation and responsibility, bringing the two parties together in ways that he perceived as too close and potentially dangerous.

In sum, Maya apparel producers are often suspicious of the state, dismissive of its rhetorics of law and order, and cynical about official corruption, and, as discussed earlier in this chapter, they sometimes take a critical view of US interventionism and international development projects and security agendas. At times, they also adopt rhetorics of blame that draw on or play into hegemonic state and transnational narratives of individualized responsibility for widespread conditions of insecurity; they question the applicability of rights to individuals and groups said to be utterly undeserving due to their criminality, for instance, while figuring themselves as people who are properly equipped to parse out blame, to separate real threats from fake ones, and to take appropriate actions to guarantee their own security and that of others in their community. Maya apparel producers scan the streets and patrol their neighborhoods in ways that reflect an overwhelming concern with crime that is understandable against a backdrop of everyday violence and endemic social suffering. Yet in doing so, they participate in practices and discourses and debates about crime, violence, and responsibility that may sometimes take away from a more critical confrontation of "the criminal and violent acts of the powerful and elite" (Scheper-Hughes 1993: 228) and the forms of "structural violence" (Farmer 2004) that limit life chances for indigenous people in Guatemala and that make them, and marginalized groups in other parts of the world, available for policing and criminalization as potential sources of dilution, pollution, and threat.

In the stories recounted here about delinquency, extortion, and threat, other places—coastal plantations and urban jails—are seen as the sources of crime and criminals. Maya apparel producers position themselves not as part of those settings but rather as members of a hardworking, steadfast, and safe community organized around a local industry that involves people in work and trade in ways that prevent the kinds of moral decay and criminality that they perceive as emerging out of other sociological and economic formations. In a context of deep material insecurity and amid perceived and actual problems of crime and disorder, apparel producers see themselves as decidedly not delinquent and definitely moral and modern, even as they also invoke themes of ethnicity, indigeneity, and locality in relation to their trade. Their claims to morality and ethnic pride are powerful correctives to national discourses that figure all indigenous people living in the highlands as partly responsible for insecurity because of their alleged drag on national progress and aversion to the rule of law and because of specters of subversive politics that go back to the internal armed conflict and obviously remain resonant for men like Julio Toc, whose story of political and personal transformation and consistency I described above. National narratives that disparage indigenous Guatemalans run together with competing tendencies in international law and rights discourse. A few decades ago, Maya people were labeled communists and subversives and targeted by the state and a transnational Cold War apparatus as threats to national and regional stability. In recent years, their indigeneity has emerged as an important cultural status and political resource as international institutions, the development industry, and the state government have endorsed indigenous and cultural rights and adopted an affirmative rhetoric around multiculturalism, even as racist discourses and forms of structural marginalization that disadvantage indigenous people in Guatemala persist. And at the same time as the status of indigenous people has been somewhat in flux, rising crime rates have been politicized as evidence of a need for the increased militarization of daily life in Guatemala and more effective criminalization of people considered to be dangerous and threatening— such as delinquents, gang members, and drug traffickers, but also pirates, who are sometimes equated with terrorists in international IP law discourse and fashion, film, software, and music industry propaganda. The claims that Maya apparel producers make about the ethics and morality of their trade challenge national political rhetoric and international legal frameworks that figure this group as part of an ongoing and evolving problem of criminality and anticitizenship on national and global levels and as a threat to a modern fashion industry. Indigenous men claim that they have been continuously industrializing, cultivating market relationships, and training others in the trade in order to promote autonomy and self-reliance and to expand opportunities for subsequent generations of indigenous people in the areas of education and enterprise. And, besides, their trade is not new. They are not recently minted "ethnic entrepreneurs" whose business plans were molded by microloan managers or set out in presentations made by NGO workers, and they do not fit into a simple and disparaging model of "pirates," as international IP law would have it, or "informal" actors, as state and international economic formalization programs make it seem, as if indigenous people in the highlands are suddenly "knocking off" brands to make a quick dollar, "copying" the United States or Europe to reap profits unfairly, or evading state regulation because of a problematic condition of unprofessionalism and attitude of noncompliance or defiance that defines a flawed culture and character. Rather, Maya apparel manufacturers have been making fashionable clothing in Tecpán for decades, engaging in livelihood struggles that have been crafted amid marginalizing, controlling, and destructive processes of all kinds, including state violence and warfare, structural discrimination, and most recently, the international criminalization of their enterprising businesses and regulating styles.

Conclusion

Late Style

This conclusion takes its title from Edward Said's 2006 book, *On Late Style,* which argues that creative work produced late in a great artist's life often breaks abruptly and definitively with the style the artist developed over his or her career—that is, the style for which the artist is well known and which has become popular and easily reproducible. Conditioned by impending debilitation and death, late style throws off the chains of self-consciousness and presents a radical program for the future.

Said took the concept of late style from Theodor Adorno (2002), who introduced the notion in his meditations on Beethoven. Adorno argued that the beloved composer's last works were distinctive from his previous compositions not because of the old man's hearing loss and senility (as so many critics have alleged) but because Beethoven had willingly and thoughtfully committed himself to dissonance, polyphony, and fragmentation—to "blank spaces" rather than "development"—toward the end of his life (Adorno 2002: 566). It was Beethoven's late work, Adorno noted, that became the prototype for a "new," modern aesthetic, the "advanced music" of Schoenberg, Webern, Stravinsky, and Berg (Adorno 2004; see Said 2006: 13). For Adorno, Beethoven's late style confirmed the aesthetic and philosophical truths of the negative dialectic. Wise in his years and disenchanted with the bourgeois social order and his own influence on its cultural sensibilities, Beethoven rejected the movement of history and the promises of progress. He surrendered himself to the reality of perpetual catastrophe. Synthesis is impossible; art is exile.

Late style is critical and courageous. It foregrounds tension and lack of harmony as it showcases "deliberately unproductive productiveness" and "going *against*" (Said 2006: 7). Maya business owners may have little in common with Beethoven, yet the concept of late style is useful for thinking about the legal problematization of knockoff fashion and the changing relationship of indigenous people to international law and politics. Piracy is a late style that materializes the all-too-easy reproducibility of contemporary cultural forms—mass-produced fashion styles, brand names and logos, digital music and movies, technologies and software. It is a structure of "unproductive productiveness" (i.e., mimicry and imitation) that confounds the globalized discourse of development, which ascribes value only to certain forms of innovation and entrepreneurship and supposedly *not* to copying. Piracy is also a creative process that instantiates new cultural and material styles. But piracy refuses to participate in the synthesis of old and new that results in a socially legitimate and, in the case of fashion branding, legally sanctioned product, the synthesis that Adorno called, conveniently enough, "development."

As I have argued in the previous chapters, the relationship of brand pirates to development discourse has been problematized by legal and business scholars, multinational corporations that hold trademark rights, the World Trade Organization and other international institutions, development and policy analysts, and social scientists seeking to determine the root causes of nonconformity and illegality. The "problem" of piracy has sparked conversations in recent decades about whether trademark law (or some other form of protection) makes sense in the case of fashion, conversations to which I have sought to contribute in the preceding chapters. More often than not, these conversations have generated defensive responses posed in terms of the moral failures of people who participate in piracy and reasoned according to the economic logics of brand dilution. Yet arguments about the detrimental impact of brand piracy on corporate bottom lines are challenged by empirical research conducted by some business scholars and economists that has demonstrated that piracy does not always or even usually decrease "brand value" and is sometimes economically beneficial for brand owners because of the free publicity it generates. The moral arguments against piracy do not hold up either. My research demonstrates that brand pirates in Guatemala are neither intentionally deceiving their clients nor ignorant of the law and therefore in need of re-education.

They are structurally marginalized vis-à-vis free trade regimes and multinational corporations, and, in the absence of a flourishing and formal national economy, they mobilize recognizable brand names as part of their designs in order to compete in a marketplace saturated by logos. In doing so, they participate in the same processes of copying and creativity that structure the fashion industry writ large, processes of taking on influence and making new and different designs, and yet they are criminalized in ways that others are not.

The modern fashion system has been constructed around an aporia— an impossibility of synthesis or closure—related to the importance of copying for the production of style and the simultaneous threat that copying poses to the industry's profitability. The copying of fashion designs cannot be outlawed entirely because it is the industry's most basic technique and conditions the system's temporality and tendency to yield "fast" fashion and big returns. The fashion system is built on copying, influence, and imitation. But copying cannot be limitless, since the production of social (i.e., racial, class, and gender) distinction and an aura of exclusivity is the grounds for modern consumer desire and corporate profits. Brand piracy stands in this gap, and its criminalization is an attempt by the industry to selectively police copying—to separate "good" copying from "bad" copying—according to neocolonial racial and gender divides that are fundamental to the world system in general and the profitability of the fashion industry in particular. For example, when indigenous people in Guatemala assert themselves as rightful participants in the fashion system by making, selling, and wearing fashionable clothing, they threaten the globalized industry's investments in branding strategies that promote a tacit (but sometimes quite explicit) white style by bringing materialized brands into contact with dark-skinned bodies and "underdeveloped" peoples in ways that put the industry's trademarks at risk for brand "pollution." Brand piracy also threatens the racialized and gendered international division of labor that makes it acceptable for some people to be style producers and consumers while others are relegated to the status of manual laborers toiling in the factories in which clothing for consumers in the Global North is assembled. Piracy refuses to accept or give in to IP law's authority to separate out "real" designers and authorized firms that are said to be valuable because of their knowledge work, design acumen, and creative vision from the populations that, in the view of IP law, merely copy and imitate, steal and pilfer, or perform the manual labor that underwrites capital accumulation.

LATE INDIGENEITY

The Maya businessmen who copy popular fashion styles, which often include trademarked brand names, in Guatemala are not "late" just because they are "pirates" or because their production is "unproductive" from the perspective of the fashion industry. There are layers of lateness that make piracy such an acute problem in Guatemala, for instance, and that seem to justify the criminalization of piracy across Latin America and around the world. Consider the association between piracy and informality. The informal economic sector continues to be described and interpreted by scholars, international finance institutions, and state agents as an anachronistic holdover from precapitalist modes of production and a drag on national economies, in spite of research that demonstrates otherwise.[1] This sector, in and of itself, is perceived to threaten developing nations and the international community because of its seeming refusal to submit to state regulatory authority. I have demonstrated how the highland apparel trade, characterized as "informal" according to the definitions used by national and international institutions, is in fact regulated by a broad range of actors, from the police and gang members who demand bribes, to tax administration agents who intervene from time to time with audits and fines, to the clients who push for better designs and lower prices, to the producers themselves, who have adopted a regulating style rooted in a set of normative discourses and practices related to pedagogy, the management of envy and individualism, the ethics of price setting, and proper and improper modes of copying. Maya apparel producers elaborate the marketplace in highland Guatemala and evaluate one another based on an evolving politics of masculinized professionalism and class-based ethnic solidarity, calibrating their business activities in line with these regulatory frameworks. What is more, the apparel trade's "informality" is not a sign or symptom of disconnection from the state. Rather, a relationship to the state that has been and continues to be marked by violence, discrimination, and marginalization motivates Maya people to conceal their lives and livelihoods from government officials. At the same time, intensifying competition linked to free trade agreements contributes to worsening conditions of economic inequality, limiting market opportunities for Maya businesses, keeping them small, and making it unlikely that they will be detected. Thus, while official narratives represent informal economic activities as late—that is, out of synch with modern systems of regulation and governance—the apparel trade is in fact powerfully shaped by interactions with the state and the dynamics of international development.

Maya pirates are also late because they are Maya. Edward Said (2006: 13) wrote that "*lateness* is the idea of surviving beyond what is acceptable and normal." In the contemporary world, where modernity is said to be at large (Appadurai 1996), indigeneity is late. The native is a remnant or holdover. In 2003, the anthropologist Adam Kuper (2003: 389) raised questions about the "return of the native" and the resurgence of the "ghostly category of 'primitive peoples'" in the guise of the United Nations' celebrations of indigenous peoples and the near global support that had been achieved for treaties that proclaim the special rights of such groups. Kuper (2003: 389) quoted former UN secretary-general Boutros Boutros-Ghali, who lamented the suffering that indigenous groups had endured and the fact that they had once "seemed doomed to extinction" and then praised the "welcome change" in attitudes and policies that was occurring on an international scale. Whereas the Western imagination has long entertained an obsession with the "last man" of native history and existence,[2] implying that indigenous people are dying out, indigenous populations have, it seems, following Kuper, bested fate and outlived themselves, hanging on for dear life.

The resurgence of indigeneity as discourse, identity, and practice over the last three decades or so poses interesting conceptual problems for anthropologists and continues to foment charged debates about truth, politics, and representation among indigenous activists, their supporters, and their critics.[3] Kuper's concerns were with the tendency toward essentialism that is inherent in the international legal and discursive framing of indigeneity and with the dangers of making kinship, descent, and, by extension, ethnic or racial difference the principal grounds for rights claims. Natives are essentialized as, well, natives, filling a "savage slot" (Trouillot 1991). Kuper's argument sparked lively debate in a few scholarly journals for several years (summarized in Barnard 2006), but his framing of the issue and many of the published responses to it lacked the nuance of more lengthy and ethnographic treatments of the everyday struggles faced by people who identify as indigenous and who advance legal and political claims on that basis. The writings of Elizabeth Povinelli (2002), Charles Hale (2007), Stuart Kirsch (2006, 2014), John and Jean Comaroff (2009), and Marisol de la Cadena (2000, 2010), to name a few, acknowledge the shortcomings, difficulties, and processes of further marginalization and commodification associated with an international legal discourse of "indigenous rights." Rather than faulting indigenous movements for essentialism (as some anthropologists and activists accused Kuper of doing), these authors have directed their criticism for the essentializing tendencies of legal and political frameworks at the liberal tradition (a political philosophy and theoretical framework that seems taken for granted in Kuper's arguments); neoliberalism and the world economic and political system, which burden indigenous populations and demand certain kinds of claims; and binaristic thinking based in Western epistemology that sets culture against nature and tradition against modernity (see Escobar 2008).

I appreciate that the debate instigated by Kuper exposed some key assumptions in anthropology and in international law having to do with time. Does indigeneity belong to the past (either to anthropology's past or to indigenous people's own past)? Is it anachronistic to speak of indigenous peoples today? I assert that thinking about indigeneity's lateness in the terms provided by Adorno and worked out by Said is a productive way to address these questions without either dismissing and discrediting the struggles in which indigenous people are involved or settling for essentialism. I am interested in the ethical and political possibilities available to people who are late—those who have apparently outlived fate or time—and in where we might be seeing those possibilities realized in the lives of indigenous Guatemalans.

Michael Ralph took up a related question in a recent article on the experience of "surplus time" among African American men in the United States. He cites the lyrics of rap artist (and fashion designer) Kanye West, performed by a chorus of children on the opening track of the album *The College Dropout* (2004), a song titled "We Don't Care": "We wasn't supposed to make it to twenty-five. / Joke's on you, we're still alive." The idea, evident across rap music since the early 1990s, argued Ralph, is that African American men often experience life and reflect on their experience in terms of the inescapability of violence and the inevitability of an early demise. Relegated to "the streets," a place defined in large measure by the drug war and urban marginalization, and thus low life chances (lower, importantly for his argument, for African American men than for African American women), rappers use lyrics to perform a hyper-masculinized utopian relationship to success, sexual conquest, and violence. Living on "surplus time" (i.e., in a condition of lateness), rap artists have promoted a life devoted to pleasure and a politics that is openly critical of the political-economic, legal, and social system that has always already sentenced them to death. The fashionable "bling" phenomenon discussed by Ralph and evidenced in rap lyrics devoted to gold chains and diamond rings is one aesthetic and stylized dimension of how African American men contend with and live out surplus time. Although Ralph does not cite it, another of Kanye West's tracks from *The College Dropout* seems particularly relevant to understanding what is at stake in the fashion and fantasy world of bling as a form of conspicuous consumption and a domain of style production and participation. On the track "All Falls Down," West raps:

> It seems we living the American Dream,
> But the people highest up got the lowest self-esteem.
> The prettiest people do the ugliest things
> For the road to riches and diamond rings.
> We shine because they hate us, floss cause they degrade us.
> We trying to buy back our forty acres.
> And for that paper, look how low we will stoop.
> Even if you in a Benz, you still a nigga in a coupe.

These lyrics deal a forceful blow to well-worn discourses about the possibilities for African Americans to assimilate through hard work, class mobility, and whitening. West insists that, contrary to the "cruel optimism" (Berlant 2011) commodified and sold to people of color, racial schemas and structures in the United States do not allow a path by which black people can cease to be racialized (and denigrated for their racial difference). African American bodies, clothed in Prada, Versace, and Tommy Hilfiger (see passages about Hilfiger and race in chapter 3), are still raced and maligned. People of color driving luxury vehicles and "living the American dream" find out very quickly, West asserts, that they are still reviled as inferior Others, and, even more so, because their economic success and its materialization are interpreted by white Americans as affronts to entrenched structures of white power and privilege—a kind of copy that pollutes a national, white style.

There are obvious and important differences between the life experiences of African Americans and those of indigenous people in highland Guatemala. Race has a distinctive politics and phenomenology in the United States as compared to Central America. It is significant, however, that trademark law is a Euro-American invention and that its globalization has happened at the behest of corporations headquartered in the United States and Western Europe. I am not convinced that the politics of international IP protections can easily be disentangled from the racialized contexts of their emergence and elaboration, especially given that much of what is being regulated by international IP law is the access of racialized populations to the white style that is produced by the likes of Ralph Lauren, Hilfiger, and Abercrombie & Fitch. Kanye West's lyrics speak to the importance of race for understanding the regulation of fashion and style not just in US cities but also on an international scale.

Ralph's analysis of surplus time also inspires me to tease out the temporality of ethnicized and racialized forms of existence and experience in Guatemala in terms of fraught associations between indigeneity and upward mobility and between death and citizenship. Empirically, indigenous Guatemalans did not express themselves to me in fatalistic terms that posited death as always near and existentially felt. But Maya people know full well that they are part of a nation-state that has been and continues to be complexly hostile to their continued existence. They contend daily with interpersonal hostilities and social systems that produce lower life chances for them and for future generations of indigenous Guatemalans. They recognize that the majority of *ladinos* would rather they just go away. Indeed, the history of Guatemala is in many ways a history of political projects aimed at the extermination of the Maya, initially through the twin efforts of slaughter and religious conversion, and then enslavement and forced labor arrangements, followed by liberal assimilationist programs and, late in the twentieth century, a full-scale genocidal military campaign. Maya people are "late," then, not because their seemingly antiquated ways of life and cultural traditions should have died out long ago but because they have somehow, someway, survived hundreds of years of willed and attempted obliteration.

Of course, anthropologists have shown how "ethnic passing" (Warren 1998) is possible in Guatemala in ways that "passing" is not generally available to African Americans. The construction of ethnic and racial categories in Central America has fluctuated over the centuries and continues to transform. At the same time, the idea that essential differences exist between indigenous and nonindigenous people in Guatemala is stridently defended by *ladinos* and indigenous people alike (for very different reasons). Movement between ethnic categories in contemporary Guatemala is sometimes less a matter of indigenous people trying to pass as *ladino* or successfully performing some kind of neutral national identity and more about a denial of identity politics and the politics of difference to people who would claim indigeneity but who publicly display ways of life that are associated with being *ladino*. I detailed how these boundaries are monitored and regulated among Maya apparel producers in chapter 2. Indigeneity can be conferred or denied by nonindigenous Guatemalans as well. For example, *ladino* residents of Guatemala City lament the influx of "dirty Indians" into their neighborhoods and the loss of class status and increases in crime that they blame on that demographic shift (Thomas et al. 2011; Camus 2011). At the same time, and in apparent contradiction, when I posed questions about this history of migration to residents of Guatemala City from various class backgrounds who identified as nonindigenous, the regular response was, "There are no indigenous people in the city." This statement is indicative of a defensive posture among urban *ladinos,* a claim to cosmopolitanism, affluence, and modernity that hinges on the city, *their* city, not being indigenous space. It is also a preemptive denial of indigenous Guatemalans' right to the city, a right that, as David Harvey (2008: 23) argues, is "far more than the individual liberty to access urban resources: it is a right to change ourselves by changing the city." Indigenous people are construed as being late to an urban scene in which they were never really welcome anyway.

Maya people may live in the city, populate online social media, engage in democratic politics, practice Christianity, attend universities, speak Spanish (and English), and wear blue jeans and Ralph Lauren polo shirts, yet they are still uncomfortably and essentially different in the eyes of many nonindigenous people and the national elite, such that the politics of race, identity, and style they confront shares some similarities with the situation that Kanye West critiques. Even Maya people who are business owners and not political activists or Maya-hackers (D. M. Nelson 1999) who openly oppose *ladino* hegemony are still suspected of undermining the economic progress, cultural advancement, and modernity of the Guatemalan nation. Maya people have been and continue to be blamed as internal threats to national security and the international rule of law; they were figured as communists during the Cold War and are suspected of being gang members, delinquents, vigilantes, and pirates today. Their presence is also elegiac, because every indigenous person in a place like Tecpán is linked through kinship and other associations to the disappearances, traumas, loss, and terror of the armed conflict. They serve as evidence of lateness, as residues and remnants of the past injustices of colonialism and postcolonial structures of exploitation and of the failures of liberal reforms. This community of survivors who belong to something of a "surplus time" is thus a "finger in the wound" (D. M. Nelson 1999) of *ladino* nationhood and nationalism, a reminder of the racist foundations of state sovereignty, the bad-faith politics of multiculturalism, and the inequality that national economic indicators and models of growth seek to hide. Indigenous Guatemalans call attention, in sum, to the perpetual catastrophe (cf. Said 2006), ongoing failings, persistent paradoxes, and troubling disjunctures of models of modernity and progress that do not confront, and indeed would rather overlook, past atrocities and the hard truths of the present.

INDIGENOUS ENTREPRENEURSHIP

I do not believe it mere coincidence that "entrepreneur" is both the preferred term used to describe wealthy African Americans in the United States and a key term in international development discourse. The mainstream media consistently portray wealthy and well-known African Americans, from Jay-Z and Beyoncé to Oprah Winfrey and Tiger Woods, as entrepreneurs. There are obviously other ways to talk about wealth, fame, success, and influence. The overwhelmingly white and male population of Wall Street financiers, for example, is more often described using terms such as "professional," "white collar," "businessmen," and "elite." They did not make it, so the story goes, because they are "gifted" or "talented" or "beautiful" like Beyoncé. They do not possess "innate skills," as is said of so many African American athletes. Wall Street executives and analysts are understood to have worked hard and earned their success. Their wealth is justified in terms of their superior intelligence, expertise, and sophistication—they are seen as belonging to a culture of "smartness," as Karen Ho (2009) has demonstrated. According to news reports, they are the backbone of the international economy, and in US national political rhetoric, they are portrayed as "job creators." All of this in spite of their direct responsibility for the recent global economic crisis.[4]

The idea of the entrepreneur has value for African Americans, just as it does for indigenous Guatemalans working in the apparel trade. It describes a long tradition of "independent self-help" enterprise among African Americans (J. Walker 2009). It reflects a tradition of making do and coping amid overwhelming obstacles and intentional projects to obstruct justice and disempower particular populations. More generally, it refers to the plain fact that class mobility and economic success are not structurally afforded to certain racialized and marginalized groups and that achieving them therefore requires a tremendous amount of individual ingenuity and personal risk and the overcoming of serious disadvantages. Thus, the term celebrates success when it happens against all odds. At the same time, in certain contexts, including mainstream media coverage and development discourse, the use of the term by reporters and policymakers and development proponents lets structures of marginalization and discrimination off the hook by calling dramatic attention to exceptional cases in which marginalized people have "made it" relative to the social and economic conditions that surround them. Michelle Alexander (2012: 248) thus writes about how, in the United States, "black success stories lend credence to the notion that anyone, no matter how poor or how black you may be, can make it to the top, if only you try hard enough." The discourse of entrepreneurship situates the responsibility for success with hardworking, individual actors, turning institutionalized discrimination and endemic poverty into the backdrop for a heroic tale of overcoming, and, at the same time, opens up conceptual and rhetorical space for blaming those who are not economically successful for their own condition, portraying them as lacking the work ethic, ingenuity, or entrepreneurial drive necessary to better themselves. The discourse of entrepreneurship thus detracts and distracts from holistic approaches to addressing structural violence and inequality while also promising "something better" (Fischer and Benson 2006) for people who adopt an entrepreneurial ethic and spirit.

Indigenous entrepreneurship emerged as a principal goal of international development programs at the turn of the millennium (DeHart 2010). The belief is that the entrepreneurial power of indigenous peoples has remained latent because they are too late, or maybe too soon, having heretofore existed outside of formal, capitalist market systems. They are figured as untapped sources of growth for developing nations if only they could incorporate themselves into the formal economy, develop, become modern, and generally "get with the program." This imagined potential does not inspire across-the-board investments in educational and economic resources for indigenous communities, however. Rather, entrepreneurship has been promoted among indigenous peoples through narrowly targeted public-private partnerships, nongovernmental development assistance programs, microcredit schemes, and market reforms, including neoliberal structural adjustment policies that involve fiscal austerity and free trade. Indigenous people are expected to take advantage of small capital loans and perhaps a bit of business training (the kind discussed in chapter 4, for instance) to develop and modify themselves, so to speak. These programs often figure indigeneity as an economic resource in and of itself—a marketing tool or branding strategy that indigenous people can use to position themselves in the marketplace and culture industry as distinctive from entrepreneurs who occupy unmarked racial or ethnic categories and as businesspeople who offer something unique and authentic to consumers because of their indigenous culture and status. A different approach would be to understand indigeneity as a category that has social significance in part because of the historical processes through which certain populations have been racialized and stereotyped as belonging to the past and tradition and socially and economically exploited and marginalized based on that difference. This approach might therefore entail a process of accounting for past injustices and rectifying conditions of inequality through robust social, economic, and political programs rather than making development into an individualized and ethnicized project of self-help and self-improvement.

John and Jean Comaroff (2009) write that the rise of "ethno-marketing" and "ethno-preneurship" (ethnicity-based marketing strategies and the legal incorporation of ethnic groups as business entities) signals the failures of broad social movements and legal and economic reforms to address conditions of poverty, inequality, and exclusion in postcolonial settings. In Latin America, the rise of such market-based solutions illustrates how much distance now stands between the radical democratic politics asserted regionally in the early twentieth century (Grandin 2004) and the entrepreneurial politics and models of entrepreneurial development now embraced—sometimes begrudgingly, sometimes enthusiastically—by indigenous people who share with previous generations their passions for and commitments to justice, fairness, and equality but who now contend with the hegemony of neoliberal multiculturalism.[5]

Formal enterprise can be and sometimes has been a route to improved life chances for indigenous people. But the focus by Latin American states, NGOs, and development institutions on indigenous entrepreneurship has the effect of depoliticizing the relationship between racial and ethnic difference and systematized subordination and planned obsolescence. It also produces a model of the ideal indigenous person that Maya activists and anthropologists (Hale 2004; Otzoy 2007; Esquít 2007) have described with the phrase, *el indio permitido,* the "acceptable Indian." The idea is that indigenous people will always be disparaged as "Indians," a deeply pejorative term that indicates their perceived backwardness—their lateness—compared with nonindigenous Guatemalans. But they may become "acceptable"—that is, permitted, tolerated, and even held up as model members of their racialized or ethnicized group— if they use indigeneity as a form of economic and cultural capital to further their entrepreneurial activities, for example, and not as a means of advancing an oppositional politics or defending a traditional way of life in a manner that is perceived to hold back national progress or symbolize a pathological Otherness. Ethnic pride and cultural traditions may be encouraged—celebrated even—by the Guatemalan state and development institutions when they serve as a veneer of difference overlaid onto a project of personal improvement that is assimilated to a national strategy of economic growth and a hegemonic model of multicultural inclusion and diversity. Indigenous entrepreneurs can be "acceptable Indians," then, when they do not actively disrupt, and when they perhaps actually contribute to, the movement of history toward a Western-style modernization, whitening, and the kind of progress touted by nation-states and the development industry.

THE LATE STYLE OF MAYA PIRATES

Where do hegemonic discourses of indigenous entrepreneurship leave Maya "pirates"? It seems we are left with a set of paradoxes. The apparel trade in the central highlands has become less formal over time in relation to the state, not more. The focus of Maya workshop owners is on what they call "community development" rather than the neoliberal models of development premised on profit maximization, individual economic advancement, and IP rights promoted on national and international levels. These pirates are self-proclaimed copycats, yet the "informal" regulation of copying and investments in innovation and creativity are essential to the processes through which style manifests in their work and in their workshops and is key to their reputations in the local industry and regional marketplace. They talk about present-day Guatemala as a country with less control, less justice, and more crime than they experienced during the internal armed conflict, in spite of the many promises of peace and reconciliation that have been made since then. Although the garment trade has turned out to be an important livelihood for Maya people in towns such as Tecpán, it has taken a very different form than the discourse of "indigenous entrepreneurship" might predict, and economic reforms aimed at unleashing entrepreneurial potential have made the trade less viable for Maya business owners, not more.

But the highland apparel trade is not, in fact, experienced by the people who participate in it as a social space or marketplace defined by irony or paradox. As I hope to have demonstrated throughout this book, the lives and livelihoods of Maya pirates are a good place from which to critique the very grounds on which these realities and fables of scandal come to seem so contradictory and perhaps unexpected. Take, for instance, the informalization of the industry over time. The history of the apparel trade evidences that formalization is not an inevitable process, especially in a setting where the state has threatened indigenous people more than it has provisioned services; where the most visible models of formal business ownership and management—the large-scale *maquiladoras* that make clothing for export—seem to Maya workshop owners to be premised on taking advantage of wage labor rather than building community; and where concealment takes on important value amid national law enforcement efforts and media campaigns that target "informal" businesses as unprofessional, and even criminal and delinquent, and given extortion threats from gang members aimed at businesses. The informalization of the apparel trade is explainable in these historical and anthropological terms. It only seems contradictory or unexpected if the master narratives and progress models premised on formalization and espoused by states and international institutions are taken for granted, expected to be teleological outcomes, and not held up to empirical scrutiny or analyzed in light of social histories, complicated institutional dynamics, the realities of everyday life, and the powerful workings of the multinational fashion industry itself.

The fact that copycats claim to be creative seems paradoxical because a great deal of cultural work and institutional and financial investment on the part of corporations and governments has gone into making originality seem like something fundamentally separate and distinct from processes of copying, mimicry, borrowing, and imitation. Understanding the production of fashion in terms of style—the dialectical relationship between instantiation and interpretation through which material culture takes shape and that involves a necessary element of influence and linkages to broader social projects, including the making of identities, distinctions, and differences through imitation and creative inflection—throws into relief the narrow definition of creativity and the narrow focus on authorship and originality that are ensconced in international IP law. What is more, appreciating trademarked brands as part of material culture—as graphic and aesthetic design elements and not only as signs that communicate information between corporations and consumers—opens up a space for appreciating the work of Maya apparel producers who creatively adopt and adapt branded designs not because they are trying to simply pilfer a corporate aura or utterance but because these elements fit and are attractive, marketable, valuable, and appealing within the regional fashion scene. The idea that Maya people should or will be made to conform to IP law's model of creativity and ownership—a model that is touted as the most rational and ethical in IP scholarship and industry propaganda—through educational interventions, entrepreneurial training, or law enforcement efforts overlooks how the regulating style that Maya workshop owners have elaborated in order to manage copying and competition within their local industry is based in a very practical understanding of the importance of borrowing and appropriation to their trade (which is also true of the fashion system writ large) and an ethical commitment to sharing resources and information in ways that respect the need of everyone involved in the trade to earn a basic living.

The romanticization of pirates and other "social bandits" has a long history (Hobsbawm 1959, 1969). Their vilification does, too. With this in mind, I argue that the lateness of Maya pirates is a mode of engagement with the world that calls attention to temporality and the lingering problems and paradoxes not of the existence and livelihoods of these individuals but of modernity. Late indigenous styles of fashion and business found in highland Guatemala reveal how the neat and tidy narratives of originality, development, economic modernization, formalization, and multiculturalism are fundamentally ideological and misleading. These narratives are not consistent with what is happening on the ground and what people want out of life. The realities of brand piracy in Guatemala show the flaws and fissures in these fables and reveal a different way of doing things, a different style.

This idea that we are in an era of lateness—one of late capitalism (Jameson 1991), late modernity (Giddens 1991), and late liberalism (Povinelli 2011)—is common in contemporary anthropology and critical theory. What is not always clear about this diagnosis is whether this means that something—capitalism, modernity, liberalism—is coming to an end or whether the lateness is itself a new stage in the unfolding of a set of processes and relations that are more or less continuous with what has come before. Lateness, Said (2006: 13) suggested, "includes the idea that one cannot really go beyond lateness at all, cannot transcend or lift oneself out of lateness, but can only deepen the lateness." Antipiracy campaigns and IP law enforcement efforts attempt to get rid of lateness, to mandate and promote creativity and eschew copying by denying that the two processes are inextricably linked and interdependent, and to eliminate backwardness by requiring everyone to be formal, modern, and assimilated. IP law is a program of "synthesis" and "development," in Adorno's terms. But ethnographic attention to the work of

Maya apparel producers engaged in late styles of indigeneity and piracy shows how the lives and livelihoods of these people are sites of deepening investments and enduring struggle, modes of persistence and perseverance, and ways of being moral and modern that reject the demands of assimilation and deny the teleology of development by dwelling instead in deep spaces of simultaneous oldness and newness.

Notes

1. What international law designates as "brand piracy" is a public and generally accepted practice in Guatemala, and Tecpán is a well-known center of clothing production, including knockoff fashion production. Nonetheless, to protect the people I interviewed, I have changed all of their names and identifying characteristics. The recent criminalization of "piracy" and the informal nature of apparel production in Guatemala posed particular methodological obstacles during my investigation. These methodological challenges and some of the ethical questions that the research raised for me are discussed at length in Benson and Thomas 2010.

2. On the globalization of fashion styles, see, e.g., Brydon and Niessen 1998; Hansen 2000; and Niessen et al. 2003. On dress as a cultural practice, see, e.g., Banerjee and Miller 2003; Kondo 1997; Moeran 2004; Polhemus and Procter 1978; and Tarlo 1996, 2010.

3. On colonialism and the politics of dress, see also Allman 2004; Gondola 1999; and Hansen and Madison 2013.

4. Kaqchikel Maya is both an ethnic identifier and a language spoken by about half a million people in the central highlands of Guatemala. People whom I include in the ethnic category Kaqchikel Maya in this book variously identified themselves to me as *indígena* (indigenous, in Spanish), Maya, Kaqchikel, *natural* (natural, in Spanish), or *winäq* (person, in Kaqchikel). Some people were more comfortable referring to themselves as *tecpanecos,* preferring a geographical referent to an ethnic identifier. I use the term Kaqchikel Maya, in keeping with other (Guatemalan and foreign) anthropologists working in the highlands, and taking a cue from cultural activists from Tecpán, who identify themselves in this way to build solidarity among indigenous speakers of Kaqchikel Maya and with other ethnolinguistic groups across Guatemala and Mexico who have

also come to identify as Maya as the result of several decades of indigenous activism and organizing.

5. Yi-Chieh Jessica Lin (2009) shows how counterfeit goods are embedded in the redefinition of both art and commodity in a rapidly changing context where new forms of economic value and social capital are being produced alongside "fakes." Ravi Sundaram (2010) and others (see essays collected in Eckstein and Schwarz 2014) advance the argument that the "cultures of piracy" that have become definitive of how media and other commodified cultural forms are consumed in postcolonial regions—from South Asia to South America—are the product of historical patterns of subordination and marginalization that have placed certain populations outside of Western modes of authorship and ownership only to see the globalization of technologies of mass reproduction integrated into localized networks of contact and exchange. Anthropologists, historians, and scholars working in the fields of cultural studies and postcolonial studies have thus advocated a view of IP piracy in relativist terms that emphasizes the relationship of dominant technologies of rule to the particular histories of people and places and the political contours of authorship and ownership across moments of Western history, as well as the travel of parochial ideas about intellectual property to colonial, postcolonial, and non-Western settings (see Larkin 2008; Luvaas 2010, 2012; Vann 2006; Rose 1993; Johns 1998, 2010; Pang 2006, 2008, 2012). Scholars have also called attention to the work that piracy does to trouble, disrupt, and destabilize hegemonic concepts that are fundamental not only to IP regimes but also to Western conceptions of personhood, property, power, and economy (see Eckstein and Schwarz 2014; Liang 2008, 2009; Philip 2005; Dent 2012a, 2012b).

6. Even legal scholars who are generally critical of the overreach of IP protections seem comfortable with this divide between creators and mere copyists. See, for example, Lawrence Lessig's (2004) claims in this regard and the discussion of Lessig's work in Liang 2011.

7. For an excellent analysis of the uses and connotations of "culture" in international law, see Sally Engle Merry's (2001, 2009) work on the making of human rights law at the United Nations.

8. Claude Levi-Strauss (1966) argued as much when he proposed that *bricolage,* the reappropriation of existing elements for new purposes, was the most basic and ordinary mode of cultural production. In a different disciplinary moment and from a different theoretical approach, Michael Taussig (1993: xiii) wrote that the mimetic faculty, the ability and propensity to copy, "is as necessary to the very process of knowing as it is to the construction and subsequent naturalization of identities." In other words, it is in and through copying that the world becomes tangible, legible, and meaningful. Far from restating Plato's classical distinction between an ungraspable, idealized form (the "real") and its corrupted (but tangible) materialization, Taussig argued for a renewed appreciation of the magic of imitation and reproduction given that the concept of the original (and its associated "aura," following Benjamin [1968]) had fallen into inevitable crisis. Working within a Continental tradition that also includes Derrida's (1976) deconstruction of authorial presence, Foucault's (1984) critique of the author function, and Baudrillard's (1994) conceptualization of simulation in

postmodern culture, Gilles Deleuze (1990: 262) similarly agitated against the hierarchy of form and representation, arguing that the simulacrum, the copy of the copy, "harbors a positive power which denies the *original and the copy, the model and the reproduction*" (see also Sundaram 2010: 106; Boon 2010: 23). Across all of this philosophical and anthropological work, there is the compelling idea that the copy is not a second and inferior term in dyadic relationship to an original (see Lempert 2014) but rather part of an inevitable process, an expanding horizon defined by impulses and dynamics of reproduction that are central to the elaboration of culture.

9. See, for example, Raustiala and Sprigman 2012; and Hemphill and Suk 2009. In legal studies and philosophy of law, two notable, recent works attempt to counter expanding copyright protections with arguments about the centrality of copying to cultural innovation. Abraham Drassinower (2015: 1–2) remarks that "a horror of the copy" institutionalized in current interpretations of copyright law ignores that "copying is culture." Drassinower's aim in making this claim is to defend a limited concept of copyright against what he views as the hyperextension of the law in recent years and the muddled rationales for such expansion put forward largely by economists and grounded in what Drassinower diagnoses as misguided calculations of an author's interests as defined in contrast to the public interest. He ends up with a constructivist view of "originality" as a legal fiction that indexes a social investment in authorship as a protected form of communication, lamenting that the term obscures the fact that individual authors necessarily (and rightfully, in his view) copy the ideas of others. A more robust defense of the copy vis-à-vis IP law's expansion has been put forth by Marcus Boon (2010: 7), who argues that "copying is a fundamental part of being human, that we could not be human without copying," and adding that "copying is not just something human—it is a part of how the universe functions and manifests." Once he acknowledges this, the philosophical question that remains for Boon is how to account for a world in which a distinction between "originals" and "copies" becomes apparent, involves interests, and requires some clarification, and he provides an answer that emphasizes a phenomenological—which is to say perspectival and empirical—approach to thinking about how things come to be understood as originals. On the much broader notion of creativity and its relationships to imitation and newness, see Hallam and Ingold 2007. For helpful reviews of and reflections on the anthropology of creativity and imitation, see Lavie et al. 1993; McLean 2009; Lempert 2014; and Wilf 2011.

10. On the local meanings that attach to soft drink brands in the Caribbean, see Miller 1997. For more on the integration of local meanings and value into the branding strategies and marketing campaigns devised by brand owners, see Iwabuchi 2002; Manning and Uplisashvili 2007; Mazzarella 2003; Meneley 2004, 2007; R. J. Foster 2005, 2007; and J. Wang 2007. For an excellent overview of the anthropology of branding, see Manning 2010.

11. See debates over the meaning of style in the field of archaeology as elaborated in Sackett 1977, 1982, 1986; Hodder 1989; and Conkey and Hastorf 1993. I follow Hodder's usage here. For discussions of style as it relates to cultural studies, see Hebdige 1979 and the studies of subculture that have

followed, including Willis 1993; Bennett 1999; Muggleton 2000; Hodkinson 2002; and McArthur 2009. For a helpful overview of the concept of style in social theory, literature, and philosophy, see Callus et al. 2013. For an analysis of the idea of style in art and literature, see Lang 1987. For examples of how the concept of style has been used in the context of fashion studies, see McRobbie 1989; E. Wilson 2003; and Warkander 2014.

12. Material culture studies in anthropology, a domain defined by the likes of Pierre Bourdieu (1984), Arjun Appadurai (1986), and Daniel Miller (1987), has drawn much needed attention to the coproduction of people and things. "Stuff actually creates us," writes Miller (2010: 10), by which he means that the material qualities of objects and how people interface with those qualities influence processes of self-making and the constitution of social relations (see also Miller 1998, 2008, 2010; Miller and Woodward 2012; Crăciun 2013). Other recent studies of materiality also advance the idea that specific modes of rationality, relationships of authority, and belief are all conditioned on interactions with objects—from calculators to paper files to religious fetishes—that get put to use in particular ways (Law 1994; Hull 2012; Keane 2007).

13. Neighboring Honduras, Belize, and El Salvador, also on the drug trafficking route, rank first, fourth, and fifth, respectively, in per capita homicides globally (United Nations Office on Drugs and Crime 2013).

14. My anecdotal evidence of the high incidence of victimization is in keeping with statistics published by the Latin American Public Opinion Project, run by researchers at Vanderbilt University (see Cruz 2009).

15. On the relationship between IP and the "commons," which is at the root of debates over cultural property and collective ownership, see Hayden 2007.

16. A related concern is that the implementation of special IP frameworks inevitably requires that indigenous peoples be subjected to extensive judicial procedures and national debates aimed at defining indigeneity, tradition, and ownership (M.F. Brown 1998). This has been true in the case of land rights struggles, where questions about what it means to be indigenous, who qualifies as such, and how citizenship and its privileges apply (or do not apply) across populations have been central to legal proceedings (Povinelli 2002; Li 2007; French 2009). Elizabeth Povinelli's (1993: 248) work on Aboriginal land claims in Northern Australia made clear how questions of identity and epistemology become deeply entwined in courtroom debates: "The land claim process teeters on the ability of the court to maintain control over the grounds of knowing what is what. The court must frame who you are, how you obtained this identity, and what knowledge and practice is a necessary or sufficient corollary to it. . . . In other words, what were the conditions by which your knowledge was produced?"

17. Besides the influential work of Janet Roitman (2005) and Julia Elyachar (2005) discussed here, I am also inspired by ethnographies of criminalized and illegal activity more broadly, including studies of "illegal" migration by Josiah Heyman (1991), Leo Chavez (2007, 2012), Pablo Vila (2000), Susan Coutin (2003, 2007), Nicholas De Genova (2005), Sarah Willen (2007), Peter Benson (2012), Ruth Gomberg-Muñoz (2011), Didier Fassin (2012), and Seth Holmes (2013); of criminal gangs, corrupt officials, smugglers, bandits, and seafaring

pirates by Carolyn Nordstrom (2007), Rebecca Galemba (2009), John Osburg (2013), and Jatin Dua (2014); and intellectual property pirates and counterfeiters by Shujen Wang (2003), Ian Condry (2004), Brian Larkin (2008), Elizabeth Vann (2006), Yi-Chieh Jessica Lin (2011), Alexander Dent (2012a), Ramon Lobato (2012), Magdalena Crăciun (2014), and Constantine Nakassis (2016). For more on the concept of illegality in anthropology and processes of criminalization, see Pandolfo 2007; Silverstein 2005; Fassin 2011; and the edited volumes Heyman 1999; Das and Poole 2004; Hansen and Stepputat 2005; and van Schendel and Abraham 2005; along with the essays featured in the November 2013 issue of *PoLAR: Political and Legal Anthropology,* which I coedited with Rebecca Galemba, and the March 2015 issue of *Critique of Anthropology,* which I coedited with Cristiana Panella. My contention regarding the anthropology of informal and illegal activity is that we need ethnographies of the people targeted by criminalizing discourses if we are to challenge the institutionalized models of "good" and "bad" actors that tend to further marginalize already disadvantaged groups, including indigenous Guatemalans.

18. See the World Bank's report, *Latin American Entrepreneurs* (Lederman et al. 2014), for a sense of how entrepreneurship is currently imagined to impel development. Note that the subtitle of the report laments the fact that there are "many firms but little innovation" in the region. My book explores an empirical context that might be described in such terms, but it also argues that the notion of "innovation" that underwrites entrepreneurial theory as well as intellectual property law misunderstands the dialectic of copying and creativity that structures the production of style.

1. ECONOMIC REGULATION AND THE VALUE OF CONCEALMENT

1. Whereas the large-scale *maquiladoras* in Guatemala that produce name-brand merchandise for export (discussed later in this chapter) typically employ young women, garment workshops in Tecpán almost exclusively employ young men, and nontraditional garment production is overwhelmingly gendered as male work. For an interesting comparison to the apparel-production sector in India, see Chari 2004.

2. This is also the title of a volume of *Yale French Studies* edited by Barbara Johnson (1982), in which she and the other contributors explore the "literarity of teaching," as she also makes the case that teaching is a compulsion that requires teacher and student to dwell in the space of the unknown. In using the phrase in this chapter, I do not intend to make a connection to Johnson's work—although the pedagogical imperative does take shape in Tecpán at the core of a dialectic between concealment and disclosure that requires the production of ignorance (on the part of the state and perhaps also on the part of producers themselves who must not know too much, so to speak, if and when called on by the state to account for their informal and illegal practices) alongside the sharing of knowledge.

3. Omar Ortez (2004) documents a similar pattern in the apparel trade's expansion in the western department of Totonicapán.

4. Unless otherwise noted, the quoted texts from informants in this chapter and subsequent chapters are my translations from Spanish. I conducted interviews in Kaqchikel Maya with people who had not been educated in Spanish (including Doña Eugenia and some workshop owners who resided in the rural *aldeas*) or who spoke Kaqchikel Maya as a matter of course in their workshops. Guillermo is a good example of an informant with whom I went back and forth between Spanish and Kaqchikel Maya, since he had been raised speaking Kaqchikel Maya but educated in Spanish and was comfortable in both. Our recorded conversations (and thus the quoted text that appears in this book) tended toward Spanish, although I sometimes spoke Kaqchikel Maya with him in his home and with his employees. Linguistic preference varied by family and by workshop, but Spanish tended to be the language of business of the generation of *tecpanecos* actively engaged as workshop owners and employees in the apparel trade.

5. On the history of the globalization of apparel manufacturing, see Rosen 2002; Collins 2003; Bonacich et al. 1994; Abernathy et al. 2004; Sklair 1989; and Tiano 1994. On the cultural and political contours of the neoliberal economic model, which has underwritten outsourcing, and the effects of the recomposition of labor around models of flexibility and new modes of subordination, see, for example, Ong 1987, 1999, 2006; Mole 2012; Freeman 2014.

6. See also Walter Little's (2009) article on the articulation of different moral economies in the Guatemalan highlands.

7. Classic texts in economic sociology, especially Karl Polanyi's (1944) *The Great Transformation,* and in economic anthropology, especially the work of Africanists Keith Hart (1973) and Jane Guyer (1981, 1993), have emphasized the embeddedness of economic activities in social relations and the impossibility of understanding markets without reference to the fundamental anthropological frames of kinship and family, household structure, political organization, and the moral dimensions of exchange (with Marcel Mauss's [1954] *The Gift* as a major influence). Stephen Gudeman's (1978, 1986) early work shaped how this substantivist position was taken up in the ethnography of Latin America, as he encouraged anthropologists to explicate locally salient models of exchange and livelihood and take entire communities rather than institutions (e.g., households) as the unit of analysis. It is worth noting that Mark Granovetter's (1985) intervention in economic sociology discouraged descriptive analysis that presumed discrete actors engaging in economic practice in favor of a network model premised on the coconstitution of agents and economies (a model further elaborated by Michel Callon [1998]), a point that has relevance for my analysis of accounting practices in chapter 4. Recent and notable work in economic anthropology has drawn attention to the circulation of currencies, commodities, credit, and other forms of economic value in the "informal" economy (Guyer 2004; Roitman 2005; Elyachar 2005; see also Hart 1973) while simultaneously historicizing that term and challenging the dichotomy it implies between state and nonstate forms of economic regulation.

8. Daniella Gandolfo (2013) provides an inspired discussion of the concept of "form" as it relates to informality. She writes, for example, that vendors in

El Hueco market in Lima, Peru, revel in informality's "freedom of form and its subordination of profit to the preservation of this freedom through webs of reciprocal obligations and forms of consumption that limit the accumulation of wealth" (Gandolfo 2013: 280). She thus offers a refreshing challenge to classic anthropological analyses of the sharing of resources within indigenous, peasant, and petty capitalist communities in Latin America, a subject I take up in the next chapter.

9. For rich discussions of the interconnections of states and informal sectors, see especially Elyachar 2005; Roitman 2005; and Portes et al. 1989: part 5.

10. On this process of the "discovery" of the "informal economy" in Latin America, see Pérez-Sáinz 1995.

11. World Bank initiatives in Guatemala include the National Competitiveness Program and the Enhancing Micro, Small, and Medium Enterprise Productivity Project. The Inter-American Development Bank oversees a number of microloan programs.

12. Ríos Montt's offer stood from May 28 to June 30, 1982, after which the Fusiles y Frijoles (Guns and Beans) program was instituted, marking the beginning of "the most ruthless phase of the war" (Garrard-Burnett 2010: 70).

13. For an excellent discussion of the concept of competition in economic anthropology, see Colloredo-Mansfeld (2002).

14. For comparison, see, for example, the rich literatures on the *pizzo* paid to extortionists in Italy (e.g., Schneider and Schneider 2003).

15. For regional comparison on this point, see Mireille Abelin's (2012) dissertation on the efforts of bureaucrats to promote a tax-paying culture in Argentina in the aftermath of the country's debt crisis. Abelin explores the multiple interpretations of taxation evident among state agents and elite citizens, the latter commonly viewing taxation as a form of theft by a government that is "unworthy" of their wealth and that fails to recognize that modern sovereignty rests ultimately with citizens rather than the state.

2. THE ETHICS OF PIRACY

1. Rosemary Coombe (2003: 300) has stated: "Intellectual property regimes were inevitably one of the first means suggested to promote the protection and use of traditional environmental knowledge, and through it, biological diversity. Conservation, it was suggested, was not being implemented in developing countries because of the lack of any incentive structure for preserving rather than destroying biological resources. Means had to be found to value them before measures could be found to protect them." Her analysis reinforces the argument that intellectual property frameworks do more than inscribe existing values into law. Although grounded in the basic assumption shared by so many economists and other social scientists that humans are self-interested actors whose decisions reflect an inherent drive toward the maximization of utility and profit, IP law, in practice, institutionalizes new values and encourages and rewards a particular kind of behavior that looks, only in hindsight, to confirm this Homo economicus ideology. On the more general notion of the performativity of economics and its

prescribed modes of regulation (including law) in relation to the market, see Mitchell 2002; Law and Urry 2004; and MacKenzie et al. 2007.

2. Rosemary Coombe (1993) and Keith Aoki (1998) note a synergy between such narratives and the discourses of "civilization" and "conversion" that underwrote colonialism.

3. On street vendors and police corruption in Guatemala, see Little (2008, 2009).

4. See also O'Neill and Thomas 2011; and Little and Smith 2009.

5. For related examples having to do with the mirroring of social relations and models of place and personhood in the production of material culture, see Dorinne Kondo's (1990) work on Japanese artisans and Michael Herzfeld's (2004) ethnography of artisans in Crete.

6. See, for example, ethnographies of creative industries by Boatema Boateng (2011), Brian Larkin (2008), and Michael Herzfeld (2004); the historical work of Adrian Johns (1998, 2010) on publishing and copyright; Mark Rose's (1993) history of copyright law; and Mary Lynn Stewart's (2008) writings on the fashion industry. Raustiala and Sprigman (2012) provide a particularly useful and wide-ranging analysis of how copying and imitation are assessed and controlled within the fashion industry, culinary world, comedy scene, and publishing industry, and they endorse flexible systems of property protection based on the creative potential that they see imitation unleashing in each of these domains. See also my further discussion of the inevitability and profitability of copying in fashion design in chapter 3.

7. See my discussions of entrepreneurship and development in previous chapters and Elyachar 2005; Freeman 2007; John L. Comaroff and Jean Comaroff 2009; and DeHart 2010.

3. BRAND POLLUTION

1. See, for example, Klein 2000; Arvidsson 2006; and Bently et al. 2008.

2. This is not to say that trademarks are no longer talked about as indicators of origin. The Lanham Act (passed in 1946), which serves as the foundation of US trademark law, specifies trademarks as indicators of source, with "source" understood in the case of fashion to refer to the designer or design firm associated with the mark (see Tsai 2005).

3. As William Mazzarella (2003: 186–187) writes, we must distinguish between two types of brand consumer: "the ones who purchase the branded goods," and the "corporate client executives who 'buy into' the categories of marketing discourse," including the definitions of brand image and brand dilution promoted in IP law.

4. Marty Neumeier's (2005) bestselling how-to guide to corporate branding, *The Brand Gap,* actually makes this point. He begins by urging executives to stop thinking about brands as something that companies design or make or sell and to start thinking of them as "a PERSON'S gut feeling, because in the end the brand is defined by individuals, not by companies, the market, or the so-called general public. . . . In other words, a brand is not what you say it is. It's what THEY say it is" (5, emphasis in original).

5. Western European nations have extended limited IP protections to fashion designs at various historical moments, and the European Union recently harmonized these protections (Scafidi 2006: 126). India and Japan have also strengthened copyright protections for fashion designs in recent years (Scafidi 2008). Still, fashion companies rarely pursue litigation against other firms (see Raustiala and Sprigman 2006; and my discussion of the topic in this chapter).

6. In *Societe Yves Saint Laurent S.A. v. Societe Louis Dreyfus Retain Mgmt., S.A.* [1994] E.C.C. 512, 514 (Trib. Comm. [Paris]), Yves Saint Laurent (YSL) brought suit against Ralph Lauren in a Parisian court for copying a YSL tuxedo dress design. The court found in YSL's favor, and Ralph Lauren was fined. Lynsey Blackmon (2007) noted that YSL had been fined in a French court ten years prior for copying a jacket designed by Jacques Esterel.

7. The likelihood of confusion is compounded when fashion firms enter the market for seconds, factory rejects, and overruns, offering these products at deep discounts in outlet malls or allowing them to spill over into the informal street markets of places where the clothing is assembled for export. "Such a marketing strategy gives credence to poorer quality counterfeits as they can claim to be 'legitimate' factory rejects" (Hilton et al. 2004: 351).

8. The Guatemalan government and national elite have long espoused an ideology of *blanquemiento* (whitening) as a "solution for the construction of a Guatemalan nation" (Casaús Arzú 2002: 103, my translation; see also Casaús Arzú 1995). In the nineteenth century, for example, the push to "whiten" the nation included a range of projects, from the privatization of communal, indigenous land holdings to the expansion of formal, Spanish-language education to the recruitment of European settlers (C. A. Smith 1990).

9. Much has been written on the social construction of race in the United States through style and consumption. On the politics of blackness and relationships to hair, fashion, and other forms of expression, see Kelley 1996; S. Walker 2007; and Byrd and Tharps 2001. On Chicano/a fashion, style, and identity, see Márez 1996; and C. Ramírez 2002.

10. For more on whiteness as a form of property in which consumers are encouraged to invest, see Lipsitz 2006; and Harris 1993. For more on the role of trademarks in propagating racial stereotypes, see Greene 2008. K. J. Greene (1999) has also written on the parallel case of copyright law, exploring the unequal protections afforded by US courts to white and black cultural forms.

11. See Chernikoff 2012. Rumors that Tommy Hilfiger had made racist statements in an interview with Oprah Winfrey about the people who wear his clothing designs began circulating as early as 1996. Yet he did not even appear on *The Oprah Winfrey Show* until 2007, when he went on television to dispel the rumors.

12. Other legal actions include a class action suit filed in July 2015 on behalf of sixty-two thousand store employees who claim they were forced to buy Abercrombie & Fitch clothing to wear on the job (see Greenhouse 2015) and a US Supreme Court case, decided against Abercrombie & Fitch in 2015, that alleged that the company had violated workplace discrimination law by turning down

a Muslim job applicant because she wore a headscarf, a style that did not comply with the company's *Look Book*. The company has settled at least two other suits involving Muslim plaintiffs who claim to have been turned away for wearing hijab (see Jamieson 2015).

13. On the intersections of race, ethnicity, and gender in Latin America and the production of "white" masculinities, see P. Wade 1997; Loveman 2014; and Gutmann 2003.

14. For an interesting comparison to the case study presented here, see David Dante Troutt's (2004) analysis of race and trademark law in the United States. Troutt (2004: 1147) frames self-branding as a form of resistance against historical denials of personhood, citizenship, and ownership over oneself and one's labor. Similarly, Beth Conklin (1997: 712) argues that owning one's image can be a powerful pushback against the burden thrust on indigenous Latin Americans to conform to the "symbolic values that . . . others identify with authentic Indianness." Troutt's analysis suggests, however, that the move to own, fix, and protect an individual or group identity using trademark law runs counter to the goals of self-determination, democratic struggle, and overcoming, which might also be important for marginalized groups.

4. FISCAL AND MORAL ACCOUNTABILITY

1. A new trial commenced on January 5, 2015, but it was halted after only a few hours of proceedings, when the defense attorneys for Ríos Montt requested that one of the three presiding judges recuse herself on grounds of bias. The court concurred, and the result was the indefinite suspension of the reopening of the trial. Six months later, the national forensic authority's medical examiner issued a report that declared eighty-nine-year-old Ríos Montt mentally incapable of standing trial because he suffers from dementia. In August 2015, a Guatemalan judge ruled that the trial could be held behind closed doors, but that, if found guilty, Ríos Montt could only be sentenced to home or hospital detention because of his mental state. The reopening of the trial was originally scheduled for January 2016, but it did not actually occur until May 2016. At the time of this writing, the proceedings are ongoing.

2. On localized forms of control as responses to the threat of broader-scale institutional controls, see Laura Nader's (1991) classic study of harmony ideology among the Zapotec people of southern Mexico. Nader interpreted the Zapotec system of dispute resolution, which kept disagreements local and relatively peaceful, as a form of resistance to potential interference from state authorities and a way of warding off the expansion of state institutions into Zapotec territory.

3. On the performative aspects of finance and accounting, see Carruthers 1995; Clark et al. 2004; Lowe 2004; Ezzamel 2012; and Strathern 2002.

4. Recent writing by some economists on the global microfinance "movement" shies away from characterizing the poor as lacking a "future orientation," opting instead for what must seem to these authors to be less offensive language about "limits to complex decision making and weak internal self-control mechanisms on the part of individuals" (Armendáriz and Murdoch 2010: 17).

5. MAKING THE HIGHLANDS SAFE FOR BUSINESS

1. For a brief history of the Partido Guatemalteco del Trabajo, especially the involvement of its various factions in the armed conflict and the peace process, see MacLeod 1999.

2. On the ultimately unsuccessful, seven-year struggle (2006–2013) by communities in the municipality of San Juan Sacatepéquez to block the large-scale Cementos Progreso plant from being constructed, see, for example, Contreras and Orozco 2013.

3. For an excellent example of this kind of entanglement between violence and justice in the administration and subsequent popular interpretation of "indigenous law," see the Chiyax case detailed in Alcaldía Comunal de Chiyax 2005.

4. For more on the patrol system and its abuses, see Manz 1988; Paul and Demarest 1988; and Schirmer 1988.

CONCLUSION

1. See Castells and Portes 1989; Portes and Schauffler 1993; and, especially, the remarkably cogent argument about such descriptions of the informal economy in Peattie 1987.

2. Orin Starn (2004) eloquently describes these obsessions and the entanglements they foster in his book *Ishi's Brain*. See also de la Cadena and Starn 2007.

3. For details of these debates in relation to indigenous Mayas in Guatemala, see, for example, Bastos and Camus 2007; Warren 1998; Fischer and Brown 1996; Fischer 1999; Nelson 1999; and Hale 2007.

4. I use the term "crisis" here for its expediency in describing a set of complex financial processes and events that received global attention beginning in 2007. They have been explored with great care by anthropologists including Karen Ho (2009), Annelise Riles (2011), and Janet Roitman (2013).

5. For rich engagements with the figure of the ethnic entrepreneur in Guatemala, see DeHart 2010; Way 2012; and Goldín 2009.

References

Abelin, Mireille. 2012. "Fiscal Sovereignty: Reconfigurations of Value and Citizenship in Post-Financial Crisis Argentina." PhD diss., Columbia University.

Abercrombie & Fitch. 2006. "Abercrombie & Fitch Expands Anti-Counterfeiting Program." www.prnewswire.com/news-releases/abercrombie--fitch-expands-anti-counterfeiting-program-55136197.html.

———. 2014. *Annual Report.* www.abercrombie.com/anf/investors/investorrelations.html.

Abernathy, Frederick H., John T. Dunlop, Janice H. Hammond, and David Weil. 2004. "Globalization in the Apparel and Textile Industries: What Is New and What Is Not?" In *Locating Global Advantage: Industry Dynamics in the Global Supply Chain,* edited by Martin Kenney and Richard Florida, 23–51. Palo Alto, CA: Stanford University Press.

Abernathy, Frederick H., Anthony Volpe, and David Weil. 2005. *The Future of the Apparel and Textile Industries: Prospects and Choices for Public and Private Actors.* Cambridge, MA: Harvard Center for Textile and Apparel Research.

Adams, Richard, and Santiago Bastos. 2003. *Las relaciones étnicas en Guatemala, 1944–2000.* Guatemala City: CIRMA.

Adorno, Theodor. 2002. *Essays on Music.* Edited and with introduction, commentary, and notes by Richard Leppert. New translations by Susan H. Gillespie. Berkeley: University of California Press.

———. 2004. *Philosophy of Modern Music.* Translated by Anne G. Mitchell and Wesley V. Blomster. New York: Continuum.

Agamben, Giorgio. 1998. *Homo Sacer: Sovereign Power and Bare Life.* Palo Alto, CA: Stanford University Press.

Aguiar, José Carlos. 2010. "La piratería como conflicto: Discursos sobre la propiedad intelectual en México." *Iconos: Revista de las Ciencias Sociales* 38: 143–156.

Ahmed, Azam, and Elisabeth Malkin. 2015. "Otto Pérez Molina of Guatemala Is Jailed Hours after Resigning Presidency." *International New York Times,* September 3.

Akerlof, George. 1970. "'The Market for 'Lemons': Quality Uncertainty and the Market Mechanism." *Quarterly Journal of Economics* 84, no. 3: 488–500.

Albers-Miller, Nancy D. 1999. "Consumer Misbehavior: Why People Buy Illicit Goods." *Journal of Consumer Marketing* 16, no. 3: 273–287.

Alcaldía Comunal de Chiyax. 2005. *Aplicación de justicia en una comunidad indígena de Totonicapán: Caso de robo agravado.* Quetzaltenango: Centro Pluricultural de la Democracia.

Alexander, Michelle. 2012. *The New Jim Crow: Mass Incarceration in the Age of Colorblindness.* New York: New Press.

Allman, Jean, ed. 2004. *Fashioning Africa: Power and the Politics of Dress.* Bloomington: Indiana University Press.

Althusser, Louis. 1971. *Lenin and Philosophy and Other Essays.* New York: Monthly Review Press.

Annis, Sheldon. 1987. *God and Production in a Guatemalan Town.* Austin: University of Texas Press.

Aoki, Keith. 1994. "Authors, Inventors and Trademark Owners: Private Intellectual Property and the Public Domain. Part II." *Columbia-VLA Journal of Law and the Arts* 18: 191–267.

———. 1998. "Neocolonialism, Anticommons Property, and Biopiracy in the (Not-So-Brave) New World Order of International Intellectual Property Protection." *Indiana Journal of Global Legal Studies* 6, no. 1: 11–58.

Appadurai, Arjun, ed. 1986. *The Social Life of Things: Commodities in Cultural Perspective.* Cambridge: Cambridge University Press.

———. 1993. "Patriotism and Its Futures." *Public Culture* 5, no. 3: 411-429.

———. 1996. *Modernity at Large: Cultural Dimensions of Globalization.* Minneapolis: University of Minnesota Press.

Armendáriz, Beatriz, and Jonathan Murdoch. 2010. *The Economics of Microfinance.* Cambridge, MA: MIT Press.

Arvidsson, Adam. 2006. *Brands: Meaning and Value in Media Culture.* New York: Routledge.

Associated Press. 2005. "Blushing Va. Pols Drop Droopy-Pants Fine." *Fox News,* February 10. www.foxnews.com/story/2005/02/10/blushing-va-pols-drop-droopy-pants-fine.html.

Banerjee, Mukulika, and Daniel Miller. 2003. *The Sari.* Oxford: Berg.

Barnard, Alan. 2006. "Kalahari Revisionism, Vienna, and the Indigenous Peoples Debate." *Social Anthropology* 14, no. 1: 1–16.

Barnett, Jonathan M. 2005. "Shopping for Gucci on Canal Street: Reflections on Status Consumption, Intellectual Property, and the Incentive Thesis." *Virginia Law Review* 91, no. 6: 1381–1423.

Barthes, Roland. 1990. *The Fashion System.* Berkeley: University of California Press.

Bastos, Santiago, and Manuela Camus. 2007. *Mayanización y vida cotidiana: La ideología multicultural en la socieded guatemalteca.* Guatemala City: FLACSO, CIRMA, Cholsamaj.

Baudrillard, Jean. 1994. *Simulacra and Simulation*. Ann Arbor: University of Michigan Press.

BBC News. 2011. "Guatemala's Colom: Users Share Blame for Drug Violence." September 7.

Beaubien, Jason. 2011. "Mexican Cartels Spread Violence To Central America." NPR, *Morning Edition*. May 30. www.npr.org/2011/05/30/136690257 /mexican-cartels-spread-violence-to-central-america.

Beck, Ulrich, Anthony Giddens, and Scott Lash. 1994. *Reflexive Modernization: Politics, Tradition, and Aesthetics in the Modern Social Order*. Cambridge: Polity Press.

Beebe, Barton. 2004. "The Semiotic Analysis of Trademark Law." *UCLA Law Review* 51: 621–704.

———. 2008. "The Semiotic Account of Trademark Doctrine and Trademark Culture." In *Trademark Law and Theory: A Handbook of Contemporary Research*, edited by Graeme B. Dinwoodie and Mark D. Janis, 42–64. Cheltenham: Edward Elgar.

———. 2010. "Intellectual Property Law and the Sumptuary Code." *Harvard Law Review* 123, no. 4: 810–889.

———. 2013. "Shanzai, Sumptuary Law, and Intellectual Property Law in Contemporary China." *UC Davis Law Review* 47: 849-874.

Benería, Lourdes. 1989. "Subcontracting and Employment Dynamics in Mexico City." In *The Informal Economy: Studies in Advanced and Less Developed Countries*, edited by Alejandro Portes, Manuel Castells, and Lauren A. Benton, 173-188. Baltimore: Johns Hopkins University Press.

Benjamin, Walter. 1968. "The Work of Art in the Age of Mechanical Reproduction." In *Illuminations*, edited by Hannah Arendt, 217-242. New York: Schocken.

Bennett, Andy. 1999. "Subcultures or Neo-Tribes? Rethinking the Relationship Between Youth, Style and Musical Taste." *Sociology* 33, no. 3: 599–617.

Benson, Peter. 2004. "Nothing to See Hear." *Anthropological Quarterly* 77, no. 3: 435–467.

———. 2012. *Tobacco Capitalism: Growers, Migrant Workers, and the Changing Face of Global Industry*. Princeton, NJ: Princeton University Press.

Benson, Peter, Edward F. Fischer, and Kedron Thomas. 2008. "Resocializing Suffering: Neoliberalism, Accusation, and the Sociopolitical Context of Guatemala's New Violence." *Latin American Perspectives* 35, no. 5: 38–58.

Benson, Peter, and Kedron Thomas. 2010. "After Cultural Competency: Research Practice and Moral Experience in the Study of Brand Pirates and Tobacco Farmers." *Qualitative Research* 10, no. 6: 679-697.

Benthall, Jonathan. 1999. "The Critique of Intellectual Property." *Anthropology Today* 15, no. 6: 1–3.

Bently, Lionel, Jennifer David, and Jane Ginsburg, eds. 2008. *Trade Marks and Brands: An Interdisciplinary Critique*. Cambridge: Cambridge University Press.

Berlant, Lauren. 2011. *Cruel Optimism*. Durham, NC: Duke University Press.

Bettig, Ronald V. 1996. *Copyrighting Culture: The Political Economy of Intellectual Property*. Boulder: Westview Press.

Bhabha, Homi. 1984. "Of Mimicry and Man: The Ambivalence of Colonial Discourse." *October* 28: 125–133.

Bharathi, S. Priya. 1996. "There Is More Than One Way to Skin a Copycat: The Emergence of Trade Dress to Combat Design Piracy of Fashion Works." *Texas Tech Law Review* 27: 1667–1694.

Biehl, João. 2007. *Will to Live: AIDS Therapies and the Politics of Survival.* Princeton, NJ: Princeton University Press.

Billingsley, Doc. 2013. "So That All Shall Know: Memory Activism and Epistemic Authority in Guatemala." PhD diss., Washington University in St. Louis.

Blackmon, Lynsey. 2007. "The Devil Wears Prado: A Look at the Design Piracy Prohibition Act and the Extension of Copyright Protection to the World of Fashion." *Pepperdine Law Review* 35, no. 1: 107–160.

Boateng, Boatema. 2011. *The Copyright Thing Doesn't Work Here: Adinkra and Kente Cloth and Intellectual Property in Ghana.* Minneapolis: University of Minnesota Press.

Bonacich, Edna, Lucie Cheng, Norma Chinchilla, Nora Hamilton, and Paul Ong, eds. 1994. *Global Production: The Apparel Industry in the Pacific Rim.* Philadelphia: Temple University Press.

Boon, Marcus. 2010. *In Praise of Copying.* Cambridge, MA: Harvard University Press.

Bourdieu, Pierre. 1984. *Distinction: A Social Critique of the Judgment of Taste.* Cambridge, MA: Harvard University Press.

———. 1998. "The Essence of Neoliberalism." Translated by Jeremy J. Shapiro. *Le Monde Diplomatique,* English edition, December. http://mondediplo .com/1998/12/08bourdieu.

Bourgois, Phillipe. 1996. *In Search of Respect: Selling Crack in El Barrio.* Cambridge: Cambridge University Press.

Braithwaite, John, and Peter Drahos. 2000. *Global Business Regulation.* Cambridge: Cambridge University Press.

Briggs, Anne Theodore. 2002. "Hung Out to Dry: Clothing Design Protection Pitfalls in United States Law." *Hastings Communications and Entertainment Law Journal* 24, no. 2: 169–214.

Brooks, Andrew. 2015. *Clothing Poverty: The Hidden World of Fast Fashion and Second-Hand Clothes.* London: Zed Books.

Brown, Michael F. 1998. "Can Culture Be Copyrighted?" *Current Anthropology* 39, no. 2: 193–222.

———. 2005. "Heritage Trouble: Recent Work on the Protection of Intangible Cultural Property." *International Journal of Cultural Property* 12: 40–61.

Brown, R. McKenna. 1996. "The Mayan Language Loyalty Movement in Guatemala." In *Maya Cultural Activism in Guatemala,* edited by Edward F. Fischer and R. McKenna Brown, 165–177. Austin: University of Texas Press.

Brush, Stephen B. 1993. "Indigenous Knowledge of Biological Resources and Intellectual Property Rights: The Role of Anthropology." *American Anthropologist* 95, no. 3: 653–671.

Brush, Stephen B., and Doreen Stabinsky, eds. 1996. *Valuing Local Knowledge: Indigenous People and Intellectual Property Rights.* Washington, DC: Island Press.

Brydon, Anne, and Sandra Niessen, eds. 1998. *Consuming Fashion: Adorning the Transnational Body*. Oxford: Berg.

Burrell, Jennifer. 2010. "In and Out of Rights: Security, Migration, and Human Rights Talk in Postwar Guatemala." *Journal of Latin American and Caribbean Anthropology* 15, no. 1: 90–115.

Butler, Judith. 1990. *Gender Trouble: Feminism and the Subversion of Identity*. New York: Routledge.

Byrd, Ayada, and Lori Tharps. 2001. *Untangling the Roots of Black Hair in America*. New York: St. Martin's Press.

Cabrera, Maynor, Nora Lustig, and Hilacías Morán. 2015. "Fiscal Policy, Inequality, and the Ethnic Divide in Guatemala." *World Development* 76: 263–279.

Cadenas Montenegro, Darico. 1981. "Esquema preliminar de ordenamiento urbano para el municipio de Tecpán Guatemala." Master's thesis, Universidad de San Carlos de Guatemala.

Caldeira, Teresa. 2001. *City of Walls: Crime, Segregation, and Citizenship in São Paulo*. Berkeley: University of California Press.

Caldwell, Paulette. 1991. "A Hair Piece: Perspectives on the Intersection of Race and Gender." *Duke Law Journal* 2: 365–396.

Callon, Michel. 1998. "Introduction: The Embeddedness of Economic Markets in Economics." *Sociological Review* 46, no. 1: 1–57.

Callus, Ivan, James Corby, and Gloria Lauri-Lucente, eds. 2013. *Style in Theory: Between Literature and Philosophy*. London: Bloomsbury.

Camerer, Colin, George Loewenstein, and Matthew Rabin, eds. 2004. *Advances in Behavioral Economics*. Princeton, NJ: Princeton University Press.

Camus, Manuela. 2011. "Primero de Julio: Urban Experiences of Class Decline and Violence." In *Securing the City: Neoliberalism, Space, and Insecurity in Postwar Guatemala*, edited by Kevin Lewis O'Neill and Kedron Thomas, 49–66. Durham, NC: Duke University Press.

Carmack, Robert M. 1988. *Harvest of Violence: The Maya Indians and the Guatemala Crisis*. Norman: University of Oklahoma Press.

Carrillo Ramirez, Alfredo. 1971. *Evolución histórica de la educación secundaria en Guatemala desde el año 1831 hasta el año 1969: 138 años de historia*. Guatemala City: Editorial José de Pineda Ibarra.

Carruthers, Bruce G. 1995. "Accounting, Ambiguity, and the New Institutionalism." *Accounting, Organizations, and Society* 20, no. 4: 313–328.

Casaús Arzú, Marta Elena. 1995. *Guatemala: linaje y racismo*. San José: FLASCO.

———. 2002. *La metamorphosis del racismo en Guatemala*. Guatemala City: Cholsamaj.

Cassis, Youssef, and Ioanna Pepelaisis Minoglou, eds. 2005. *Entrepreneurship in Theory and History*. New York: Palgrave Macmillan.

Casson, Mark, and Andrew Godley. 2005. "Entrepreneurship and Historical Explanation." In *Entrepreneurship in Theory and History*, edited by Youssef Cassis and Ioanna Pepelaisis Minaglou, 25–60. New York: Palgrave Macmillan.

Castells, Manuel, and Alejandro Portes. 1989. "World Underneath: The Origins, Dynamics, and Effects of the Informal Economy." In *The Informal*

Economy: Studies in Advanced and Less Developed Countries, edited by Alejandro Portes, Manuel Castells, and Lauren A. Benton, 11–40. Baltimore: Johns Hopkins University Press.

Castillo, Mike, Osman Rodasy, and Fernando Magzul. 2011. "Reportan 24 linchamientos en Huehuetenango." *Prensa Libre,* October 27.

Chakrabarty, Dipesh. 2000. *Provincializing Europe: Postcolonial Thought and Historical Difference.* Princeton, NJ: Princeton University Press.

Chari, Sharad. 2004. *Fraternal Capital: Peasant-Workers, Self-Made Men, and Globalization in Provincial India.* Palo Alto, CA: Stanford University Press.

Chavez, Leo. 2007. "Conditions of Illegality." *International Migration* 45, no. 3: 192–196.

———. 2012. *Shadowed Lives: Undocumented Immigrants in American Society.* Belmont: Wadsworth, Cengage Learning.

Chen, Yongmin, and Thitima Puttitanun. 2005. "Intellectual Property Rights and Innovation in Developing Countries." *Journal of Development Economics* 78, no. 2: 474–493.

Chernikoff, Leah. 2012. "Tommy Hilfiger to Address Those Racist Rumors from 1996 One More Time." *Fashionista,* March 12. www.fashionista.com/2012/03/tommy-hilfiger-addresses-those-racist-rumors-from-1996-one-more-time.

Clark, Gordon, Nigel Thrift, and Adam Tickell. 2004. "Performing Finance: The Industry, the Media, and Its Image." *Review of International Political Economy* 11, no. 2: 289–310.

Clifford, James. 2000. "Taking Identity Politics Seriously: The Contradictory Stony Ground . . ." In *Without Guarantees: Essays in Honour of Stuart Hall,* edited by Paul Gilroy, Lawrence Grossberg, and Angela McRobbie, 94–112. London: Verso.

Collins, Jane. 2003. *Threads: Gender, Labor, and Power in the Global Apparel Industry.* Chicago: University of Chicago Press.

Colloredo-Mansfeld, Rudi. 2002. "An Ethnography of Neoliberalism: Understanding Competition in Artisan Economies." *Current Anthropology* 43, no. 1: 113–137.

Comaroff, Jean. 1996. "The Empire's Old Clothes: Fashioning the Colonial Subject." In *Cross Cultural Consumption: Global Markets, Local Realities,* edited by David Howes, 19–38. New York: Routledge.

———. 2007. "Beyond Bare Life: AIDS, (Bio)Politics, and the Neoliberal Order." *Public Culture* 19, no. 1: 197–219.

Comaroff, Jean, and John L. Comaroff, eds. 2006. *Law and Disorder in the Postcolony.* Chicago: University of Chicago Press.

———. 1999. "Occult Economies and the Violence of Abstraction: Notes from the South African Postcolony." *American Ethnologist* 26, no. 2: 279–303.

Comaroff, John L., and Jean Comaroff. 1997. *Of Revelation and Revolution.* Vol. 2, *The Dialectics of Modernity on a South African Frontier.* Chicago: University of Chicago Press.

———. 2009. *Ethnicity, Inc.* Chicago: University of Chicago Press.

Comisión para el Esclarecimiento Histórico. 1999. *Guatemala: Memoria del Silencio.* Guatemala City: United Nations.

Condry, Ian. 2004. "Cultures of Music Piracy: An Ethnographic Comparison of the US and Japan." *International Journal of Cultural Studies* 7, no. 3: 343–363.

Conkey, Margaret W., and Christine A. Hastorf, eds. 1993. *The Uses of Style in Archaeology*. Cambridge: Cambridge University Press.

Conklin, Beth A. 1997. "Body Paint, Feathers, and VCRs: Aesthetics and Authenticity in Amazonian Activism." *American Ethnologist* 24, no. 4: 711–737.

Contreras, Geovanni, and Andrea Orozco. 2013. "Inicia construcción de cementera en San Juan Sacatepéquez." *Prensa Libre*, July 19.

Coombe, Rosemary J. 1993. "Tactics of Appropriation and the Politics of Recognition in Late Modern Democracies." *Political Theory* 21, no. 3: 411–433.

———. 1996. "Embodied Trademarks: Mimesis and Alterity on American Commercial Frontiers." *Cultural Anthropology* 11, no. 2: 202–224.

———. 1998. *The Cultural Life of Intellectual Properties: Authorship, Appropriation, and the Law*. Durham, NC: Duke University Press.

———. 2003. "Works in Progress: Traditional Knowledge, Biological Diversity, and Intellectual Property in a Neoliberal Era." In *Globalization Under Construction: Governmentality, Law, and Identity*, edited by Richard Warren Perry and Bill Maurer, 273–314. Minneapolis: University of Minnesota Press.

Cooper, Frederick, and Ann Laura Stoler, eds. 1997. *Tensions of Empire: Colonial Cultures in a Bourgeois World*. Berkeley: University of California Press.

Cooper, William. 2008. "Saggy Pants Law Overwhelmingly Approved in Riviera Beach." *Palm Beach Post*, March 11.

Coronado, Eddy. 2013. "Empresarios, preocupados por piratería." *Prensa Libre*, June 12.

Correa, Carlos M. 2000. *Intellectual Property Rights, the WTO and Developing Countries: The TRIPS Agreement and Policy Options*. London: Zed Books.

———. 2001. "The TRIPS Agreement: How Much Room for Maneuver?" *Journal of Human Development* 2, no. 1: 79–107.

Cosminsky, Sheila. 1977. "The Impact of Methods on the Analysis of Illness Concepts in a Guatemalan Community." *Social Science and Medicine* 11, no. 5: 325–332.

Coutin, Susan Bibler. 2003. *Legalizing Moves: Salvadoran Immigrants' Struggle for U.S. Residency*. Ann Arbor: University of Michigan Press.

———. 2007. *Nations of Emigrants: Shifting Boundaries of Citizenship in El Salvador and the United States*. Ithaca: Cornell University Press.

Crăciun, Magdalena. 2014. *Material Culture and Authenticity: Fake Branded Fashion in Europe*. London: Bloomsbury.

Crossley, Émilie. 2012. "Poor but Happy: Volunteer Tourists' Encounters with Poverty." *Tourism Geographies* 14, no. 2: 235–253.

Cruz, José Miguel. 2009. "Public Insecurity in Central America and Mexico." *AmericasBarometer Insights* 28: 1–7.

Crystal, Valerie, Shin Imai, and Bernadette Maheandiran. 2014. "Access to Justice and Corporate Accountability: A Legal Case Study of HudBay in Guatemala." *Canadian Journal of Development Studies* 35, no. 2: 286–303.

Das, Veena, and Deborah Poole, eds. 2004. *Anthropology in the Margins of the State*. Santa Fe: School of American Research Press.

Dávila, Arlene M. 2001. *Latinos, Inc.: The Marketing and Making of a People*. Berkeley: University of California Press.

Davis, Jennifer. 2008. "Between a Sign and a Brand." In *Trade Marks and Brands: An Interdisciplinary Critique*, edited by Lionel Bently, Jennifer Davis, and Jane C. Ginsburg, 65–91. Cambridge: Cambridge University Press.

De Genova, Nicholas. 2005. *Working the Boundaries: Race, Space, and "Illegality" in Mexican Chicago*. Durham, NC: Duke University Press.

de la Cadena, Marisol. 2000. *Indigenous Mestizos: The Politics of Race and Culture in Cuzco, Peru, 1919-1991*. Durham, NC: Duke University Press.

———. 2010. "Indigenous Cosmopolitics in the Andes: Conceptual Reflections Beyond 'Politics.'" *Cultural Anthropology* 25, no. 2: 334–370.

de la Cadena, Marisol, and Orin Starn, eds. 2007. *Indigenous Experience Today*. Oxford: Berg.

de Soto, Hernando. 1989. *The Other Path: The Invisible Revolution in the Third World*. New York: Harper and Row.

DeCastro, Julio O., David A. Balkin, and Dean A. Shepherd. 2008. "Can Entrepreneurial Firms Benefit from Product Piracy?" *Journal of Business Venturing* 23, no. 1: 75–90.

DeHart, Monica C. 2010. *Ethnic Entrepreneurs: Identity and Development Politics in Latin America*. Palo Alto, CA: Stanford University Press.

Deleuze, Gilles. 1990. *The Logic of Sense*. Translated by Mark Lester. New York: Columbia University Press.

Dent, Alexander S. 2012a. "Introduction: Understanding the War on Piracy, or Why We Need More Anthropology of Pirates." *Anthropological Quarterly* 85, no. 3: 659–672.

———. 2012b. "Piracy, Circulatory Legitimacy, and Neoliberal Subjectivity in Brazil." *Cultural Anthropology* 27, no. 1: 28–49.

Derrida, Jacques. 1976. *Of Grammatology*. Baltimore: Johns Hopkins University Press.

Dotson, Rachel. 2014. "Citizen-Auditors and Visible Subjects: Mi Familia Progresa and Transparency Politics in Guatemala." *PoLAR: Political and Legal Anthropology Review* 37, no. 2: 350–370.

Douglas, Mary. 1966. *Purity and Danger: An Analysis of the Concepts of Pollution and Taboo*. London: Routledge.

———. 1992. *Risk and Blame: Essays in Cultural Theory*. London: Routledge.

Dow, James. 1981. "The Image of Limited Production: Envy and the Domestic Mode of Production in Peasant Society." *Human Organization* 40, no. 4: 360–363.

Downes, David R. 2000. "How Intellectual Property Could Be a Tool to Protect Traditional Knowledge." *Columbia Journal of Environmental Law* 25: 253–282.

Drassinower, Abraham. 2015. *What's Wrong with Copying?* Cambridge, MA: Harvard University Press.

Dua, Jatin. 2014. "Regulating the Ocean: Piracy and Protection along the East African Coast." PhD diss., Duke University.

Dudley, Kathryn M. 1996. "The Problem of Community in Rural America." *Culture and Agriculture* 18, no. 2: 47–57.

Eckstein, Lars, and Anja Schwarz, eds. 2014. *Postcolonial Piracy: Media Distribution and Cultural Production in the Global South.* London: Bloomsburg.

Ehlers, Tracy Bachrach. 2000. *Silent Looms: Women and Production in a Guatemalan Town.* Austin: University of Texas Press.

Ekern, Stener. 2008. "Are Human Rights Destroying the Natural Balance of All Things? The Difficult Encounter Between International Law and Community Law in Mayan Guatemala." In *Human Rights in the Maya Region: Global Politics, Cultural Contentions, and Moral Engagements,* edited by Pedro Pitarch, Shannon Speed, and Xochitl Leyva Solano, 123–144. Durham, NC: Duke University Press.

El Harbi, Sana, and Gilles Grolleau. 2008. "Profiting from Being Pirated by 'Pirating' the Pirates." *Kyklos* 61, no. 3: 385–390.

Eldridge, Richard Thomas. 1989. *On Moral Personhood: Philosophy, Literature, Criticism, and Self-Understanding.* Chicago: University of Chicago Press.

Elyachar, Julia. 2005. *Markets of Dispossession: NGOs, Economic Development, and the State in Cairo.* Durham, NC: Duke University Press.

English, Bonnie. 2013. *A Cultural History of Fashion in the 20th and 21st Centuries: From Catwalk to Sidewalk.* London: Bloomsburg.

Entwhistle, Joanne. 2000. *The Fashioned Body: Fashion, Dress and Modern Social Theory.* Cambridge: Blackwell.

Escobar, Arturo. 1995. *Encountering Development: The Making and Unmaking of the Third World.* Princeton, NJ: Princeton University Press.

———. 2008. *Territories of Difference: Place, Movements, Life,* Redes. Durham, NC: Duke University Press.

Esquít, Edgar. 2007. "El indio sumiso en el pasado y los güisaches como indígenas «superados»: Orígenes de otras formas de la cultura y la política subalternas." *Estudios Centroamericanos* 62, nos. 709–710: 1048–1051.

Esquít, Edgar, and Iván García. 1998. *El derecho consuetudinario, la reforma judicial y la implementación de los acuerdos de paz.* Guatemala City: FLACSO.

Ezzamel, Mahmoud. 2012. *Accounting and Order.* New York: Routledge.

Farmer, Paul. 2004. "An Anthropology of Structural Violence." *Current Anthropology* 45, no. 3: 305–325.

Fassin, Didier. 2011. "Policing Borders, Producing Boundaries: The Governmentality of Immigration in Dark Times." *Annual Review of Anthropology* 40: 213–226.

———. 2012. "Compassion and Repression: The Moral Economy of Immigration Policies in France." *Cultural Anthropology* 20, no. 3: 363–387.

Ferguson, Ann Arnett. 2000. *Bad Boys: Public Schools in the Making of Black Masculinity.* Ann Arbor: University of Michigan Press.

Ferguson, James. 1990. *The Anti-Politics Machine: "Development," Depoliticization, and Bureaucratic Power in Lesotho.* Cambridge: Cambridge University Press.

———. 1999. *Expectations of Modernity: Myths and Meanings of Urban Life on the Zambian Copperbelt.* Berkeley: University of California Press.

————. 2006. *Global Shadows: Africa in the Neoliberal World Order.* Durham, NC: Duke University Press.

Fernández García, María Cristina. 2004. *Lynching in Guatemala: Legacy of War and Impunity.* Cambridge, MA: Weatherhead Center for International Affairs, Harvard University.

Fernández-Kelly, Patricia, and Anna M. García. 1989. "Informalization at the Core: Hispanic Women, Homework and the Advanced Capitalist State." In *The Informal Economy: Studies in Advanced and Less Developed Countries,* edited by Alejandro Portes, Manuel Castells, and Lauren A. Benton, 247–264. Baltimore: Johns Hopkins University Press.

Fink, Carsten. 2005. "Entering the Jungle of Intellectual Property Rights Exclusion and Parallel Importation." In *Intellectual Property and Development: Lessons from Recent Economic Research,* edited by Carsten Fink and Keith E. Mascus, 171–188. New York: World Bank and Oxford University Press.

Fink, Carsten, and Patrick Reichenmiller. 2005. *Tightening TRIPS: The Intellectual Property Provisions of Recent US Free Trade Agreements.* World Bank Trade Note 20. Washington, DC: World Bank.

Fink, Carsten, and Keith E. Maskus, eds. 2005. *Intellectual Property and Development: Lessons from Recent Economic Research.* New York: World Bank and Oxford University Press.

Fischer, Edward F. 1996. "Induced Culture Change as a Strategy for Socioeconomic Development: The Pan-Maya Movement in Guatemala." In *Maya Cultural Activism in Guatemala,* edited by Edward F. Fischer and R. McKenna Brown, 51–73. Austin: University of Texas Press.

————. 1999. "Cultural Logic and Maya Identity: Rethinking Constructivism and Essentialism." *Current Anthropology* 40, no. 4: 473–500.

————. 2001. *Cultural Logics and Global Economics: Maya Identity in Thought and Practice.* Austin: University of Texas Press.

Fischer, Edward F., and Peter Benson. 2006. *Broccoli and Desire: Global Connections and Maya Struggles in Postwar Guatemala.* Palo Alto, CA: Stanford University Press.

Fischer, Edward F., and R. McKenna Brown, eds. 1996. *Maya Cultural Activism in Guatemala.* Austin: University of Texas Press.

Fischer, Edward F., and Carol Hendrickson. 2002. *Tecpán Guatemala: A Modern Maya Town in Global and Local Context.* Boulder: Westview Press.

Ford, Talissa Jane. 2008. "Prophets and Pirates: The Space of Empire in British Romance Literature." PhD diss., University of California, Berkeley.

Foster, George M. 1953. "Cofradía and Compadrazgo in Spain and Spanish America." *Southwestern Journal of Anthropology* 9, no. 1: 1–28.

————. 1965. "Peasant Society and the Image of Limited Good." *American Anthropologist* 67, no. 2: 293–315.

————. 1972. "The Anatomy of Envy: A Study in Symbolic Behavior." *Current Anthropology* 13, no. 2: 165–202.

Foster, Robert J. 2005. "Commodity Futures: Labour, Love, and Value." *Anthropology Today* 21, no. 4: 8–12.

————. 2007. "The Work of the New Economy: Consumers, Brands, and Value Creation." *Cultural Anthropology* 22, no. 4: 707–731.

——. 2008. *Coca-Globalization: Following Soft Drinks from New York to New Guinea*. New York: Palgrave Macmillan.

Foucault, Michel. 1977. *Discipline and Punish: The Birth of the Prison*. Translated by Alan Sheridan. New York: Random House.

——. 1984. "What Is an Author?" In *The Foucault Reader*, edited by Paul Rabinow, 101–120. New York: Pantheon.

——. 1990. *History of Sexuality*. Vol. 2, *The Use of Pleasure*. Translated by Robert Hurley. New York: Random House.

——. 2010. *Security, Territory, Population: Lectures at the Collège de France, 1977–1978*. Edited by Michel Senellart. Translated by Graham Burchell. New York: Picador.

Franklyn, David. 2004. "Debunking Dilution Doctrine: Toward a Coherent Theory of the Anti-Free-Rider Principle in American Trademark Law." *Hastings Law Journal* 56: 117–168.

Freeman, Carla. 2001. "Is Local: Global as Feminine: Masculine? Rethinking the Gender of Globalization." *Signs* 26, no. 4: 1007–1037.

——. 2007. "The Reputation of Neoliberalism." *American Ethnologist* 34, no. 2: 252–267.

——. 2014. *Entrepreneurial Selves: Neoliberal Respectability and the Making of a Caribbean Middle Class*. Durham, NC: Duke University Press.

French, Jan Hoffman. 2009. *Legalizing Identities: Becoming Black or Indian in Brazil's Northeast*. Chapel Hill: University of North Carolina Press.

Frimer, Jeremy A., and Lawrence J. Walker. 2008. "Towards a New Paradigm of Moral Personhood." *Journal of Moral Education* 37, no. 3: 333–356.

Fultz, Katherine. 2015. "Economies of Representation: Communication, Conflict, and Mining in Guatemala." PhD diss., University of Michigan.

Galemba, Rebecca. 2009. "Cultures of Contraband: Contesting Illegality at the Mexico-Guatemala Border." PhD diss., Brown University.

Gallant, Thomas W. 1999. "Brigandage, Piracy, Capitalism, and State-Formation: Transnational Crime from a Historical World-Systems Perspective." In *States and Illegal Practices*, edited by Josiah McC. Heyman, 25–62. Oxford: Berg.

Gandolfo, Daniella. 2013. "Formless: A Day at Lima's Office of Formalization." *Cultural Anthropology* 28, no. 2: 278–298.

Garber, Marjorie. 1992. *Vested Interests: Cross-Dressing and Cultural Anxiety*. New York: Routledge.

Gardner, Kathy, and David Lewis. 1996. *Anthropology, Development and the Post-Modern Challenge*. London: Pluto Press.

Garrard-Burnett, Virginia. 1998. *Protestantism in Guatemala: Living in the New Jerusalem*. Austin: University of Texas Press.

——. 2010. *Terror in the Land of the Holy Spirit: Guatemala Under General Efraín Ríos Montt, 1982–1983*. Oxford: Oxford University Press.

Giddens, Anthony. 1991. *Modernity and Self-Identity: Self and Society in the Late Modern Age*. Palo Alto, CA: Stanford University Press.

Gilroy, Paul. 1987. *"There Ain't No Black in the Union Jack": The Cultural Politics of Race and Nation*. Chicago: University of Chicago Press.

Glebbeek, Marie-Louis. 2009. "Post-War Violence and Police Reform in Guatemala." In *Policing Insecurity: Police Reform, Security, and Human Rights in Latin America,* edited by Niels Uildriks, 79–94. Lanham: Lexington Books.

Godoy, Angelina Snodgrass. 2002. "Lynchings and the Democratization of Terror in Postwar Guatemala: Implications for Human Rights." *Human Rights Quarterly* 24, no. 3: 2002.

———. 2006. *Popular Injustice: Violence, Community, and Law in Latin America.* Palo Alto, CA: Stanford University Press.

———. 2013. *Of Medicines and Markets: Intellectual Property and Human Rights in the Free Trade Era.* Palo Alto, CA: Stanford University Press.

Goldín, Liliana R. 1992. "Work and Ideology in the Maya Highlands of Guatemala: Economic Beliefs in the Context of Occupational Change." *Economic Development and Cultural Change* 41, no. 1: 103–123.

———. 2001. "Maquila Age Maya: Changing Households and Communities of the Central Highlands of Guatemala." *Journal of Latin American Anthropology* 6, no. 1: 30–57.

———. 2009. *Global Maya: Work and Ideology in Rural Guatemala.* Tucson: University of Arizona Press.

Goldín, Liliana R., and Brent Metz. 1991. "An Expression of Cultural Change: Invisible Converts to Protestantism among Highland Guatemala Mayas." *Ethnology* 30, no. 4: 325–338.

Goldstein, Daniel M. 2007. "Human Rights as Culprit, Human Rights as Victim." In *The Practice of Human Rights: Tracking Law Between the Global and the Local,* edited by Mark Goodale and Sally Engle Merry, 49–77. Cambridge: Cambridge University Press.

———. 2012. *Outlawed: Between Security and Rights in a Bolivian City.* Durham, NC: Duke University Press.

Goldstein, Daniel M., Gloria Achá, Eric Hinojosa, and Theo Rocken. 2009. "La Mano Dura and the Violence of Civil Society in Bolivia." In *Indigenous Peoples, Civil Society, and the Neo-Liberal State in Latin America,* edited by Edward F. Fischer, 43–63. New York: Berghahn Books.

Gomberg-Muñoz, Ruth. 2011. *Labor and Legality: An Ethnography of a Mexican Immigrant Network.* Oxford: Oxford University Press.

Gondola, Ch. Didier. 1999. "Dream and Drama: The Search for Elegance among Congolese Youth." *African Studies Review* 42, no. 1: 23–48.

Goodale, Mark. 2009. *Surrendering to Utopia: An Anthropology of Human Rights.* Palo Alto, CA: Stanford University Press.

Gordon, Kathleen E. 2011. "What Is Important to Me Is My Business, Nothing More: Neoliberalism, Ideology and the Work of Selling in Highland Bolivia." *Anthropology of Work Review* 32, no. 1: 30–39.

Gould, David, and William Gruben. 1996. "The Role of Intellectual Property Rights in Economic Growth." *Journal of Economic Development* 48: 323–350.

Grandin, Greg. 2000. *The Blood of Guatemala: A History of Race and Nation.* Durham, NC: Duke University Press.

———. 2004. *The Last Colonial Massacre: Latin America in the Cold War.* Chicago: University of Chicago Press.

Granovetter, Mark. 1985. "Economic Action and Social Structure: The Problem of Embeddedness." *American Journal of Sociology* 91, no. 3: 481–510.

Green, Linda. 1999. *Fear as a Way of Life: Mayan Widows in Rural Guatemala*. New York: Columbia University Press.

———. 2003. "Notes on Mayan Youth and Rural Industrialization in Guatemala." *Critique of Anthropology* 23, no. 1: 51–73.

Green, Robert, and Tasman Smith. 2002. "Executive Insights: Countering Brand Counterfeiters." *Journal of International Marketing* 10: 89–106.

Greene, K. J. 1999. "Copyright, Culture and Black Music: A Legacy of Unequal Protection." *Hastings Communications and Entertainment Law Journal* 21, no. 2: 339–392.

———. 2008. "Intellectual Property at the Intersection of Race and Gender: Lady Sings the Blues." *Journal of Gender, Social Policy and the Law* 16, no. 3: 365–385.

Greenhouse, Jared. 2015. "Why 62,000 Abercrombie & Fitch Employees Are Suing the Company." *Huffington Post*, July 22. www.huffingtonpost.com/entry/abercrombie-fitch-lawsuit-look-policy_us_55ae70e6e4b08f57d5d29286.

Greenwald, Richard A. 2005. *The Triangle Fire, the Protocols of Peace, and Industrial Democracy in Progressive Era New York*. Philadelphia: Temple University Press.

Grossman, Gene M., and Elhanan Helpman. 1993. *Innovation and Growth in the Global Economy*. Cambridge, MA: MIT Press.

Gudeman, Stephen. 1978. "Anthropological Economies: The Question of Distribution." *Annual Review of Anthropology* 7: 347–377.

———. 1986. *Economics as Culture: Models and Metaphors of Livelihood*. London: Routledge and K. Paul.

Gupta, Akhil, and James Ferguson, eds. 1997. *Culture, Power, Place: Explorations in Critical Anthropology*. Durham, NC: Duke University Press.

Gutmann, Matthew C., ed. 2003. *Changing Men and Masculinities in Latin America*. Durham, NC: Duke University Press.

Guyer, Jane I. 1981. "Household and Community in African Studies." *African Studies Review* 24: 87–137.

———. 1993. "Wealth in People and Self-Realization in Equatorial Africa." *Man* 28: 243–265.

———. 2004. *Marginal Gains: Monetary Transactions in Atlantic Africa*. Chicago: University of Chicago Press.

Hage, Ghassan. 1996. "The Spatial Imaginary of National Practices: Dwelling–Domesticating/Being–Exterminating." *Environment and Planning D* 14, no. 4: 463–485.

Hale, Charles R. 2004. "Rethinking Indigenous Politics in the Era of the 'Indio Permitido.'" *NACLA Report on the Americas* 38, no. 2: 16–37.

———. 2005. "Neoliberal Multiculturalism: The Remaking of Cultural Rights and Racial Dominance in Central America." *PoLAR: Political and Legal Anthropology Review* 28, no. 1: 10-19.

———. 2007. *Más Que un Indio: Racial Ambivalence and Neoliberal Multiculturalism in Guatemala*. Santa Fe: School for American Research.

Hall, Stuart. 1999. "Whose Heritage? Unsettling 'The Heritage,' Re-Imagining the Post-Nation." *Third Text* 49: 3–13.

Hallam, Elizabeth, and Tim Ingold, eds. 2007. *Creativity and Cultural Improvisation.* Oxford: Berg.

Handy, Jim. 1989. "A Sea of Indians: Ethnic Conflict and the Guatemalan Revolution, 1944–1952." *The Americas* 46, no. 2: 189–204.

———. 2004. "Chicken Thieves, Witches, and Judges: Vigilante Justice and Customary Law in Guatemala." *Journal of Latin American Studies* 36, no. 3: 533–561.

Hann, C. M., ed. 1998. *Property Relations: Renewing the Anthropological Tradition.* Cambridge: Cambridge University Press.

Hansen, Karen Tranberg. 2000. *Salaula: The World of Secondhand Clothing and Zambia.* Chicago: University of Chicago Press.

———. 2004. "The World in Dress: Anthropological Perspectives on Clothing, Fashion, and Culture." *Annual Review of Anthropology* 33: 369–392.

Hansen, Karen Tranberg, and D. Soyini Madison, eds. 2013. *African Dress: Fashion, Agency, Performance.* London: Bloomsbury.

Hansen, Thomas Blom, and Finn Stepputat, eds. 2005. *States of Imagination: Ethnographic Explorations of the Postcolonial State.* Durham, NC: Duke University Press.

Harris, Cheryl. 1993. "Whiteness as Property." *Harvard Law Review* 106, no. 8: 1707–1791.

Hart, Keith. 1973. "Informal Economic Opportunities and Urban Employment in Ghana." *Journal of Modern African Studies* 11, no. 1: 61–89.

Harvey, David. 2005. *A Brief History of Neoliberalism.* Oxford: Oxford University Press.

———. 2008. "The Right to the City." *New Left Review* 23: 23–40.

Hayden, Cori. 2003. *When Nature Goes Public: The Making and Unmaking of Bio-Prospecting in Mexico.* Princeton, NJ: Princeton University Press.

———. 2007. "A Generic Solution? Pharmaceuticals and the Politics of the Similar in Mexico." *Current Anthropology* 48, no. 4: 475–495.

Hebdige, Dick. 1979. *Subculture: The Meaning of Style.* London: Methuen.

Helpman, Elhanan. 1992. "Endogenous Microeconomic Growth Theory." *European Economic Review* 36: 237–267.

Hemphill, C. Scott, and Jeannie Suk. 2009. "The Law, Culture, and Economics of Fashion." *Stanford Law Review* 61, no. 5: 1147–1199.

Hendrickson, Carol E. 1995. *Weaving Identities: Construction of Dress and Self in a Highland Guatemala Town.* Austin: University of Texas Press.

———. 1996. "Women, Weaving and Education Revitalization." In *Maya Cultural Activism in Guatemala,* edited by Edward F. Fischer and R. McKenna Brown, 156–164. Austin: University of Texas Press.

Herzfeld, Michael. 1992. *The Social Production of Indifference: Exploring the Symbolic Roots of Western Bureaucracy.* Chicago: University of Chicago Press.

———. 2004. *The Body Impolitic: Artisans and Artifice in the Global Hierarchy of Value.* Chicago: University of Chicago Press.

Heyman, Josiah McC. 1991. *Life and Labor on the Border: Working People of Northeastern Sonora, Mexico, 1886–1986*. Tucson: University of Arizona Press.

———, ed. 1999. *States and Illegal Practices*. Oxford: Berg.

Hiebert, Timothy H. 1994. *Parallel Importation in US Trademark Law*. Contributions in Legal Studies 74. Westport, CT: Greenwood Publishing Group.

Hill, Jane H. 2008. *The Everyday Language of White Racism*. Oxford: Wiley-Blackwell.

Hilton, Brian, Chong Ju Choi, and Stephen Chen. 2004. "The Ethics of Counterfeiting in the Fashion Industry: Quality, Credence and Profit Issues." *Journal of Business Ethics* 55, no. 4: 343–352.

Hirsch, Eric, and Marilyn Strathern, eds. 2004. *Transactions and Creations: Property Debates and the Stimulus Of Melanesia*. New York: Berghahn Books.

Ho, Karen. 2009. *Liquidated: An Ethnography of Wall Street*. Durham, NC: Duke University Press.

Hobsbawm, Eric. 1959. *Primitive Rebels: Studies in Archaic Forms of Social Movement in the 19th and 20th Centuries*. New York: W. W. Norton.

———. 1969. *Bandits*. London: Weidenfeld and Nicolson.

Hodder, Ian. 1982. *Symbols in Action: Ethnoarchaeological Studies of Material Culture*. Cambridge: Cambridge University Press.

———, ed. 1989. *The Meaning of Things: Material Culture and Symbolic Expression*. Abingdon: Harper Collins Academic.

———. 1990. "Style as Historical Quality." In *The Uses of Style in Archaeology*, edited by Margaret W. Conkey and Christine A. Hastorf, 44–51. Cambridge: Cambridge University Press.

Hodkinson, Paul. 2002. *Goth: Identity, Style, and Subculture*. Oxford: Berg.

Holmes, Seth. 2013. *Fresh Fruit, Broken Bodies: Migrant Farmworkers in the United States*. Berkeley: University of California Press.

Huang, Jen-Hung, Bruce C. Lee, and Chih-Tung Hsiao. 2008. "Managing Channel Quality: The Consequential Impacts of the Grey Market." *Total Quality Management* 19, no. 12: 1235–1247.

Hull, Matthew S. 2012. *Government of Paper: The Materiality of Bureaucracy in Urban Pakistan*. Berkeley: University of California Press.

Hunt, Alan. 1996. *Governance of the Consuming Passions: A History of Sumptuary Law*. Basingstoke: Macmillan.

Husted, Bryan W. 2000. "The Impact of National Culture on Software Piracy." *Journal of Business Ethics* 26, no. 3: 197–211.

International Labor Organization. 1971. *Employment, Incomes and Inequality: A Strategy for Increasing Productive Employment in Kenya*. Geneva: ILO.

Isik, Damla. 2010. "Personal and Global Economies: Male Carpet Manufacturers as Entrepreneurs in the Weaving Neighborhoods of Konya, Turkey." *American Ethnologist* 37, no. 1: 53-68.

Iwabuchi, Koichi. 2002. *Recentering Globalization: Popular Culture and Japanese Transnationalism*. Durham, NC: Duke University Press.

Jaffe, Alexandra, ed. 2009. *Stance: Sociolinguistic Perspectives.* Oxford: Oxford University Press.

James, Erica Caple. 2010. *Democratic Insecurities: Violence, Trauma, and Intervention in Haiti.* Berkeley: University of California Press.

Jameson, Fredric. 1991. *Postmodernism; or, the Cultural Logic of Late Capitalism.* Durham, NC: Duke University Press.

Jamieson, Dave. 2015. "Supreme Court Rules against Abercrombie & Fitch in Discrimination Case." *Huffington Post,* June 1. www.huffingtonpost.com/2015 /06/01/supreme-court-abercrombie_n_7464534.html.

Johns, Adrian. 1998. *The Nature of the Book: Print and Knowledge in the Making.* Chicago: University of Chicago Press.

———. 2010. *Piracy: The Intellectual Property Wars from Gutenberg to Gates.* Chicago: University of Chicago Press.

Johnson, Barbara, ed. 1982. "The Pedagogical Imperative: Teaching as a Literary Genre." Special issue, *Yale French Studies* 63.

Karaganis, Joe, ed. 2011. *Media Piracy in Emerging Economies.* Social Science Research Council. www.ssrc.org/publications/view/C4A69B1C-8051-E011-9A1B-001CC477EC84.

Karlan, Dean, and Martin Valdivia. 2011. "Teaching Entrepreneurship: Impact of Business Training on Microfinance Clients and Institutions." *Review of Economics and Statistics* 93, no. 2: 510–527.

Keane, Webb. 2007. *Christian Moderns: Freedom and Fetish in the Mission Encounter.* Berkeley: University of California Press.

Kelley, Robin D. G. 1996. *Race Rebels: Culture, Politics and the Black Working Class.* New York: Free Press.

Klein, Naomi. 2000. *No Logo: Taking Aim at the Brand Bullies.* New York: Picador USA.

Kleinberg, Eliot. 2008. "Judge: Riviera Beach 'Saggy Pants' Ban Unconstitutional." *Palm Beach Post,* September 15.

Kleinman, Arthur. 1999. "Experience and Its Moral Modes: Culture, Human Conditions, and Disorder." In *The Tanner Lectures on Human Values,* vol. 20, edited by G.B. Peterson, 355–420. Salt Lake City: University of Utah Press.

Kleinman, Arthur, Veena Das, and Margaret Lock, eds. 1997. *Social Suffering.* Berkeley: University of California Press.

Kirsch, Stuart. 2004. "Property Limits: Debates on the Body, Nature, and Culture." In *Transactions and Creations: Property Debates and the Stimulus of Melanesia,* edited by Eric Hirsch and Marilyn Strathern, 21–39. New York: Berghahn Books.

———. 2006. *Reverse Anthropology: Indigenous Analysis of Social and Environmental Relations in New Guinea.* Palo Alto, CA: Stanford University Press.

———. 2014. *Mining Capitalism: The Relationship between Corporations and Their Critics.* Berkeley: University of California Press.

Kobrak, Pablo, and Marta Gutiérrez. 2001. *Los linchamientos pos conflicto y violencia colectiva en Huehuetenango Guatemala.* Guatemala City: CEDFOG.

Kondo, Dorinne K. 1990. *Crafting Selves: Power, Gender, and Discourses of Identity in a Japanese Workplace*. Chicago: University of Chicago Press.

―――. 1997. *About Face: Performing Race in Fashion and Theater*. New York: Routledge.

Konstam, Angus. 2008. *Piracy: The Complete History*. New York: Osprey.

Kort, Peter, Jonathan Caulkins, Richard Hartl, and Gustav Feichtinger. 2006. "Brand Image and Brand Dilution in the Fashion Industry." *Automatica* 42, no. 8: 1363–1370.

Kuper, Adam. 2003. "The Return of the Native." *Current Anthropology* 44, no. 3: 389–402.

Lai, Edwin. 1998. "International Intellectual Property Rights Protection and the Rate of Product Innovation." *Journal of Development Economics* 55, no. 1: 133–153.

Lakhani, Nina. 2015. "Guatemalan President's Downfall Marks Success for Corruption Investigators." *Guardian*, September 9.

Lambek, Michael, ed. 2010. *Ordinary Ethics: Anthropology, Language, and Action*. New York: Fordham University Press.

Lang, Berel, ed. 1987. *The Concept of Style*. Ithaca: Cornell University Press.

Laplante, Lisa J. 2014. "Memory Battles: Guatemala's Public Debates and the Genocidal Trial of José Efraín Ríos Montt." *Quinnipiac Law Review* 32: 621–673.

Larios, Roxana. 2011. "Pantalones de lona lideran la piratería." *Siglo 21*, January 17.

Larkin, Brian. 2008. *Signal and Noise: Media, Infrastructure, and Urban Culture in Nigeria*. Durham, NC: Duke University Press.

Lavie, Smadar, Kirin Narayan, and Renato Rosaldo, eds. 1993. *Creativity/Anthropology*. Ithaca: Cornell University Press.

Law, John. 1994. *Organizing Modernity: Social Ordering and Social Theory*. Oxford: Blackwell.

―――. 2002. "Economics as Interference." In *Cultural Economy: Cultural Analysis and Commercial Life,* edited by Paul du Gay and Michael Pryke, 21–38. London: Sage.

Law, John, and Annemarie Mol. 1995. "Notes on Materiality and Sociality." *Sociological Review* 43: 274–294.

Law, John, and John Urry. 2004. "Enacting the Social." *Economy and Society* 33, no. 3: 390–410.

Lederman, Daniel, Julián Messina, Samuel Pienknagura, and Jamele Rigolini. 2014. *Latin American Entrepreneurs: Many Firms but Little Innovation*. Washington, DC: World Bank.

Lempert, Michael. 2014. "Imitation." *Annual Review of Anthropology* 43: 379–395.

Leonardo, José Roberto. 2011. "Celebran el 'Día Mundial de la Propiedad Intelectual.'" *Prensa Libre*, April 26.

Lessig, Lawrence. 2004. *Free Culture: How Big Media Uses Technology and the Law to Lock Down Culture and Control Creativity*. New York: Penguin.

Levi-Strauss, Claude. 1966. *The Savage Mind*. Chicago: University of Chicago Press.

Li, Tania Murray. 2007. *The Will to Improve: Governmentality, Development, and the Practice of Politics*. Durham, NC: Duke University Press.

Liang, Lawrence. 2008. "Meet John Doe's Order: Piracy, Temporality, and the Question of Asia." *Journal of the Moving Image* 7: 154–170.

———. 2009. "Piracy, Creativity and Infrastructure: Rethinking Access to Culture." http://papers.ssrn.com/sol3/papers.cfm?abstract_id=1436229.

———. 2011. "Beyond Representation: The Figure of the Pirate." In *Making and Unmaking Intellectual Property: Creative Production in Legal and Cultural Perspective*, edited by Mario Biagioli, Peter Jaszi, and Martha Woodmansee, 167–180. Chicago: University of Chicago Press.

Lin, Yi-Chieh Jessica. 2009. *Knockoff: A Cultural Biography of Transnational Counterfeit Goods*. PhD diss., Harvard University.

———. 2011. *Fake Stuff: China and the Rise of Counterfeit Goods*. New York: Routledge.

Lippert, Owen. 1999. *Competitive Strategies for the Protection of Intellectual Property*. Vancouver: Fraser Institute.

Lipsitz, George. 2006. "Learning from New Orleans: The Social Warrant of Hostile Privatism and Competitive Consumer Citizenship." *Cultural Anthropology* 21, no. 3: 451–468.

Little, Walter E. 2004. *Mayas in the Marketplace: Tourism, Globalization, and Cultural Identity*. Austin: University of Texas Press.

———. 2008. "Crime, Maya Handicraft Vendors, and the Social Re/Construction of Market Spaces in a Tourism Town." In *Economies and the Transformation of Landscape*, vol. 25, edited by Lisa Cliggett and Christopher A. Pool, 267–290. Lanham: Altamira Press.

———. 2009. "Living and Selling in the 'New Violence' of Guatemala." In *Mayas in Post-War Guatemala:* Harvest of Violence *Revisited,* edited by Walter E. Little and Timothy J. Smith, 54–66. Birmingham: University of Alabama Press.

Little, Walter E., and Timothy J. Smith, eds. 2009. *Mayas in Post-War Guatemala:* Harvest of Violence *Revisited.* Birmingham: University of Alabama Press.

Livingston, Julie. 2012. *Improvising Medicine: An African Oncology Ward in an Emerging Cancer Epidemic*. Durham, NC: Duke University Press.

Lobato, Ramon. 2012. "A Sideways View of the Film Economy in an Age of Digital Piracy." *Necsus: European Journal of Media Studies* 1, no. 1: 85–97.

López, Julie. 2010. "Guatemala's Crossroads: Democratization of Violence and Second Chances." Working Paper Series on Organized Crime in Central America, Woodrow Wilson International Center for Scholars, Latin American Program.

Loveman, Mara. 2014. *National Colors: Racial Classification and the State in Latin America*. Oxford: Oxford University Press.

Low, Setha. 2003. *Behind the Gates: Life, Security, and the Pursuit of Happiness in Fortress America*. New York: Routledge.

Lowe, Alan. 2004. "Postsocial Relations: Toward a Performative View of Accounting Knowledge." *Accounting, Auditing, and Accountability Journal* 17, no. 4: 604–628.

Lury, Celia. 2004. *Brands: The Logos of the Global Economy*. New York: Taylor and Francis.

Luvaas, Brent. 2010. "Designer Vandalism: Indonesian Indie Fashion and the Cultural Practice of Cut 'N' Paste." *Visual Anthropology Review* 26, no. 1: 1–16.

———. 2012. *DIY Style: Fashion, Music and Global Digital Cultures*. Oxford: Berg.

———. 2013. "Material Interventions: Indonesian DIY Fashion and the Regime of the Global Brand." *Cultural Anthropology* 28, no. 1: 127–143.

MacKenzie, Donald, Fabian Muniesa, and Lucia Siu, eds. 2007. *Do Economists Make Markets? On the Performativity of Economics*. Princeton, NJ: Princeton University Press.

Mackintosh, John T., and Thomas R. Graham. 1986. "Grey Market Imports: Burgeoning Crisis or Emerging Policy." *North Carolina Journal of International Law and Commercial Regulation* 11: 293–320.

MacLeod, Philip S. 1999. "A Brief History of the Partido Guatemalteco del Trabajo: A Companion to an Exhibition of the Partido Guatemalteco del Trabajo Papers." Latin American Library, Tulane University. http://lal.tulane.edu/happenings/exhibits/exhibition-partido-guatemalteco-del-trabajo-papers.

Magid, Julie Manning, Anthony D. Cox, and Dena S. Cox. 2006. "Quantifying Brand Image: Empirical Evidence of Trademark Dilution." *American Business Law Journal* 43, no. 1: 1–42.

Manning, Paul. 2010. "The Semiotics of Brand." *Annual Review of Anthropology* 39, no. 1: 33–49.

Manning, Paul, and Ann Uplisashvili. 2007. "'Our Beer': Ethnographic Brands in Postsocialist Georgia." *American Anthropologist* 109, no. 4: 626–641.

Manz, Beatriz. 1988. *Refugees of a Hidden War: The Aftermath of Counterinsurgency in Guatemala*. Albany: SUNY Press.

———. 2005. *Paradise in Ashes: A Guatemalan Journey of Courage, Terror, and Hope*. Berkeley: University of California Press.

Márez, Curtis. 1996. "Brown: The Politics of Working-Class Chicano Style." *Social Text* 48: 109–132.

Marron, D. B., and D. G. Steele. 2000. "Which Countries Protect Intellectual Property? The Case of Software Piracy." *Economic Inquiry* 38, no. 2: 159–174.

Marroquín, Jenniffer. 2010. "Leve baja en piratería." *Siglo 21*, May 11.

Maskus, Keith E. 2000. *Intellectual Property Rights in the Global Economy*. Washington DC: Institute for International Economics.

———. 2012. *Private Rights and Public Problems: The Global Economics of Intellectual Property in the 21st Century*. Washington DC: Peterson Institute for International Economics.

Mason, Matt. 2008. *The Pirate's Dilemma: How Youth Culture Is Reinventing Capitalism*. New York: Free Press.

Maxwell, David. 1998. "Delivered From the Spirit of Poverty? Pentecostalism, Prosperity, and Modernity in Zimbabwe." *Journal of Religion in Africa* 28, no. 3: 350–373.

Maurer, Bill. 2002. "Anthropological and Accounting Knowledge in Islamic Banking and Finance: Rethinking Critical Accounts." *Journal of the Royal Anthropological Institute* 8, no. 4: 645–667.

Mauricio Martínez, Francisco. 2004. "Negocios de película." *Prensa Libre,* October 3.

Mauss, Marcel. 1954. *The Gift: Forms and Functions of Exchange in Archaic Societies.* Translated by Ian Cunnison. Glencoe, IL: Free Press.

Mayén, Gisela. 1995. *Derecho consuetudinario indígena en Guatemala.* Guatemala City: Asociación de Investigación y Estudios Sociales.

Mazzarella, William. 2003. *Shoveling Smoke: Advertising and Globalization in Contemporary India.* Durham, NC: Duke University Press.

McArthur, J. A. 2009. "Digital Subculture: A Geek Meaning of Style." *Journal of Communication Inquiry* 33, no. 1: 58–70.

McBride, Dwight A. 2005. *Why I Hate Abercrombie & Fitch: Essays on Race and Sexuality.* New York: New York University Press.

McAllister, Carlota, and Diane Nelson, eds. 2013. *War by Other Means: Aftermath in Post-Genocide Guatemala.* Durham, NC: Duke University Press.

McCreery, David. 1994. *Rural Guatemala: 1760–1940.* Palo Alto, CA: Stanford University Press.

McLean, Stuart. 2009. "Stories and Cosmogonies: Imagining Creativity Beyond 'Nature' and 'Culture.'" *Cultural Anthropology* 24, no. 2: 213–245.

McRobbie, Angela, ed. 1989. *Zoot Suits and Second-Hand Dresses: An Anthology of Fashion and Music.* London: Macmillan.

Meagher, Kate. 1995. "Crisis, Informalization, and the Urban Informal Sector in Sub-Saharan Africa." *Development and Change* 26, no. 2: 259–284.

Meneley, Anne. 2004. "Extra Virgin Olive Oil and Slow Food." *Anthropologica* 46, no. 2: 165–176.

———. 2007. "Like an Extra Virgin." *American Anthropologist* 109, no. 4: 678–687.

Menocal, Carlos. 2005. "Guatemala es paraíso de la falsificación." *Prensa Libre,* August 7.

Mercer, Kobena. 1987. "Black Hair/Style Politics." *New Formations* 3: 33–54.

———. 1994. *Welcome to the Jungle: New Positions in Black Cultural Studies.* New York: Routledge.

Merry, Sally Engle. 2001. "Changing Rights, Changing Culture." In *Culture and Rights,* edited by Jane K. Cowan, Marie-Bénédicte Dembour, and Richard A. Wilson, 31–55. Cambridge: Cambridge University Press.

———. 2009. *Human Rights and Gender Violence: Translating International Law into Local Justice.* Chicago: University of Chicago Press.

Miller, Daniel. 1987. *Material Culture and Mass Consumption.* New York: Basil Blackwell.

———. 1997. *Capitalism: An Ethnographic Approach.* Oxford: Berg.

———, ed. 1998. *Material Cultures: Why Some Things Matter.* Chicago: University of Chicago Press.

———. 2008. *The Comfort of Things.* Cambridge: Polity Press.

———. 2010. *Stuff.* Cambridge: Polity Press.

Miller, Daniel, and Sophie Woodward. 2012. *Blue Jeans: The Art of the Ordinary.* Berkeley: University of California Press.

Ministerio de Educación de Guatemala. 2008. *Chimaltenango: Agenda Educativa 2008–2009.* Guatemala City: Gobierno de Guatemala.

Mitchell, Timothy. 1991. *Colonising Egypt*. Berkeley: University of California Press.

———. 2002. *Rule of Experts: Egypt, Techno-Politics, Modernity*. Berkeley: University of California Press.

Moeran, Brian. 2004. "A Japanese Discourse of Fashion and Taste." *Fashion Theory* 8, no. 1: 35–62.

Mohanty, Chandra. 1988. "Under Western Eyes: Feminist Scholarship and Colonial Discourses." *Feminist Review* 30: 61–88.

Mole, Noelle. 2012. *Labor Disorders in Neoliberal Italy: Mobbing, Well-Being, and the Workplace*. Bloomington: Indiana University Press.

Morgan, George, and Kalervo Gulson. 2010. "Indigenous People and Urbanization." *Environment and Planning A* 42, no. 2: 265–267.

Morris, Edward W. 2005. "'Tuck in That Shirt!': Race, Class, Gender, and Discipline in an Urban School." *Sociological Perspectives* 48, no. 1: 25–48.

Muggleton, David. 2000. *Inside Subculture: The Postmodern Meaning of Style*. Oxford: Berg.

Muñoz, Geldi. 2012. "Guatemala les dice adios a las maquilas." *Siglo 21*, July 17.

Nader, Laura. 1991. *Harmony Ideology: Justice and Control in a Zapotec Mountain Village*. Palo Alto, CA: Stanford University Press.

———. 1999. "Controlling Processes: Tracing the Dynamic Components of Power." *Current Anthropology* 38, no. 5: 711–738.

Nakassis, Constantine. 2010. "Youth and Status in Tamil Nadu, India." PhD diss., University of Pennsylvania.

———. 2012. "Counterfeiting What? Aesthetics of Brandedness and BRAND in Tamil Nadu, India." *Anthropological Quarterly* 85, no. 3: 701–722.

———. 2013. "The Quality of a Copy." In *Fashion India: Spectacular Capitalism*, edited by Tereza Kuldova, 142–165. Oslo: Akademika.

———. 2016. *Doing Style: Youth and Mass Meditation in South India*. Chicago: University of Chicago Press.

Nash, June. 1979. *We Eat the Mines and the Mines Eat Us: Dependency and Exploitation in Bolivian Tin Mines*. New York: Columbia University Press.

———. 1981. "Ethnographic Aspects of the World Capitalist System." *Annual Review of Anthropology* 10: 393–423.

———, ed. 1993. *Crafts in the World Market: The Impact of Global Exchange on Middle American Artisans*. Albany: SUNY Press.

Nelson, Diane M. 1999. *A Finger in the Wound: Body Politics in Quincentennial Guatemala*. Berkeley: University of California Press.

———. 2001. "Stumped Identities: Body Image, Bodies Politic, and the Mujer Maya as Prosthetic." *Cultural Anthropology* 16, no. 3: 314–353.

———. 2009. *Reckoning: The Ends of War in Guatemala*. Durham, NC: Duke University Press.

Nelson, Sara Sadler. 2003. "The Wages of Ubiquity." *Iowa Law Review* 88, no. 731: 776–783.

Neumeier, Marty. 2006. *The Brand Gap: How to Bridge the Distance Between Business Strategy and Design*. Berkeley: New Riders.

Newell, Sasha. 2012. *The Modernity Bluff: Crime, Consumption, and Citizenship in Côte d'Ivoire*. Chicago: University of Chicago Press.

Niessen, Sandra A., Ann Marie Leshkowich, and Carla Jones, eds. 2003. *Re-Orienting Fashion: The Globalization of Asian Dress.* Oxford: Berg.

Nill, Alexander, and Clifford Shultz. 1996. "The Scourge of Global Counterfeiting." *Business Horizons* 39, no. 6: 37–42.

Nolin, Catherine, and Jacqui Stephens. 2010. "'We Have to Protect the Investors': 'Development' and Canadian Mining Companies in Guatemala." *Journal of Rural and Community Development* 5, no. 3: 37–70.

Nordstrom, Carolyn. 2004. *Shadows of War: Violence, Power, and International Profiteering in the Twenty-First Century.* Berkeley: University of California Press.

———. 2007. *Global Outlaws: Crime, Money, and Power in the Contemporary World.* Berkeley: University of California Press.

Nurmi, Jari-Erik. 2005. "Thinking about and Acting on the Future: Development of Future Orientation across the Lifespan." In *Understanding Behavior in the Context of Time: Theory, Research, and Application,* edited by Alan Strathman and Jeff Joireman, 31–58. Hove, UK: Psychology Press.

Observatory of Economic Complexity. 2016. "Where Does Guatemala Import From?" http://atlas.media.mit.edu/en/visualize/tree_map/hs92/import/gtm /show/all/2014/.

Ochoa García, Carlos. 2002. *Derecho consuetudinario y pluralismo jurídico.* Guatemala City: Cholsamaj.

Offit, Thomas. 2011. "Cacique for a Neoliberal Age: A Maya Retail Empire in the Streets of Guatemala City." In *Securing the City: Neoliberalism, Space, and Insecurity in Postwar Guatemala,* edited by Kevin Lewis O'Neill and Kedron Thomas, 67–82. Durham, NC: Duke University Press.

O'Neill, Kevin Lewis. 2009. *City of God: Christian Citizenship in Postwar Guatemala.* Berkeley: University of California Press.

———. 2010. "The Reckless Will: Prison Chaplaincy and the Problem of Mara Salvatrucha." *Public Culture* 22, no. 1: 67–88.

———. 2011. "Delinquent Realities: Christianity, Formality, and Security in the Americas." *American Quarterly* 63, no. 2: 337–365.

O'Neill, Kevin Lewis, and Kedron Thomas, eds. 2011. *Securing the City: Neoliberalism, Space, and Insecurity in Postwar Guatemala.* Durham, NC: Duke University Press.

Ong, Aihwa. 1987. *Spirits of Resistance and Capitalist Discipline: Factory Women in Malaysia.* Albany: SUNY Press.

———. 1999. *Flexible Citizenship: The Cultural Logics of Transnationality.* Durham, NC: Duke University Press.

———. 2006. *Neoliberalism as Exception: Mutations in Citizenship and Sovereignty.* Durham, NC: Duke University Press.

Ortez, Omar. 2004. "Spreading Manufacturing Growth Gains through Local Jobs: Lessons from the Guatemalan Highlands." *Development in Practice* 14, no. 1: 163–170.

Osburg, John. 2013. *Anxious Wealth: Money and Morality among China's New Rich.* Palo Alto, CA: Stanford University Press.

Otzoy, Irma. 1996. "Maya Clothing and Identity." In *Maya Cultural Activism in Guatemala,* edited by Edward F. Fischer and R. McKenna Brown, 141–155. Austin: University of Texas Press.

———. 2007. "Sipakapa y el límite de la democracia." *ISTOR* 6, no. 24: 29–42.

Pandolfo, Stefania. 2007. "The Burning: Finitude and the Politico-Theological Imagination of Illegal Migration." *Anthropological Theory* 7, no. 3: 329–363.

Pang, Laikwan. 2006. *Cultural Control and Globalization in Asia: Copyright, Piracy, and Cinema.* New York: Routledge.

———. 2008. "'China Who Makes and Fakes': A Semiotics of the Counterfeit." *Theory, Culture and Society* 25, no. 6: 117–140.

———. 2012. *Creativity and Its Discontents: China's Creative Industries and Intellectual Property Rights Offenses.* Durham, NC: Duke University Press.

Pasquino, Pasquale. 1991. "Criminology: The Birth of a Special Knowledge." In *The Foucault Effect: Studies in Governmentality,* edited by Graham Burchell, Colin Gordon, and Peter Miller, 235–250. Chicago: University of Chicago Press.

Patzán, José Manuel. 2014. "Piratería causa graves pérdidas." *Prensa Libre,* December 27.

Paul, Benjamin D., and William J. Demarest. 1988. "The Operation of a Death Squad in San Pedro La Laguna." In *Harvest of Violence: The Maya Indians and the Guatemalan Crisis,* edited by Robert M. Carmack, 119–154. Norman: University of Oklahoma Press.

Peattie, Lisa. 1987. "A Concept in Good Currency and How It Grew: The Informal Sector." *World Development* 15, no. 7: 851–860.

Peltier, Michael. 2008. "State Passes Droopy Pants Law." *Reuters,* March 2.

Pérez-Sáinz, Juan Pablo. 1995. "Globalización y neoinformalidad en América Latina." *Nueva Sociedad* 135: 36–41.

Petersen, Kurt. 1992. *The Maquiladora Revolution in Guatemala.* New Haven, CT: Orville H. Schell, Jr., Center for International Human Rights at Yale Law School.

Phau, Ian, Gerard Prendergast, and Leung Hing Chuen. 2001. "Profiling Brand-Piracy-Prone Consumers: An Exploratory Study in Hong Kong's Clothing Industry." *Journal of Fashion Marketing and Management* 5, no. 1: 45–55.

Philip, Kavita. 2005. "What Is a Technological Author? The Pirate Function and Intellectual Property." *Postcolonial Studies* 8, no. 2: 199-218.

Pine, Jason. 2012. *The Art of Making Do in Naples.* Minneapolis: University of Minnesota Press.

Pitarch, Pedro, Shannon Speed, and Xochitl Leyva Solano, eds. 2008. *Human Rights in the Maya Region: Global Politics, Cultural Contentions, and Moral Engagements.* Durham, NC: Duke University Press.

Polanyi, Karl. 1944. *The Great Transformation: The Political and Economic Origins of Our Time.* Boston: Beacon.

Polhemus, Ted, and Lynn Procter. 1978. *Fashion and Anti-Fashion: Anthropology of Clothing and Adornment.* London: Thames and Hudson.

Ponte, Lucille M. 2009. "Echoes of the Sumptuary Impulse: Considering the Threads of Social Identity, Economic Protectionism, and Public Morality in the Proposed Design Piracy Prohibition Act." *Vanderbilt Journal of Entertainment and Technology Law* 12, no. 1: 45–92.

Portes, Alejandro, Manuel Castells, and Lauren A. Benton, eds. 1989. *The Informal Economy: Studies in Advanced and Less Developed Countries.* Baltimore: Johns Hopkins University Press.

Portes, Alejandro, and Richard Schauffler. 1993. "Competing Perspectives on the Latin American Informal Sector." *Population and Development Review* 19, no. 1: 33–60.

Povinelli, Elizabeth A. 1993. *Labor's Lot: The Power, History, and Culture of Aboriginal Action.* Chicago: University of Chicago Press.

———. 2001. "Radical Worlds: The Anthropology of Incommensurability and Inconceivability." *Annual Review of Anthropology* 30: 319–334.

———. 2002. *The Cunning of Recognition: Indigenous Alterities and the Making of Australian Multiculturalism.* Durham, NC: Duke University Press.

———. 2011. *Economies of Abandonment: Social Belonging and Endurance in Late Liberalism.* Durham, NC: Duke University Press.

Power, Michael. 1994. *The Audit Explosion.* London: Demos.

———. 1997. *The Audit Society: Rituals of Verification.* Oxford: Oxford University Press.

Prensa Libre. 2008. "Empresas piden acciones contra ingente piratería." January 7.

———. 2011a. "Guatemala deja de percibir US$48 miliones anuales por piratería." April 26.

———. 2011b. "Los Zetas dedicados a piratería intelectual en México y Centroamérica." January 13.

———. 2011c. "Mañana se llevará a cabo un foro acerca de la cultura pirata." March 11.

Preston, Julia. 2014. "In First for Court, Woman Is Ruled Eligible for Asylum in US on Basis of Domestic Abuse." *New York Times,* August 24.

Ralph, Michael. 2006. "'Flirt[ing] with Death' but 'Still Alive': The Sexual Dimension of Surplus Time in Hip Hop Fantasy." *Cultural Dynamics* 18, no. 1: 61–88.

Ramírez, Catherine. 2002. "Crimes of Fashion: The Pachuca and Chicana Style Politics." *Meridians: Feminism, Race, Transnationalism* 2, no. 2: 1–35.

Ramírez, Guillermo Isaí. 2015. "Piratería deja pérdidas al país." *Prensa Libre,* April 24.

Raustiala, Kal, and Chris Sprigman. 2006. "The Piracy Paradox: Innovation and Intellectual Property in Fashion Design." *Virginia Law Review* 92, no. 8: 1687–1777.

———. 2012. *The Knockoff Economy: How Imitation Sparks Innovation.* Oxford: Oxford University Press.

Raynor, Joel O. 1969. "Future Orientation and Motivation of Immediate Activity: An Elaboration of the Theory of Achievement Motivation." *Psychological Review* 76, no. 6: 606–610.

Reid, Amanda S. 2004. "Trademark Dilution Law: A Cross-Disciplinary Examination of Dilution and Brand Equity Scholarship." PhD diss., University of Florida.

Richards, Michael. 1985. "Cosmopolitan World View and Counterinsurgency in Guatemala." *Anthropological Quarterly* 58, no. 3: 90–107.

Riles, Annelise. 2011. *Collateral Knowledge: Legal Reasoning in the Global Financial Markets.* Chicago: University of Chicago Press.

Ritson, Mark. 2007. "Fakes Can Genuinely Aid Luxury Brands." *Marketing,* July 25.

Roediger, David. 1991. *The Wages of Whiteness: Race and the Making of the American Working Class.* London: Verso.

Rohloff, Peter, Anne Kraemer Díaz, and Shom Dasgupta. 2011. "'Beyond Development': A Critical Appraisal of the Emergence of Small Health Care Non-Governmental Organizations in Rural Guatemala." *Human Organization* 70, no. 4: 427–437.

Roitman, Janet L. 2005. *Fiscal Disobedience: An Anthropology of Economic Regulation in Central Africa.* Princeton, NJ: Princeton University Press.

———. 2013. *Anti-Crisis.* Durham, NC: Duke University Press.

Rose, Mark. 1993. *Authors and Owners: The Invention of Copyright.* Cambridge, MA: Harvard University Press.

Rosen, Ellen Israel. 2002. *Making Sweatshops: The Globalization of the US Apparel Industry.* Berkeley: University of California Press.

Rosette, Ashleigh, and Tracy Dumas. 2007. "The Hair Dilemma: Conform to Mainstream Expectations or Emphasize Racial Identity." *Duke Journal of Gender Law and Policy* 14: 407–422.

Rothschild, Michael, and Joseph Stiglitz. 1976. "Equilibrium in Competitive Insurance Markets: An Essay on the Economics of Imperfect Information." *Quarterly Journal of Economics* 90, no. 4: 629–649.

Sackett, James. 1977. "The Meaning of Style in Archaeology: A General Model." *American Antiquity* 42, no. 3: 369–380.

———. 1982. "Approaches to Style in Lithic Archaeology." *Journal of Anthropological Archaeology* 1, no. 1: 59–112.

———. 1986. "Isochrestism and Style: A Clarification." *Journal of Anthropological Archaeology* 5, no. 3: 266–277.

Said, Edward W. 2006. *On Late Style: Music and Literature Against the Grain.* New York: Vintage.

———. 2008. "Two Visions in Heart of Darkness." In *Bloom's Modern Critical Interpretations: Joseph Conrad's* Heart of Darkness, edited and with an introduction by Harold Bloom, 22–31. New York: Infobase.

Sandoval, Greg. 2010. "Biden to File Sharers: 'Piracy is Theft.'" *CNET,* June 22. www.cnet.com/news/biden-to-file-sharers-piracy-is-theft/.

Sanford, Victoria. 2003. *Buried Secrets: Truth and Human Rights in Guatemala.* New York: Palgrave Macmillan.

Scafidi, Susan. 2005. *Who Owns Culture? Appropriation and Authenticity in American Law.* New Brunswick, NJ: Rutgers University Press.

———. 2006. "Intellectual Property and Fashion Design." In *Intellectual Property and Information Wealth: Issues and Practices in the Digital Age,* edited by Peter K. Yu, 115–131. Westport: Praeger.

———. 2008. "F.I.T.: Fashion as Information Technology." *Syracuse Law Review* 59: 69–82.

Schechter, Frank I. 1927. "The Rational Basis of Trademark Protection." *Harvard Law Review* 40, no. 6: 813–833.

Scheper-Hughes, Nancy. 1993. *Death without Weeping: The Violence of Everyday Life in Brazil*. Berkeley: University of California Press.

Schneider, Jane C., and Peter T. Schneider. 2003. *Reversible Destiny: Mafia, Antimafia, and the Struggle for Palermo*. Berkeley: University of California Press.

Schirmer, Jennifer. 1988. *The Guatemalan Military Project: A Violence Called Democracy*. Philadelphia: University of Pennsylvania Press.

Scott, James C. 1976. *The Moral Economy of the Peasant: Rebellion and Subsistence in Southeast Asia*. New Haven: Yale University Press.

Sell, Susan. 1995. "Intellectual Property Protection and Antitrust in the Developing World: Crisis, Coercion, and Choice." *International Organization* 49, no. 2: 315–349.

Shore, Cris. 2008. "Audit Culture and Illiberal Governance: Universities and the Politics of Accountability." *Anthropological Theory* 8, no. 3: 278–298.

Sieder, Rachel. 1996. *Derecho consuetudinario y transición democrática en Guatemala*. Guatemala City: FLACSO.

———. 2003. "Renegotiating 'Law and Order': Judicial Reform and Citizen Responses in Post-War Guatemala." *Democratization* 10, no. 4: 137–160.

———. 2011. "Contested Sovereignties: Indigenous Law, Violence and State Effects in Postwar Guatemala." *Critique of Anthropology* 31, no. 3: 161–184.

Silverstein, Paul. 2005. "Immigrant Racialization and the New Savage Slot: Race, Migration, and Immigration in the New Europe." *Annual Review of Anthropology* 34: 363–384.

Simmel, Georg. 1906. "The Sociology of Secrecy and Secret Societies." *American Journal of Sociology* 11, no. 4: 441–498.

Sklair, Leslie. 1989. *Assembling for Development: The Maquila Industry in Mexico and the United States*. New York: Routledge.

Smith, Adrian. 2005. "Capitalism from Below? Small Firms, Petty Capitalists, and Regional Transformation in Eastern Europe." In *Petty Capitalists and Globalization: Flexibility, Entrepreneurship, and Economic Development*, edited by Alan Smart and Josephine Smart, 83–98. Albany: SUNY Press.

Smith, Carol A. 1984. "Local History in Global Context: Social and Economic Transitions in Western Guatemala." *Comparative Studies in Society and History* 26, no. 2: 193–228.

———. 1989. "Survival Strategies Among Petty Commodity Producers in Guatemala." *International Labour Review* 128, no. 6: 791–814.

———, ed. 1990. *Guatemalan Indians and the State, 1540 to 1988*. Austin: University of Texas Press.

———. 1995. "Race-Class-Gender Ideology in Guatemala: Modern and Anti-Modern Forms." *Comparative Studies in Society and History* 37, no. 4: 723–749.

Smith, Timothy J., and Thomas Offit. 2010. "Confronting Violence in Postwar Guatemala: An Introduction." *Journal of Latin American and Caribbean Anthropology* 15, no. 1: 1–15.

Smulovitz, Catalina. 2003. "Citizen Insecurity and Fear: Public and Private Responses in Argentina." In *Crime and Violence in Latin America: Citizen*

Security, Democracy, and the State, edited by Hugo Frühling and Joseph S. Tulchin with Heather A. Golding, 125–152. Washington, DC: Woodrow Wilson Center Press and Johns Hopkins University Press.

Starn, Orin. 2004. *Ishi's Brain: In Search of America's Last "Wild" Indian.* New York: W. W. Norton.

Stewart, Mary Lynn. 2008. *Dressing Modern Frenchwomen: Marketing Haute Couture, 1919-1939.* Baltimore: Johns Hopkins University Press.

Stiglitz, Joseph. 1979. "Equilibrium in Product Markets with Imperfect Information." *American Economic Review* 69, no. 2: 339–345.

Strathern, Marilyn, ed. 2000. *Audit Cultures: Anthropological Studies in Accountability, Ethics, and the Academy.* London: Routledge.

———. 2002. "Externalities in Comparative Guise." *Economy and Society* 31, no. 2: 250–267.

Strathern, Marilyn, and Eric Hirsch. 2004. "Introduction." In *Transactions and Creations: Property Debates and the Stimulus Of Melanesia,* edited by Eric Hirsch and Marilyn Strathern, 1–20. New York: Berghahn Books.

Sundaram, Ravi. 2010. *Pirate Modernity: Delhi's Media Urbanism.* New York: Routledge.

Superintendencia de Administración Tributaria. 2013. "Cultura Tributaria." Official website. http://portal.sat.gob.gt/culturatributaria/.

———. 2014a. "Cultura Tributaria." Facebook page. www.facebook.com /CTSATGuatemala.

———. 2014b. *Micos y Pericos.* Television series. http://portal.sat.gob.gt /culturatributaria/?page_id=140.

Swann, Jerre B., and Theodore H. Davis, Jr. 1994. "Dilution, an Idea Whose Time Has Gone; Brand Equity as Protectable Property, The New/Old Paradigm." *Journal of Intellectual Property Law* 1, no. 2: 219–257.

Tarlo, Emma. 1996. *Clothing Matters: Dress and Identity in India.* Chicago: University of Chicago Press.

———. 2010. *Visibly Muslim: Fashion, Politics, Faith.* Oxford: Berg.

Tate, Winifred. 2007. *Counting the Dead: The Culture and Politics of Human Rights Activism in Colombia.* Berkeley: University of California Press.

Taussig, Michael. 1980. *The Devil and Commodity Fetishism in South America.* Chapel Hill: University of North Carolina Press.

———. 1993. *Mimesis and Alterity: A Particular History of the Senses.* New York: Routledge.

Tax, Sol. 1957. "Changing Consumption in Indian Guatemala." *Economic Development and Cultural Change* 5, no. 2: 147–158.

Thomas, Kedron. 2009. "Structural Adjustment, Spatial Imaginaries, and 'Piracy' in Guatemala's Apparel Industry." *Anthropology of Work Review* 30, no. 1: 1–10.

———. 2012. "Intellectual Property Law and the Ethics of Imitation in Guatemala." *Anthropological Quarterly* 85, no. 3: 785–815.

———. 2013. "Brand 'Piracy' and Postwar Statecraft in Guatemala." *Cultural Anthropology* 28, no. 1: 144-160.

Thomas, Kedron, Kevin Lewis O'Neill, and Thomas Offit. 2011. "Securing the City: An Introduction." In *Securing the City: Neoliberalism, Space, and*

Insecurity in Postwar Guatemala, edited by Kevin Lewis O'Neill and Kedron Thomas, 1–24. Durham, NC: Duke University Press.

Tiano, Susan. 1994. *Patriarchy on the Line: Labor, Gender, and Ideology in the Mexican Maquila Industry.* Philadelphia: Temple University Press.

Traub-Werner, Marion, and Altha J. Cravey. 2002. "Spatiality, Sweatshops, and Solidarity in Guatemala." *Social and Cultural Geography* 3, no. 4: 383–401.

Treverton, Gregory, Carl Matthies, Karla Cunningham, Jeremiah Goulka, Greg Ridgeway, and Anny Wong. 2009. *Film Piracy, Organized Crime, and Terrorism.* Santa Monica, CA: RAND Corporation.

Trommsdorff, Gisela. 1983. "Future Orientation and Socialization." *International Journal of Psychology* 18, nos. 1–4: 381–406.

Trouillot, Michel-Rolph. 1991. "Anthropology and the Savage Slot: The Poetics and Politics of Otherness." In *Recapturing Anthropology: Working in the Present,* edited by Richard G. Fox, 17–44. Santa Fe: School of American Research Press.

Troutt, David Dante. 2004. "A Portrait of the Trademark as a Black Man: Intellectual Property, Commodification, and Redescription." *UC Davis Law Review* 38: 1141–1207.

Tsai, Julie P. 2005. "Fashioning Protection: A Note on the Protection of Fashion Designs in the United States." *Lewis and Clark Law Review* 9, no. 2: 447–468.

Tsing, Anna Lowenhaupt. 2004. *Friction: An Ethnography of Global Connection.* Princeton, NJ: Princeton University Press.

Turner, Michelle. 2000. "The Braided Uproar: A Defense of My Sister's Hair and a Contemporary Indictment of *Rogers v. American Airlines.*" *Cardozo Women's Law Journal* 7: 115–162.

United Nations Development Programme. 2015. "Guatemala." www.gt.undp.org/content/guatemala/es/home.html.

United Nations Office on Drugs and Crime. 2013. *Global Study on Homicide 2013: Trends, Contexts, Data.* www.unodc.org/documents/gsh/pdfs/2014_GLOBAL_HOMICIDE_BOOK_web.pdf.

United States Trade Representative. 2010. *National Trade Estimate Report on Foreign Trade Barriers.* www.ustr.gov/sites/default/files/uploads/reports/2010/NTE/NTE_COMPLETE_WITH_APPENDnonameack.pdf.

Urkidi, Leire. 2011. "The Defense of Community in the Anti-Mining Movement of Guatemala." *Journal of Agrarian Change* 11, no. 4: 556–580.

van Schendel, Willem, and Itty Abraham, eds. 2005. *Illicit Flows and Criminal Things: States, Borders, and the Other Side of Globalization.* Bloomington: Indiana University Press.

Vann, Elizabeth F. 2006. "The Limits of Authenticity in Vietnamese Consumer Markets." *American Anthropologist* 108, no. 2: 286–296.

Véliz, Rodrigo J., and Kevin Lewis O'Neill. 2011. "Privatization of Public Space: The Displacement of Street Vendors in Guatemala City." In *Securing the City: Neoliberalism, Space, and Insecurity in Postwar Guatemala,* edited by Kevin Lewis O'Neill and Kedron Thomas, 83–101. Durham, NC: Duke University Press.

Vila, Pablo. 2000. *Crossing Borders, Reinforcing Borders: Social Categories, Metaphors, and Narrative Identities on the U.S.-Mexico Frontier.* Austin: University of Texas Press.

Vogt, Evon Z. 1961. "Some Aspects of Zinacantán Settlement Patterns and Ceremonial Organization." *Estudios de Cultura Maya* 1: 131–145.

———. 1969. *Zinacantán: A Maya Community in the Highlands of Chiapas.* Cambridge, MA: Belknap Press of Harvard University Press.

Wade, Margaret. 2011. "The Sartorial Dilemma of Knockoffs: Protecting Moral Rights Without Disturbing the Fashion Dynamic." *Minnesota Law Review* 96, no. 1: 336–369.

Wade, Peter. 1997. *Race and Ethnicity in Latin America.* London: Pluto Press.

Walker, Juliet. 2009. *The History of Black Business in America: Capitalism, Race, Entrepreneurship.* Chapel Hill: University of North Carolina Press.

Walker, Susannah. 2007. *Style and Status: Selling Beauty to African American Women, 1920–1975.* Lexington: University Press of Kentucky.

Wallerstein, Immanuel. 1974. *The Modern World System I: Capitalist Agriculture and the Origins of the European World-Economy in the Sixteenth Century.* Berkeley: University of California Press.

Wang, Jing. 2007. *Brand New China: Advertising, Media, and Commercial Culture.* Cambridge, MA: Harvard University Press.

Wang, Shujen. 2003. *Framing Piracy: Globalization and Film Distribution in Greater China.* Lanham: Rowman and Littlefield.

Warkander, Philip. 2014. "'No Pansies!!': Exploring the Concept of 'Style' through Ethnographic Fieldwork." *Fashion Theory* 18, no. 3: 233–250.

Warren, Kay B. 1978. *The Symbolism of Subordination: Indian Identity in a Guatemalan Town.* Austin: University of Texas Press.

———. 1998. *Indigenous Movements and Their Critics: Pan-Maya Activism in Guatemala.* Princeton, NJ: Princeton University Press.

Watanabe, John M. 1992. *Maya Saints and Souls in a Changing World.* Austin: University of Texas Press.

Watson, Kathy. 2015. "Guatemala Sets Pace in Corruption Fight." *BBC*, September 14. www.bbc.com/news/world-latin-america-34195758.

Way, J. T. 2012. *The Mayan in the Mall: Globalization, Development, and the Making of Modern Guatemala.* Durham, NC: Duke University Press.

Weber, Max. 1947. *The Theory of Social and Economic Organization.* Translated by A. M. Henderson and Talcott Parsons. New York: Free Press.

White, Shane, and Graham White. 1998. *Stylin': African American Expressive Culture from Its Beginnings to the Zoot Suit.* Ithaca: Cornell University Press.

Whitwell, Stuart. 2006. "Brand Piracy: Faking It Can Be Good." *Brand Strategy*, May 8. www.intangiblebusiness.com/news/marketing/2006/05/brand-piracy-faking-it-can-be-good.

Wilf, Eitan. 2011. "Sincerity Versus Self-Expression: Modern Creative Agency and the Materiality of Semiotic Forms." *Cultural Anthropology* 26, no. 3: 462–484.

Wilk, Richard R. 1983. "Little House in the Jungle: The Causes of Variation in House Size Among Modern Kekchi Maya." *Journal of Anthropological Archaeology* 2, no. 2: 99–116.

Willen, Sarah S. 2007. "Toward a Critical Phenomenology of 'Illegality': State Power, Criminalization, and Abjectivity among Undocumented Migrant Workers in Tel Aviv, Israel." *International Migration* 45, no. 3: 3–38.

Williams, Raymond. 1977. *Marxism and Literature*. Oxford: Oxford University Press.

Willis, Susan. 1993. "Hardcore: Subculture American Style." *Critical Inquiry* 19, no. 2: 365–383.

Wilson, Elizabeth. 2003. *Adorned in Dreams: Fashion and Modernity*. London: I. B. Tauris.

Wilson, Fiona. 1993. "Workshops as Domestic Domains: Reflections on Small-Scale Industry in Mexico." *World Development* 21, no. 1: 67–80.

Wilson, Maya. 2009. "Guatemala: Crime Capital of Central America." Washington, DC: Council on Hemispheric Affairs.

Winthrop, Robert. 2002. "Exploring Cultural Rights: An Introduction." *Cultural Dynamics* 14, no. 2: 115–120.

Wolf, Eric R. 1957. "Closed Corporate Peasant Communities in Mesoamerica and Central Java." *Southwestern Journal of Anthropology* 13, no. 1: 1–18.

———. 1983. *Europe and the People without History*. Berkeley: University of California Press.

World Bank. 2015. "Data: Guatemala." http://data.worldbank.org/country /guatemala.

World Intellectual Property Organization. 1999. *Intellectual Property and Human Rights*. www.wipo.int/edocs/pubdocs/en/intproperty/762/wipo_pub_ 762.pdf.

Yagenova, Simona V., and Rocío Garcia. 2009. "Indigenous People's Struggles against Transnational Mining Companies in Guatemala: The Sipakapa People vs. GoldCorp Mining Company." *Socialism and Democracy* 23, no. 3: 157–166.

Zaloom, Caitlin. 2010. *Out of the Pits: Traders and Technology from Chicago to London*. Chicago: University of Chicago Press.

Index